The Bumper Book

of British Sleaze

First published in Great Britain in 2007

by Foxcote Books Ltd, London

10 9 8 7 6 5 4 3 2 1

A CIP catalogue record for this book is available
from the British Library.

ISBN 1-905880-00-6

ISBN-13 978-1-905880-00-3

Designed and typeset by Foxcote Books

Cover design by OnFire Creative, London

Illustrations by iCandi Media / © Foxcote Books Ltd, 2007

Printed and bound in Germany by GGP Media GmbH, Pößneck

www.foxcotebooks.com

The Bumper Book

of British Sleaze

by

Richard Morton Jack

and

Owen O' Rorke

foxcote

If you feel you have been unfairly omitted from this book, please contact the publisher and every effort will be made to include you in the next edition.

for Mostyn Neil Hamilton

Preface

Karl Marx once argued, satirically but rather convincingly, that criminals are society's most useful and productive members. Imagine that crime didn't exist: no *Double Indemnity* or *The Godfather*, no James Bond or Sherlock Holmes, no employment for judges, police, lawyers, locksmiths, probation officers or John Grisham. And, of course, no members of parliament and no sleaze: when law is redundant, who needs legislators?

No great loss, you might say. But think again. Like Marx's criminals, sleazy politicians perform a public service by arousing all the most pleasurable emotions – self-righteousness, schadenfreude, moral indignation and communal hilarity. Recall your ecstatic laugh when you first learned that John Major and Edwina Currie had been stripping off and swapping DNA samples, or when you saw John Prescott with Tracey Temple's legs round his neck, or when you read the *Guardian*'s gleefully libel-proof front page on the morning after Jonathan Aitken's conviction: 'He Lied and Lied and Lied'. Recall the entire public career of Lord (*sic*) Archer, from his expenses fiddles in the 1960s to that glorious summer's day in 2001 when Mr Justice Potts told the warders: "Take the prisoner down." Through this book we can relive these magic moments again and again. What joy to be reminded of even a bit-part player such as Piers Merchant MP, who resigned in 1997 after twice being caught canoodling with an 18-year-old former nightclub hostess – a liaison he explained away as "as part of research into a book on tabloid intrusion".

David Mellor and Antonia de Sancha, Neil and Christine Hamilton, Cash for Questions and Back to Basics: the mid-1990s were a golden age of sleaze. When Tony Blair moved into Downing Street he promised a "purer than pure" government and some poor saps actually believed him. But normal business soon resumed: Labour was caught lying about secret million-pound donations from Bernie Ecclestone, Robin Cook ditched his wife and ran off with his secretary after a late-night ultimatum from Alastair Campbell, Peter Mandelson started limbering up for the first of his many resignations. Yet as late as June 2001 Blake Morrison suggested in the *Guardian* that lack of sleaze might be a reason for voter apathy: "Having been governed for all these years by dissolutes, we've elected leaders who are better behaved than we are…vicar Blair and his fastidious sidesmen."

Fastidious! Not the first adjective that springs to mind for Ron Davies, Geoffrey Robinson, Peter Mandelson, David Blunkett or John Prescott. Nor should we forget the minister for whom the 2002 Local Government and Women's Conference in Cardiff was such a powerful aphrodisiac (see page 66); the image of Stephen Byers leaping aboard Councillor Barbara Corish in nothing but a pair of black cotton socks is irresistible and indelible.

In celebrating sleaze, we should also celebrate the word itself. Call an MP corrupt and you'll receive a writ within the hour; 'sleazy' is safer because imprecise. It covers everything from outright bribery, through freebie holidays and dodgy peerages, to extra-marital romps with farmyard animals. John Prescott's cowboy outfit and Peter Mandelson's mortgage are both effortlessly encompassed. And if you do get sued you can always take refuge in the etymological defence, since sleaze originally meant nothing more sinister than rough Silesian cloth.

I owe this detail to a source close to John Major – his charming brother Terry Major-Ball, who gave me a scholarly lecture on the word's history when I met him at a party in 1994. Suddenly all those headlines about 'a government drowning in sleaze' seemed both inappropriate and slightly surreal: one might as well accuse ministers of wallowing in tweed, or swimming in Crimplene. Fearful that familiarity might breed boredom – 'sleaze' appeared in newspapers 2,435 times in 1994, the high point of Tory misbehaviour – I began trying out alternative and equally antique nouns such as mockado, an inferior Flemish cloth ('Labour Puts the Mockers on Ministerial Mockado'), or kite, used by Shakespeare to mean a scavenger on a London dunghill. Neither caught on, because neither had sleaze's onomatopoeic resonances: sleek, sleight-of-hand, slither; slick wheeze, slimy cheese.

Sleaze it is, then. We can deplore the scallywags and mountebanks and money-grubbers and skirt-chasers whom it describes so evocatively, but just imagine how tooth-achingly grim public life would be without any Archers or Prescotts or even the occasional Piers Merchant. Sleazebags of the world, unite: you may lose your jobs, but you win a round of applause and a handsome retirement present. *The Bumper Book of British Sleaze* is it.

Francis Wheen, 2007

Actualité

French word roughly meaning 'events as they happen,' as opposed to the solid Anglo-Saxon word 'truth'. A commodity with which to be economical.

see *Clark, Alan / Matrix-Churchill*

Adams, Irene
b. Dec 27th 1947
MP (Lab), Paisley North, 1990-2005

Under-siege Paisley MP who thought she'd seen the last of Tommy Graham (*qv*) and his attempts to turn her constituency against her after he was lambasted and expelled from Labour in September 1998. Sadly, the very next month she found three more 'Grahams' had secured key positions within her local party (his extended family Joan, John and Tommy Jnr) – leading to fears that her rival was trying to 'control the constituency from the outside'. "This looks like Custer's last stand," she fumed. "Mrs Graham is a member of the Labour Party… I do not think anyone has a problem with that. Mr Graham, on the other hand, is expelled from the Labour Party and I hope his wife is not his puppet." She added that Paisley South MP Douglas Alexander and Port Glasgow's Norman Godman had both complained to her that they were having to turn away problems from constituents in Graham's own patch who didn't want to have to deal with the sweaty pariah.

see *Graham, Tommy / Paisley*

Additional Costs Allowance

Kitty intended to help far-flung constituency MPs cover the cost of London living. From 2006 the rules were softened to allow members to claim mortgage interest paid on their pieds à terre, as well as interior decoration outlay on their second, third or fourth homes. Had this helping hand only been available a decade earlier, Peter Mandelson (*qv*) might not have needed to resort to a private loan to plant both feet on the property ladder. Roughly a third of MPs now claim the maximum of over £20k reserved for those who have furthest to travel, such as Windsor MP Michael Trend (*qv*).

Aitken, Jonathan

b. Aug 30th 1942
MP (Con), Thanet East, 1974-83 /
Thanet South, 1983-97

Sleaze beacon who combined ministerial duties in Defence Procurement with a priapic sex drive and extensive Middle East concerns, by no means all of which made it to the Register of Members' Interests. When forced to resign his TV-am directorship in 1988, he blustered that he hadn't been aware of 'the need for candour' – a statement that could be taken as a touchstone for his political career, which ended with a 1999 perjury conviction and jail term.

The suave Old Etonian's attempt to become Oxford Union President foundered in 1962, as had a bid to heal a family rift with the mega-rich Beaverbrook clan: his rich uncle assured young Jonathan that he wouldn't get a penny. Instead he set out to make his mark as a journalist, taking LSD for the *Evening Standard* in 1966 and penning the vapid *Young Meteors* in 1967. When Aitken took an interest in the Nigerian-Biafran conflict, the sympathetic General Henry Alexander handed him a copy of the Scott Report (*qv*) in strict confidence in 1969. He copied it and passed it to veteran Tory MP Hugh Fraser and the *Sunday Telegraph*. When the story broke, Aitken – who'd already embarked on an affair with his young wife, Lady Antonia – made out that Fraser had leaked the report to the newspaper. A 1970 trial on charges under the Official Secrets Act clarified that point, but resulted in acquittal for Aitken after a sympathetic summing up by Mr Justice Caulfield (*qv*).

The scandal had cost him his first bash at fighting a seat, so he decided to focus on business instead, acting as chairman of Slater Walker Securities and forming Aitken Hume International with his cousin Tim. Over lunch in Paris in 1973 he hit it off with Saudi Prince Mohammed bin Faud (*qv*) and was introduced to his secretary, Said Ayas (*qv*). Ayas became a close friend, and gestures such as arranging UK medical care for his family were much appreciated – and generously rewarded with further Saudi contacts and openings. Saudi money would follow Aitken throughout his career, from the 1981 TV-am deal to his arms procurement under John Major. As his elderly mother Penelope put it: "He's been hawking with them in the desert, and all kind of things that businessmen don't normally do." He became an MP in 1974, but his winning ways were wasted on Margaret Thatcher – if not her daughter. By becoming 'the man who made Carol cry', Aitken booked himself 18 years on the backbenches. In fact he thrived there: he could cultivate Middle East contacts and philander to his heart's content, without having his dealings scrutinised too closely. In 1979 he married a neighbour of the Ayas family, Olivera Lolicia Azucki, who presented him with twins the following year. At his 1997 libel trial, he spoke movingly of his vigil by her bedside during the complicated labour; he was slower to mention the affair with sado-masochistic hooker Paula Strudwick (*qv*) he'd embarked upon just weeks after his daughters' birth.

On the surface, at least, the 80s were golden for Aitken: his home in Westminster's Lord North Street was a glamorous political salon, he organised the Conservative Philosophy Group and even became churchwarden at St Margaret's, Westminster. Aitken Hume PLC was booming, too, though in reality it had become little more than a front for Saudi royal investments, such as the hostile takeover of TV-am (*qv*) in 1981. This resulted in newsreader Anna Ford hurling a glass of wine at Aitken, and when the true source of his funding emerged in 1988 he was obliged to resign his directorship.

"He was effectively the Saudis' ambassador to Europe. He may not have pimped for their prostitutes, but he was at the beck and call of the royal family"

In the late 80s he was named 'Backbencher of the Year' by the *Spectator* for his 'arresting challenges to Mrs.Thatcher's treatment of press freedom', and in 1992, after she'd been ousted, he received a surprise promotion to the post of Minister for Defence Procurement. He promptly gave up a number of lucrative directorships, but some felt that his reliance on foreign patronage still compromised his position. One senior civil servant raged: "He was effectively the Saudis' ambassador to Europe. He may not have pimped for their prostitutes, but he was at the beck and call of the royal family. He thought he was one of them."

When he joined the Cabinet in 1994 as Chief Secretary to the Treasury, a whole new can of sleaze was opened – an investigation into his business affairs involving the

Independent, Guardian and *World In Action.* On April 10th 1995 the *Guardian* printed numerous allegations against him, including the charge that he'd stayed at the Paris Ritz (*qv*) courtesy of Saudi businessmen in September 1993, thereby violating ministerial rules. That afternoon he called a press conference at Conservative HQ at which he announced his notorious intention "to cut out the cancer of bent and twisted journalism in our country with the simple sword of truth and the trusty shield of British fair play." Maintaining that his wife had paid the bill, in July he announced his intention to step down in order to fight the claims. The subsequent libel action began in April 1997, after Aitken rejected an offer to settle from the *Guardian* just before he lost his seat.

"I will cut out the cancer of bent and twisted journalism in our country with the simple sword of truth and the trusty shield of British fair play"

In court the undeclared hospitality was investigated, as were claims of pimping and illegal arms deals (see *World In Action / Guardian trial*); but painstaking detective work by the newspaper proved that he had severely perjured himself (and persuaded his young daughter Victoria to lie on his behalf),

and in June the proceedings collapsed. Aitken resigned from the Privy Council and contemplated his colossal legal bills.

The only use for his 'sword of truth' so far had been to commit hara kari – but even worse was to come. It was decided to bring a criminal trial for perjury and perverting the course of justice, at which he pleaded guilty in January 1999, commenting at one court appearance: "I have learned my lessons. I hope I never tell any lies again. Sometimes you become a prisoner of your own lie. Ultimately I have no excuses." On June 8th he was convicted and imprisoned for 18 months. He split from his wife and filed for bankruptcy (actions undertaken to spite his creditors, some have speculated), and at the end of the year it emerged that he'd sired a lovechild by the wife of a business contact, Adnan Khashoggi, eighteen years before. In jail he embraced God, and served just under half his sentence before taking a theology course back in Oxford and penning an execrable pair of memoirs, *Pride and Perjury* and *Porridge and Passion.*

A rumoured return to politics was scotched in February 2004 by Tory leader Michael Howard ("Jonathan Aitken has very many admirable qualities, but I am afraid his days as a Conservative Member of Parliament are over"), and Aitken responded with equanimity. "The leader has spoken. I accept his judgement with good grace," he said, and switched allegiance to UKIP (*qv*).

al-Fayed, Mohammed

see *Fayed, Mohammed*

Alexander, Richard
b. June 29th 1934
MP (Con), Newark On Trent, 1979-97

Tory MP who visited Romania, amongst other jollies, as part of a small gift-giving delegation to dictator Nicolae Ceausescu in 1985. Shortly before the 1989 summer recess he placed the following plaintive ad in the parliamentary *House* magazine: 'Hardworking backbench Tory MP of 10 years' standing seeks consultancy in order to widen his range of activities. Please contact Richard Alexander at the House of Commons on 01 219 4207.' The needy blue explained that 'advertising was one way of making it clear to others that I was available to be their spokesman if I wished... it was one way of drawing the nation's attention to the fact that I only had one consultancy and could take on more if they wished'. No work resulted from the ad, and he lost his seat to Fiona Jones (*qv*) in 1997.

Following her 1999 conviction for electoral malpractice (subsequently overturned), he won the Tory nomination for the anticipated by-election – but it wasn't to be.

Allason, Rupert
b. Nov 8th 1951
MP (Con), Torbay, 1987-97

Buccaneering serial litigant Allason, the son and grandson of Tory MPs, was expelled from Catholic public school Downside in his teens, but compensated by serving as a Special Constable from 1975-1982. Having cobbled together numerous works about spying under the nom de plume Nigel West, he became the MP for one-time Tory stronghold Torbay. There he steadily haemorrhaged voters until finally losing his seat by 12 votes to Lib Dem Adrian Sanders, a defeat he grudgingly conceded after the maximum three recounts (see *Thatched Tavern, the*). In 1993 he was the only Tory MP to miss the vital vote on the Maastricht Treaty, as he was sunning himself in the Caribbean. He thereby incurred the displeasure of Prime Minister John Major (*qv*), and lost the party whip. Increasingly, however, his time was consumed in pursuing pig-headed libel actions against adversaries such as the *Mirror* newspaper, the BBC and the publisher Random House, during which he would defend himself.

The *Mirror* claim arose from a front page editorial about Allason and George Galloway (*qv*) on October 23rd 1991, headlined 'Dishonourable Men and Dirty Tricks'. The article concerned questions the MPs had raised in the House about Israeli whistle-blower Mordechai Vanunu, and stated that the two had 'as much honour as a pair of jackals scavenging in a rubbish tip, which is where they both belong.' They promptly sued the paper's proprietor Robert Maxwell (*qv*), and were awarded £200,000 damages and £30,000 costs. By the time the matter was settled in November 1992, however, Maxwell was dead. Allegedly prompted by *Mirror* hacks including Alastair Campbell (*qv*), the following day a brace of Labour MPs decided to chair an Early Day Motion pressuring Allason to donate his damages to the cheated Maxwell pensioners. An article duly appeared in the *Mirror* on November 20th, erroneously giving the number of MPs supporting the EDM as 50. Allason demanded an apology, which was printed on November 26th, but after numerous further exchanges, he declared that 'Campbell's conduct amounted to a misconceived and malicious attempt to embarrass me in my constituency'. On February 9th 1993 he issued a writ claiming damages for malicious falsehood, personally serving papers on Mirror Group chief executive David Montgomery. Over three years later, in May 1996, he won a verdict that ran only partially in his favour, so appealed the following year, claiming amongst other things that the loss of his seat was attributable to the *Mirror's* actions. In July 1998 he was awarded the princely sum of £1050 in damages. Mr Justice Popplewell added that his claim to have suffered financially as a result of the *Mirror's* conduct was 'utterly unconvincing'.

The *Mirror* responded by splashing pictures of Allason holidaying in St. Tropez with nubile twenty-something Jane Burgess, which came as a surprise to his wife Nikki – though she later told the *Evening Standard*: 'I thanked my lucky stars for the affair because without her he wasn't going to give me a divorce.' In 1997, meanwhile, a spin-off diary from the BBC's flagship satire programme *Have I Got News For You* strongly implied he was a 'conniving little shit,' an epithet he called 'vicious and revolting' after his mother pointed it out to him. Needless to say, he sued BBC Worldwide and Hat Trick Productions, but lost, thus putting him in the unique position of being fair game for the insult in the eyes of the law. Seemingly spoiling for another court appearance, Allason penned an article for the *Sunday Express* in May 2000, repeating far-fetched claims that Roger Windsor, former chief executive of the National Union of Mineworkers, was an agent of MI5. Windsor sued for libel, and won.

Nothing daunted, in October 2001 the writ-happy former MP pursued a copyright action against publishing behemoth Random House, accusing them of failing to acknowledge his copyright in the tedious 1997 memoirs of alleged 'Cambridge Spy' John Cairncross. Mr Justice Laddie found against him, describing his evidence as 'profoundly and cynically dishonest', and branding him 'one of the most dishonest witnesses I have ever seen,' in a judgement hailed by the *Independent* as 'one of the most scathing verdicts ever delivered in court against a public figure'. The beak's broadside was largely provoked by the fact that Allason had denied being a director of another publishing company that had negotiated with Cairncross for the book rights, St. Ermin's Press. The judge, however, found Allason described as an 'editorial director' on its website. When he looked again the next day, it had been amended to read 'editorial consultant'. Disgusted, he ordered Allason to pay a sum not dissimilar to that which he'd claimed from Robert Maxwell ten years earlier, and referred the matter to the Director of Public Prosecutions.

"Profoundly and cynically dishonest"

By August 2005 Allason (who'd once bragged in *Who's Who* that his hobby was 'sailing close to the wind') was enduring a buffeting to brace the hardiest of seafarers. When the former MP failed to cough up the damages, Mr Justice Neuberger branded his evidence 'wholly unsatisfactory,' found him in contempt of court and imposed a six-month suspended sentence, giving him 42 days to produce details of his assets (believed at one time to include properties in London, Berkshire, Devon, Switzerland and the Caribbean), family trusts, share ownership and companies (Westintel Research and Westintel Ltd.), as well as income from Nigel West works, including bad novels such as *Murder In The Commons* (1992) and *Murder In The Lords* (1996). As of the time of writing, Allason is thought not to have complied with this order – nor to be on British soil.

al-Marashi, Ibrahim
b. 1973

Postgraduate whose doctoral thesis *Iraq's Security & Intelligence Network: A Guide & Analysis* was pillaged, restyled as a British government report called *Iraq: Its Infrastructure of Concealment, Deception and Intimidation* and released to the press by No.10 on February 3rd 2003 (see *Dodgy Dossier [ii]*). This was acknowledged to be a huge blunder when Cambridge lecturer Glen Rangwala revealed how vast chunks of al-Marashi's homework had been faithfully lifted – right down to the typos. Such parts that were not straight steals were either cribbed from the plane-spotters' bible *Jane's Intelligence Review* or had been creatively restyled for impact (where al-Marashi had used 'monitoring', the British government had put 'spying'; 'aiding opposition groups' became 'supporting terrorist organisations,' and so on).

As for al-Marashi, he was more concerned about the UK government's flagrant abuse of copyright than the fact that his essay was being used to start a war. "I was a bit disenchanted because they never cited my article," he griped. "Any academic, when you publish anything, the only thing you ask for in return is that they include a citation of your work."

Blair later issued an apology to the US Naval college lecturer, but the British public is still waiting.

al-Yamamah

Meaning 'the Dove' – it's a joke, of sorts – this is the name given to a series of UK arms sales to Saudi Arabia, beginning in September 1985 and memorably dubbed 'the biggest sale of anything to anyone ever.' Paid for by up to 600,000 barrels of Saudi oil a day, according to some reports, the contracts are said to have netted BAE (formerly British Aerospace) a total of £43bn in the last twenty years.

Pushed through after vigorous lobbying by Margaret Thatcher, the contract bore its first fruit in 1989, followed over the next two decades by megadeals for British Tornados and Eurofighter Typhoons. In 1994, a genuine 'Dove' – Labour anti-war stalwart Tam Dalyell – submitted evidence to Parliament which he claimed proved Thatcher's son Mark had benefited from a multi-million pound commission on the original £20bn (that's £20,000,000,000) deal. 'Sir Mark', as he is now, has strenuously denied the suggestion that he ever profited from his mother's position. Dalyell was dismayed to discover the Tory government was not prepared to investigate. The National Audit

Office had made a full review of the contracts two years earlier, but it has never been published. As such, it is the only such document the NAO has ever withheld – implying that it is more sensitive even than the report detailing the plans for the Secret Service buildings in London. Labour MP Harry Cohen, who tabled an Early Day Motion in 2002 tentatively linking Saudi commissions from these deals to Al-Qaeda funding, also noted a 'serious conflict of interest' in that the man appointed to head up the NAO since 1987, Sir John Bourn, had himself done 'a lot of work at the MoD on Al Yamamah'.

'The Dove' flapped back onto the front pages in September 2003, when it emerged that BAE was under investigation by the Serious Fraud Office in connection with a supposed £60m 'slush fund'. It was alleged that the company had showered Saudi royals (see *Prince Bandar*) with perks including gold Rolls-Royces to sweeten the tooth-rotting deal still further. Prince Turki bin Nasser, the Saudi minister for arms procurement, was also alleged to be a beneficiary. The SFO made two arrests in November 2004, but no charges resulted. A year later BAE further jacked up the heat by refusing to comply with compulsory demands to disclose any payments to the Middle East.

But on December 14th 2006 the British government suddenly discontinued the investigation 'in the interest of national and international security', and ordered that all files be handed in. This U-turn came after a month of threats from the Saudi government that a lucrative Eurofighter contract would be awarded to France if the SFO didn't back off (especially in regard to poking around certain Swiss bank accounts). The Attorney General Lord Goldsmith reassured a stunned public: "No weight has been given to commercial interests or to the national economic interest."

One familiar name quickly offering his ha'pence-worth was Jonathan Aitken (*qv*), who welcomed the move in the name of Anglo-Saudi relations. Prime Minister Tony Blair stood firmly alongside Aitken on the issue commenting the day after the plug was pulled: "Strategic interest comes first."

SLEAZE

"This candidate is a candidate of probity and integrity, and I'm going to back him to the full"

– *William Hague on Jeffrey Archer's London Mayoral bid, 1997*

SLOT

SLEAZE

"We paid inordinate attention in the early days of New Labour to courting, assuaging and persuading the media"

– *Tony Blair, June 12th 2007*

SLOT

Amess, David

b. March 26th 1952
MP (Con), Basildon 1983-97 /
Southend West 1997-

This inadvertent TV star is man of contradictions: a pro-lifer who supports the death penalty, a loyalist Tory passionate about banning fox-hunting, a leading Conservative Friend of Israel who wanted to see Tony Blair impeached for invading Iraq. He is also known, if he is known at all, as the clot duped in the 'Cake For Questions' affair. Thanks to Amess's credulity, on July 23rd 1996 TV prankster Chris Morris (*qv*) managed to get a question asked in the Commons without recourse to brown envelopes (*qv*). Amess's subsequent interview on Morris's *Brass Eye* conclusively demonstrated that, provided a camera is running, an MP will hold forth with confidence on any subject – in this case, an outsized, yellow, non-existent drug called 'cake'.

Amos, Alan

b. Nov 10th 1952
MP (Con), Hexham, 1987-92

Party-hopping grafter who was distributing Tory leaflets at the age of 14, and went on to become president of the Conservative Association at Oxford University (where he was a contemporary of Tony Blair at St. John's College). His views in local government were robust – pro-birching, anti-abortion – and he developed a reputation for uncompromising toil as an MP. In March 1992, however, he resigned his seat when he was arrested and cautioned for indecency behind the notorious Jack Straw's Castle, a pub on London's Hampstead Heath. He dismissed the incident as 'a silly mistake', but it caused him radically to rethink his politics. "I had always been loyal to the Conservative Party; I had always been loyal to the police. Both were then disloyal to me," he told the *Spectator* in 1997. He surprised former colleagues the same year by appearing on ITV's pointless debate *The Monarchy – The Nation Decides,* ranting that the Queen was the 'head of a rotten, class-ridden, corrupt social and political environment', and that her family were 'parasites and hypocrites'. The passing of the years did little to cool his ire: in February 2001 he told the *Guardian* "I realised I no longer wanted to be part of a minority-bashing, foreigner-hating party," and at that year's Election he unsuccessfully contested Hitchin & Harpenden for Labour. The following year he became a Labour councillor in Tower Hamlets, only to lose his seat at the local elections in 2006.

Anderson, Sally
b. 1976

Blonde estate agent who enjoyed a whirlwind friendship with beleaguered Work and Pensions Secretary David Blunkett (*qv*) following their meeting in Annabel's (*qv*) in June 2005. The difference in their ages prompted unfavourable media comment, causing her mother Kathy (herself five years Blunkett's junior) to leap to her defence in the *Daily Mail* that September. "Sally is a very beautiful, intelligent and talented young lady who is entitled to have a friendship with whomever she pleases," she blasted, adding: "I have the very highest regard for Mr Blunkett as a politician." Anderson's fiancé Neil Gomersal had less, pronouncing himself 'gutted' when she moved out of his £500,000 Ascot home soon afterwards.

In October the *Sunday Times* claimed that Blunkett was hoping to have a child with Anderson, but he countered that their relationship was platonic, and when she sold her story to the *People* a few days later (with the assistance of Max Clifford), he announced that he had been 'a sucker'. In March 2006 the tabloid was obliged to print a statement that read in part: "Ms Anderson claimed that she had had sex with Mr Blunkett and that when she told him she might be pregnant he abandoned her. Ms Anderson also claimed that Mr Blunkett had used her for sex and had offered valuable gifts as an inducement. We now accept that these allegations are untrue and that Mr Blunkett did not lie about them."

Anglia Television

Norwich-based independent TV station which began broadcasting in 1959 and decided to accept a multi-million takeover bid from the Meridian group early in 1994. Just before the deal went public, Jeffrey Archer (*qv*) embarked on a share-buying spree, prompting concerns that his wife, a director of the company, could have furnished him with confidential inside information – though there has never been enough evidence for a prosecution.

Following a series of directors' meetings to discuss the top-secret takeover deal, attended by Mary Archer, her husband impulsively snapped up 25,000 shares. That was on January 13th 1994, the day after one such meeting. On Friday January 14th Archer snaffled another 25,000 – just in time for the weekend, after which the board would reconvene to confirm the takeover. Jeffrey (who, in line with a company directive, had written to his wife in 1992 to confirm 'I have no Anglia shares and have no intention of buying any in the future') officially purchased the shares 'on behalf of a friend'. That friend was Broosk Saib, a Kurdish Iraqi whose sizeable city portfolio suggested no need for a middle-man to do his dealing, least of all one in a potentially compromised position. Even more strangely, the well-positioned hubby had employed the services of a one-off broker, with whom he never worked again, to buy the shares on a 'new time' basis: that is, putting up no capital at all in the expectation of an immediate sale. And sell he did, within moments of the takeover's being made public on the morning of Tuesday 18th January.

Predictably, the shares had leapt in value, and Archer made a tidy £77,219.62 without ever putting up a penny of his own money. A Stock Exchange inquiry was launched into the affair, but the Department of Trade and Industry (overseen by fellow Tory Michael Heseltine) later announced that the peer would not be prosecuted, on the grounds that it was not possible to prove that husband and wife had consulted. A 'grateful' Lord Archer declared himself 'exonerated' – although privately the scandal was blamed for his snub as Party Chairman by John Major, in favour of ultra-safe pair of hands Jeremy Hanley.

Annabel's

Snooty Mayfair nightspot in which, on any given night, one might reasonably expect to encounter film stars, pop singers, minor royalty and former socialist David Blunkett (*qv*). Overwhelmed by the demands of his Cabinet post, however – and despite his prodigious memory – Blunkett neglected to declare his honorary membership in the 2005 Register of Members' Interests. Tariq Siddiqi, who introduced him to the club, has since had his membership rescinded – and Blunkett, for his part, insists his and Sadie's disco-dancing days are done. As for how he spent his time in the club, his sometime companion Sally Anderson (*qv*) offered this insight into Blunkett's and Siddiqi's repartee in the *Mail on Sunday* in October 2005: "They were quite open about discussing the business of the DNA company and what David could do for them. I didn't pay much attention to most of it because it was so boring."

see *DNA Bioscience*

Anschutz, Philip
b. 1939

Casino tycoon famously dubbed America's 'greediest executive' by *Fortune* magazine in 2002. Following government relaxation of gambling laws in October 2005, his entertainment group, AEG, registered a serious interest in converting the Millennium Dome (*qv*) into Britain's first 'Super-Casino'. Anschutz met Deputy Prime Minister John Prescott (*qv*) on several occasions from 2004, treating him to a two-night stay at his Colorado ranch in July 2005 – where he gifted him Wild West accessories including off-the-rack cowboy boots, Stetson bluejeans, a hat, a personalised silver belt buckle and a leather notebook. The total value of the tat was estimated as high as £11,000. Some felt it inappropriate that Prescott had accepted such hospitality when the contract was up for grabs, but a Labour spokeswoman reassured the nation by stating that the DPM was "very clear he has done nothing wrong", before adding: "He is very relaxed about it." Prescott belatedly recorded the trip in the Register of Members' Interests in July 2006, and made a meagre donation to a 7/7 charity from the public purse in lieu of payment for the beano (though his department initially put it about that he'd reached into his own pocket).

The following month AEG had to apologise for fabricating church support for the casino project (see *Dodgy Dome Dossier, the*). Nonetheless, theological concerns are of some importance to the Christian gaming billionaire: as well as channelling his fortune into overturning gay rights legislation in Colorado, Anschutz has generously funded evangelical evolution-deniers The Discovery Institute.

Apathy-Greed Index

see *Smith, Sir Dudley*

Aquablast

There are currently around 2,000 companies using the name Aquablast, covering services from power hoses and leisure accessories to pool cleaning and dental hygiene. Only one matters to sleaze lovers, however: the pie-in-the-sky Canadian venture that destroyed Jeffrey Archer's first political career in 1973, setting him on the road to fame and *Fortune* (*qv*) as a writer of dreadful novels.

Having already borrowed money from rich friends to dabble in commodities such as sugar, cocoa and copper, the bumptious Member for Louth was quick to sniff the potential in a 'miracle' gadget designed to slip into car exhausts and somehow reduce petrol consumption. And when Aquablast sought investment, he was first at the trough – not only sinking his own life savings into the lunatic scheme, but tapping friends once again and even trawling overseas to net every last titbit going. By December 1972, Archer's estimated £427,000 spree had inflated the share price to such an extent that the Canadian authorities started to take an interest.

In January, however, it started to drop, and when it became clear that the prototype had no practical or market value whatsoever, the shares went into freefall. By the end of 1973 the company was, like the widget itself, absolutely worthless. Archer's loss was literature's, too: faced with bankruptcy, to say nothing of a fraud investigation, he pledged to repay his army of angry creditors by employing his not considerable writing talents to earn back their money.

Archer, an

Slang among city traders for the sum of £2000 (see *Coghlan, Monica)*

Archer, Jeffrey
b. April 15th 1940 (allegedly)
MP (Con), Louth, 1969-74

Described by Margaret Thatcher as 'the extrovert's extrovert', this bull-necked fantasist has been a sleaze icon for nearly forty years.

"The kind of bloke who'd bottle your piss and sell it"

In that time he has successively been an MP, Deputy Tory Chairman and a peer, as well as bankrupted, expelled from his party and jailed. His own accounts of his life and times have consistently been exposed as inaccurate, but the handsome proceeds of a torrent of bad novels have afforded him the trappings, if not the public esteem, of an old-fashioned Tory grandee.

The son of an itinerant fraudster and bigamist who masqueraded as an army officer, Archer was educated at Wellington School, Somerset (not Wellington College, Berkshire) and Oxford's Department Of Education (not Brasenose College), though the 'about the author' sections of his literary works continue to perpetrate confusion on this issue (mind you, they also call him 'a master storyteller'). He met his frosty spouse Mary (*qv*) at this time, as well as playing a small part in persuading the Beatles to visit Oxford in Oxfam's name, a task for which he trousered an over-generous commission and was hailed by Ringo Starr as "the kind of bloke who'd bottle your piss and sell it." With endorsements like this, a career in politics was inevitable, despite further rumblings about his practice of creaming off a percentage of charity funds he'd raised.

Having served on the Greater London Council, where he became known as 'Mr 10%' for his habit of preparing his colleagues' expense claims on commission, he won Louth for the Conservatives in a 1969 by-election, aged 29. Though he claimed to be the UK's youngest-ever MP, he wasn't even the youngest in the Commons at the time. His term was marked by mutterings about fiddled expenses, and he was obliged to step down in 1974 when a foolhardy investment in Canadian firm Aquablast (qv) brought him to the brink of bankruptcy. In the same year he was also detained on suspicion of shoplifting in Toronto, but escaped prosecution. Energetic rather than able, sly rather than intelligent, in the late 70s and early 80s he rebuilt his finances as (appropriately enough) a writer of inept fiction, and went on to amass a huge fortune via a string of poorly-conceived novels, said to require a fleet of editors to make them readable. Between resigning as a Conservative MP and being appointed Party Deputy Chairman by Mrs Thatcher in 1985, he held no official political post, but used his flair for self-publicity to keep his name close to that of the Tory government.

His hubris reached its apex in July 1987, when he succeeded in half-inching £500k from the *Daily Star* (qv). The libel action in question was brought by Archer over an article alleging he'd paid Monica Coghlan (qv) for sex one night in September 1986. The trial judge, Mr Justice Caulfield (qv), simply couldn't believe that a man with such a wife could require the services of a prostitute, and was no doubt relieved to hear evidence from Archer's pal Ted Francis that they were together on at least one of the two nights for which Archer had prepared an alibi. The damages were paid, and though Archer vowed to give them to charity, no visible gesture towards doing so was made. Indeed, the two central mysteries of the trial still haven't been publicly resolved: whether the fibbing fundraiser actually availed himself of Ms Coghlan's professional services, and whether (as she furiously maintained) he has a pock-marked back.

Tickled pink by his victory, Archer set about ingratiating himself with John Major (often by acting as a party fundraiser or auctioneer) and was given a peerage in 1992, becoming Lord Archer of Weston-Super-Mare. His ennoblement was ostensibly in recognition of his efforts on behalf of displaced Kurds, though his claims to have raised almost £60 million for them have never come close to being verified (see *de Burgh, Chris / Simple Truth, the*). He was soon in the eye of another storm – this time over allegations of insider share trading in Anglia Television (*qv*), which broke at the outset of 1994. No charges were brought, but the whiff of wheeler-dealing was still pungent when he announced his candidature as Conservative Mayoral candidate for London in October 1999. His cocoon quickly began to unravel.

"Jeffrey is one of those chaps who doesn't understand when the game is up"

Citing Archer's gall in running for public office, his embittered former chum Ted Francis and former mistress Andrina Colquhoun (*qv*) decided to expose the real story of the 1987 trial – a litany of reluctant favours, gross misrepresentations and straightforward lies. William Hague (*qv*) swiftly withdrew his support for Archer as a candidate of 'probity and integrity', and endorsed serial philanderer Steve Norris (*qv*) instead. Archer was expelled from the Conservative Party amid two charges of perjury, two of obstruction of justice and one of using a false instrument (see *Dodgy Diary, the*) – and less concrete claims from his secretary that he had inadvertently arranged Jill Dando's murder. Whilst awaiting trial, he showcased his lifelong gall by starring in his own play, *The Accused*. A theatrical travesty whose plot mimicked his own tribulations, it led to calls for a separate prosecution for contempt of court. On 19th July 2001 he was found guilty of perjury and perverting the course of justice, and sentenced to four years' imprisonment, as well as being ordered to repay the damages with interest. His nemesis, Mr Justice Potts, commented: "These charges represent as serious an offence of perjury as I have had experience of, and have been able to find in the books… it has been an extremely distasteful case."

Whilst banged up Archer penned three dire volumes of diaries, leading the *Mail on Sunday* to acclaim him as 'a prison Pepys'. Two months after his July 2003 release, new legislation was mooted to prevent convicted criminals from voting in the Lords. One last ditch effort to rejoin Conservative party life was blocked in November 2005 by David Cameron (*qv*), who crisply stated: "I think that his days as a front line politician are over." Former colleague David Mellor (*qv*) added that "Jeffrey is one of those chaps who doesn't understand when the game is up." By 2006 the message seemed to be getting through: in an appearance on Andrew Marr's *Sunday AM* TV programme on 26th February, Archer confirmed the news that literary critics had been dreading: he had no ambitions to return to public life, and intended to focus on writing instead.

Rather than for any achievements, Jeffrey Archer's political career will probably be remembered for the light it cast on the judgement of senior Tories (including three successive leaders – Thatcher, Major and Hague) who continued to support him despite every indication that he was a wrong'un. Former MP and ubiquitous TV prat Gyles Brandreth relates how his prep school headmaster described the young Archer as 'the best athletics coach he had ever come across.' Perhaps the fallen peer occasionally reflects that, had he only stuck at what he was good at, he might now be a comfortably retired PE department head, instead of the single most ludicrous figure in modern British political history.

Archer, Mary
b. Dec 22nd 1944

Mary 'Lady' Archer's fragrance intoxicates judge and convict alike. She has, however, courted trouble for herself on her husband's behalf, standing not only by her man, but his demonstrably untrue version of events. Her sleaziest hour came in January 1994, in her capacity as a director of Anglia Television (*qv*), when it was ungallantly suggested that her position as a director of the company made it suspicious that Jeffrey had made a killing on shares just before its takeover deal went public.

His Lordship has commented of their marriage: "I have put her through some hellishly tough times, and she has been remarkable throughout them all. But the other side of the coin, as she herself says, is that she has had a remarkable life with me, with remarkable privileges." As for her husband, she summarises thus: "We are all human, but Jeffrey manages to be more human than most."

When hostessing, the icy academic has been known to showcase her warmer front by sprawling over her husband's grand piano to purr cabaret standards at startled guests.

Arctic Monkeys, the

Sheffield indie sensations (not to be confused with fellow pop primates Chimp Eats Banana – see *Nobacon, Danbert*) briefly linked to Labour leadership hopeful Gordon Brown, as he enviously eyed David Cameron's record collection in 2006. Their music 'really wakes you up in the mornings', he enthused to *New Woman* magazine that summer. By September he was able to clarify the matter, boasting to lads' mag *GQ*: "I mean, I've heard Arctic Monkeys and they're very loud."

"I mean, I've heard Arctic Monkeys and they're very loud"

By the end of the month, however, he'd tired of the high-octane simians. "It will not be a surprise to you to learn I'm more interested in the future of the Arctic circle than the future of the Arctic Monkeys," he told a conference crowd, adding that he was unable to name a single one of their songs.

Arms to Africa

Murky business involving UK arms exports to war-torn Sierra Leone, which caused embarrassment for Foreign Secretary Robin Cook in 1998, following his personal assurance to the Commons that the government would not deal with mercenaries. While the democratically-elected but deposed Sierra Leonean President Kabbah plotted his return to power, an embargo was in force. British 'military consultants' Sandline International, meanwhile, arranged an export of arms to the Equatorial trouble-spot – and told Customs its goons had got the nod from the Foreign Office. Most of the ensuing blame was directed by the government department at Sandline's 'shifty' Colonel Tim Spicer and High Commissioner Peter Penfold, who'd supposedly encouraged President Kabbah to 'buy British'.

Cheeks reddened again when the Foreign Affairs Committee prepared to announce its findings in February 1999. BBC correspondent Nicholas Jones, who'd predicted the report would come down especially hard on Cook, received a phone call from the man himself just prior to publication, eager to put him straight on its contents. According to Jones's memoirs, *The Control Freaks*, the Cabinet love-rat ended the chat with: "Remember, this conversation didn't take place." This came after his junior minister Tony Lloyd had told MPs that no-one in the Foreign Office had seen the report until the day of its release. It turned out that Cook had in fact enjoyed a sneak preview courtesy of his minion (and investigating committee member) Ernie Ross. Despite Cook's claims that he'd been praised by the Committee for his co-operation, the report didn't make cosy reading. Shadow Foreign Secretary Michael Howard said the inquiry had blasted ministers for 'deliberately misstating the scope and the nature of the arms embargo to Sierra Leone', continuing: "This was especially serious as the Government made an order implementing the embargo, which created a criminal offence with a maximum penalty of seven years' imprisonment." 'Cock Robin' could take solace in the fact that the report found no 'connivance' or 'conspiracy' in his department, and that it had criticised Colonel Spicer's lack of candour (or knowledge of the rules) in the first place – but he could hardly argue when the Committee diagnosed an 'appalling failure' overall from the Foreign Office. The whole affair sounded a bum note for a new government that had promised an 'ethical foreign policy'.

Arms To Iraq

Everyone knows Iraq had no weapons of mass destruction in 2003 – but this wasn't without the best efforts of the British government in the late 1980s. The Matrix Churchill affair (*qv*) was only the tip

of a disastrous policy jointly pursued by MI6 and the CIA to meet the threat of Arab nationalism by keeping the Middle East destabilised.

With the benefit of hindsight, protecting world peace by arming the region's most aggressive dictatorship might seem a little rash. However, since the policy relied on all potential enemies of Western civilisation blowing chunks out of each other, it made sense to keep the Iran-Iraq war ticking over.

"It is in Western interests for the Iranians and the Iraqis to fight each other – the longer the better"

Shameless Tory MP Alan Clark (*qv*) admitted during the 1992 Matrix Churchill trial that it was "in Western interests for the Iranians and the Iraqis to fight each other – the longer the better." Realising this happy dream required shipping arms through the more established trade route of Saudi Arabia, incorporating hefty commissions to Saudi and Iraqi warmongers en route – none of which made anyone look terribly clever when Saddam Hussein (*qv*) invaded Kuwait in 1990, making him public enemy number one for the next two decades.

see *Matrix Churchill*

Ashby, David

b. May 14th 1940

MP (Con), Leicestershire North West, 1983-97

Married barrister whose quiet backbench career was interrupted in January 1994 by allegations in the *Sunday Times* that he'd shared a double bed with a male friend, Dr Ciaran Kilduff, on a French chateau break. The claims sat awkwardly with his 1992 election literature, which stated he was 'married with a family, and therefore understands the needs of families… a man of integrity who believes in traditional moral values.' Remarkably, the source for the newspaper's story had been his estranged Italian wife, Silvana. When it declined to retract its insinuation that he was a lying gay hypocrite, Ashby sued. The absurd trial that followed at the end of 1995 saw the volatile Silvana accusing him (while giving testimony on behalf of the *Sunday Times*) of trying to murder her, their daughter Alexandra saying her mother had accused her of being a lesbian, and the MP himself brandishing a bizarre helmet (with hosepipe attachment) that he said helped get him off to sleep. Ashby insisted that the gimcrack contraption would scotch any possibility of homosexual activity, as would his impotence. But what wasn't denied was that he'd already shared rooms with a number of other MPs – for reasons of thrift, he explained. The action was unsuccessful, and when the verdict was announced Ashby shoved his wife away and wept. She announced outside the court: "I love my husband very much and will always be behind him," though whether this was a threat is unclear. Soon afterwards Ashby lost the support of his local party and resigned his seat, perhaps to focus on settling the ruinous costs he'd incurred during the four-week trial.

Ashcroft, Michael

b. March 4th 1942

Belize-based billionaire and British peer who likes nothing better than gifting cash to the Conservative Party – £3.6m at the last count (a compulsory disclosure from the Tories in the wake of the Cash for Honours scandal, *qv*). It might have been more had he not clashed with Michael Howard in 2004 over a proposed £2m donation conditional upon his distributing the funds as he saw fit, rather than leaving it to the discretion of elected policy makers. Some felt it inappropriate, too, that he arranged UK political donations from foreign nationals.

Although John Major (*qv*) kept him at arm's length, Ashcroft became party treasurer under the next leadership, weathering serious allegations of impropriety made in the *Times* (see *Belize*). Just reward came in March 2000, when William Hague (*qv*) nominated him for a life peerage – a proposal that had already been rejected once by the honours' scrutiny committee. Acknowledging that most of Ashcroft's business and political interests were in Central America, Hague added the condition that he become a tax-registered UK resident – but the tycoon publicly stated that he intended to take the title 'Baron Ashcroft of Belize'. He later insisted this was a 'joke' (he became Baron Ashcroft of Chichester), but the gesture was appreciated by the Belizian government: three months later, at their behest, he was awarded a knighthood to add to his peerage, 'for public service to the community and country of Belize'. A friend observed in June that Ashcroft had "given up a huge amount of time and energy to tackling the problems of this small, developing country" – neglecting to include the term 'tax-free' – and added: "Although he is British to the core, Belize is where his heart is."

Belize was also where most of his assets were, despite Hague's stipulation. While maintaining a giddy ranking on newspaper rich lists, he paid a surprisingly modest amount of tax in the UK. When International Development Secretary Clare Short tried to clamp down in 2001, it created a bloody fight, and in July her department had to release a statement denying that she had called the Tory a 'scumbag'. Bar-

oness Jay had already branded His Lordship 'stinking', while Labour opponent Peter Bradley MP demanded: "Is it right that somebody who seeks such a central role in one of our political parties should be so closely involved with the government of a foreign country?" And it wasn't just the People's United Party of Belize where he wielded power – in recent years he has become the biggest single donor to the Liberal Party of Australia, from his new address in the House of Lords, Westminster.

"Although he is British to the core, Belize is where his heart is"

The DEA scandal (see *Belize*) was put to bed when Murdoch personally interceded in 1999, just as Ashcroft's £100m suit against his flagship UK paper threatened to turn nasty. The Aussie Eurosceptic had no desire to turn the Conservative party against the *Times*, as both were key tools in his battle against Brussels. After the mogul's intervention the matter was settled out of court, with both sides claiming vindication. An Ashcroft supporter said: "This has never been about money. It has been about defending accusations that he was a drug dealer and a money launderer." A *Times* editorial source responded: "We have made no apology, paid no compensation, and Ashcroft has picked up his own costs."

Ashdown, Paddy

b. Feb 27th 1941
MP (Lib Dem), Yeovil, 1983-2001

This SAS hero (and leader of the newly-united Liberal Democrat party from 1988-99) is now Baron Ashdown of Norton-sub-Hamdon, but is more likely to be remembered as 'Paddy Pantsdown' after a rampant five-month affair with his secretary Tricia Howard in 1987. It only came to light in 1992, following a break-in at the offices of Ashdown's solicitors, with whom he'd cannily lodged an account of their relationship. The ensuing publicity allegedly boosted his personal rating by 13%, though his image was undermined when Howard was quoted in the *Mirror* stating: "We timed it, and it lasted nine-and-a-half seconds. For him, anyway."

Criticism of a more serious nature arose in July 2005, when Ashdown's witness statement at Slobodan Milosevic's war crimes trial was called into question. On March 14th 2002, acting in his role as the so-called 'Viceroy of Bosnia', he told the International Criminal Tribunal that he'd personally witnessed a number of Serbian atrocities through his binoculars – but three years on a defence witness appeared to show he could not have seen them from his standpoint. The Prosecution duly re-submitted the co-ordinates for Ashdown's whereabouts in June 1998, hoping to circumvent the mountain and forests said to be in his line of vision, only to position him over the sealed Kosovan border. The prosecution blustered about the necessity of being approximate, but the controversy didn't affect the outcome of the trial, which was cut short by Milosevic's death.

Ashton, Joe

b. Oct 9th 1933
MP (Lab), Bassetlaw, 1968-2001

Gritty Yorkshire MP whose long parliamentary career drew to an undignified close when he was found by police relaxing in Northampton's Siam Sauna massage parlour in November 1998. He denied paying for sex ("I did not partake in or pay for any services"), but was accused in the tabloids of having enjoyed 'bubble bath romps' with a 21-year-old prostitute. He subsequently admitted he had given the police misleading personal information at the scene, and announced he would not be standing at the next Election.

Ayas, Said
b. 1942

Personal secretary to Prince Mohammed bin Faud (*qv*) of Saudi Arabia, and fixer to Jonathan Aitken (*qv*) since the 1970s. Ayas may have been the one who paid the famous September 1993 bill at the Paris Ritz (*qv*), or it may have been his employer, or it may have been an anonymous benefactor. Whoever it was, it certainly wasn't Lolicia Aitken, as her husband claimed in court – she was in Switzerland at the time. And amongst all the allegations flying around during the 1997 libel action, one thing was never suggested for a moment: that Aitken had settled his own bill.

Robert 'Bob' Boothby

b. Feb 12th 1900 / d. July 16th 1986

MP (Con), Aberdeen & Kincardine / Aberdeenshire East, 1924-58

Characterised as 'a bounder, but not a cad' by the Queen Mother and 'a shit of the highest order' (see *Clark, Alan*) by his cousin Ludovic Kennedy, this burly rascal set out his sleaze stall early by conducting an epic affair with future PM Harold Macmillan's wife Dorothy, dating from 1929. Boothby was meant to be comforting 'Supermac' for having lost his seat – yet while the dull, gracious Macmillan channelled his dejection into political supremacy, his bisexual love rival sank into booze, gaming, a failed marriage and a faltering career. By 1964, it is widely believed, he'd even sunk into the arms of East End entrepreneur Ron Kray (see fellow pioneer Tom Driberg on page 120) – but the politician maintained that they were merely business contacts, and controversially extracted a whopping £40,000 payout from the *Mirror* in 1964 for suggesting otherwise. Either way, the great love of Boothby's life was demonstrably other men's wives: by Kennedy's account he fathered at least three children by them.

Boothby's claim to sleaze immortality came with an early, defining 'conflict of interest' (*qv*). Having chaired a 1939 committee concerning the retrieval of assets from occupied Czechoslovakia, he neglected to mention his stake in the personal case of one Richard Weininger, who'd fled Germany leaving his wealth tied up in Prague banks. At the same time as pressuring the Treasury and the House for a speedy resolution to the matter, Boothby assured various creditors that his unpaid loans (arising from gambling losses) would be covered by his forthcoming payout from Weininger. When wartime security measures saw Weininger arrested in 1940, the paperwork was enough to damn the MP. He later reflected on the matter with the timeless words: "The single sentence 'I have an interest to declare' would, it seems, have cleared me. I can only say that it never occurred to me to say it." He wouldn't be the last.

'B'

b. March 9th 1943
MP (Con), Huntingdon, 1983-2001

Puzzling cryptogram employed by Edwina Currie (*qv*) to refer to her mysterious lover in her *Diaries* 1987-92.

B, Mr

b. Sept. 29th 1936

Puzzling cryptogram employed by David Mills (*qv*) to refer to his mysterious paymaster in his business correspondence.

Back To Basics

"It is time to get back to basics: to self-discipline and respect for the law, to consideration for others", sermonised PM John Major in his address to the Tory party conference on October 8th 1993. A seemingly endless procession of stories about his MPs had started to appear in the national press almost before the bunting was torn down, and the ultimate consequence of the hubristic policy was crushing defeat at the 1997 General Election. At least no administration that boasted John Major heading up a family values campaign, Neil Hamilton taking care of business ethics and Nicholas Soames as Minister for Food could be accused of not having a sense of humour.

Edwina Currie, for one, failed to see the joke. "I think the worst thing that ever happened, for which he was entirely responsible, was Back to Basics," she fumed to BBC Radio 5 Live in 2002. "He then, as a policy, decided to have Back to Basics all about family morality, about how awful single parents were – I thought that was evil, really rotten, really cruel, and it was then open house on the way that his ministers had been behaving."

see *Currie, Edwina / Hamilton, Neil / Mellor, David / Milligan, Stephen / Yeo, Tim* and entries *passim*

SLEAZE

"I have expressed a degree of regret that could be equated with an apology"

– Defence Secretary Des Browne on allowing sailors released from captivity in Iran to sell their stories, April 2007

SLOT

Badger

Any of several small, carnivorous burrowing mammals of the family Mustelidae, having short legs, long claws and a heavy, grizzled coat. Popular with nocturnal nature enthusiasts in the UK (see *Davies, Ron*). Not to be confused with Norman Lamont (*qv*).

Bai-Lin tea

Supposedly health-giving cuppa sold at sky-high prices by Cherie Blair's sometime financial adviser, Peter Foster. Though the Aussie lag claimed the potion possessed miraculous slimming properties, boffins at Queensland's Department of Health found it to be no different from ordinary tea, and as a result he was in hot water himself.

see *Cho-Low tea*

Baker, Terence
b. 1939 / d. 1991

Jeffrey 'Lord' Archer's screen agent and ready alibi, who admitted privately that he'd lied during the 1987 *Daily Star* libel trial to protect his client – and his book rights. Unfortunately, owing to a blunder in Monica Coghlan's testimony (slavishly followed by the mendacious Archer), Baker was asked to lie about the wrong night. He died in 1991, to the future peer's undisguised relief.

see *Francis, Ted*

Bandar, Prince
b. *March 2nd 1949*

This well-rounded Saudi's full name is His Royal Highness Prince Bandar bin Sultan bin Abdul Aziz Al Saud, but he's plain old Prince Bandar to his friends. Many of these are in Britain: the RAF-trained fighter pilot was said to have been one of the chief beneficiaries of BAe's controversial al-Yamamah deal (*qv*). After Attorney-General Lord Goldsmith put the brakes on the Serious Fraud Office's lengthy investigation into it in December 2006, it became impossible to establish exactly how and if Bandar did benefit, and whether his reported £120m annual payments over 10 years ever arrived – especially since, as investigators concluded, there was "no distinction between the accounts of the embassy, or official government accounts... and the accounts of the royal family." The Prince has always strenuously denied any wrongdoing, and one person wholeheartedly backing Goldsmith was PM Tony Blair. "I don't believe the investigation would have led anywhere except to the complete wreckage of a vital strategic relationship for our country," he told a meeting of the G8 on June 7th 2007. "This investigation, if it had gone ahead, would have involved the most serious allegations and investigations being made into the Saudi royal family."

Barker, Gregory
b. March 8th 1966
MP (Con), Bexhill and Battle, 2001-

Wiry TA officer who weathered a CV-fiddling fuss to wrench his safe-as-houses seat from the reluctant grasp of Charles Wardle (*qv*). A loyal pal of David Cameron, the minted former financier (and advisor to billionaire oligarch Roman Abramovich) was appointed Shadow Environment Minister in December 2005, in which capacity he accompanied the newly-annointed leader on a pollution-belching mission to Norway in April 2006.

That October he quietly removed 'family man' references from his website when it emerged that he'd split from his wife and three children following a torrid affair with William Banks-Blaney, the interior decorator of their Sussex home. The affair came as a particular surprise to gay rights groups, who rated his voting on pro-gay matters at 30.2%, as opposed to an anti-gay score of 60.2%. As fellow MP Chris Bryant (*qv*) put it: "Greg's private life is nobody's business but his own. But it's a shame he has not felt able to have consistently backed gay rights." Comfort for Barker's wife Celeste was offered in the form of an open letter by Belinda Oaten (wife of tainted Lib Dem Mark Oaten, *qv*), generously published by the *Daily Mail*. "What I'd really like to do is come round to your house, give you a big hug and then make you the strongest gin and tonic you've had in your life," she wrote. "I don't know if you're a smoker, but I'll bring some cigarettes, too."

Bastards

1. Archaic term of abuse used to describe children born out of wedlock (see entries *passim*).

2. Current term of abuse used to describe Cabinet ministers (see *Major, John*).

BAT

British American Tobacco controls a sixth of the world's tobacco market, principally a third-world growth area and (says the World Health Organisation) an industry responsible for an estimated 10% of all adult deaths. Despite this – and conceding that BAT profited from smuggled cigarettes in developing markets – cigar-chomping Tory Kenneth Clarke (qv) insisted to the House of Commons health committee in February 2000 that BAT was "a company of integrity… an extremely good corporate citizen." By coincidence, he was also BAT's Deputy Chairman at the time, and his doomed 2001 party leadership attempt was part-funded by the firm's former boss, snout mogul Sir Patrick Sheehy.

SLEAZE

The Sun: So, how fit are you, Tony?

Cherie: Very!

The Sun: What, five times a night?

Tony: At least. I can do it more, depending how I feel.

The Sun: Are you up to it?

Cherie: He always is!

- *May 4th 2005*

SLOT

Bazoft, Farzad
b. May 22nd 1958 / d. March 15th 1990

Iran-born, British-based *Observer* journalist, operating legitimately in Iraq but executed on trumped-up charges of being an Israeli agent in 1990, after making a forced confession. Though the Cabinet made a belated attempt to secure his release, no one seems to have contemplated freezing business relations with the Gulf state (see *Arms to Iraq*). Bazoft's grim fate provoked international condemnation and a widely-suspected smear campaign by the British government. Newspapers including the *Sun* and the *Mail On Sunday* printed articles strongly implying that he was indeed a spy, though anonymous British intelligence sources told the *Sunday Times* that it was 'inconceivable' that they or Mossad would have taken him on as an agent. Following Bazoft's murder, the *Observer* accused a number of MPs of having 'used their privileged position to give substance to Iraqi propaganda in favour of this barbarity without any proof'.

These included Anthony Beaumont-Dark, Rupert Allason and Terry Dicks (all qv), the latter two of whom did their bit by appearing on TV-am (qv) to fight Iraq's corner. The utterly unconvincing Allason decreed it 'highly likely' that Bazoft would have 'tried to capitalise on his knowledge and background by offering information to the Israelis', adding the absurd remark that 'Mossad almost certainly snapped him up' (this was widely agreed to be uncharacteristic of Mossad's modus operandi).

"An innocent reporter who died a horrible death after a totally unfair trial"

Hard-right jester Dicks, meanwhile, glibly opined that a reporter should know the risks when following up a story – in this case, reports of an explosion in a military compound outside Baghdad, in which up to 700 workers were alleged to have died. He was also quoted as suggesting that Bazoft 'deserved to be hanged' on the eve of the execution. *Observer* editor Donald Trelford found their comments 'beneath contempt'. "This man was an innocent reporter who died a horrible death after a totally unfair trial," he stated. "It is monstrous that people should use this opportunity to damage his reputation."

Bearded One, The

Term of endearment used by hard-hitting canine pundit Sadie (*qv*) in her weekly *Sun* slot when describing the shenanigans of her bungling master, David Blunkett (*qv*).

Beaumont-Dark, Sir Anthony
b. Oct 11th 1932 / d. April 2nd 2006
MP (Con), Birmingham Selly Oak, 1979–92

Jut-jawed 'king of the rentaquote', renowned for aphorisms such as 'I wouldn't want twenty coloured people living next door to me' (when a Birmingham city councillor in the 1960s) and 'it's too good for the people!' (when Tony Banks suggested the House of Commons be open to the public). In fact the wealthy stockbroker was as happy goading the right as the left: slamming the Poll Tax but cheering the invasion of Iraq, one moment suggesting Prince Charles give away half his wealth, the next branding the African National Congress a terrorist organisation. He once opined that Catholics who opposed contraception should pay higher housing rates, and in 1978 moved to block a would-be bishop who didn't agree with his strict stand against homosexuality. He was so confident of his re-election in 1987 that he punted thousands on the result, but so resigned to defeat five years later that he took to insulting his own constituents on the campaign trail. Beaumont-Dark, who earned widespread condemnation for his solidarity with Rupert Allason and Terry Dicks (both *qv*) over the murder of Farzad Bazoft (*qv*), retired from public life with a knighthood "to keep me warm," and his parting remark "I certainly don't feel I shall have left footprints in the sands of time" has proven spot on.

Beggar's Belief (*sic*)

Agit-prop dope shop in North Wales, masterminded by in Rhyl's answer to Howard Marks, Jeffrey Ditchfield, and busted in its first hour of trading in September 2003, following complaints from ther Labour MP for the Vale of Clwyd, Chris Ruane. By way of protest, Ditchfield set up mail-order firm 'Bud Buddies' and attempted to supply the entire Cabinet with cannabis.

see *Ditchfield, Jeffrey*

┌─── WIGGINGS ───

"For nearly four years you wove a web of deceit in which you entangled yourself and from which there was no way out unless you were prepared to come clean and tell the truth. Unfortunately you were not... this was no passing error of judgment. It was calculated perjury pursued over a period of time"

– *Mr Justice Scott Baker to Jonathan Aitken, 1999*

└─ FROM THE BEAK ─┘

Belize

Commonwealth tax haven in Central America, to most intents and purposes owned by its UN Ambassador, Conservative peer Michael Ashcroft.

In 1999 allegations were made in the *Times* about the tycoon's offshore business interests, based on a leak revealing that the US Drug Enforcement Agency kept a file on the international party donor. Jonathan Randel, a mole in the DEA, raised concerns that the Agency was turning a blind eye to money laundering under the Ashcroft business umbrella in Belize. However, it was Randel who was indicted – for breaching national security – and eventually sent to federal prison in January 2003, while Ashcroft brought a £100m suit against the newspaper.

The *Times* settled out of court after intercession by Rupert Murdoch, withdrawing the unsubstantiated suggestion that Ashcroft had been directly "suspected of money laundering or drug-related crimes." However, in 2001 the *Guardian* published details of a US Government document released under the Freedom of Information Act, showing just why the authorities were so suspicious: lax administration in Belize and huge quantities of hard-to-regulate cashflow through the ex-Tory Treasurer's many companies were suggested. As the *Guardian* website put it (while carefully pointing out that they were not pointing fingers at Ashcroft himself), 'the loosely regulated offshore tax haven he set up in Belize has been the repeated focus of complaints that it makes life easy for criminals.'

Billionaire Ashcroft responded to the fallout by announcing an intention "to reorganise his affairs in order to return to live in Britain," though his Commons opponents still feel he should register far more of his taxable income in the UK.

see *Ashcroft, Michael*

Bell, Martin

b. Aug 31st 1938
MP (independent), Tatton,
1997 – 2001

Former BBC foreign correspondent and white-suited crusader who successfully deposed the wretched Neil Hamilton (*qv*) from the fifth-safest Conservative seat in the country on an 'anti-sleaze' ticket in 1997. Even John Major was said to have been 'speechless' when Hamilton rode roughshod over party feeling to stand for election. Such was the cross-bench feeling against Hamilton, however, that the Labour and Lib Dem candidates stood aside to let Bell scoop up their voters. Few outside the husband-and-wife Hamilton campaign team were sorry when he registered a whopping 11,077 majority over the beleaguered Tory, smugly proclaiming his victory 'a beacon which will shed light in dark corners'.

An August 1998 article in the *Sunday Express* pointed out that Bell's Parliamentary attendance record compared dismally with his sleazy predecessor's. 'One MP with a surprisingly poor score is independent Martin Bell, with only 32 per cent,' it stated. 'In marked contrast, his disgraced predecessor Neil Hamilton managed 74 per cent.'

Having insisted that he would not seek re-election, in 2001 Bell relocated to Brentwood & Ongar and did just that, unsuccessfully – a trick he repeated at the 2004 European Parliament elections.

SLEAZE

"My primary concern in fighting the case is to clear my name — but I am also determined to remove the slur the cash-for-questions case has cast over parliament as a whole"
- *Neil Hamilton upon going to Court, November 1999.*

SLOT

Berlusconi, Silvio
b. Sept. 29th 1936

Italy's longest-serving post-war prime minister described himself as 'the Jesus Christ of politics' at the launch of his failed bid to retain office in 2006, though his detractors in the home of Catholicism struggle to see the comparison.

A right-wing billionaire and plastic surgery enthusiast with colossal media interests, he has successively been tried for embezzlement, tax fraud, false accounting, bribing the police and corrupting the judiciary, but despite a string of convictions he has largely gone unpunished. The statute of limitations which he brought into force has been a good friend to him, as has Tony Blair – following their decision to support one another in Europe and over the Iraq war, Blair condescended to holiday in Berlusconi's 27-bedroom clifftop villa in Sardinia. Berlusconi also forged a close link with lawyer David Mills (*qv*) in the 1990s, leading to accusations of corruption that threatened to derail the career of Mills's wife Tessa Jowell (*qv*). In October 2006 the pair were committed for trial in Italy for corruption, having already been charged with tax evasion and embezzlement. However, that November a fainting fit on the part of Berlusconi – acted out live during a TV debate – saw the legal process suspended, possibly for good.

Best, Keith
b. June 10th 1949
MP (Con), Anglesey, 1979-83 /
Ynys Mon, 1983-87

Former soldier and lawyer whose promising parliamentary career fizzled out in 1987 when it emerged that he had fraudulently acquired more than his fair share of shares in British Telecom when it was privatised in 1984. A long-term advocate of privatisation, Best had legitimately snapped up shares in Enterprise Oil, Cable & Wireless, British Aerospace and Britoil before the big one was floated. Frustrated by the 800-shares per person restriction, however, he hit upon the brilliant expedient of applying under multiple addresses, bank accounts and names ('Keith Best', 'Lander Best', 'Keith Lander Best'), bagging 4800 shares and a profit of £4800.

When *Labour Research* magazine exposed the dealings on April 1st 1987, he acted quickly to limit the damage. "At the time of making the applications, I did not consider that I was acting improperly," he blustered, pledging to give any profits to charity. When it emerged that he'd used a similar gambit to purchase shares in Jaguar, however, he announced that he'd stand down at the next Election.

It wasn't enough for Scotland Yard, and in October 1987 he was tried, convicted, fined and jailed for four months (he served five days). Sentencing him, Judge Butler remarked: "You engaged in carefully calculated acts of dishonesty, designed to provide a substantial profit. Nor have you expressed one word of regret." Kinder words came from fellow MP David Evans (*qv*). "I think Keith was just somebody who got caught," he trilled. "I think most people are at it. I don't think he is a criminal in any way." Voters in Anglesey begged to differ, and his seat was soon claimed by Plaid Cymru.

Betsygate

If sleaze could be measured on a sliding scale, Watergate would be at one end and this at the other. The truly stultifying scandal, which broke in October 2003, involved Ian Duncan Smith's wife working for the Tory party whilst also drawing a public salary. Or something. While it was undoubtedly preferable for a Tory to be carrying on with his Diary Secretary (*qv*) when he also happened to be married to her, the petty Newsnight exposé (masterminded by Jeffrey Archer's scourge Michael Crick) chose to focus on the suggestion that the avowedly 'non-political' Betsy was not doing enough to justify her parliamentary wage. Watchdog Sir Philip Mawer duly spent months propping up his eyelids while researching the claim, and concluded in March 2004 that the hapless Betsy was indeed just about worth her modest £15k pay-packet.

see *Duncan Smith, Iain*

Betts, Clive
b. Jan 13th 1950
MP (Lab), Sheffield Attercliffe, 1992 -

Classic 'moment of madness' MP who endured an unenviable stint on Sheffield City Council as deputy to David Blunkett (*qv*) before joining the House. His progress was steady until

February 2003, when allegations emerged that he'd photocopied a doctored immigration officer's letter. This was an attempt to fox passport authorities into allowing his Brazilian 'assistant' José Gasparo to re-enter Britain – an offence that carried a potential £5,000 fine or six months' imprisonment. He was also accused of applying for a security pass so that Gasparo could work as a researcher in his Westminster office, without telling authorities that Gasparo was also a male escort, and thus automatically classed as a security risk. Unusually, Betts – whose activities were fearlessly exposed by the *Sun* and the *Daily Mail* – reported himself to the Parliamentary authorities for investigation. The Committee on Standards and Privileges swung into action, and ruled in July that Betts had 'connived in a course of action which might have led to the immigration officer being deceived,' that his 'conduct fell well below the standard expected of a Member' and that he had 'undoubtedly acted extremely foolishly.' Their report also wearily noted that 'past experience indicates how the employment in the Palace Of Westminster of a person with a history of work in the sex industry can become a cause of public scandal,' and Betts was suspended from the House for a week.

Bissett-Scott, Sarah
b. 1949

Former Labour candidate who claimed to have had a two-year affair with beefy lothario John Prescott (*qv*) in the late 80s. "I was totally bowled over by him," she reminisced in the *Sunday Mirror* on April 30th 2006. "He did all the running, but I loved him and I think he loved me too… He might be fat and ugly now, but when I knew him was a very attractive man."

Black, Conrad
b. Aug 25th 1944

Former *Telegraph* proprietor, convicted fraudster and Tory peer who was so keen to become Baron Black of Crossharbour – on Tony Blair's recommendation – that he renounced Canadian citizenship in 2001. His new status came under threat on July 13th 2007, when he was found guilty on four counts in his Chicago fraud trial, accounting for around three million dollars worth of till-dipping. This followed a government White Paper proposing an 'Archer law', whereby peers who'd done porridge could be stripped of their gladrags; in any event the Tory whip was removed from his grasping fingers.

see *Maxwell, Robert / Archer, Jeffrey*

Black Book, the

The original bumper book of British sleaze, this legendary tome – compiled by whips – allegedly recorded sensitive information about MPs' personal, sexual and financial foibles. Thought to have been instituted by the Tories to encourage intransigent members to toe the party line, it was apparently abandoned when Nick Brown (*qv*) took over as Chief Whip in May 1997.

Black Monday

Name given to November 16th 1992, when bungling Tory Chancellor Norman Lamont (*qv*) was falsely said to have visited a branch of Thresher to splash out on a bottle of fizz and 20 Raffles.

see *Threshergate / Onanuga, John*

Black Wednesday

Name given to September 16th 1992, when bungling Tory Chancellor Norman Lamont (*qv*) decided to withdraw the pound from the Exchange Rate Mechanism (ERM), prompting nationwide fiscal meltdown. Tory hesitancy over when Britain should join, and unfavourable domestic conditions when she did, left her vulnerable to investors like George Soros speculating triumphantly on the pound's devaluation, while trading losses to British business totalled £800m over two months, and were finally estimated by the Treasury in 1997 to stand at £3.3bn. One financial ace doling out advice to Lamont at the time was the young David Cameron (*qv*).

SLEAZE

"You wake up and you receive a phone call – Shipman's topped himself. You have just got to think for a minute: is it too early to open a bottle?"
– *Home Secretary David Blunkett on Harold Shipman's suicide, January 2004*

"He said what he said – and it is what he genuinely thinks. I suspect it's how most ordinary people feel, too"
– *Home Office spokesman*

"Mr Blunkett has nothing to celebrate in the fact the prison service is incapable of detaining people properly for their crimes and has an appalling suicide record"
– *Mark Oaten MP*

SLOT

Blair, Cherie

b. Sept 23rd 1954

Gaffe-prone New Labour 'First Lady', whose links with crooks and cranks (see *Foster, Peter / Temple, Jack / Caplin, Carole*) steadily undermined the gravitas of her husband's office. In addition, a perceived inability to resist freebies (and lucrative speaking engagements) led to accusations of exploiting his position – something she steadfastly denied.

The daughter of softcore stud Tony Booth (*qv*), Cherie was a gifted law student and married Tony Blair in 1980. Having unsuccessfully contested Thanet North as a Labour candidate at the 1983 Election, she built a prominent career as an advocate. Hours after her husband claimed the top job in April 1997, she gave the public an early taste of indignities to come by answering the door to No. 10 in her nightie, wild-eyed and mad-haired, to accept a bunch of flowers from waiting tabloid photographers ("I thought, 'Oh my God, Tony is gonna kill me'," she later revealed). By 2000 she was one of the highest-paid QCs in the land, and was fined a tenner for travelling on a train without a ticket.

"I thought, Oh my god, Tony is gonna kill me"

Her nadir came two years later, when her fingers got spectacularly burnt over the 'Cheriegate' scandal. This followed the fateful decision to take financial advice from Australian entrepreneur Peter Foster (*qv*), lover of her best friend Carole Caplin (*qv*). The pair of flats she bought with his assistance not only called her judgement into question once and for all, but also prompted the memorable press call at which she explained she was 'not a superwoman' (*qv*).

At the 2002 Labour Party conference she stunned delegates by collecting free goods for her children from stalls, and the following April a polite offer to take one or two items gratis from a Melbourne store resulted in a frenzied trolley-dash. Attendants watched open-mouthed as the PM's wife selected clothes aplenty, as well as an alarm clock, a beach play set, a lunchbox and some pillow cases, eventually departing with some 68 items. Her eye for the main chance was never more prominent than during her speaking tours promoting *The Goldfish Bowl* (*qv*), a ditchwatery canter through the spouses of great British leaders, published in September 2004. In order to stimulate the sluggish sales of the deadly tome, Mrs Blair embarked on a sensational world tour. Having broken what was described as a 'self-imposed TV interview ban' to flog the project in front of relentless interrogators Richard Madeley and Judy Finnegan (a concept that may have been floated during their visit to Chequers in May 2003), she also attracted criticism for accepting fabulously lucrative speaking engagements.

Especially painful was a tour of New Zealand and Australia in February 2005 (dubbed 'the PR trip from hell' by the *Independent*), where she greeted the Kiwis as Aussies, enthused about her book at length (instead of the children's cancer charity involved) and trouser-suited a cool £102,000. A subsequent inquiry by Aussie watchdog Consumer Affairs Victoria suggested that the five-date tour had raised significantly less than Cherie's fee. This led to fears that the charity would have to deregister: a stipulation of charitable status required 60% of proceeds going to research, but at one Melbourne dinner only £6,690 of the £81,270 receipts ended up helping the stricken tots. British-based event organiser Max Markson also took a hefty £40k cut from the tour.

"Gob-smackingly, spine-chillingly, hair-raisingly extraordinary"

Later that year, while in the States on official business with her husband, she nipped off to perform a £30k gig in Washington's Kennedy Centre, which killjoys interpreted as a gross misuse of government transport resources. Further embarrassment came with her May 2006 idea of auctioning a signed (by her) copy of the Hutton Report (*qv*) to raise money for the cash-strapped Labour party. Tony Blair responded to the ensuing outcry by assuring the Commons that "I do not believe that any offence to anyone was intended," prompting Ed Vaizey, MP for the family of David Kelly (*qv*), to respond: "I can assure him that it was caused." The ghoulish lot raised a meagre £400. Her inability to avoid controversy was paraded again as she left 10 Downing Street for the last time on July 27th 2007, when she mouthed at the assembled press "goodbye, I don't think we'll miss you" – a sentiment the BBC's political editor Nick Robinson called 'gob-smackingly, spine-chillingly, hair-raisingly extraordinary'.

Blair, Tony

b. 6th May 1953
MP (Lab), Sedgefield, 1983-2007
Prime Minister 1997-2007

Whether one sees Anthony Charles Lyndon Blair as the greatest leader this country has ever known or the very embodiment of phony socialism, a soft-porn star's son-in-law made good (see *Booth, Tony*) or 'a pretty straight sort of guy' (as he described himself in 1997), many are troubled by a nagging doubt that his inauguration pledge of making the Labour Party 'purer than pure' was not 100% honoured.

Trouble began for the public school-educated barrister within weeks of gaining power, with the Bernie Ecclestone scandal *(qv)*. That prompted him to come as close as he ever would to an apology, conceding: "I didn't get it all wrong". Having astonished the party by sending his own children to a fee-paying school outside his borough (see *London Oratory, the)*, his election pledge to sack sleazy MPs 'on the spot' was sorely tested in 1998, when Robin Cook *(qv)* and Ron Davies *(qv)* showed that it wasn't just Tories who liked to put it about, and kingmaker Peter Mandelson *(qv)* inexorably morphed into New Labour's answer to Jeffrey Archer *(qv)* – an embarrassment who kept being given another chance. Preferential treatment of his closest mates in the party – Lord Irvine, Lord Levy, Lord Falconer, Steven Byers – led to cries of Cronyism *(qv)*, and his dependence on the sinister, unelected Alastair Campbell *(qv)* further undermined the public's faith in his ability to trust his own convictions. Dogged support of the Millennium Dome *(qv)* didn't help matters much, either ("in the Dome we have a creation that, I believe, will truly be a beacon to the world", he stated at its February 1998 launch).

Blair's legacy, however, will always be most marked by two especially stubborn sleaze stains – Cash for Honours and the Dodgy Dossier (both *qv*). The former resulted in his being interviewed thrice as a witness by police, in December 2006 and January and June 2007 (becoming the first time a serving British leader had ever been quizzed in relation to a criminal investigation), and the latter became comfortably the most talked-about aspect of his three terms in power. The spurious basis on which the country was led into an unpopular war without UN authority (see *45 Minutes, WMDs*), it was the catalyst for many unnecessary deaths, perhaps most notoriously that of government weapons expert Dr David Kelly (*qv*). It also prompted an attempt to impeach the Prime Minister in August 2004, instigated by Plaid Cymru MP Adam Price – the first such Commons petition for 150 years.

"I didn't get it all wrong"

Domestic issues did little to brighten the reputation of brand Blair in the new millennium either. Trusted deputies like David Blunkett and John Prescott (both *qv*) saw out long careers mired in sleaze; the Home Office was in abject disarray; Stephen Byers (*qv*), culpable of misleading Railtrack shareholders in 2002, admitted that Britain's railways had become 'worse' since Labour came to power; the Health Service remained a sore point, and the goodwill generated by a rare 10 Downing Street baby in May 2000 diminished when little Leo became the focus of a fuss concerning the MMR vaccine (*qv*). To many, this epitomised the 'do-as-I-say, not-as-I-do' Blair image. As former rival Paddy Ashdown (*qv*) noted in his diaries, "he tends to say what

people want to hear" (except, he might have added, 'we're pulling out of Iraq').

Blair clung grimly to power whilst trying to make up for his misjudgements, finding time to run the country between TV turns on *The Simpsons* and a Catherine 'are you disrespectin' me?' Tate skit (during which he informed the 'am I bovvered?' comedienne that he 'really needed to get on' and was 'a bit pushed for time'). But despite making the 'thoughtful' gift of a £90 Burberry jumper to George Bush in July 2006, Blair could not persuade the US President to let him muscle in on the big issues, such as the Israeli-Lebanon crisis that same month.

This lent credibility to the ever-growing suspicion that Britain's slick Premier was something of a lightweight when it came to the issues that really mattered – and when the dust settles over New Labour, one nagging question may remain: just what the hell *did* Tony Blair believe in?

Perhaps his memoirs will clarify the point: according to the *Telegraph* on August 20th 2007, the former PM 'has instructed a leading American lawyer to negotiate a publishing deal for his political memoirs, which could make him up to £8 million.'

Bletchley Motors Group

Many politicians have been likened to car salesmen, but Luton North MP 'Honest' John Carlisle (*qv*) took things a stage further in 1995 by converting the hallowed floor of the Commons into a Rover showroom. In fulfilling his declared duty as a director of this Milton Keynes-based dealership, the rabid right-winger offered 'members of both Houses of Parliament, their families and their staff' mates' rates on new wheels. The brochure confirmed he'd be 'happy to arrange a demonstration in London or your own home', and could be easily contacted 'at the House' (when not serving the needs of his constituents, of course).

Bliar

Humorous anagram devised by puzzle boffins for use on satirical T-shirts. Coldplay idol Chris Martin and reality TV icon George Galloway (*qv*) are celebrity fans of the joke, whose strong implication is that former Prime Minister Tony Blair is a liar.

SLEAZE

> "John is John and I'm lucky to have him as my deputy"
>
> – *Tony Blair on John Prescott thumping the electorate, May 2001*

SLOT

Blind Trust

1. An investment whose details are kept from the investor, usually used by MPs to save any possibility of being accused of conflicts of interest; what Cherie Blair appears to have used to purchase two Bristol flats in 2002 (see *Cheriegate*).

2. Total faith, without precaution or proviso. What Cherie Blair placed in convicted criminal Peter Foster over her property investments; what her husband placed in many of his MPs (see *Mandelson, Peter / Blunkett, David / Prescott, John* etc.).

Blunkett, David
b. June 6th 1947
MP (Lab), Sheffield Brightside, 1987-

No blind Briton since Milton has achieved as much as this Sheffield-born socialist – but Milton didn't sleep with married women (including, scholars suspect, his own wife). Nor was he accused of fast-tracking visa applications, punting on shares in which he held interests, or neglecting to declare free membership of upper-class discothèques.

After a long apprenticeship in local politics (he was a member of Sheffield City Council from 1970 and its leader from 1980-87), Blunkett entered the Commons in 1987 and progressed through the Shadow ranks, becoming Education Secretary after the 1997 election. He established his hardline credentials by decrying civil rights for foreign nationals as 'airy-fairy' and 'libertarian' in November 2001, and was made Home Secretary in the first reshuffle of the second term. His irascible disposition made him most ill-suited to the post, and his tenure was marked by a stream of intemperate public statements (such as revealing that his first response to Harold Shipman's prison suicide was "is it too early to open a bottle?"). Things came to a head in November 2004 when it emerged that his office had assisted the 'fast-tracking' of the immigration application of his married lover's nanny, 'Luz' Casalme (*qv*).

Despite investigator Sir Alan Budd having confidently established 'a chain of events linking Blunkett to the change in the decision on Ms Casalme's application,' the Home Secretary continued to insist he'd done nothing wrong. 'Where [Sir Alan's] findings differ from my recollections, this is simply due to failure on my part to recall details,' he bumbled, and when he did eventually go (on December 15th 2004, with £18,725 in severance pay), he insisted he was only doing so to spare his pal Tony further embarrassments. He was not sufficiently embarrassed himself to leave his grace-and-favour £3m Belgravia mansion for a further year, despite mutterings about rent and taxes from his new neighbours on the backbenches.

Most embarrassing for all concerned, however, was an ongoing love polygon linking American-born Kimberly Quinn, her estranged husband, and a string of alleged lovers: Blunkett, Fleet Street adonis Simon Hoggart, an Indian media honcho and a breakfast radio presenter. All but Blunkett distanced themselves from the undignified mess. Though Blunkett had been divorced since 1990, Quinn (publisher of crusty Bible the *Spectator*) was married, and reconciled with husband Stephen while pregnant in August 2004. Subsequent DNA testing proved that her two-year old tot William was indeed Blunkett's, but that he was not the father of newly-born Lorcan.

Having been forgiven for disporting with Tory publishers, Blunkett was himself 'fast-tracked' back into government when the voters returned Labour the following May. Just hours after the reshuffle on May 7th 2005, he was appointed Secretary of State for Work and Pensions – but was back in the soup almost immediately. Speculation about his freebie membership of posh London nightclub Annabel's and a relationship with vivacious 29-year-old blonde Sally Anderson (*qv*) followed. But it wasn't this that kippered him; two weeks before accepting the Cabinet post, Blunkett had accepted a paid directorship of DNA Bioscience, buying £15k worth of shares in the company – which specialised in paternity-testing technology – without consulting the relevant advisory committee. It was revealed on November 1st 2005 that he'd ignored no fewer than three letters from the committee's chairman, Lord Mayhew of Twysden, inviting him to consult them. Despite maintaining there was no conflict of interests, and pushing a series of loophole arguments about family trusts, the former 'Iron Home Secretary' was scuttled the moment the story broke. He resigned again on November 2nd 2005, banking his second £18,725 severance

payment in 12 months. "I think he's more or less admitted that he should have followed the rules," mused Lord Nolan in a *Yorkshire Post* interview. "But I think it's the fault of the Government that he has been allowed to see if he can get away with it."

It wasn't all bad news, though: having followed Peter Mandelson (*qv*) in resigning from successive Cabinet posts, on December 1st he began penning a wretched weekly column for the *Sun* (whose flame-haired editor, Rebekah Wade, he counts as a close friend). For this he was paid around £150,000 a year – considerably more than his ministerial salary. This little earner wasn't cleared by the Advisory Committee on Business Appointments until after he'd started either, prompting the *Independent On Sunday* to observe on December 4th: 'Although Mr Blunkett can say that he observed the precise wording of the code, that 'ministers should seek advice on business appointments', he has certainly flouted its spirit in not waiting for a reply'.

Trouble flared up again in April 2006, when it emerged that he was spurning his constituency home in favour of a cottage on the Duke of Devonshire's Chatsworth estate, towards whose rent he'd claimed £20,000 from the public purse.

James Frayne, of the Taxpayers' Alliance, commented in the *Sunday Times*: "Taxpayers should not have to pay for this when he has a much cheaper property so close." In September 2006 he published his stultifying journals (see *Dreary Diary, the*), confessing in the entry for October 9th 2005: "If I could turn the clock back... I would run a mile from DNA Bioscience and suppers with Sally Anderson." But it was far, far too late – by then he had long since rivalled John Prescott for the title of New Labour's leading liability.

Bofors affair

The greatest scandal in Indian government history, involving a protracted investigation into major Labour donors Srichand and Gopichand Hinduja (*qv*). It is illegal in India to profit from commission on the sale of arms (in this case some 400 howitzers peddled to the Indian military by Swedish firm Bofors in 1986), but it seemed that several senior figures in the Indian establishment had done just that. The Hindujas were finally able to convince a court that payments received from the Swedes stemmed from a long-term consultancy contract, not a billion-dollar guns bonanza – to the considerable relief of their many friends in government in the UK. The fiasco finally fizzled out after the 14-year, £30m trial collapsed in chaos. Following their May 2005 dismissal, three of the four brothers returned to their homes in Europe – but many Indians feel there's still a case to answer back home.

Booth, Cherie
b. Sept 23rd 1954

High-powered human rights lawyer with London's Matrix Chambers. Not to be confused with hausfrau, author and public orator Cherie Blair (*qv*).

Booth, Hartley
b. July 17th 1946
MP (Con), Finchley, 1992 – 1997

Married Methodist lay preacher (and grandson of William Booth, founder of the Salvation Army) who inherited his coveted North London seat from Margaret Thatcher. Early in 1994 it emerged that he had become 'infatuated' with his Parliamentary Researcher (*qv*), part-time nude model Emily Barr, and the ensuing bother prompted his resignation as PPS to Douglas Hogg. Booth denied their relationship was ever physical, a claim Barr flatly contradicted ("if it got to an orgasmic situation, I'd feel a little guilty saying no"); but the lovelorn member damned himself by penning a syrupy volume of poems to the 22-year-old under the witless *nom de plume* Justin Thyme (*'You said you seduced me / He who is tall / Has further to fall – and I fell / How I fell'*).

Pleading poverty, he proceeded to spend some months haranguing the student for the return of modest sums of money he had spent on her (including a big-hearted £400 towards an abortion scare), and lost his seat at the next opportunity. Barr, meanwhile, worked for Peter Mandelson (*qv*) before moving to France and becoming a mid-ranking purveyor of 'chick lit'.

Booth, Lauren
b. July 22nd 1967

Coat-turning model-cum-pundit whose meal ticket is in no way dependent on being half-sister-in-law to Tony Blair (*qv*).

At the 1997 Election she was (in her own words) a 'card-carrying Blairite', but by September 2006 she was screeching 'Yo, Blair! Time to go!' at a rally, assuring the crowd that her relationship with the PM was a "coincidence of marriage that makes neither of us very happy." Whether her journalistic career would outlive his premiership was always a moot point, and it surprised no one when she appeared in 2006's *I'm A Celebrity, Get Me Out Of Here*, boasting in its publicity material that her 'special talents' included 'burping'. This isn't the only social convention she's happy to flout: she told the *Independent* in October 2001 that "I've been smoking cannabis since I was 14, and it hasn't done me any harm" – a predilection she apparently shares with her father (see *Booth, Tony*).

Booth, Tony
b. Oct 9th 1931

Hellraising star of the small screen and would-be socialist icon whose pungent 2002 autobiography *What's Left?* proudly states that he is 'now recognised as the Prime Minister's father-in-law', following daughter Cherie's 1980 love-match with Tony Blair.

"I have noticed on visits to Downing Street that whenever I begin to talk politics with Tony, an aide will materialise with an urgent request for his attention"

Subtitled *A Political Memoir*, it outlines his vision for a better Britain, recasting his booze-fuelled showbiz career as the history of a left-wing firebrand. In it, Booth claims personal responsibility for, amongst other things, New Labour's 'windfall tax' scheme, after bending Blair's ear about big business in 1997. Nevertheless, he poignantly observes: "Perhaps it is no more than coincidence, but I have noticed on visits to Downing Street that whenever I begin to talk politics with Tony, an aide will materialise with an urgent request for his attention." Blair's caution perhaps stems from his father-in-law's tendency to smoke cannabis on his premises (to relieve pain in his legs), as revealed in the *Mail on Sunday* in 2001.

For all his political fervour, Booth is best loved for his tawdry turn as small-town Don Juan 'Sidney Noggett' in low-rent Carry On rip-offs like *Confessions Of A Window Cleaner*. In the 1978 classic *Confessions From A Holiday Camp*, he services a fellow holidaymaker so frenziedly in a toolshed that the structure collapses. Ever the idealist, Booth stoutly maintains: "If the films had been made in France or Italy, they would have been revered as 'art'."

Bophuthatswana

South African puppet state incorporating the 'racist Vegas' - Sun City, a vast tourist playground described by Tory MP Tim Rathbone in 1986 as being "born out of the womb of the obnoxious policy of apartheid". In September 1987 Andrew Hunter MP (*qv*) chaired a Bophuthatswana Parliamentary Group in the Commons, dedicated to winning the territory recognition as a nation-state (and therefore immunity from international sanctions imposed on South Africa). The government would never have countenanced the concept, as the profitable region (a haven for prostitution, cheap labour and police brutality) was still subject to Pretoria both economically and in rule of law. But that didn't stop BPG members accepting its hospitality throughout the late 1980s, in exchange for lobbying their colleagues, either at Westminster's plush L'Amico restaurant or in the unofficial Bophuthatswanan 'embassy' in Holland Park (purchased and set up in 1981-2). Despite years more of such freebies, the international community stood firm, and the operation was eventually wound up after protracted controversy over the whereabouts of its funds (see *Emery, Sir Peter*). By that time a large number of MPs had enjoyed free Bophuthatswanan jaunts that came to be known in parliament as 'the Bop run'.

Bordes, Pamella
b. 1961

Sultry sub-continental strumpet who pole-vaulted into the headlines early in 1989 when it emerged that she'd stepped out with junior minister Colin Moynihan, having had an affair with a Libyan security official named Ahmed Gadaff Al-Daim. This alleged mistress-sharing raised hysterical newspaper speculation similar to that surrounding John Profumo in 1961. The water was further muddied when it was established that Tory MP Henry Bellingham had obtained a Commons pass for Bordes, so she could act as a Parliamentary Researcher (*qv*) for his Honourable Friend David Shaw. "From my point of view, this has all become too silly for words," Shaw sighed to the *Evening Standard* in March. A former Miss India, Bordes was also the sometime companion of newspaper editors Donald Trelford (the *Observer*) and Andrew Neil (the *Sunday Times*), whose hair-dye she controversially alleged had stained his pillow-cases, and whose flat and wardrobe she notoriously trashed. She never confirmed nor denied allegations that she was a prostitute, and returned to India when the scandal died down, where she is now thought to work as a photographer.

Bowden, Sir Andrew

b. April 8th 1930
MP (Con), Brighton Kemptown,
1970-97

Old school Tory implicated in the Cash For Questions affair (*qv*). His parliamentary feathers had gone unruffled until old crony Ian Greer (*qv*) introduced him to Mohammed Fayed (*qv*) in February 1987. Bowden was subsequently accused of requesting £50,000 in exchange for lobbying on the Egyptian's behalf in the Commons. He vigorously denied that Greer's whopping £5,319 donation to his election fund had originated from Fayed, though the payment neatly dovetailed with six parliamentary questions he'd tabled relating to the tycoon. The Downey Report (*qv*) eventually concluded that it had probably been 'intended as a reward for lobbying, and Sir Andrew probably knew it came originally from Mr Fayed,' and Bowden was criticised for giving 'a positively misleading explanation' of his dealings with the House of Fraser. There was insufficient evidence of his demanding cash for formal censure, but the report did criticise him for failing adequately to declare his interests to ministers.

Since being unseated in 1997, the ageing knight has found a preferable way of making a fast buck – he's been ranked 72nd best poker player in Europe. "I am a reasonably gifted amateur, but that is the best I would say," he told the *Independent* in June 2006 – an assessment that might seem generous if applied to his political career.

Brazier, Julian

b. July 24th 1953
MP (Con), Canterbury, 1987-

Tory Eurosceptic who killed a motorcyclist, Carlo Civitelli, whilst driving on the wrong side of the road on holiday in Tuscany in 2002. The Territorial Army officer blamed the accident on a 'lapse of attention', and was banned from driving in Italy for six months, as well as receiving a four-month suspended prison term. In June 2005 Michael Howard made him Shadow Transport Spokesman, a move condemned by the *Sunday Mirror* as 'the most insensitive political appointment in living memory'. Brazier was quick to reassure naysayers, explaining: "I've joined the all-party group on road safety and sat my advanced driving test. I am looking forward to the job very much."

Brit Awards

Critically-derided music industry prizegiving where, in 1996, PM-in-waiting Tony Blair garlanded his hero David Bowie, sticking around long enough to hob-nob with Oasis – though Hobnobs are not thought to have been among the refreshments on offer at their table. "There were literally ounces of cocaine just a couple of feet away," bragged a band source later. The group's leader Noel Gallagher dubbed Blair 'the man' on accepting his own gong, and before long he was round at No.10, cracking gags with Blair about their respective ways of managing to 'stay up all night'. Downing Street stopped sending representatives to the

Brits in 1998, however, after John Prescott was doused (see *Nobacon, Danbert*). Still, New Labour can't claim pole position for embarrassment at the awards – in 1990 pop pederast Jonathan King somehow persuaded Margaret Thatcher to croon *How Much Is That Doggy In The Window?* in a video link, prompting several sickened artists to return their prizes.

British Consul in Singapore

Non-existent position never held by Jeffrey Archer's father.

see *Viceroy of Brunei*

SLEAZE

"Many of those who have spoken in the Football Disorder Bill debate are either lawyers or football fans. I have to confess I am neither"
– David Cameron in the Commons, October 2001

"It was just very gently pointed out that Gordon Brown watched from a box and that David was more like a real fan"
– a David Cameron aide on England's World Cup opener, June 2006

SLOT

SLEAZE

> "I think that his days as a front line politician are over"
>
> – *David Cameron on Jeffrey Archer, November 2005*

SLOT

Brown Envelopes

Discreet paper conveyances capable of holding letters, photographs, dirty magazines or wadges of £5 notes.

see *Fayed, Mohammed / Coghlan, Monica / Hamilton, Neil / Smith, Tim / Cash For Questions*

Brown, Gordon
b. Feb 20th 1951
MP (Lab), Dunfermline East, 1983-2005 / Kirkcaldy & Cowdenbeath 2005-
Prime Minister 2007-

Christened James Brown (and there comparisons with the Sex Machine must end), this burly bean-counter, eternal pension optimist and bargain-basement bullion barterer had a momentous 2007: it was the year he became the first frontbench politician from any nation to urge public support for one Big Brother contestant over another. "A vote for Shilpa is a vote for Britain, and British tolerance," urged the PM-in-waiting as millions of UK voters hit the phones ahead of the January 18th *Celebrity Big Brother* eviction. Brown's guidance was sadly confused, however: viewers were voting for the housemate they wished to evict, so a vote for Bollywood second-stringer Shilpa Shetty would have played into the hands of her tormentor, Essex foghorn Jade Goody (*qv*).

see *Spence, Laura*

Brown, Michael (i)
b. July 3rd 1951
MP (Con), Brigg & Scunthorpe, 1979-83 / Brigg & Cleethorpes, 1983-97

Grubby member who was steadily shinning up the greasy pole when he was outed by the tabloids and implicated in the Cash For Questions affair (*qv*), which combined to KO his political prospects.

From 1989 to 1990 Brown had served as PPS to Trade & Industry Minister Douglas Hogg (he later boasted in the *Sunday Telegraph* of having fellated an unnamed lobby journalist in Hogg's Commons office). His career was still in the ascendant when, in May 1994, the *News of the World* jubilantly ran a story under the headline 'lawmaker is lawbreaker' showing him holidaying in Barbados with a 20-year-old man, at a time when the gay age of consent was 21. He'd already been accused of participating in a threesome with his beach companion, and resigned as a junior government whip. As the paltry story coincided with John Major's 'Back To Basics' farrago, however, it dragged on far longer than it deserved. It had just about been forgotten by July 1997, when the Downey Report (*qv*) roasted him for failing to register money received from uber-lobbyist Ian Greer regarding US Tobacco. "Mr Brown persistently and deliberately failed to declare his interests in dealing with Ministers and officials over the Skoal Bandits issue," it said, and few were surprised when Brown failed to retain his seat at the General Election on May 1st 1997.

Brown, Michael (ii)
b. April 19th 1966

Slovenly Scottish-born crook who dubbed the Lib Dems 'muppets' when his unprecedented £2.4m donation to their funds in 2005 ended up being investigated by the Electoral Commission. The pony-tailed property millionaire was hardly in a position to pass judgement, though: he was in breach of probation in Florida for bouncing cheques before fleeing the country in the mid-90s, and technically remained a fugitive. He told the *Times* that it was only a matter of three small cheques made out for tins of noodles when he was starving, but US authorities revealed that the deception ran into many thousands of dollars (his lawyer, Tamara Lynne Jones, who'd kept Brown out of jail on the charge of grand theft, lost patience with the case when he twice bounced $2,500 cheques to cover her own services).

The row over the Glaswegian school drop-out's political contribution centred on the fact that he had nothing registered at UK Companies House at the time it was made, therefore making it roughly £2.4m more than was lawful from an overseas businessman. When the papers got hold of the story, he angrily demanded that the Lib Dems return his money – but his troubles were only just beginning. In April 2006, after £26m in cash loans to his 5th Avenue Partners company had gone walkabout, lawyers for HSBC caught up with him at his new home in Majorca as he prepared for his 40th birthday beano.

With Brown left biting the pillow in a Spanish jail awaiting extradition to the UK, the investigation escalated to incorporate criminal charges, including an impressive 53 counts of forgery alone. Covering over half a billion pounds of supposed trade, the accusations encompassed forgery and false accounting relating to the time he was almost single-handedly funding the Lib Dems' headlong charge towards third place in the 2005 election.

When the High Court ruled that 5th Avenue Partners was fraudulent and had never traded (Brown had needed a nominal UK business in order to qualify as a legitimate donor in the first place), prominent Lib Dems began to regret their glee in the mammoth pay-out. Reddest-faced would have been treasurer Reg Clark and then-leader Charles Kennedy, who'd enjoyed £30k of free flights on Brown's private jet during the campaign, as well as copping a giant gift hamper on the birth of his son. In October 2006, Brown received a two-year prison sentence – 18 months on the charge of 'very deliberate and well thought-through perjury', according to Judge Geoffrey Rivlin QC, and 6 months for the other 'serious offence' of obtaining a false passport (this was a 'pointed flouting of a direct court order' – Brown applied for a fresh one after claiming to have lost his old one in the washing machine).

Unsurprisingly, Lib Dem peers were now calling for the donation's return: "It was not a desirable source of funding, and we should not take funding from sources like that," grumbled Lord Taverne, as the horse bolted over the horizon. It is feared, however, that should Brown, the courts or his creditors ever formally demand to have the cash returned, the bronze-winning political bridesmaids might be bankrupted for good.

Brown, Nick
b. June 13th 1950
MP (Lab), Newcastle-upon-Tyne East, 1983-

A long-term ally of Gordon Brown, this former adman was forced out of the closet in November 1998, shortly before the *News of the World* implied that his relationship with a young kiss-and-tell was in fact that between punter and prostitute. "I deny totally that I paid money for sex. I have never done so," stated the one-time *Jackie* contributor. "As in any other friendship, there were gifts. As I earned more than he did, there were occasions when I gave him small sums of money as gifts of friendship." But when it emerged that the unnamed rat in question had been threatening to talk to the media for months, these 'gifts' started to smack of extortion. In fact, it was only after the Ron Davies (*qv*) affair that the tabloids deemed the splash on the obscure MP newsworthy, and in the ensuing brouhaha the *Sun*'s 'political editor' Trevor Kavanagh advanced the infamous theory that a 'gay mafia' was running the country, claiming that four out of sixteen men in the Cabinet had lifestyles unsuitable for the readers of a family newspaper. This prompted 'out' MP Ben Bradshaw to liken the red-top's handling of the issue to Nazi scaremongering about Jews in the 1930s.

Ironically, Brown's first act after Tony Blair appointed him Chief Whip in May 1997 had been to abolish the feted Black Book (*qv*), in which the sexual indiscretions and personal foibles of MPs were said to be recorded. He had the misfortune both to be Agricultural Secretary during the 2001 foot-and-mouth crisis (having already been assaulted with an éclair by self-professed "environmental activist and socialite" Birgit Cunningham) and too loud a supporter of his namesake Gordon during the wilderness years, and (after a series of demotions) he left the government altogether in June 2003 – only to be appointed Deputy Chief Whip by new PM Gordon Brown four years later.

Brown, Ron

b. June 29th 1940 / d. Aug 3rd 2007
MP (Lab), Edinburgh Leith, 1979-92

Irascible liability who set the sleaze bar impressively high for the 90s Tories. An old-school leftie, the facially-disfigured Brown made a string of unofficial visits to Colonel Gaddafi in Libya starting in the 1970s, and by the early 80s had been targeted by the KGB as a potential mouthpiece for Kremlin propaganda. Unfortunately, his impenetrable accent proved a bar to the appointment ("He seemed very promising," Soviet Defector Oleg Gordievsky sighed to *Scotland*

on Sunday in 2004. "He was very friendly indeed. The only problem was that we couldn't understand him at all because of the accent. We tried and we tried and we tried to figure out what on earth he was saying.") During a late debate about welfare cuts on April 22nd 1988, the Thatcher-baiting Scot earned lasting notoriety for bounding down from the backbenches, hurling papers at startled Tories, seizing the ceremonial Commons mace and brandishing it at Michael Heseltine. The priceless bauble was dented in the process, and his defiant refusal to apologise cost him the party whip. "I'd only had a pint of Younger's Tartan," he mused later. "The bloody thing was heavier than I'd expected."

"She may be from a strict Welsh Methodist background, but she's thrilling in bed"

He went on to wave a similar object in a promotional clip for pop trio Bananarama, and not long afterwards he was caught by fellow MPs enjoying a wash in the Commons showers with his feisty Welsh researcher, Nonna Longden. She was said to have subsequently pursued him through the Commons, yelling "I want your baby!" – a notion he dismissed on the grounds that "it would be physically impossible" (see *Ashby, David / Lehaney, 'Sir' Barry*).

Brown (and his fondness for the odd drink) returned to the headlines in 1989, when he was arrested for drunkenly purloining underwear and jewellery from Longden's lodgings in Hastings. At the trial that ensued the following year he was accused of smashing windows, mirrors and glasses at the flat, but escaped with a £1000 fine – a "moral victory" he celebrated by cracking open champagne on the court steps, quipping: "I don't think I'll be offered a front bench job". The *News of the World* subsequently printed allegations that she'd aborted his child, been nicknamed 'Hot Lips' by him and accompanied him to Libya, while the *Sunday Mirror* quoted her estranged husband Peter saying: "That man is lower than a rat. He has wrecked our marriage and destroyed Nonna's life. I used to think that MPs were the bastions of society. But he is just a bastard." On a more reflective note, he added: "She may be from a strict Welsh Methodist background, but she's thrilling in bed... I can understand how Brown became so infatuated with her. She knows how to satisfy a man."

The party had had enough, and Brown was expelled in April 1990. At the 1992 election he contested his seat as an independent, and romped in fifth with a disappointing 10.3% of the vote. By 1999 he'd rallied sufficiently to stand for Tommy 'Hairball' Sheridan's breakaway Scottish Socialist Party in the inaugural Scottish General Election. He remained unelectable, though, with a mere 2.5% of the vote. Having sought work as a drinks steward in a Hong Kong golf club and a cabbie, in April 2002 he made a welcome return to public attention when his bank account was frozen over his refusal to pay council tax (prompted by his disgust at the state of Edinburgh's streets). His subsequent activities (including a stint as agony uncle for a local paper) were sadly hampered by ill health, and he finally succumbed to liver disease.

see *Knickergate*

Browne, John
b. Oct 17th 1938
MP (Con), Winchester, 1979-1992

Career cad who listed 'gold' as an interest in *Who's Who* – and whose political career was pole-axed in the pursuit of it.

Having established a vast network of contacts in the Middle East throughout the 1970s, Browne set up an umbrella company in 1978, Falcon Rose Ltd., in order to oversee the range of interests he planned to pursue as an MP. Under its auspices he undertook work for a startling number of businesses, including the aptly-titled Worms Investments, without disclosing his major shareholding in it to Parliament. Much of the 80s was spent oiling wheels for Lebanese lobbyist Charles Chidiac (who paid him a monthly retainer to further his clients' interests in Parliament), as well as for a dizzying array of banks, oil companies, estate agents, construction companies and so on, precious few of which made it into the Register Of Members' Interests.

Towards the end of the 80s investigative journalists began to scrutinise his affairs, prompted by his shabby treatment of his ex-wife, Elizabeth (he was prepared to see her jailed for her failure to pay an outstanding £49,000 in divorce settlement). She helpfully furnished interested parties with documents relating to his interests, but it was only when he attempted to introduce a 'Protection of Privacy' act to Parliament (that would have limited journalists' access to MPs'

business affairs) in April 1989 that the press really got the knives out. *Observer* scribe John Leigh personally complained that Browne had failed to declare his earnings from foreign sources (especially one whopping $88,000 sum from Saudi Arabia), offshore trusts and various firms, and that he'd asked questions in the House without declaring his interest in their outcome. Browne vouched that he only declared payments that he deemed to be in conflict with his official duties, but the Members' Interests Committee found his discretion wanting, and suspended him from the Commons for twenty days in March 1990.

He was deselected just before the 1992 General Election, but boldly stood as an independent. The people of Winchester eloquently expressed their loyalty by awarding him less than 5% of the vote, causing him to lose his deposit. Uncowed, he contested the 1993 Newbury by-election on an anti-Maastricht ticket (and had the gall to bill himself as a 'Conservative Rebel', stating that 'our present Cabinet has shown neither principle nor policy') – but that didn't wash either. In 1997 he had another crack as an independent, bellyaching to the Hampshire Chronicle that 'the Conservative Party has been hijacked by mediocrity' and showcasing his robustness by polling the same amount of votes as the Monster Raving Loony Party candidate (307, or 0.5% of the total). Still not getting the message, he mounted unsuccessful campaigns as a UKIP candidate in Falmouth & Camborne (2001) and North Devon (2005), where he upped his vote share to 2.8% and 5.3% respectively. Seemingly addicted to humiliation on the hustings, Browne is expected to announce an intention to stand for Veritas (*qv*) at any moment.

Bryant, Chris
b. Jan 11th 1962
MP (Lab), Rhondda, 2001-

Randy former curate who ill-advisedly cavorted on a webcam in his underpants in late 2003. When it emerged that he'd emailed a 'horny bastard' he'd encountered on gaydar.com with an open invitation to give him 'a good long fuck', Bryant acknowledged that the leaked excerpts were bona fide, but reminded the electorate that he'd "never sought to make an issue of my private life", pledging: "I will not myself be distracted from standing up for the people of the Rhondda."

"I'm shocked - but to be honest, I can't help laughing. He's no Pierce Brosnan, is he? And those underpants are awful"

Local pensioner Mary Walker, 74, perhaps spoke for the whole constituency when she remarked: "I'm shocked - but to be honest, I can't help laughing. He's no Pierce Brosnan, is he? And those underpants are awful."

Despite the best efforts of ranting rent-a-quote Richard Littlejohn (who called his emails 'unprintable in a family newspaper' in the *Sun* and slammed him for 'hawking his backside round the internet wearing nothing but a pair of grubby underpants' in the *Daily Mail*), Bryant survived to become a ringleader of the failed September 2006 Labour rebellion against Tony Blair.

Buck, Sir Antony
b. Dec 19th 1929 / d. Oct 6th 2003
MP (Con), Colchester, 1961-83 / Colchester North, 1983-92

Good-natured gull whose marital misadventures helped shore up the image of Tory sleaze even after he'd left the Commons. Having parted from his Australian wife of 34 years in 1989, he fell for the charms of one Bienvenida Pérez, a 32-year-old Spanish seductress with designs on British society. Not long afterwards, she embarked upon a torrid affair with the Chief of the Defence Staff, Sir Peter Harding. When it became public she flogged her side of the story to the *News of the World* for £150,000, including details of their 'champagne kiss of love' – a passionate embrace incorporating a mouthful of the sparkling treat. Despite her claim that he was 'a tornado in bed', Harding was forced to resign in March 1994.

Sir Antony found solace in the arms of Russian asylum seeker Tamara Norashkaryan, who became the subject of questions in the Commons in June 1994 as to the extent of his influence in her immigration application (see *Casalme, Leoncia*).

"I am like a teabag. You don't know how strong I am till you put me in boiling water"

Her predecessor, meanwhile, penned a slim volume of autobiography, *Bienvenida: The Making of a Modern Mistress* ('the tale of the rise of a contemporary courtesan, who emerged triumphant from the poverty of the backstreets of Valencia to enjoy the five-star lifestyle of the upper echelons of British and American society') and – after a couple more marriages and reports in the *Sun* that she'd worked as a prostitute – opened a seduction school. "I wish for women to go into a relationship as if entering a business," she told the *Guardian* of the venture in 2000, going on to warn: "I am like a teabag. You don't know how strong I am till you put me in boiling water."

Bullingdon, The

Oxford University binge-drinking society whose rigorous membership qualifications are being rich and boorish. Occasionally exposed in the quality dailies for harmless student japes such as trashing restaurants, its alumni include Alan Clark, Boris Johnson, David Cameron and George Osborne (all *qv*).

Butler Report, the

Off-whitewash (see *Hutton Report, the*) which concluded in October 2004 that there were 'serious flaws' in the intelligence used to go to war with Iraq, but that there was no one to blame in high office. "Our conclusion was that you could not pick out anyone who bore special responsibility," Lord Butler pronounced, before adding reassuringly: "I think that is often the case in government." If that sounded like a guarded rebuke, then the peer's true feelings emerged that December, when he unleashed a stinging slap across Tony Blair's chops in the *Spectator* for the way he ran the country – his emphasis on 'selling' himself, his litany of 'extremely bad bills', and the fact that executive power was being taken away from Parliament, even the Cabinet. "The Cabinet now – and I don't think there is any secret about this – does not make decisions," he thundered.

SLEAZE

"The public does not have an automatic right to know what Members of Parliament get up to"
– *Sir Patrick McNair-Wilson MP, July 1989*

SLOT

Buttercross Café

Peterborough cake-trap acclaimed online for having 'a pleasant area just for sitting and relaxing'. It wa also, famously, the scene of 'Jostlegate' (*qv*) in October 2004.

see *Clark, Helen*

Byers, Stephen
b. April 13th 1953
MP (Lab), Wallsend / Tyneside North, 1992-

Mendacious minister whose increasingly desperate fibs did nothing to dig him out of a succession of potholes of his own making.

On entering Parliament in 1992 he was quick to align himself with the ascendant Tony Blair – an association he had cause to be grateful for in 1997, when he became Minister of State at the Department of Education and Employment. Upon joining the front benches he was asked to shave off his spivvy moustache, and was tripped up on Radio 5 Live over his shaky grasp of the eight-times table soon afterwards.

"The most clear example in human history of someone being caught out lying"

In July 1998 he entered the Cabinet as Chief Secretary to the Treasury, and became a Member of the Privy Council. After the resignation of Peter Mandelson (*qv*) that December, he was made Secretary of State for Trade and Industry. Cracks soon began to appear in his smooth façade: in particular he was heavily criticised for advocating the Phoenix Consortium's takeover of MG Rover, which squeezed substantial profits out of the moribund British firm. It was in his final departmental role that he came into his own, however. After the General Election in June 2001 he was appointed Secretary of State for Transport, Local Government & the Regions (widely perceived as a demotion). On October 6th he took the rash decision to ask the courts to place the privatised railway infrastructure company Railtrack into administration, in order to create Network Rail, a unilateral decision that enraged its many shareholders. At the same time, Byers attracted criticism for making his communications staff Jo Moore and Martin Sixsmith (both *qv*) take the hit for the team after a series of unpopular leaks from his department. When the forced resignations got messy in February 2002, it became clear that he'd misled the house on the matter, and his Tory shadow, Tim Collins, suggested with only slight hyperbole that it represented 'the most clear example in human history of someone being caught out lying'. But when forced to make an official statement to the Commons on May 9th, the feeble Byers still refused to offer an apology. By May 21st a *Guardian*/ICM poll 2002 was suggesting that Byers was now more unpopular than Margaret Thatcher at her nadir, with an approval rating of minus 49 points. On May 27th he was forced under questioning to disclose documents relating to the controversial 2001 sale of Express Newspapers to porn dealer Richard Desmond (*qv*), while he'd been in charge of Trade and Industry. The very next day the party – and the country – finally got its wish, as Byers reluctantly handed in his notice to the Prime Minister.

Like a loyal dog, sleaze seemed to follow wherever he went. At the end of the month, a highly critical report about the Railtrack farrago was published by the Transport Select Committee. The report reserved especial criticism for the government's betrayal of its shareholders, 49,500 of whom united to bring the largest class action ever conducted in the English courts. Then, at the height of his unpopularity in June 2002, he admitted to having cheated on his partner of 15 years with Barbara Corish (*qv*) on February 2nd. Corish opted for a scathing kiss-and-tell, which turned out to be almost as critical of Byers' performance as the Railtrack report. In July 2005 the class action finally came to the High Court. Prosecuting lawyer Keith Rowley QC alleged that Byers had "devised a scheme by which he intended to injure the shareholders of Railtrack Group by impairing the value of their interests in that company without paying compensation, and without the approval of Parliament".

Byers was eventually cleared of misfeasance, but on October 17th he apologised in the Commons for his 'factually inaccurate' reply to the Select Committee – though he took care to emphasise that he hadn't set out to mislead them. The Committee was not satisfied, so on January 31st 2006 he suffered the humiliation of having to make a further statement. "I accept the committee's conclusion, and I therefore offer my unreserved apologies to the House," he said, mealy-mouthed to the last.

Byrne, Liam

b. Oct 2nd 1970
MP (Lab), Birmingham Hodge Hill, 2004-

Harmless Northener who found himself in hot water when reports of his shareholdings broke in September 2006. It emerged that he hadn't sold his stake in a government-contracted firm since joining government ranks himself in May 2005. In that time a possible conflict of interest evolved when he moved from the Department of Health to become (briefly) Minister of State for policing: his company e-Government Solutions was already providing computer services for eight police forces around the country. Byrne was reshuffled from the high-profile role after just two weeks, but (despite having pledged on his first appointment to sell his holding), well over a year later he still hadn't managed to wash his hands of it. The mild-mannered MP, who'd set up the company in 2000, insisted it wasn't easy to dispose of. A Home Office spokesman promised that he was 'in the active process of disposing of the shares' – but opposition MPs couldn't help wondering aloud why it was taking such a long time.

did you not have a wank thinking 'Margaret Thatcher'?" demanded inquisitor Jonathan Ross on the June 23rd 2006 edition of his BBC *Friday Night* show – an idea even the *Daily Mail* found 'repellent'.

Sleaze-watchers eagerly await his response to future party scandals – should there be any.

Cameron, David
b. Oct 9th 1966
MP (Con), Witney, 2001-

The unelectable personification of 'compassionate Conservatism' has remained tight-lipped over whisperings about hard drug use as a young man, but concedes he used to 'err and stray' in his life before politics. Cameron has, however, laddishly confessed in *Cosmopolitan* magazine to attending a VD clinic at Oxford, where he was also a member of the obnoxious Bullingdon Club (*qv*). Having resigned his £28,000-a-year directorship of bar chain Urbium (of which his father-in-law, Lord Astor, is a director), in order to toe the party line on binge-drinking, he became party leader in December 2005 and promptly embarked on a jet-setting global green initiative, condemning Tony Blair for having 'tarnished politics'.

One suggestion he has flatly rejected is that he ever sexually fantasised about Mrs Thatcher. "Did you or

Campbell, Alastair
b. May 25th 1957

Bullying, bedpan-mouthed former tabloid hack, widely thought to have been Tony Blair's puppeteer in his unelected role as Downing Street's 'Director of Communications & Strategy' from 1997 until his long-awaited resignation in August 2003.

Campbell honed his 'style over substance' approach to life at Gonville & Caius College, Cambridge, where he cobbled essays together without reading the books and enjoyed any opportunity "to beat up an upper class twit" (as he later bragged). In France he embarked on a short-lived career in pornography, contributing (as the 'the Riviera Gigolo') to *Forum*, a shandy mag owned by Richard Desmond (*qv*). Back in the UK he found employment as a showbiz correspondent, ferreting out gossip and doorstepping celebrities until the *Daily Mirror* took him on as political correspondent in 1985. Over the following years he conquered an alcohol problem and developed a close working relationship with belly-flopping fraudster Robert Maxwell (*qv*). By the the time of Maxwell's death in November 1991, Campbell had become the paper's political editor, but soon moved to the long-defunct *Today* newspaper and became one of then-Labour leader Neil Kinnock's closest advisers.

At this time he also came into ever-closer contact with fresh-faced Labour leadership candidate Tony Blair, whose team he joined for the 1997 General Election campaign. He worked tightly with Peter Mandelson, and perfected the hectoring manner that would come to define him: if newspapers criticised the campaign he complained bitterly, and he was not above attacking individual journalists if he deemed them insufficiently supportive of the project known as 'New Labour'. Over the next few years he tightly controlled media access to Blair, making numerous enemies en route, such as Andrew Gilligan (*qv*), with whom he picked a fight in 2000 over a report on plans for the EU constitution. Gilligan never forgot his harsh words, and three years later embroiled the volatile Scot in the Dodgy Dossiers (*qv*) furore, accusing him of attempting to 'sex it up'. Campbell angrily responded by pressuring the BBC to reveal the sensitive source for the story, confiding to his diary with typical eloquence that 'it would fuck Gilligan if he [Dr David Kelly] were his source'. Campbell announced his resignation from Downing Street in August 2003, a month after Kelly's suicide, and embarked on a self-justifying speaking tour of regional theatres. By the time he and the government had received their ringing endorsement on the affair from Lord Hutton in January 2004, Dr Kelly (*qv*) lay dead, half the BBC had lost their jobs and Britain was still at war.

His long-threatened 'tell-all' memoirs were expected to hammer the final nail in New Labour's coffin, though Campbell was on record as saying: "I would consider it wrong to publish in a manner or at a time detrimental to the interests of the government or the party I served." Sure enough, he waited until several days after Tony Blair was out of No.10 before going to press on July 9th 2007. Sadly, however, for the most part his 'Disappointing Diary' (*qv*) consists of worries about Blair's wardrobe and the fragile state of his own mind, peppered with his trademark expletives.

Campbell, Ronnie
b. Aug 14th 1943
MP (Lab), Blyth Valley, 1987-

Port wine-stained Welshman said to have turned 'purple with rage' during a curry house scuffle in June 2001. It wasn't his first brush with authority – on March 3rd 1998 he became the first MP since Blair's victory to be ordered from the Commons, after losing his temper during a debate and repeatedly howling 'hypocrite' at Shadow Agriculture Minister Michael Jack. The 'curry rage' incident arose when the MP was enjoying a quiet biriyani with his son Aidan at the well-regarded Pan Ahar restaurant in his constituency. He soon found himself being harangued by well-oiled fellow diner Denise Longman, who insulted his wife and accused him of intending not to pay for his meal. She claimed he then called her a 'slut' and broke her companion's jaw. Though all sides admitted a fracas had ensued, the incident was dismissed as mere 'handbags' by the no-nonsense former miner, who was 'hugely relieved' when a court found in May 2002 that no-one could be sure which Campbell had socked the complainant's jaw (a waiter said it was his son). Either way, no hard feelings were held against the Pan Ahar: four years after the trial, Campbell nominated it for the inaugural Tiffin Cup Final – a celebration of South Asian culinary excellence organised by sleaze leviathan Keith Vaz MP (*qv*).

Caplin, Carole
b. Jan 8th 1962

Pert 'lifestyle guru' who graduated from the pages of *Men Only* to the portals of 10 Downing Street in her role as confidante to Cherie Blair, whom she'd met in an Islington gymnasium in 1989. Her Rasputin-like hold over the Prime Minister's wife, as well as her compulsive indiscretion, has led to some of the most entertaining stories ever circulated about life behind Britain's most famous door. These include the revelation that Mrs Blair's surprise 1999 pregnancy was the product of 'New Age sexual techniques', that the women shared showers together (incorporating a 'mud massage'), that Caplin and the Blairs engaged in an erotic fruit-fight in a Mexican steambath (furiously denied by Cherie), and that holistic crackpot Jack Temple (*qv*) had been given a collection of the Prime Minister's toenail clippings at her behest (these he pickled, before drawing useful conclusions with the aid of a crystal pendulum).

Prior to obtaining £60,000-a-year employment with the Blairs for personal services 'across the board' (as she told *Hello!* magazine in 2003), Caplin worked as a dancer, topless model and recruiter for discredited new age therapists Exegesis – a cash-rich cult condemned by David Mellor (*qv*) in 1994 as 'puerile, dangerous and profoundly wrong'.

"Tony relied on Carole... She picked his clothes, right down to his underpants"

Her finest hour, however, came as girlfriend to inept international conman Peter Foster (*qv*), whom she introduced to Britain's upper echelons of power. The Australian crook is still roosting atop a tell-all book, at the heart of which lies 'the extraordinary influence that Carole has over Tony'. In it he allegedly claims that "Tony relied on Carole... She picked his clothes, right down to his underpants." Canny Alastair Campbell (*qv*) never approved: following 'Cheriegate' (*qv*) in December 2002, and a security review, Caplin was stripped of her official Downing Street pass in April 2003. More extraordinary to many was the fact that she had the pass in the first place. After being frozen out, the trash TV stalwart could only fret from afar about the PM. "He's in dire straits, he's put on weight," she fretted to a tabloid reporter in 2005. "I can't believe the change in him since I've not been here."

Caprice, Le

Swanky London eaterie where Jeffrey Archer supped with his agent, Terence Baker, on September 8th 1986, before he is thought to have met prostitute Monica Coghlan. Owing to an alibi bungle, however, he actually claimed they were there on September 9th. Archer therefore felt obliged to enlist pliable pal Ted Francis to lie about the previous evening as well. Francis dutifully pretended to have enjoyed his Lordship's sparkling company at a different restaurant, Sambuca – leaving his host to hope no-one had actually spotted him at Le Caprice.

With characteristic gall, in 2003 the Mayfair nosh-spot became Archer's first port of call on release from prison, where he had been serving time for the above lies since July 2001. He said he couldn't resist the fishcakes.

Carlisle, John
b. Aug 28th 1942
MP (Con), Luton West / North,
1979-97

Unreconstructed bigot who won few friends by saying "they should never have released Nelson Mandela", and whose pungent contribution to the Criminal Justice debates of the early 90s was: "All gypsies should be banished into the wilderness."

Having headed the Foreign Affairs Committee of the all-male Monday Club (*qv*) and chaired the pro-apartheid British-South Africa Group, Carlisle earned a degree of goodwill by masterminding a press campaign to deny braying termagant Janet Street-Porter appointment as the BBC's new 'Head of Arts and Culture' in April 1991.

"John Carlisle is one of the most offensive men in the House of Commons"

He was back to square one a year later, however, when he informed a constituent that "students such as yourselves are nothing more than middle-class parasites living off working-class taxpayers." His next outburst ('women are natural bitches') heralded a vicious attack on his female colleagues, whom he branded insecure and backbiting, asserting that "the day's work here at the Commons is more naturally tackled by a man. Once you start giving women special privileges and pushing them forward – and it is the same with ethnic minorities – you give them a false sense that they are equal to the task."

Following a stint flogging cut-price motors in the Commons (see *Bletchley Motors Group*), it became clear that Carlisle was the one unequal to the task. In the wake of the 1996 Dunblane school massacre he called the victims' parents calls for a total handgun ban 'hysterical', prompting a *Mirror* leader to state: 'No contempt is enough to dump on John Carlisle... How anyone could be so callous is beyond understanding. How anyone like Carlisle could become an MP is beyond belief.' He stood down from his seat as the Tories suffered a catastrophic 9,626 vote reverse in the 1997 Election, and left Parliament (to take up a directorship with the Tobacco Manufacturers' Association) with this tribute from SNP leader Alex Salmond ringing in his ears: "John Carlisle is one of the most offensive men in the House of Commons."

Casalme, Leoncia 'Luz'
b. 1968

Former Filipina factota to Kimberly Quinn (*qv*), over whom David Blunkett first lost his place in the Cabinet, following claims he'd tried to fast-track her 2004 bid for UK residency. 'Luz' told the *Daily Mail* that her man-eating boss had mentioned a 'friend' who might be able to help with the visa application, though this was denied. Despite his lusty reputation, there has never been any suggestion of impropriety between David and Leoncia.

see *Nannygate*

SLEAZE

"I feel a deep sense of responsibility and humility. You put your trust in me and I intend to repay that trust. I will not let you down"

– Tony Blair addresses the electorate on Election night, May 2nd 1997

SLOT

Cash for Access

Alternative term for the paltry 1998 'Lobbygate' affair.

see *Draper, Derek*

Cash for Dinners

Not a schools catering scheme, but a term desperately coined by the *Mirror* in November 2006 to describe David Cameron's willingness to break bread in the Commons with wealthy businessmen in exchange for generous donations – or, if he wasn't peckish, to fob them off with a personal phone call.

With uncharacteristic candour, Tory HQ confessed that it was perfectly true, and that there was 'nothing secret' about it. In fact, begging letters were being openly sent to targeted donors. In May 2007 the tabloid reported that the Commons Administration Committee had banned all parties from using Commons dining rooms to raise money, seemingly spelling an end to the groundbreaking concept.

Cash for Honours

Term given to the long-standing parliamentary tradition of trading party funding for political office (see page 188), which reared its head again after the 2005 General Election.

"Basically the Prime Minister's office would recommend someone like Malcolm for an OBE, a CBE or a knighthood"

Though the subsequent police investigation resulted in no charges, the affair seemed especially rich given the section in Labour's 1997 manifesto pledging 'we will clean up politics', in which they heaped scorn on the Tories over 'Cash For Questions' (*qv*) and angrily promised to reform party funding.

The 2006 outbreak first came to public attention via Tony Blair's appointment of his tennis partner, Michael 'Lord' Levy (*qv*), as Labour's fundraising guru in the run-up to his wallet-crushing 1997 Election victory. Levy proved more than equal to the task, but in the wake of 2005's similarly ruinous

Election campaign, his adeptness at finding sources of funding began to attract suspicion. This hardened in January 2006 when Des Smith (a former headmaster and council member of the Specialist Schools and Academies Trust) told an undercover *Sunday Times* reporter over champagne that "basically... the Prime Minister's office would recommend someone like Malcolm [a fictional potential donor] for an OBE, a CBE or a knighthood." Smith resigned when the report appeared, but it was too late to avert a scandal.

In February, stockbroker Barry Townsley (who'd donated £6,000 and loaned £1m to the Labour Party, as well as contributing £1.5m to a City Academy), withdrew his acceptance of a peerage nomination, citing press intrusion. In March property millionaire Sir David Garrard withdrew his candidature shortly before a number of Blair's nominees for life peerages were rejected by the House Of Lords. One of these was British-Indian food millionaire Sir Gulam Noon, who'd also been put forward after making donations and lending money. Another was Dr Chai Patel, director of the Priory healthcare group, who was considerably aggrieved by the coverage of the affair. Several of the people implicated were also major donors to charities with which Lord Levy had been involved, and all had contributed significant sums to Labour.

It was too much for SNP sniffer dog Angus MacNeil MP (*qv*), who decided to report the matter to the police in March 2006, thereby setting in train a devastating series of arrests and enquiries. Over the course of March it emerged that New Labour had borrowed £3.5m from private individuals in 2005, and that a total of £14m had been loaned by wealthy philanthropists in support of their General Election campaign. This suggested that the vast majority of the £18m the party spent on its campaign had come from loans from individuals, the terms of which were undisclosed. Strictly speaking, this was not in violation of party funding rules, which merely require that anyone donating £5,000 or more must be named, but that loans of any amount do not have to be declared, so long as they are made on commercial terms.

The plot thickened when Party Treasurer Jack Dromey announced he'd had no knowledge of the loans, and had learnt of them solely through the press. He also stated that he was launching an internal investigation and asking the Electoral Commission to look into the matter. By July it was being claimed that Lord Levy had told

Sir Gulam Noon not to tell the Lords vetting committee about his £250,000 loan to the Labour party.

"It's something we have never seen before in political history. This is a potential political scandal of massive proportions"

The enormous interest on loans of this size prompted the question: why did Lord Levy prefer loans to donations? And why were Tony Blair, Lord Levy and Matt Carter (General Secretary of the British Labour Party) the only people privy to details of the transactions? The time had come for collars to be felt, and on July 12th Levy was marched off for questioning. As 2006 drew to a close, numerous others were questioned too: Patricia Hewitt MP (November 22nd), Tony Blair himself (December 14th) and Jack McConnell (December 15th), for example. 2007 saw the inquiry gathering steam: John McTernan (Director of Political Operations at No. 10) was questioned, Ruth Turner (Director of Government Relations at No. 10) was arrested, and at the end of the month Levy was re-arrested and Blair interviewed as a witness again. As CNN's European Political Editor, Robin Oakley, commented: "It's something we have never seen before in political history. This is a potential political scandal of massive proportions".

In April 2007 the Yard's Assistant Commissioner, John Yates, handed over a 216-page long evidence file to the Crown Prosecution Service, as well as over 6,300 documents. In the course of his investigation 136 people had been interviewed, and costs in excess of £1m had been incurred. On June 28th – the day after he left 10 Downing Street – it emerged that Blair had been questioned for a third time. On July 20th the CPS disappointed many by announcing that it would not be bringing any charges, stating: 'For a case to proceed, the prosecution must have a realistic prospect of being able to prove that the two people agreed that the gift, etc, was in exchange for an honour... there is no direct evidence of any such agreement between any two people subject of this investigation.' It was hardly the exoneration Labour had dreamt of.

see *Levy, Lord Michael / Smith, Des*

Cash for Questions

The simple equation that obliterated a Tory government, almost exactly three hundred years after the House of Commons Journal stated in 1695: "The offer of money, or other advantage, to a Member of Parliament for the promoting of any matter whatsoever, depending or to be transacted in Parliament, is a high crime and misdemeanour."

The phrase was coined in 1994 by the *Sunday Times* for a sting implicating MPs Graham Riddick and David Tredinnick (both *qv*). The stitch-up followed a remark made by a prominent businessman at a boozy press lunch, to the effect that he always went to his chequebook if he wanted issues raised in Parliament. But while the *Sunday Times* got their story by offering bogus bungs to back-benchers, the seeds of a bona fide sensation went back much further – to 1985, and the threat of a Department of Trade and Industry investigation into Mohammed Fayed's purchase of Harrods. Incensed by the DTI's cheek, Fayed retained the services of Ian Greer (*qv*) to promote his cause in Parliament for £25,000 a year. Greer swiftly recruited MPs Sir Peter Hordern, Michael Grylls, Tim Smith and Neil Hamilton, and the quartet undertook a number of activities on Fayed's behalf during the late 80s (Hordern, it should be emphasised, fully declared his interest in The House of Fraser, and never acted improperly). These included organising meetings with ministers, writing letters and, most infamously, asking questions in the Commons – some 22 queries linked to Fayed's interests were posed by Hamilton and Smith between 1987 and 1989.

The co-operative MPs enjoyed various rewards, ranging from small gifts or stays in Fayed's Villa Windsor or Paris Ritz hotel to (it was alleged) cash in brown envelopes (*qv*). The scandal was blown wide open when Fayed spoke to the *Guardian* on October 20th 1994. The ranting conspiracy theorist was still smarting like a jilted lover after Hamilton declined to respond to a friendly letter of congratulations on his 1992 appointment to the Department of Trade (only on the DTI's advice did the MP resist this latest offer of a free lunch). "I felt it was now my public duty to make these facts known," said Fayed, who claimed each question cost him £2k and quoted Greer boasting: "You need to rent an MP just like you rent a London taxi." It is a claim Greer denies – but the strongest possible public judgement was passed on all parties after the Hamilton v Fayed libel trial, fondly remembered today as 'Liar versus Liar'.

see *Fayed, Mohammed / Greer, Ian / Grylls, Michael / Hamilton, Neil / Smith, Tim / Paris Ritz / Riddick, Graham / Tredinnick, David / Thising's Disease*

Cash for Sex

The oldest transaction known to man.

see *Archer, Jeffrey* and entries *passim*

┌─── **WIGGINGS** ───┐

"Not by any means a wholly satisfactory or convincing witness... he has been less than completely open and frank... he did not impress me as a witness in whom I could feel 100% confident"

– Judge Sir Maurice Drake on Alastair Campbell, 1996

└─ **FROM THE BEAK** ─┘

Castro, Fidel
b. Aug 13th 1926

Cigar-chomping revolutionary widely accused of running Cuba into the ground since seizing power in 1959. Especial condemnation has been reserved for his execution of political opponents (up to 50,000, according to some sources) and incarceration of homosexuals. In 2006 he became the subject of an adulatory biography, *The Fidel Castro Handbook*, by cigar-chomping *Big Brother* contestant George Galloway (*qv*). "The Cubans are the only people in the entire world who have a leader who can say that he doesn't possess one dollar to his name", asserted the fiery socialist in May that year, following claims that his idol had amassed a personal fortune of almost a billion US dollars at the expense of his people. In the book he also states his belief that the bearded dictator is 'one of the greatest men of the twentieth century', and that 'he will be remembered and revered.'

see *Hussein, Saddam / Courage / Strength / Indefatigability*

Caulfield, His Honour Judge Bernard
b. April 24th 1914 / d. Oct 17th 1994

Lovesick beak who astounded a courtroom – and a nation – during the 1987 Archer libel trial, by openly salivating over the claimant's wife. In particular, his erotically-charged tribute to Mary Archer's 'fragrance' has passed into comic history.

"Cold, unloving, rubber-insulated sex in a seedy hotel room"

Caulfield, a devout Catholic, simply couldn't believe that a man in Archer's position could wish to pay for "cold, unloving, rubber-insulated sex in a seedy hotel room, round about quarter to one on a Tuesday morning, after an evening at the Caprice", and told the jury that any damages they awarded would be 'a message to the world that the accusations were false'. He was memorably forced to recall the jury after protests from the *Daily Star's* counsel that there had been no fewer than twelve 'inaccuracies and mistakes' in his summing-up, but they got the message all the same.

see *Archer, Jeffrey* / *Coghlan, Monica* / *Daily Star, the*

Cercle, Le

Hush-hush right wing 'think-tank' linked to the arms trade, which meets twice a year: once in Washington, once in a location known only to members (but rumoured to be a rotating series of Ramada Inn banqueting suites). Conspiracy theorists insist that its members are part of the illuminati; sleaze stars linked with the group have included Paul Channon, Alan Clark and its former chairman, Jonathan Aitken – a 'distinguished list', as Clark proudly put it. "Jonathan Aitken, who knows absolutely everybody in the world, has, amusingly and indiscreetly, guided me through it," he reported in his *Diaries*. When Aitken's more famous 'indiscretions' led to the libel courts, he was replaced as chairman – but at the trial called upon his former UK secretary at Le Cercle, Geoffrey Tantum, to be star witness for the losing side. Norman Lamont (*qv*) subsequently took over his role.

Champagne

1. French fizzy drink associated with special occasions – e.g. the Prime Minister having Noel Gallagher round to No.10, the Home Secretary hearing that Harold Shipman had succeeded in committing suicide under his department's care, Lord Levy hearing he wouldn't be charged for attempting to sell honours.

2. Prefix applied to a type of socialist whose lifestyle seemingly clashes with the politics he espouses.

Channon, Paul
b. Oct 9th 1935 / d. Jan 27th 2007
MP (Con), Southend West, 1959-1997

Long-serving Tory who, aged 23, inherited his fortune and seat (despite 129 other aspirants) from his lusty father – MP, diarist and snob 'Chips' Channon, who'd married into the filthy rich Guinness dynasty (see page 101). It was unfortunate for Channon Jr that his eventual appointment to government – as Secretary of State for Trade and Industry in January 1986 – would coincide with a scandal engulfing his mother's family, triggered by an illegal attempt to inflate the Guinness share price. With such a deafening clash of interests, Channon's position in Trade became uniquely impotent. Unable to lift a finger to police either his family accounts or the biggest domestic issue his department would probably ever face, he was deftly shuffled sideways to Transport.

All went well until 2003, when the *Guardian* revealed that his trade role under Thatcher had also extended to arming Iraq. At the time it had been known that Saddam Hussein was gassing his opponents by the thousand, and it was perfectly possible that Falluja 2 (a chemical factory built in Iraq by Britain in 1985, behind America's back) had been used to manufacture chemical weapons. But Channon pressed for the British company involved (Uhde Ltd) to receive insurance and Export Credit guarantees – the latter ensuring its activities were hidden from the public and the US. "I consider it essential everything possible be done to oppose the proposed sale and to deny the company concerned cover," one Foreign Office minister wrote to the government. The MP responded: "A ban would do our other trade prospects in Iraq no good."

In 2003 the coalition forces cited Falluja 2 in their justification for invading Iraq, pointing out its obvious use in manufacturing WMDs (*qv*). When the *Guardian* tried to confront him with this information, Channon – now Lord Kelvedon – declined to reply. He was bronzing himself in Mustique.

Cheeky Girls

b. Oct 31st 1982

Eastern European pop tarts whose 2002 debut single, *The Cheeky Song* (*Touch My Bum*), was voted the worst record of all time in a January 2004 Channel 4 poll.

see *Öpik, Lembit / Irimia, Gabriela*

Chequers

Buckinghamshire pile that has served as grace-and-favour country residence for British Prime Ministers since 1917. In that time it has played host to some of the key figures of the 20th Century, including US Presidents, world royalty and Mick Hucknall. Weekend guests of the Blairs there included bad film director Michael Winner, TV inquisitor Des O'Connor and stultifying sesquipedalian Sir Stephen Fry.

In March 2007 it emerged that the public cost of maintaining the luxury home in 2005/06 was £900,000.

see *Montrose, Petrina*

Cheriegate

Stink made public on December 1st 2002, involving a mortgage saving of up to £69,000 made by the Blair family on two Bristol properties.

This was achieved through the involvement of former fugitive from British justice and would-be 'slimming tea' magnate Peter Foster (*qv*).

The stocky ex-lag entered Cherie Blair's life through her sometime shower partner Carole Caplin (*qv*) in 2002, but the stench only really hit the nation's nostrils on February 5th 2003, when the Prime Minister's wife officially denied Foster's involvement in her property dealings. Unfortunately, the Gold Coast crook had the emails to prove her wrong, and a tearful Mrs Blair duly expressed her 'regret' that the pressures of motherhood, her husband's high office, and pretty much everything else except poor judgment, had forced her into allowing "someone I barely knew, and had not then met, to get involved in my family's affairs."

Further accusations in the *Mail On Sunday* included improper use of a 'blind trust' (*qv*) to make the purchase, and the much more serious allegation of interfering on Foster's behalf in his latest extradition case. Mrs Blair denied these 'frenzied' charges of string-pulling, such as running checks on Foster's solicitors and the judge who would be hearing the case, but further revelations in the *Scotsman* suggested that she'd had all the details of the Foster case faxed to a private office in Number 10. Reflecting on the whole sorry farrago at a press conference on December 10th 2002, she tearfully conceded "maybe I should have asked more questions, but I didn't" – thus unwittingly composing New Labour's epitaph.

Cho-Low tea

Herbal refreshment ascribed miraculous cholesterol-reducing properties by Peter Foster (*qv*) in 1989. The chubby fraudster took out 100 adverts in US newspapers to publicise the claim, and paid for none of them. When it was discovered that, despite receiving advance monies totalling $100,000, he didn't even have any of the $50-a-box brew to shift, Foster – who later helped the Blair family broker a big-money mortgage deal in Bristol – revealed he and business partner Trevor Brine hadn't yet had time to repackage the heaps of budget tea found in his basement.

When they nicked him, police had to coax Foster out from under a sauna bench, where he was wedged in hiding. He was duly convicted of grand theft and false advertising, sentenced to 120 days in jail, fined $300,000 and given 900 hours' community service, which he spent picking up litter.

see *Bai-Lin tea*

---WIGGINGS---

"A large amount of alcohol appears to have been consumed, but that neither excuses nor fully explains your behaviour"

- *Sheriff Kathrine Mackie to Lord Watson of Invergowrie, 2005*

---FROM THE BEAK---

Churchill, Winston
b. Oct 10th 1940
MP (Con), Stretford / Davyhulme, 1970-1997

Not to be confused with the man who saved the world from Nazism, this philandering grandson of our 'Greatest Briton' was in fact born Winston Spencer-Churchill. Though he edited a collection of his grandfather's speeches entitled *Never Give In*, his own best-known rhetorical effort owed more to Enoch Powell: during a visit to Bolton in May 1993 he railed at the 'relentless flow' of immigrants who were diluting the 'British way of life'. In particular he groused that half the population of Bradford and Leeds consisted of immigrants, when the true figures were 6% and 15% respectively. Home Secretary Michael Howard (himself the child of immigrants) was swift to condemn the remarks, stating: "Up and down our country, people from ethnic minorities and from all races are making a tremendous contribution to our national life." Two years later Winston minor attracted further opprobrium, this time for flogging £12.5m worth of his illustrious forebear's papers – effectively forcing the hand of heritage authorities to buy them back with Lottery money, rather than see them leave the country. In 1997 his marriage of three decades to long-suffering Minnie wound up acrimoniously, with numerous infidelities aired – notably with Soraya Khashoggi (see *Aitken, Jonathan*).

Clark, Alan
b. April 13th 1928 / d. Sept 5th 1999
MP (Con), Plymouth Sutton, 1974–92
Kensington and Chelsea, 1997–99

Pickled philanderer and serial 'S-H-1-T' (as his wife Jane described him in 1992) who staggered through a twenty-year Parliamentary career with his trousers down and his pecker up.

"Alan had never hidden his admiration for Adolf Hitler"

From an early age, recalled brother Colin, "Alan had never hidden his admiration for Adolf Hitler." Indeed, he went on to name his German Shepherd dog 'Eva' in tribute to the Führer's moll, indicating his lifelong disregard for public opinion. After achieving a measure of prominence in 1961 for *The Donkeys*, a discredited critique of WW1 Generals, Clark moved into politics and soon began to propound his salty views on race and class. In 1971, for instance, his candid message to Ugandan Asian refugees was "you cannot come here because you are not white"; and he had the winning habit of referring to any given African country as 'Bongo-Bongo Land', whether in private or at the Commons.

Although liked by Margaret Thatcher, whose sexual allure he was open about, she never trusted him with anything greater than the junior ministerial role he achieved in 1983. If anything, she overestimated him: that year he became the first and only MP to be accused of being drunk at the despatch box, after slurring his way through an employment bill. The Tory benches furiously denied the suggestion by a young Clare Short (*qv*), but she was perfectly correct: Clark had warmed up for the debate at a friend's wine-tasting. This much he admitted in his *Diaries*, where he recalled his befuddled panic en route for Parliament, and boozy contempt for the document itself: "Sometimes I turned over two pages at once, sometimes three. What did it matter?" It was an assessment many would make of his *Diaries 1983-1992* a decade later.

After Thatcher's fall in 1990, Clark's reputation waned, though not as a womaniser. The 1993 publication of his trivial *Diaries* exposed a litany of lust: he stated that 'girls have to be succulent, and that means under 25', and according to close friend Jonathan Aitken he'd celebrated his appointment as Parliamentary Under Secretary for Employment by seducing a woman on the train between Canterbury and Folkstone (apparently he was worried that the 'creative use' to which he put his red dispatch box during the encounter might have revealed him as a minister). Cad status was assured in 1994 when the *News of the World* gleefully printed details of what the *Diaries* called his 'coven' – namely the entire female population of an unfortunate judge's family (see *Harkess, James*). Clark's long-suffering wife Jane merely tutted that such upsets are inevitable if you 'sleep with what I call below-stairs types' (Jane, who was 16 when she married the 30-year-old

Clark, used her middle name at his insistence – it was the same as his mother's). In the same year Clark admitted at the Matrix Churchill trial (*qv*) that he and others had lied over arms sales to Iraq – or, as he put it, been 'economical with the actualité' – thereby precipitating the damning Scott Report (*qv*).

As well as precipitating Thatcher's ousting, the Arms-to-Iraq storm had meant there was no chance of him standing for re-election back in 1992, and many assumed his *Diaries* would rule him out for good. They had insulted – amongst others – King Hussein of Jordan ('an oily little runt'), Douglas Hurd ('might as well have a corn-cob up his arse... pompous, trite, high-sounding'), Malcolm Rifkind ('a weasel'), Michael Heseltine ('the sort of person who buys his own furniture') and Kenneth Clarke (a 'podgy little puffball'). His attitude to the electorate was little more favourable – "sometimes I get a wild urge to relieve my bladder out of the window, spattering on the ant-like minions below," he reflected upon leaving his Ministerial office in April 1992. Buoyed by his new-found status as a celebrity cad, however, Clark returned to the Commons as MP for Chelsea and Westminster in 1997, only to succumb to cancer two years later. Tributes poured in, led by fellow Tory MP David Heathcoat-Amory:

"He wasn't a particularly nice man, I don't think. He could be very cruel with colleagues. I don't think he was very empathetic." The most generous anecdote he could muster was the time they were doing a whip-round for a colleague, and Clark refused to chip in. Self-obsessed Edwina Currie (*qv*) wasn't a fan either: "He was a complete rogue. I was very relieved that I was not his type of woman." His editor at *Classic Cars* magazine, meanwhile, had this to add: "He annoyed many readers... he was a right-wing nut. His columns generated more irate letters than anything." Old pal Aitken had happier memories, however, fondly telling *BBC Magazine* in January 2004 of the times Clark would come to him with 'girl trouble' – though as for the details, Aitken sighed, 'memory fails me' (and not for the first time).

"There is no doubt that he was a great character. We need people like that in politics. Just not too many"

Despite Clark's dubious reputation, his *Diaries* have assured him a cult status among those who like their heroes raddled, libidinous and nationalistic. Or, as Heathcoat-Amory put it: "There is no doubt that he was a great character. We need people like that in politics. Just not too many."

Clark, Helen
b. Dec 23rd 1954
MP (Lab), Peterborough, 1997-2005

Sometime drinking partner of rat-keeper Jane Griffiths (*qv*) who suffered a humiliating revolt within her own constituency in 2004, before becoming involved in a spot of bother with her political rival.

Elected as Helen Brinton in 1997, her politics turned after she married Alan Clark (no relation). Party members were soon appalled by her apparently pro-Tory outbursts and fully expected her to defect, most likely citing the Iraq war. But though the ashen 'Blair Babe' narrowly survived their 2004 vote to deselect her, it was merely a stay of execution before Conservative Stewart Jackson toppled her in 2005. Intriguingly, she had attempted to take him to court on assault charges a few months earlier, and made a pointed electoral pledge about "getting more funding for the police and reducing anti-social crime" – though some witnesses alleged the aggressor was her (see *Jostlegate*). Either way, talk of charges for on grounds of malicious falsehood and wasting police time came to nothing.

She finally defected just days after her defeat, something her former colleagues called a 'slap in the face' – albeit not a very painful one. It puzzled many TV viewers, too, as they'd heard her urge on Election night: "We must applaud and cheer the Labour Government." Four days later, on May 9th, her wording had changed to: "I have become increasingly frustrated with the conduct of the Labour government." The next month it emerged that, although she had indeed walked out on her old party, it was unclear whether she was moving across the divide, or even how much the Tories wanted her. Still, her nemesis Jackson would have been cheered by how 'gutted' Clark admitted to being on losing not just her seat but her 'considerable salary' in an interview with the *Guardian* three weeks later. "Losing a seat is easy," she sighed. "Living after losing a seat is not. You wake up the next morning with the task of filling it – and the afternoon and the evening. You can't taste food and you can't sleep. Dressing is difficult… I hate all my clothes."

SLEAZE

"Children who need to be taught to respect traditional moral values are being taught that they have an inalienable right to be gay"

– Margaret Thatcher at the 1987 Conservative Party Conference

SLOT

SLEAZE

"You need never pay for your own lunch or dinner as a Member of Parliament"

- *Neil Hamilton, 1999*

SLOT

Clarke, Kenneth
b. July 2nd 1940
MP (Con), Rushcliffe, 1970-

Corpulent Tory mainstay whose interests include birdwatching, jazz and losing Tory leadership elections (three to date – 1997, 2001 and 2005).

'Ken' Clarke's blokey everyman image is reinforced by his love of classic motors and fine cigars. He has a reputation as a moderate pro-European, despite one anomaly in his student years: in 1962 he invited Oswald Mosley to return to the Cambridge Union, a move that sufficiently infuriated the young Michael Howard to make him stand against him for Union President. In a pattern that would become depressingly familiar to Clarke, his rival greasy pole-climber pipped him to the top job. Enduring passions for Clarke include drinking and smoking, as reflected in his espousal of the Campaign For Real Ale (CAMRA) and British American Tobacco (BAT). One is a pressure group loath to see lager in British pubs, the other a multinational loath to stomach government health regulations.

When BAT was hit by a smuggling scandal in February 2000, Clarke (as the firm's six-figure-salaried Non-Executive Deputy Chairman) found himself trying to convince the Commons health committee what a 'good corporate citizen' the firm really was. He told them that, as part of his remit, "I seek to ensure that the company follows the highest standards of probity" – which apparently included a crafty loophole enabling BAT to "act, completely within the law, on the basis that our brands will be available in the smuggled as well as the legitimate market." It might seem odd for a former Chancellor to espouse untaxed trade, but he blamed high tobacco duty for the murky methods – something he would doubtless move to correct in the unlikely event of his returning to power.

At the height of another acrimonious leadership contest in summer 2001, Clarke jetted off to Vietnam on BAT business – but denied the trip was anything to do with a projected multi-million link-up with the state-owned tobacco firm, Vinataba, which BAT clinched soon afterwards. More revelations emerged in August about how BAT had been using a hush-hush subsidiary and bank account in Switzerland to cream cash off the worldwide smuggling trade, though the firm's Non-Executive Deputy Chairman insists he didn't have 'any detailed knowledge of the day-to-day activities' of the Swiss scam. Equally, questions were asked about how Clarke, as chair of corporate social responsibility at the firm, could in good conscience have failed to act as it expanded operations into North Korea – from 2001 onwards – without ever mentioning the fact in its annual reports. BAT confirmed that Clarke's remit saw him 'oversee human rights reports on all countries where we operate'; two years previously the firm was forced to abandon trade in Burma after UK government pressure, with even Clarke admitting: "Burma is not one of the world's most attractive regimes."

There were calls by Labour to investigate red-faced Ken in October 2005 for apparent 'contradictions' in his evidence five years previously: namely his dismissal of claims that BAT was involved in smuggling as 'unfounded' and 'nonsense', when the company itself had already privately admitted several aspects of the allegations. Having long refuted that his BAT link was anything to be ashamed of, his camp finally conceded that Clarke would renounce the post if he won his most recent bid (at the time of writing) for the Tory leadership in late 2005. He didn't, and as he crashed out of contention once more in the first round, the hush-puppied fat-cat must have been privately blessing his nice little earner.

Clelland, David
b. June 27th 1943
MP (Lab), Tyne Bridge, 1985-

Pipe-smoking, guitar-playing love rat in the best traditions of the House. Once dubbed 'the nattiest cloth cap Parliament has seen for some time', the salt-of-the-earth Tyne MP was carrying on with his parliamentary secretary Brenda Graham for many months, behind his wife Maureen's back. He confirmed the cruel whispers on October 29th 1998, the same week Ron Davies (*qv*) resigned from the Cabinet – and just before Labour was to release a green paper on family values. After a 'very painful experience' for all parties, he divorced Maureen, his wife of 33 years, stating: "I would like to emphasise that this will in no way impinge upon my work as Member of Parliament for Tyne Bridge or my dedication to the people of the constituency." A leisurely six years later, he and Brenda completed their bliss by marrying in the holiday paradise of Peyia in Cyprus.

SLEAZE

"My project will be complete when the Labour Party learns to love Peter Mandelson"

– Tony Blair, the Daily Telegraph, March 1996

SLOT

Clifford, Max
b. April 6th 1943

Silver-topped, silver-tongued 'high priest of sleaze' (according to the *Daily Telegraph*) who (according to his own publicity) 'hates hypocrisy in public life'. A longtime Labour supporter, the veteran PR fixer cheerfully took credit for the rash of Tory scandals that followed John Major's kamikaze 'Back To Basics' policy – a 'personal vendetta' he attributed in part to the NHS's handling of his daughter's rheumatoid arthritis. He derived especial pleasure from orchestrating the humiliation of Neil Hamilton (*qv*) – to whom he later paid substantial damages over unfounded rape allegations – but is not above exposing a Ron Davies or a John Prescott when the mood takes him.

He left David Blunkett especially sore – after resigning from the Cabinet for the second time in November 2005, 'the bearded one' (*qv*) darkly muttered: "The so-called revelations of Max Clifford are just that – they are complete lies. One day, but obviously not now, they will be dealt with."

Clifford's breathtakingly self-serving, third-person autobiography, *Read All About It* (2005), offers a wealth of absorbing information about him. He likes 'nothing better than sitting in front of the television with a bowl of whelks', for example, and his sitting room boasts 'comfy sofas in a rich Devon cream'. We also learn that 'being with him is a bit like accompanying Father Christmas on an out-of-season tour... moving a hundred yards down the street can take almost an hour', and that he was for years a prolific arranger of orgies, unbeknownst to his late wife ("sexual procuring has never bothered me"). In July 2007 he summarised his life's work in the *Observer* thus: "Scandal is something that brings society together... I like to think I've made a contribution to this country in terms of filth and frivolity."

see *Davies, Ron / de Sancha, Antonia / Prescott, John / Blunkett, David / Mellor, David / Hamilton, Neil / Hamilton, Christine / Archer, Jeffrey / Back to Basics / Milroy-Sloane, Nadine*

Cocktail Sausage

1. Shrivelled meat snack served at Labour office parties.

2. Shrivelled meat snack serviced at Labour office parties (and afterwards, according to tabloid sources).

see *Prescott, John*

Coghlan, Monica

b. May 3rd 1951 / d. April 27th 2001

Petite prostitute who never lived to see her dream of seeing Jeffrey Archer 'squirm' in court. She did, however, have the satisfaction of re-telling her story to the *Mirror* in November 1999, including the £20 she says he slipped her for 'extra time' (*qv*). "He seemed the perfect upper-class client," she recalled of the man who claimed to be a car salesman. "Everything from his smell to the style of his shoes said he was a gentleman."

At Archer's 1987 libel action against the *Daily Star* (*qv*), he accepted that his pal Michael Stacpoole had met the 4'11" stunner at Victoria Station on October 24th 1986, and handed her a brown envelope (*qv*) containing at least £2000 of his money in order to leave the country. But he could scarcely have denied it: the handover was recorded as part of a *News of the World* sting. The *Star*'s editorial policy was bolder, however, prompting him furiously to deny in court that he'd ever met Coghlan, let alone had 'perverted sex' with her. The jury believed His Lordship's stooges over Coghlan's saucy testimony ("he was quite taken by my nipples"), and concluded that at about 12.45am on a Tuesday morning in September the Tory toad was indeed at Le Caprice (*qv*) with his theatrical agent Ted Francis – not paying her £70 for "cold, unloving, rubber-insulated sex in a seedy hotel room" (© Caulfield, Judge Bernard, *qv*).

"They made me feel cheap, worthless and dirty – something I'd never felt through all my years on the streets"

"He humiliated me, they all did," Coghlan told the *Mirror*. "Him, his wife, the barristers, the judge. They made me feel cheap, worthless and dirty – something I'd never felt through all my years on the streets." Her 'professional' reputation in tatters, the fun-sized temptress was forced into bingo-calling. "Jeffrey Archer took everything away from me," she complained. "I lost my home, my dignity, my self-respect, and any hope of a future." She was prepared to go back to the courtroom and face 'the man I hate' to see justice done, but was killed in a road accident on April 27th 2001, just before she had the chance. "I want him to suffer like I've suffered," she said. "But mostly I want him to tell the truth." That was always a forlorn hope, but on July 19th Archer was nonetheless convicted of systematic perjury at an Old Bailey rematch, and packed off to jail.

Colquhoun, Andrina
b. 1952

Mistress and secretary to Jeffrey Archer (*qv*) from 1982-5, appointed to the latter post to justify the amount of time the two were spending together. It is said that whenever the lovestruck PA (who called him 'Moon') visited his London flat, she took down all photographs of Archer's lady wife, Mary. Following an admonition from Mrs Thatcher to 'tidy up his life', the would-be Tory Deputy Chairman dumped Colquhoun in 1984, sugaring the pill by giving her his BMW (number plate: ANY 1). Though she tactfully left his employ soon after, the two remained close. So close, in fact, that one of the duties required of Archer's new PA, Angela Peppiatt, was buying Gucci trinkets for her predecessor – and at his 2001 perjury trial it emerged that she'd also been detailed to purchase identical love-tokens for Mary. Archer was nervous about his 'London wife' becoming public knowledge (especially after fellow love rat Cecil Parkinson was forced to resign from the Cabinet in October 1983), but the affair continued a little while longer, under cover of 'writing' trips to the Bahamas. This fizzled out when Colquhoun met her future husband Robert Waddington, so when in 1999 it emerged that the fictionalist had been using her name as an alibi in the Ted Francis cover story, dating from September 1986, she was 'horrified' – and only too happy to give 75 minutes of fulminating evidence against her former lover at the Old Bailey in 2001. It emerged that she'd been in Greece with Waddington at the time Archer claimed he was meeting her behind his wife's back.

Colquhoun, incidentally, had previously been linked with none other than Lord Lucan, whom she was supposed to be meeting at the Clermont Club the night he disappeared – though she maintained to police at the time of the Archer trial that she wasn't the sort to get involved with a married man.

Committee On Standards In Public Life

Augean Stable door-shutting body set up by a panicked John Major in October 1994, to stem the sleaze tsunami swamping his government following his 'Back To Basics' initiative. "It is to act as a running authority of reference," he blathered. "Almost, you might say, an ethical workshop called in to do running repairs." The patch-up wasn't enough to save his party at the polls.

see *Nolan Report, the*

Conflict of Interest

A situation in which a public servant is deemed not to be in a position to carry out a duty without being compromised by private concerns, especially financial. Despite tireless efforts to define such hazards by the Committee On Standards In Public Life (*qv*), the accusation – most easily avoided by transparency in one's financial affairs – is typically accompanied by howls of protest and spontaneous outbreaks of amnesia.

see entries *passim*

Conniving Little Shit

see *Allason, Rupert*

Conway, Derek
b. Feb 15th 1953
MP (Con), Shrewsbury & Atcham, 1983-97 / Old Bexley & Sidcup, 2001-

Former Vice-Chamberlain of Her Majesty's Household who came in for a double dose of stick from the media over allowances in 2006 and 2007. Until then the backbench bruiser – who lost his first seat to sleaze meteor Paul Marsden (*qv*) in 1997 – had been under the press radar for a decade, following a 1996 accusation of Commons vote-rigging in a fishing policy debate. In 2006, however, he came in for grief over his mileage claim for the preceding 12 months. This is supposed to cover trips between Westminster, an MP's constituency and his home, as well as trips up to 20 miles beyond the constituency on official business. Conway's whopping £4072 claim equated to around 1000 trips between Westminster and his constituency.

Then, on May 27th 2007, the *Sunday Times* revealed he was paying his son Frederick £981 a month out of his annual £84,081 parliamentary staffing allowance. The tutting that ensued was mainly directed at the fact that young Fred was supposedly also a full-time geography finalist at Newcastle University. Also on Conway's payroll was his wife Colette, down for £3271 a month. Employing family members to help fulfil parliamentary duties is nothing new, though: Quentin Davies (qv) employs missus Chantal, and the Sunday Times report also found the wives of Labour MPs Stuart Bell and Nick Ainger on the public payroll. As Conway put it: "It's not something I'm going to be drawn into talking about… I am not going to comment" – and, as Betsygate (qv) demonstrated, no-one really cares anyway.

Cook, Margaret
b. 1945

Avenging banshee who ensured maximum embarrassment for her husband Robin and the Labour government when the Minister left her for his secretary, Gaynor Regan (qv), after 28 years of marriage. 'Cock Robin' may have thought he was exercising damage-limitation by abruptly canning a US holiday in August 1997 (in a Heathrow lounge) and issuing divorce demands instead – but it backfired horribly. Desperate to stop the rot, Tony Blair went to some personal trouble to contain the stink, deigning to send Margaret (a doctor and academic) a signed note of sympathy from Tuscany

and arranging a house call from, of all people, Peter Mandelson (whom she later claimed her husband 'hated'). Neither the autograph nor the Mandygram did the trick, and she proceeded to tell all to the tabs: the other mistresses, the alcohol abuse, the hotel stupors. She even published a memoir in 1999, A Slight and Delicate Creature, assuring the Sunday Times (who serialised it): "I am really not motivated by revenge of any description." Cook was unconvinced. He called the book 'vindictive and undignified', and feared his ex-wife would 'destroy' him. Despite her best efforts, however, public enthusiasm for tittle-tattle about the stunted stud soon petered out, and shortly afterwards she admitted to Woman's Own: "It's a dreadful thing to have done… The reaction towards me has been by no means favourable." By September 2002 she seemed to have come to terms with his actions, writing in the Scotsman that "plenty of scientific studies have shown a clear correlation between longevity, youthfulness and a high level of sustained sexual activity."

Cook, Robin
b. Feb 28th 1946 / d. Aug 6th 2005
MP (Lab), Edinburgh Central, 1974-83 / Livingston, 1983-2005

Horny homunculus who brought sadly-missed intellectual gravitas to Westminster, distinguishing himself as a statesman by damning two governments' policies on Iraq, and as a lover-man by giving the Blair administration its first major sex scandal.

On Friday August 1st 1997 he was en route to Colorado with his wife of 28 years Margaret (*qv*), when he received a call from Alastair Campbell (*qv*) warning him he was 'in the shit' with the *News of the World*. He'd been enjoying a lengthy affair with his diary secretary, Gaynor Regan (*qv*), and the tabloid had the pictures to prove it. The turf-loving Foreign Secretary promptly commandeered Heathrow's VIP lounge, sat Margaret down and announced that the holiday and the marriage were both off. He then rode out a month-long tabloid blitz, perhaps ruing Ms Regan's failure to get a resident's parking permit (had she only done so, he wouldn't have needed to dash out of her flat at 8am to feed a meter, giving the paper the shots it needed). They married later that year. Margaret subsequently branded him a boozing philanderer in a series of newspaper interviews and a bad book (whose index included separate listings for his 'heavy drinking', 'weight problems' and

'sexual difficulties'), and the Arms to Africa affair (*qv*) offered him another buffeting the same year.

The public forgave all, however, when he stepped down over Iraq on March 17th 2003 (see *Short, Clare*). While his resignation speech went easy on Blair, his stand is still seen by many as the most damning protest by an MP against the manner in which his former boss took Britain into war, and his Edinburgh gravestone reads: 'I may not have succeeded in halting the war, but I did secure the right of Parliament to decide on war'.

Cool Britannia

Culturally bankrupt media concept hijacked by New Labour in 1997 to cash in on the global popularity of the Spice Girls. Blair-endorsed enterprises under its banner included inviting proud Class-A drug users such as Noel Gallagher and Alan McGee to drinks at Number 10, appointing Stella McCartney and Mick Hucknall to toothless think-tanks, and dispatching John Prescott to the Brit Awards (*qv*).

see *Nobacon, Danbert*

Corish, Barbara
b. 1950

Scouse Labour councillor who succumbed to the charms of beleaguered Transport Secretary Stephen Byers (*qv*) after the Local Government and Women's Conference in Cardiff on February 2nd 2002.

According to her, he seduced her wearing nothing but a pair of black cotton socks. According to other accounts, he was also wearing beer goggles: he'd allegedly been sinking pints of Brains Bitter all evening at the Marriott Hotel bar.

"It was the most disgusting thing I've ever had a man say to me in my life"

One particular piece of pillow talk from the crapulent Cabinet Minister sickened the blowsy delegate: "It was the most disgusting thing I've ever had a man say to me in my life," she said of the mystery request. "I had to stop straight away. It just killed all passion dead."

Coulson, Andy
b. 1968

Shadowy hack who graduated in 2003 from showbiz gossip to the most prestigious job in journalism: editing the *News of the World*. His subsequent achievements in the field of paedo-bashing (to say nothing of hard-hitting investigations into footballers' sex lives) were sadly overshadowed by a criminal investigation which prompted his resignation in February 2007. His royal correspondent, Clive Goodman, had just been jailed for employing tactics that he acknowledged were 'improper, unethical and reprehensible' (such as tapping royal telephone calls) – and which the courts deemed 'sustained and criminal conduct' at the expense of People's Princes William and Harry. "If you are asking, is this the proudest moment in the 163-year history of the *News of the World* then no, clearly it's not," stuttered one senior Wapping Executive.

David Cameron (*qv*) didn't mind, though: he snapped up the former 'Bizarre' compiler to be his 'Director of Communications' that May, at a reported annual salary of £475,000. Though Coulson had never previously shown an interest in politics (other than asking the Blairs in 2001 whether they'd joined the mile high club), the Tory leader gushed "Andy is a hugely experienced journalist," before adding soberly: "We are not looking for an Alastair Campbell figure – his reliance on spin and aggressive media management has been discredited."

Another admirer of Coulson was former *Mirror* editor Piers Morgan, himself discredited for running fake pictures of US soldiers urinating on Iraqi prisoners. "The best quality for any tabloid journalist is charm," he told the *Guardian* in April 2005. "Andy's charming, great fun, the kind of guy you'd want to have a laugh with."

Courage

1. Quality of mind or spirit that enables one to face fear or danger, whether physical or moral, with self-possession, confidence, and resolution; bravery.

2. Quality attributed to Saddam Hussein by George Galloway MP (*qv*).

see also *Indefatigability, Strength*

Cowboy

1. Rugged farmhand in America's Wild West, whose iconic costume of Stetson, belt, jeans and boots is beloved of small boys and Cabinet ministers (see *Anschutz, Philip*). The term was used by John Prescott (*qv*) to describe US President George W. Bush in August 2006.

2. Pejorative term for an incompetent who takes your hard-earned money in exchange for shoddy work (see *Prescott, John*).

Cox, Anna
b. 1979

Chest-enhanced researcher for Piers Merchant MP (*qv*) in the run-up to the 1997 Election. Described by the *Sun* as a 'Soho nightclub hostess,' her duties apparently included al fresco lovemaking and planning reform of the Young Conservatives (for which organisation, at 17, she still comfortably qualified).

When rumours about their relationship refused to go away, Merchant announced they were co-authoring a book on tabloid intrusion. Ten years later, it has yet to appear.

Cricket Test

1. A five-day cricket international, such as that attended by John Major at the Oval on May 2nd 1997, hours after sustaining the most crushing General Election defeat in modern British political history.

2. Stringent measure proposed by Norman Tebbit (*qv*) in 1990, for establishing the loyalties of immigrants. "A large proportion of Britain's Asian population fail to pass the cricket test," he expounded to the *Los Angeles Times*. "Which side do they cheer for? It's an interesting test."

SLEAZE

> "This is wholesale deception. How can the British public trust the Government if it is up to these sort of tricks? People will treat any other information they publish with a lot of scepticism from now on"
>
> *– Ibraham al-Marashi on the Government's cribbing of his university thesis, 2003*

SLOT

Cronyism

Slow-burning scandal concerning Labour's suspected practice of dishing out honours or office as rewards for being chums with Tony Blair or his lieutenants. Rumblings were heard as far back as 1997, when lawyer Charlie Falconer, Blair's childhood pal and ex-flatmate, received a peerage the day after the General Election, becoming Solicitor-General. Having assumed responsibility for the Millennium Dome (*qv*) from Peter Mandelson, Falconer went on to become Lord Chancellor in 2003. Bottomless-pocketed supermarket tycoon Lord Sainsbury, meanwhile, was appointed industry minister after giving away up to £3m to the party chest. Other donors ennobled at Blair's request include TV presenter Melvyn Bragg, film producer David Puttnam and crime writer Ruth Rendell, while Granada boss Gerry Robinson became head of the Arts Council. More commonly-cited examples include tennis ace Lord Levy (*qv*), Blair's legal mentor Derry Irvine (*qv*) – who was also appointed Lord Chancellor – and Garry Hart, godfather to the Blairs' daughter, who was controversially made a special adviser to the Lord Chancellor without the role being advertised.

see *Cash for Honours*

Cunningham, Jack
b. Aug 4th 1939
MP (Lab), Whitehaven, 1970-83 / Copeland, 1983-2005

Undistinguished Agriculture Minister and latterly 'Cabinet Enforcer' in Tony Blair's 1998 government. His crusade to outlaw beef on the bone led one farmer to mutter: "He's an ignorant pig and he won't listen to our point of view." As MP for Copeland, 'Nuclear' Jack's more salubrious contacts included the local philanthropists at Sellafield and chemical firm Albright & Wilson. A&W paid him £10,000 in 1996 for "advice on contacts with ministers and others with whom we do not normally have meetings," according to the Register of Members' Interests. The firm is a member of the Chemical Industries Association (which was lobbying for deregulation at the time), but in October that year its Bristol plant exploded, releasing a cloud of hydrogen chloride so toxic that both Severn bridges had to be closed. Thankfully, no amount of consultancies could buy their longed-for emancipation from public accountability – but Cunningham carried on collecting his fees.

As regards his role as President of the 'Friends of Sellafield Society', the *Ecologist* magazine noted in 1999: "Dr Jack Cunningham has gone further than almost any other Labour politician in supporting nuclear power. It is the extent, however, of his pro-nuclear stance and the intimacy of his relationship with British Nuclear Fuels (BNFL) that has rendered the objectivity of his decisions as a Minister open to question."

Until stepping down as an MP in 2005, he was a frequent freebie flyer to the US for energy consultancy junkets, leading to newspaper allegations that he was indulging himself at the taxpayer's expense – in the first two years of Blair's premiership, the tally already stood at £77,000. This included two jaunts to the agriculture council in Luxembourg, which alone cost more than £28,000. His successor as Agriculture Minister, Nick Brown (*qv*), splashed out a mere £537 on visits to the next two agriculture councils.

'Junket Jack' wasn't the first family member to be implicated in scandal: his father, Andy, was a prominent Labour party figure until brought down in 1974 by the Poulson bribery scandal, which also claimed the reputation of Tory Home Secretary Reginald Maudling (see page 240). He is not, however, to be confused with the Andy Cunningham who plays Simon Bodger in the CBBC series 'Bodger and Badger' (see *Davies, Ron*).

Currie, Edwina
b. Oct 13th 1946
MP (Con), South Derbyshire, 1983-97

Flatulent political footnote whose *Diaries 1987-92*, featuring explicit revelations about the nation's favourite uncle, John Major, almost made the public forget her career-killing blunder over rotten eggs. And, when not eulogising the prowess of 'the man in blue underpants', the little-read journals movingly unfolded a portrait of a woman pole-axed by digestive discomfort (see *Dirty Diary, the*).

By the time of the egg fiasco in 1988, Currie already had a solid reputation as a relentless self-publicist with a flair for tactlessness. She turned off viewers by appearing on TV in 1986 demonstrating how to put on a condom, advised shivering pensioners to cope with Arctic winter temperatures by "wearing long johns", enraged Northerners by saying they were dying of "ignorance and chips", and outraged everyone by stating that "good Christian people who would not dream of misbehaving will not catch Aids". This seemed especially rich when it emerged that she herself had been conducting a mutually adulterous affair with Major from 1984 to 1988.

1988 was an especially bad year for her, in fact. Not only did her lover give her the flick, but (in her capacity as a junior health minister) she repeatedly informed the nation that the majority of its eggs was riddled with the potentially fatal gut-buster salmonella. Poultry farmers begged to differ, and as their sales plummeted, the British Egg Council threatened to sue over the "factually incorrect and highly irresponsible" remarks. She finally resigned on December 16th after Mrs Thatcher floored her with the devastating one-liner: "I had eggs for breakfast."

Currie's credibility never recovered, so she decided to replace her ministerial career with a literary one. Having counselled fellow authors to 'stick to what you know', she followed the maxim rigidly: her 1994 debut novel *A Parliamentary Affair* dripped with sub-Jilly Cooper sex. Non-fiction pot-boilers such as *What Women Want* and *Three Line Quips* were followed by a steady trickle of pulp – *A Woman's Place, Chasing Men, This Honourable House*. Since getting the boot at the ballot box in 1997, Currie has fought valiantly to remain in the public eye. Her media career has been sustained either by weak plays on her cuckolded ex-husband's surname (*Late Night Currie, Currie Night*), or appearances on low-brow TV shows including *Hell's Kitchen* and *The Weakest Link* (a special 'headline grabbers' edition, alongside former colleague Neil Hamilton, qv). On Irish television in 2002 she actually referred to her new husband (chain-smoking ex-copper John 'JJ' Jones) as 'John Major' – to widespread disbelief – and in 2006 she made a tear-stained appearance on *Celebrity Wife Swap*, where she was brow-beaten by unconventionally handsome racing pundit John McCririck (qv).

When her *Diaries* appeared in 2002, it came as little surprise to find that they shared the same teenage style as her novels: what was a shock was the identity of 'B' (*qv*), the other man in her life. "With me he could philosophise and explore new talents in bed," she bragged of the 'Back To Basics' PM. He remembered the affair rather differently, terming it "the one event in my life of which I am most ashamed". It was an assessment endorsed by Mary Archer (*qv*), who miaowed with no apparent self-awareness: "I am a little surprised, not at Mrs Currie's indiscretion, but at a temporary lapse in John Major's taste."

For all Currie's protestations that her decision to publish was motivated by a desire to serve history, David Mellor (*qv*), perhaps mindful of his own experience, spoke for many in commenting: "She sold John Major down the river for cash, like a cheap little trollop."

"Good Christian people who would not dream of misbehaving will not catch Aids"

In weaker moments, the gassy Tory has admitted that she still pines for her superman. "The most hurtful thing was to look at John's autobiography and find that I wasn't even in the index," she sniffled to the *Times* in 2002. While his judgement in many things may have been questionable, here Major seems to have captured her place in history absolutely.

Sir Henry 'Chips' Channon

b. March 7th 1897 / d. Oct 7th 1958

MP (Con), Southend / Southend West, 1935-58

Described in the *Independent* in April 2007 as 'a rich American snob who passed himself off as an English gentleman', this preening poseur laid on a salty sleaze buffet for posterity, admitting: 'I hate and am uninterested in all the things most men like such as sport, business, statistics, debates, speeches, war and the weather; but I am riveted by lust, furniture, glamour, society and jewels.' Though politically inconsequential, 'Chips' set the useful precedent of a minor political player gaining notoriety through the gratuitous frankness of his or her journals (see *Clark, Alan*; *Currie, Edwina*; *Temple, Tracey*). 'I do not really think the House of Commons is my cup of tea', he reflected on December 5th 1935. The brew he preferred consisted of behind-the-scenes backbiting, drinking and impropriety, much of which was detailed in his diary, but omitted from the version published in 1967. At the forefront of the antics was Chips himself, whose larks included spiking his guests' drinks – he wrote of one 1947 soirée: 'I laced the cocktails with Benzedrine, which I always find makes a party go.'

In line with his wishes, his juiciest jottings have been held back until 2018, but it has been speculated that they may cast light upon whispers of an affair between him and the Duke of Kent (younger brother of King George VI), as well as grapples with playwright Terence Rattigan, society gardener Peter 'Petti' Coats and others. Perhaps surprisingly, Chips managed to sire a scandal-hit son in Paul Channon (*qv*), who – aged 23 and still a second-year Oxford undergraduate – sank cosily into his old man's still-warm Essex seat, defying 129 other applicants for the nomination and an anti-nepotism campaign run by the then-credible *Daily Express*. It was no more than family tradition: 'Chips' had himself inherited the seat in 1935 from his mother-in-law, who'd assumed democratic duties from her husband when he retired to take up his father's seat in the Lords (an institution famously distinguished from the Commons by its basis in heredity). Though no opponent of privilege herself, Nancy Mitford summarised him thus: "One always thought Chips was rather a dear, but he was black inside."

and I am delighted with the jail sentence." In October 2002 Archer stumped up an estimated £3m to Express newspapers, representing his libel award, the paper's legal costs and interest on both sums. Jill also confirmed that, were her husband still alive, they'd have cracked open a bottle of bubbly themselves.

Daily Star, the

Tawdry tabloid taken to the cleaners by Jeffrey Archer (*qv*) in 1987 over claims that he'd bedded prostitute Monica Coghlan (*qv*). Their story, which appeared in November 1986, followed revelations in the *News of the World* on October 26th about Archer's chum Michael Stacpoole handing cash to Coghlan at Victoria station – but where the *Star* fell down was in giving details of Archer's unproven encounter with her. On July 24th Mr Justice Caulfield (*qv*) awarded him damages of £500,000, and ordered the paper to pay costs of £700,000. The overjoyed novelist shook each juror by the hand and – having signed a few autographs – left the court with his wife Mary, who told journalists: "We might open a bottle of champagne."

Editor Lloyd Turner was sacked, and succumbed to a heart attack in 1996. His widow Jill had this thought when Archer's perjury caught up with him in 2001: "Lloyd always believed that justice would be done,

Dale, Sara
b. 1951

Sex therapist and former tenant of Norman Lamont (*qv*). Dale's 'healing techniques', incorporating whips, chains and ticklers, stretched the definition of holistic to breaking point, so when word of her ancient profession reached the tabloids in April 1991, the musteline Chancellor began proceedings to evict her from his Notting Hill basement. The £50-a-time sadomasochist, meanwhile, attempted to clean up by releasing an 18-rated VHS, *Sara Dale's Sensual Massage*, with a soothing soundtrack by 'Sleazy' from Nazi-fixated pop act Throbbing Gristle. Her current whereabouts are unknown.

— *RED HOT* —

"The thing about a strawberry is you can balance one on the end of your, well, you know."

- Edwina Currie, quoted in the Sunday Mirror, September 2002

— *CURRIE* —

┌──── WIGGINGS ────┐

"What you did was a disgraceful exhibition of uncontrollable temper, and you should be thoroughly ashamed"

– Judge John Gower to Ron Brown, 1990

└── FROM THE BEAK ──┘

Danish Minimum Wage, the

Engrossing topic which Tommy Sheridan insisted he and Scandinavian temptress Katrine Trolle had been discussing – at some length – in the numerous calls between them that showed up on his mobile phone bill. This was accepted during his 2006 libel action against the *News of the World*, much to Katrine's indignation: as experts in European social policy will know, Denmark does not even have a minimum wage.

see Sheridan, Tommy / Trolle, Katrine

Davies, Quentin
b. May 29th 1944
MP (Con/Lab), Stamford & Spalding, 1987-97 / Grantham & Stamford, 1997-

Tory turncoat (see *Woodward, Shaun*) whose reputation took a dip in 1991, when Lincolnshire magistrates fined him £1500 for allowing sheep on his land to descend into what the *Economist* described as a 'pathetic' condition. The smallholder blamed his shepherd, but this carried little weight with his parliamentary colleagues: for a time their baa-ing whenever he stood up to speak made it hard for him to be taken seriously, and he no longer lists the beasts in the Register of Members' Interests.

On June 26th 2007 Davies defected, hailing Gordon Brown as 'a leader I have always admired… with a towering record' while expressing contempt for Tory boss David Cameron's 'superficiality', 'unreliability' and 'apparent lack of any clear convictions'. The assessment was remarkably similar to one he'd earlier made of Brown, whom he accused of being 'extraordinarily incompetent', 'extraordinarily naïve', 'incredibly imprudent' and 'spectacularly complacent' in a Commons debate on March 16th 2005. "I trust and believe that something nasty will happen to the Chancellor in electoral terms before too long," he had ranted – and two years later he fulfilled his own hex. Davies insists he could not 'honestly' have r emained a Tory, but it remains to be seen just how kindly Labour MPs will take to a pro-hunting colleague who proudly belongs to no fewer than three gentlemen's clubs (Brooks's, the Travellers and the Beefsteak).

Davies, Ron

b. August 6th 1944
MP (Lab), Caerphilly, 1983-2001
Secretary of State for Wales, 1997-8

This rotund rambler from Rhymney wasn't the first New Labour frontbencher to be caught in a sex scandal (see *Cook, Robin*), but was the first to fall on his sword. He was also the second. Indeed, Davies comfortably holds the all-party record for resignations (five), well ahead of fellow Labour lemmings Peter Mandelson and David Blunkett.

His first brace of departures followed the mysterious events of the night of October 26th 1998. In the early hours, Davies presented himself at Brixton police station, to announce that he'd been robbed of his car, wallet, mobile phone, Labour Party card and conference pass. Earlier in the evening, he explained, he'd gone for a stress-busting stroll on Clapham Common and met a stranger who later transpired to be Donald 'Boogie' Fearon (*qv*). Having agreed to go for a drink and a bite, they hopped into Davies's car and picked up a couple of Fearon's associates en route. At this point, Davies claimed, a knife was produced and he was robbed. His assailants had panicked and fled only when they realised that they were attacking the most powerful man in Wales.

"I have actually been there when I have been watching badgers"

The police soon exposed inconsistencies in his version of events, and by the following morning he'd realised the game was up. After an intense meeting with Tony Blair and Alastair Campbell, he agreed to resign and – though he denied any gay intent in visiting Clapham Common – informed a puzzled Commons: "We are all different, the product both of our genes and our experiences."

Davies-watchers – and there were plenty in the tabloid press – had to wait until June 30th 1999 for his next resignation. He'd been elected a Welsh Assembly member on May 6th, but rumours persisted about his private life and his successor as Secretary of State for Wales, Alun Michael, had refused to give him his expected place in the Welsh Cabinet. The *News of the World* was on his case, and on June 13th it ran a story about his cruising activities at a place called Llwyn-Hir, a mile from the home he shared with his then-wife

Christina. Learning of the imminent scoop, Davies was forced to make a pre-emptive statement, announcing: "I am left with no alternative but to confirm that I am, and have been for some time, bisexual." Before he stood down, he told the press that he was receiving treatment for a 'compulsive disorder' which meant he was 'addicted to high-risk situations' – constantly returning to public life, perhaps.

That August he split from his wife, and in September announced that he'd be resigning as an MP at the next Election to focus exclusively on Welsh issues. To widespread surprise, he remarried in August 2002 and had a baby the following February – but in March he suffered his final, career-defining bout of temporary insanity. A tabloid honey-trap forced him to deny he'd engaged in a gay sex act with a stranger, this time on Tog Hill, a beauty spot off the M4. Though he admitted familiarity with the celebrated pick-up venue, he insisted his intentions were innocent. "I have actually been there when I have been watching badgers," he desperately explained, and stood down as a Labour candidate in the forthcoming assembly elections. He forfeited party membership altogether in 2004, citing press intrusion, the Iraq war, the incompetence of the Welsh Assembly, university top-up fees and almost everything else he could think of except his own status as a chronic liability. Since then he has restricted his political activities to a low-profile group called Forward Wales and a failed bid to join the European Parliament.

de Burgh, Chris
b. Oct 15th 1948

Terminally unhip crooner who big-heartedly agreed to front Jeffrey Archer's 'Simple Truth' (sic) campaign in April 1991, and headlined the resulting concert (alongside MC Hammer) in May. In June the fibbing novelist claimed it had raised £57m for Kurdish refugees, but by August 16th 2001 a tetchy Red Cross official was stating: "The fifty-seven million never existed." The actual figure stood at just £1m – less than 2% of the amount claimed, which would have trounced the total raised by Live Aid. Though the larger figure may have represented the sum of all donations received worldwide by the UN High Commission, only a 'tiny, tiny proportion' were attributable to Archer's efforts (including the MOR concert).

Baroness Nicholson, who demanded re-accounting, fumed: "Clearly both the Red Cross and Jeffrey Archer, deliberately or not, misled the Iraqi Kurds at their time of greatest need." The 5' 6" *Lady In Red* idol could not be blamed for the debacle, however – and had his own misgivings about the affair, expressed in an October 1991 interview with fanzine the *Getaway Gazette*. "The only other thing I was disappointed by was the relative lack of success of The Simple Truth single itself," he sighed, referring to the flop charity reissue of his 1987 classic (not written with the Kurdish situation in mind, but 'dead on. Dead on', in his opinion). The housewives' favourite went on to bemoan the lack of a promotional video as a reason for "the disappointing chart position of the record in the UK" – and added that Archer "said he was a big fan of my music". It is not known whether this was yet another of the peer's famous fabrications.

de Sancha, Antonia
b. Sept 14th 1961

Striking bit-part actress (see *Farmiloe, Sally*) who conducted a notorious affair with heinous Heritage Secretary David Mellor in the early 90s. The lanky siren (measurements 36-23-35, according to *Celebrity Sleuth* magazine) initially bonded with Mellor over a shared love of *South Pacific*, and a passionate affair ensued. Her friend Rowan Pelling, editor of the *Erotic Review* (for which de Sancha later penned a sex advice column) explained in 2004: "She liked sleeping with ugly men because there could be a powerful beauty and beast chemistry."

"She liked sleeping with ugly men because there could be a powerful beauty and beast chemistry"

The liaison soured when "he refused to acknowledge the fact that I felt like hell, and he wasn't very interested in me at all," and she'd soon contracted with sleaze broker Max Clifford (*qv*), who flogged her sorry tale to the *People* for £30,000. In the ensuing splash she informed its horrified readers that she'd sucked Mellor's hairy big toe, and was subsequently persuaded by Clifford – who characterised his relationship with her as that of 'father and daughter' – to add another wholly fictitious detail: that the soccer-mad MP liked to don a Chelsea strip before ravishing her. The ensuing furore forced him to resign, and did little for her acting career.

In an interview with the *Independent* on July 17th 2002 she denied the toe-sucking and the Chelsea strip, and confirmed that "absolutely nothing attracted me to him physically… The excitement was, to be perfectly frank, from being with somebody who was in a peak position of power." The article also recounts their only subsequent encounter, when she was eating in a restaurant with Paul Halloran – the journalist who'd introduced them in the first place. "He saw me and he saw Paul and he freaked out," she says of the 2001 incident. "He went to the loo for about 20 minutes, then went and sat down at his table. I have never seen a man eat so quickly. He totally ignored us and, as he walked past us, Paul said: 'Hello David, say hello to Antonia'. He spluttered hello, went bright red and ran up the stairs. It was just pathetic."

see *Mellor, David / Pie-Man, the*

Desmond, Richard
b. Dec 8th 1951

Porn dealer who creamed off a tiny fraction of his filthy lucre to make telling donations to the Labour Party in 2001. The £100,000 hand-out coincided with a successful bid by the publisher of periodicals such as *Mega Boobs* and *Horny Housewives* to move downmarket by buying the *Daily Express* and its sister papers. Sure enough, the much-anticipated referral of the takeover to the Competition Commission never materialised, and the cheque cleared just in time to avoid sober new legislation ensuring immediate disclosure of all such donations to the public. Labour insisted that the timing was not deliberate, and that such measures had not been taken to head off the inevitable criticism that would come from handling such sticky notes. The disgusted naysayers came from within the party as well as out (though the Conservatives had previously accepted a smaller donation of their own from the millionaire muckspreader). Long-term anti-porn campaigner Clare Short (*qv*) was particularly angry, and when the story broke in 2002 she suggested that new donor vetting procedures were "established because of the embarrassment over that affair." Tessa Jowell (*qv*), meanwhile, told the *Financial Times*: "I don't feel comfortable that the party accepts a donation from somebody who earns certainly part of his income from pornography." But former Desmond associate Derek Botham – now going solo in the masturbation market – countered (somewhat unhelpfully to all parties): "In the stakes of sleaze Richard Desmond is a much more upright character than half the people in the government."

As the owner of several newspapers, Desmond had earned the ear of

Tony Blair, but would turn the tables in April 2004 by announcing his titles' switch in support to the Conservatives. There was nothing the Tories could do but wince and anticipate an even more crushing defeat at the next election, especially when stories emerged on the same day that Desmond had launched a foul-mouthed tirade against the putative German bidders for the rival *Telegraph* Group (he announced that Germans were 'all Nazis', despite having accepted sizeable Commerzbank backing when he acquired his own media stock). But as his brother-in-arms Botham said at the time: "When push comes to shove, Richard can stand up straight as an honest citizen, and very few people in any government of the last 20 years have actually been able to do that."

Diary Secretary

Assistant charged with helping MPs fill their schedules, and usefully occupy their time outside Parliament.

see *Parliamentary Researcher* / entries *passim*

Dicks, Terry
b. March 17th 1937
MP (Con), Hayes and Harlington, 1983-97

Controversial Blue who outraged

many with his pro-Section 28 couplet 'Heterosexual sex is normal, homosexual is abnormal', but confused the issue by campaigning under the slogan 'We Love Dicks'.

"He brought shame on the political process of this country by his blatant espousal of racism and his various corrupt dealings"

He'd already shown his colours when, sharing TV-am's sofa with Rupert Allason (*qv*) in 1991, he vigorously defended Iraq's decision to murder British-based journalist Farzad Bazoft (*qv*). A recent visitor to Iraq himself, Dicks was on record criticising his own government for being too quick to condemn Saddam Hussein over the 'alleged' gassing of Kurds. He attracted especial censure for the statement that Bazoft 'deserved to be hanged,' the day before the state-sponsored killing. *Observer* editor Donald Trelford, whose staff were staging a vigil with the NUJ and Amnesty International outside the Iraqi embassy, spoke for many in stating: "To say the day before a man is executed he deserves to be hanged, when he has no evidence, is despicable." Unchastened, in 1994 Dicks savaged the University of Sussex for offering a module on 'Sexual Dissidence and Cultural Change', calling it 'a degree in gay' and recommending that "the place should be shut down and disinfected."

He went on to have a memorable clash with Labour motormouth Tony Banks during a December 16th debate on lottery cash. When he described AIDS as a 'self-inflicted luvvies illness' and the Terence Higgins Trust as 'not a genuine charity,' Banks branded him 'The Honorable Member for Hell' and 'living proof that a pig's bladder on a stick can get elected to Parliament'.

Dicks – who called Nelson Mandela a 'black terrorist' and West Indians 'in general bone idle', as well as acclaiming the 1994 flogging of British subject Gavin Sherrard-Smith for selling alcohol in Qatar – was little mourned by his successor in Hayes and Harlington, Labour's John McDonnell. In his maiden speech on June 6th 1997 – traditionally an opportunity for new MPs to pay tribute, however insincerely, to their predecessors – he stated: "Terry Dicks was a stain on the character of this House, the Conservative party which harboured him and the good name of my constituency. He brought shame on the political process of this country by his blatant espousal of racism and his various corrupt dealings. He demeaned the House by his presence, and I deeply regret that the Conservative party failed to take action to stem his flow of vile bigotry. Thankfully, my constituents can now say good riddance to this malignant creature."

Dirty Diary, the (i)

Soubriquet for Edwina Currie's *Diaries 1987-1992*, published in 2002, which describe how she broke away from a husband 'slumped snoring in front of the television' to find solace in adultery: first with a 'right slob, with kinky preferences', then – astoundingly – with John Major (*qv*). "He may have been grey to the world," she announced, "but he was a very exciting lover." The Mills & Boon stylings of the journal offered the former minister all the practice she needed to become a writer of 'erotic' fiction. "With me he could explore new talents in bed," she cooed, telling of how she longed for Major's 'sweet taste, and the giggles' when they were apart, wishing she were 'warm and sticky' with him instead, and wistfully pining when they were apart: "I wish my flat was filled with one big man in his blue underpants."

"The 'orrible smell suggests H²S, and therefore eggs"

She is more graphic still when referring to her stomach. March 30th 1991 finds her 'woozy' and 'very full' after she 'overdid it' on tuna salad and veal on a French trip.

'Yuk, I feel grotty', she confides on April 25th, 'feeling sick' and 'very crampy', something she ascribes to 'gut ache'. On May 7th, coolly disregarding salmonella risks, she confesses 'I like egg sandwiches very much' – but they're not doing her any good, as in no time she has 'a very upset tum'. She considers blaming 'those prawn sandwiches at lunchtime', but concludes "the 'orrible smell suggests H²S, and therefore eggs". By December 5th she is 'dog tired' because her 'period is coming on', and – yet again – her 'gut aches'. The next spring is no less turbulent. On March 3rd she reveals that she has 'picked up a bug in France' which has given her the 'squitters' and (still worse) left her 'queasy and full of wind'. And so on it rumbles – though her gastrointestinal concerns aren't solely confined to herself. Watching John Major pile on the condiments in the Commons tea room on February 7th 1991, she frets that he'll give himself an ulcer.

Elsewhere in the journal she finds time to consider her own chances of leading the country. "Major is tough and brainy and nice underneath, but there is a definite lack of charisma," she confides. "I reckon I would run him close in a straight fight after a few more years of government." Sadly the prize bout never arose, leaving her free to pursue reality TV interests instead.

Dirty Diary, the (ii)

Sub-Pepysian document detailing the infantile innermost thoughts of John Prescott's erstwhile Diary Secretary, Tracey Temple (*qv*), and shared with readers of the *Daily Mirror* in April 2006. "God forbid – whatever made me I don't know," she groans when remembering the first time she agreed to go back to her boss's flat, after the 2002 office Christmas bash. The ill-spelt log also showed in painful detail just how willing the DPM (*qv*) was to give up the work in his in-tray (usually 'things to do with regeneration or the environment') in exchange for slap and tickle. Among the more embarrassing episodes is the account of the memorial service for dead servicemen in Iraq on October 10th 2003 – also the occasion of Temple's 43rd birthday. She describes the event in terms of wide-eyed celeb-spotting ('It was great... Royalty was there, the PM and Cherie etc'), and afterwards recalls the 'randy old sod' demanding more sex ('he was so up for it').

Disappointing Diary, the

Hotly-anticipated memoirs of life behind the doors of No.10 by the one closest to the Prime Minister – not Cherie Blair with *The Goldfish Bowl*, but Alastair Campbell and his *Blair Years* (published in July 2007, a full two weeks after Tony Blair's departure from office, to minimise damage to Gordon Brown). Hopes that the pugnacious Scot might blow the new administration apart with a volley of brutally frank revelations were hardly satisfied by the book's weary trudge through his many spats with enemies in the media and the Commons. Though the journals were bowdlerised, a few moments of historical import remain, such as Trousergate (qv). Beyond that, the book devotes plenty of time to the storm brewing between Blair and Brown (who didn't take long to get impatient for power: Campbell moans about Blair's 'bad-tempered conversations with GB' as early as May 1997). It also offers potent imagery, such as the time in December 1994 when 'I went into see TB, who was standing stark naked reading the *Mail*,' or the time in 1995 when 'I pushed open the door and there [Mo Mowlam] was in all her glory, lying in the bath with nothing but a big plastic hat on.'

Naked revelations aside, the book also detailed internecine strife, reporting that Peter Mandelson needed to be 'reined in', that Alan Duncan (qv) said Clare Short was 'like a bag lady' while John Prescott (qv) felt: 'That woman is fucking mad.' Gordon Brown, meanwhile, apparently commented in March 2003 that 'the War Cabinet meetings were hopeless. You had

Clare [Short] blathering away, DB [David Blunkett] and JR [John Reid] behaving like armchair generals and giving out weakness vibes to the real generals.' In July, as the scandal over David Kelly (qv) grows, we are told: 'I called Geoff Hoon [Defence Secretary]. He was not remotely on top of the case.' Nor, it seems, was Campbell: following Kelly's suicide, the big-hearted press scourge tells us: 'I wept because of the pressures I was under, and the sadness I felt for Kelly's family.'

Ditchfield, Jeffrey
b. 1966

Haggard Welshman behind a 2004-05 scheme to supply soft drugs to the Cabinet. The Rhyl-based herbal entrepreneur had founded politically-motivated dope dealerships Bud Buddies and Beggar's Belief (qv) in 2003, and despite beating various charges on medicinal grounds, was convicted of possessing and supplying cannabis in September 2006. During Ditchfield's trial Defence Minister John Reid (qv) was named as one of the intended recipients of his largesse, which came as no surprise – the toking taff had tried the same stunt on several Cabinet ministers (including the PM), and his supporters continued to target Reid when he became Home Secretary in May 2006. Ironically, they could claim no credit when a belief-beggaringly minuscule quantity was discovered in his holiday cottage just weeks later.

DNA Bioscience

Having undergone a paternity test of his own (see *Quinn, Kimberly*), 'Minister Without Dignity' David Blunkett took an understandable interest in DNA technology. After befriending entrepreneur Tariq Saddiqi and his wife Lucy late in 2004, he leapt at their offer to become a director of this firm (offering 'peace of mind' from £159 a pop) on April 21st 2005, and splashed out £15,000 on shares. Unfortunately, however – and despite his prodigious memory – he forgot to consult the government's Advisory Committee on Business Appointments first, despite receiving three reminders from its chairman, Lord Mayhew of Twysden. Though he was only on the board for a fortnight before resigning after the General Election on May 5th (when he was readmitted to the Cabinet as Work and Pensions Secretary), it was suggested that he could have used inside knowledge of government to further the company's interests. Blunkett vigorously refuted this, but he'd committed a technical breach of the Ministerial Code and (under pressure from all sides) reluctantly resigned from the Cabinet at the start of November.

When the story broke he quickly announced an intention to dispose of the shares (which he'd apparently bought as a nest-egg for his sons), acknowledging that the holding caused 'continuing misinterpretation of the position'. But with no hope of holding onto his Cabinet post, he opted to retain his stake instead. With a flotation scheduled for the first quarter of 2006, it was rumoured that the value of his 3% slice had soared as high as £500,000 – but as the bubble burst (with some blaming the unfortunate publicity he'd generated), Blunkett's spokesman conceded that the valuation was 'not realistic'. In December 2005 DNA Bioscience's remaining directors recommended that the firm be placed into voluntary liquidation (which would have rendered his holding worthless) - but at the time of writing the firm appears still to be trading.

Dodgy Diary, the

Bogus document compiled in May 1987 by Angela Peppiatt (*qv*) for her boss Jeffrey Archer – and one of the most lucrative works of fiction he has ever got someone else to write for him. The 1986 *Economist* diary was obtained by a friend of Peppiatt's, Gavin Pearce, on January 8th 1987, two weeks after the *Star* had lodged its defence – mistakenly in regard to the night of September 9th 1986. Archer duly switched his alibi to the wrong night, only for the error to be exposed, forcing him to concoct a second dinner-date alibi for the evening before. At the end of April 1987 he asked Peppiatt to fill in the blank pages in the dodgy diary covering 5th – 12th September, with details of the names and times he gave her. Thereafter all pages except those relating to the 8th and 9th were sealed, prior to inspection by the defence, who little suspected they were blank. Peppiatt says the 'duplicate' was justified to her for reasons of security in light of the Brighton bomb, but Archer swore in court that the diaries were contemporary documents. Smelling a rat, she took the precaution of making 'before and after' photocopies dated with a copy of the day's *Times* – documents the police found very useful 13 years later, when the time came to tuck the recently-ennobled weasel behind bars.

SLEAZE

> "I have not smoked cannabis. But I did eat a tiny bit of cannabis cake and all I can say is I enjoyed the cake, but that is all"
>
> – *ex-Chancellor Lord Lamont on his drug use, 2000*

SLOT

Dodgy Dome Dossier, the

As part of the seemingly unstoppable drive of AEG boss Philip Anschutz (*qv*) to rebrand the defunct Millennium Dome (*qv*) as a giant casino, this flimsy PR dossier was 'sexed up' in August 2006 to include endorsements from major local religious figures – who were in fact implacably opposed to the scheme. The Reverend Malcolm Torry, of Greenwich Peninsula Chaplaincy, cited a 'serious breach of trust' after his group was quoted falsely and out of context on the Department for Culture, Media and Sport's website, the ministerial page fed hype by AEG. Echoing the February 2003 Iraq Dossier, the document was stitched together from an unwitting academic source: in this case, a 2005 anti-casino paper published by the GPC, arguing that 'gambling can prevent human flourishing and that it should therefore be avoided'. "The paper which our trustees put out is negative," raged Torry, whereas the AEG dossier claimed his people were 'fully committed' to the regeneration plans and 'fully recognise the right of people to gamble in a free country'. More bizarrely, it suggested that Muslim and Sikh leaders had joined Christians in 'welcoming' the new enterprise, whereas all three faiths in fact explicitly condemn gambling. The Frankenstein report, cobbled together by one of Anschutz's senior AEG managers, was 'simply made up without our knowledge and agreement', said Torry – and local imam Sheikh Hassan Ali Barakat, Muslim representative of the Greenwich chaplaincy, agreed. "I don't support the casino, I never have and it's wrong for Anschutz to say that I do," he stormed. Fortunately, the 4,600 ungodly jobs planned by AEG went to a pop auditorium instead.

Dodgy Dossier, the (i)
(*aka* 'the September Dossier')

Shoddy government report thrown together to justify an invasion of Iraq, which the UK had helped arm throughout the 80s and early 90s. Published on September 24th 2002 and officially titled *Iraq's Weapons of Mass Destruction: The Assessment of the British Government*, the dossier's main problem was that it relied on assumptions about Iraqi WMDs (*qv*), whose existence had not yet been proven.

One area of grave doubt was controversially recycled by President Bush in his January State of the Union address - namely that Saddam had sought to buy "significant quantities of uranium from Africa". The chief source for this appeared to be a collection of flagrant forgeries from Niger, though Tony Blair later testified to

the Commons Liaison Committee that this was not the case. Once the CIA concluded that the intelligence should not have been repeated, it severely damaged the credibility of UK intelligence operatives.

Then, on May 29th 2003, Andrew Gilligan alleged on the *Today* programme that an early version of the dossier had been returned by Downing Street with the suggestion it needed to be 'sexed up' before the public would swallow it. Specifically, one reference to Iraq being able to mobilise WMDs 'within 45 minutes' was sure to have the tabloids in a panic. Attempting to downplay its significance, one government spokesman affected not to recall any particular media attention over the sensationalist phrase – despite it making the front page of the *Evening Standard* within hours of the dossier's release. The following day's *Sun* headline read '45 MINUTES FROM DOOM'; the respected *Daily Star*, meanwhile, ran with 'MAD SADDAM READY TO ATTACK: 45 Minutes From A Chemical War'.

"45 MINUTES FROM DOOM"

The real importance to the government of the '45 minute' statistic was made clearer when it emerged that spin doctor Tom Kelly (*qv*) had complained to Alastair Campbell six days before publication: "The weakness, obviously, is our inability to say he [Saddam Hussein] could pull the nuclear trigger any time soon." So came the arbitrary figure of three quarters of an hour, which Gilligan suggested the government knew to be false before public release. Though the risky allegation was softened in a later broadcast to 'questionable', it was a red rag to Labour, who set out to see the BBC humiliated by way of revenge.

Dodgy Dossier, the (ii)
(*aka* the February Dossier)

The term 'Dodgy Dossier' was first coined by Channel 4 News to describe the February 2003 paper *Iraq: Its Infrastructure of Concealment, Deception and Intimidation* – a waste of ink cribbed partly from a Californian postgraduate thesis (see *al-Marashi, Ibrahim*). Nonetheless, allied to the September 2002 dossier, it was considered evidence enough on which to go to war. The term 'dodgy' is now often applied equally to the earlier dossier (see above), which redefined the length of time represented by forty-five minutes (meaning 'probably never'). The existence of two such dodgy documents can be confusing even to scrupulous professionals: Andrew Gilligan (*qv*), defending himself during the Hutton Inquiry, referred throughout his interview to both reports.

Donnygate

Condemned by whistleblowing former councillor Ron Rose as "the most extensive local government scandal in British history", this sorry saga ended in a string of prison sentences in March 2002.

The affair centred on two senior Doncaster Councillors, former mayor Raymond Stockhill and planning chief Peter Birks, routinely taking bribes (Birks accepted a £160,000 farmhouse in exchange for pushing through local businessman Alan Hughes's unsound multi-million pound planning application in 1992, for example). The council had been under police investigation since 1997, over expenses scams ranging from foreign trips to buying racehorses, and 74 arrests were made in total, including Council Leader Malcolm Glover (appointed as a 'clean pair of hands' in 1997). Local MP Kevin Hughes (*qv*) sprang to his defence – "they'll be arresting people for taking a cup of coffee next," he quipped – but Glover was duly handed a suspended prison sentence for fiddling expenses.

In all some 25 Labour councillors were convicted, many desperately pleading old age and decrepitude in mitigation. At Nottingham Crown Court, Mr Justice Hunt was unimpressed. "Public life requires a standard of its own," he thundered.

"Power corrupts, and corruption in government by those elected by the public strikes at its integrity and at the root of democracy." Ron Rose was in full agreement, adding: "Despite the enormous scale of the wrongdoing, there has been no serious Labour Party investigation into the Doncaster scandals."

Donoughue, Lord Bernard
b. 1934

Despite lucrative involvement with Robert Maxwell, this self-made economist was appointed to a government position by Tony Blair from 1997 to 1999. Having been a senior policy adviser to Harold Wilson and James Callaghan, Donoughue was appointed executive vice-chairman of Maxwell's London & Bishopsgate Investment firm in 1988, at a time when (unbeknownst to him) it was busily implementing the corpulent crook's criminal share dealings. Having trousered a £500,000 fee (and despite his self-professed intellect), he failed to act on the company's lack of proper records or adequate control systems, and was subsequently damned by a DTI report. "He ought to have ascertained sufficient information," it said. "Had he done so he might have identified the abuse by Robert Maxwell." Donoughue was cautiously repentant in response. "With hindsight, I regret it," he blathered. "I don't want to make an excuse for myself, but I am not an experienced City person." Satisfied, Blair appointed him to the Ministry of Agriculture in 1997, a post he left in a 1999 reshuffle – partly to enjoy watching his racehorse, Robber Baron.

Douglas, Dorrett
b. 1964

Working girl who told the BBC's *Panorama* in 2001 that Monica Coghlan (*qv*) was not alone in having been solicited by pathological punter Jeffrey Archer. 'Little' Dorrett claimed to have accepted £50 and a glass of champagne to 'do the deed' one summer's night in 1985. He was 'nice, clean and well-mannered,' she recalled, but 'no stranger to the procedures.' Douglas, who backed up her story with a host of uncanny details about Archer's flat, remembered the serial seducer parting his dressing gown and asking: "Well, what do you think of this, then?" Her answer is not recorded.

SLEAZE

"An allegation of bribery for purposes of buying a peerage is destructive of the body politics (*sic*) of the government and the country"

– Robert Maxwell, November 1986

SLOT

Downey Report

Sharply-worded swing at the barn door that was Cash For Questions (*qv*), compiled by senior civil servant Sir Gordon Downey in July 1997. Despite clearing protagonists such as Ian Greer (*qv*) of provable corruption, it included withering critiques of most of those involved, and Greer's lobbying business collapsed that year. John Major was sufficiently concerned by the Report to prorogue Parliament into a May 1st polling day, hoping to avoid the terrible stink until after the Election – a tactic he'd used five years earlier over the Matrix Churchill affair (*qv*). This time it made little difference.

DPM

1. Abbreviation used in plumbing to describe a Damp Proof Membrane, a vast stretch of oily skin that protects the integrity of a house.

2. Abbreviation used in the diary of Tracey Temple (*qv*) to describe the Deputy Prime Minister, a vast stretch of oily skin which protects itself whilst undermining the integrity of the House.

Draper, Derek
b. 1969

Self-styled 'Mr Fixit' at the centre of the miserable Cash For Access (or 'Lobbygate') scandal (*qv*), which made an early bid to undermine public confidence in the Blair dream in 1998.

Draper's lobbying business, Prima, was doing such a roaring trade after the 1997 Election victory that by June 1998 an undercover reporter named Gregory Palast decided to pose as a US energy executive and seek his lubrication skills. The bumptious Mandelson protégé duly bragged of knowing the 'people that count' in government – by his reckoning exactly seventeen of them – and added: "To say I am intimate with all of them is the understatement of the century." But precisely none of them was willing to back their buddy in the subsequent stink.

His associate Roger Liddle – a former Prima director who'd decamped to the Downing Street Policy Unit – was also present at the interview. After Palast had assisted him to several glasses of champagne, Liddle slurred darkly about how things were done at New Labour HQ. "There is a circle, and Derek is part of the circle," he darkly intoned. "Anyone who says he isn't is the enemy… Just tell me what you want, who you want to meet, and Derek will make the call for you." Palast's exposé made the front of the *Observer* on July 5th 1998, but he later described Draper as 'nothing more than a messenger boy, a factotum, a purveyor, a self-loving, over-scented clerk.'

Draper is now a psychotherapist in America, and pens a column for the *Mail on Sunday*, as well as appearing on hard-hitting self-improvement show *Kyle's Academy*, helmed by TV agony uncle Jeremy Kyle. Reflecting on his former life, he has concluded: "My message was quite simple, really. 'I'm rich and a bit of a wanker. Who cares? You can still be that and be Labour'."

D:Ream

Camp Northern Irish house duo who scored a 1994 chart-topper with *Things Can Only Get Better* (*qv*), later to serve as the hopelessly optimistic soundtrack to New Labour's 1997 Election campaign – on the back of which it soared all the way back to #19 in the UK charts.

Dreary Diary, the

Name given to *The Blunkett Tapes: My Life In The Bear Pit*, the soporific journals of former Home/Pensions Secretary David Blunkett (*qv*), published in October 2006. A self-justifying whinge stretched over 500 numbing pages, its appearance was commemorated by serialisation in the *Guardian* and the *Daily Mail*, a two-part documentary on Channel 4, extensive extracts on Radio 4 and an unprecedented outpouring of public apathy.

"This book is a disgrace... why do disgraced and useless individuals get a publishing deal and profit from their bad behaviour?"

By mid-November booksellers had shifted a grand total of 1,196 copies, and at the end of the month its sales ranking on amazon.co.uk was a miserable 2,179. By January 2007 it had plummeted to 35,935, with one disgruntled reader commenting: "This book is a disgrace... why do disgraced and useless individuals get a publishing deal and profit from their bad behaviour?"

Blunkett's famous memory came in for criticism, too – his recollection of an exchange with the Director-General of the Prison Service, Martyn Narey, in October 2002, for example, was that he'd said there should be 'no dithering' in dealing with rioting lags in Lincoln prison. When the book appeared, however, Narey advanced a different version. "He shrieked at me that he didn't care about lives, told me to call in the army and 'machine gun' prisoners and, still shrieking, again ordered me to take the prison back immediately," he told the *Times*. "I refused. David hung up."

Duncan, Alan
b. March 31st 1957
MP (Con), Rutland & Melton, 1992-

Voted 'best-looking politician 2005' by *Pink News* subscribers, this diminutive Tory made a fortune in oil during the first Gulf War before joining his former flatmate William Hague in Westminster. His parliamentary career suffered an early setback, however, when he was forced to resign his junior government role in January 1994 – within 17 days of appointment – over the dubious expansion of his property portfolio. In May 1990 he'd advanced £140k to an elderly Westminster neighbour, Harry Ball-Wilson, to facilitate the purchase of the ex-fighter ace's council-owned Georgian home. The underlying concept was to take advantage of the council's 'right to buy' scheme for long-term residents – on the understanding that the property (soon to be worth twice as much) would revert to him upon Ball-Wilson's death. In fact the red-blooded pensioner remarried and moved out, leaving Duncan free to purchase the property at a knockdown rate. The deal was legal but unseemly, and though 15 Tories signed a Commons motion in his support, 200 Opposition MPs backed a more stinging one. He had the good grace to step down as

parliamentary private secretary to Health Minister Brian Mawhinney at once.

Duncan Smith, Iain
b. April 9th 1954
MP (Con), Chingford, 1992-97 / Chingford and Woodford Green, 1997-

Only the second Conservative Party leader never to become Prime Minister (see *Hague, William*), the achievements of the self-styled 'Quiet Man' in the field of sleaze are characteristically modest. On a particularly slow day for stories, *Newsnight* revealed that the mild-mannered no-hoper had been 'creative' with his CV, suggesting he'd attended seats of learning even Jeffrey Archer might have blushed to mention (the University of Perugia and Durnsford College of Management). His sleaze

zenith came in October 2003 with 'Betsygate' (*qv*), unequivocally the most trifling scandal in British political history. It wasn't long before the party had forgotten all about it, and indeed him. When he lost his colleagues' vote of confidence later that month, his publishers rushed out his deplorable novel *The Devil's Tune* – but his literary abilities were deemed only marginally superior to his leadership skills, and the wretched volume never made it to paperback. In February 2004 he embarked upon a sideline in cabaret with a one-man show entitled 'An Audience with Iain Duncan Smith', but the debut performance at Liverpool's 1600-seat Philharmonic Hall attracted only 67 punters. After this he returned to the back benches, which many felt was his natural habitat, re-emerging in December 2006 as head of David Cameron's 'social justice policy unit'. In no time he was telling the *Sunday Telegraph* that gay couples 'don't even register on the Richter scale of how to bring up children', and went on to slam co-habiting parents – views that did little to advance the cause of Compassionate Conservatism.

Dustbingate

Tag given to the 1998 fuss over Wyke Property Services, partly owned by Johnathan Prescott (*qv*) and entirely devoted to the non-socialist practice of buying repossessed homes at knockdown prices. Not to be confused with his brush with the headlines in 2006 (see *Prescott, John Jr*), this squall originated when five shift-workers from Hull sniffed a fast buck. The penniless entrepreneurs, among them a toilet cleaner, got wind of a rumour from a local gasman that the son of the Deputy PM might be cashing in on other people's misery, and decided to beat the press to the punch. Having identified properties in Leeds and Hull apparently acquired by Johnathan (*sic*), the vigilantes set about looking for evidence by befriending neighbours, raiding garages, even dragging dustbins into the street and upending them (despite the name, no damning material was found thus). Ringleader Ian Newton claimed to have made £96,000 from various deals stemming from his wombling, including advances for a book and a film. He even bought a sports car – though plans for *Dustbingate: The Movie* collapsed after bitter disputes in casting the role of Prescott Sr. (*Hi-De-Hi* star Paul Shane was presumably unavailable).

Tom Driberg

b. May 22nd 1905 / d. Aug 12th 1976

MP (independent / Lab), Maldon, (1942-55) / Barking (1959-74)

Defiantly unconventional gay sex addict who claimed to have performed his first act of gross indecency in a lavatory at the age of ten, and maintained the habit throughout a three-decade Parliamentary career. Having been a gossip columnist and Communist activist, Driberg entered the House during the war and remained there for over three decades. The highest offices were denied him, however, for the obvious reason that he represented such a security risk – though he worried little for his own safety. He always carried a fat wad of notes on his person, in the stated assumption that every member of His Majesty's constabulary could be bought. Indeed, policemen were a particular peccadillo of the left-winger: one of his favourite anecdotes involved spontaneously fellating a uniformed bobby on Hungerford Bridge. His 1951 marriage to the unfortunate Ena Binfield prompted Churchill to quip 'buggers can't be choosers', but the holy bonds of matrimony did little to quell his appetite for cruising.

Driberg (latterly Baron Bradwell) somehow managed to keep his proclivities out of the public eye until his posthumous 1976 autobiography, Ruling Passions, blew the lid off the Westminster cottaging scene. MPs on both sides were openly relieved not to have been exposed in the tawdry opus, memorably described by the *Sun* as 'the biggest outpouring of literary dung a public figure has ever flung into print'. Though some pointed to his many contacts in MI5 (on whose behalf he spied on his own party), Driberg put his evasion of scandal down to fear: nobody wanted to cut a maverick loose when he could bring half the House down with him. Unfortunately for sleaze sleuths, the unfinished memoirs stopped short of naming names – but Labour heavyweight Nye Bevan is said to have been treated to oral sex from Driberg in his office (see *Brown, Michael*). Labour PM Jim Callaghan claimed to have been groped by him, but the randy rogue's affections were far from restricted to the great and good. Generally he preferred the touch of strangers – and one place where new boys were always on tap was round Cockney businessman Ronnie Kray's (see fellow pioneer Bob Boothby, page 34). And another matter Ruling Passions failed to clarify was whether Driberg was a Soviet spy, as claimed by KGB loose cannon Vasili Mitrokhin after his death.

Ecclestone, Bernie
b. Oct 28th 1930

One of Britain's shortest, richest men, an eager supporter of New Labour, and the unwitting architect of the party's first major sleaze scandal.

In January 1997, when Tony's rabble seemed a shoo-in for power, Bernie dug deep and wrote them a cheque for £1m, with the advice of his trusted lawyer David Mills (*qv*). The donation was not, however, entirely altruistic. Much of Ecclestone's wealth was tied up in Formula 1 racing, and much of Formula 1 racing's wealth was tied up in tobacco sponsorship. Unfortunately, the party had made it abundantly clear in both their 1992 and 1997 manifestos that a Labour government would enforce an outright ban on tobacco advertising. After frenzied backpedalling, Labour finally announced that Formula 1 was to be exempt from the projected ban

until at least 2006. Seditious media elements immediately suggested that the turnabout was in effect a straight transaction between Bernie, Blair and Brown, so the party panicked and agreed to return the money (though the returned cheque was said to have been postdated to avoid embarrassment with the bank manager).

The whole affair enraged the stumpy F1 tycoon, who is unlikely to have been mollified by Blair's grudging public apology on November 17th 1997. "I didn't get it all wrong," he mumbled. "But it hasn't been handled well, and I apologise for that."

EDM

Abbreviation for Early Day Motion, a way for MPs to raise concerns which otherwise might not be debated in Westminster, but which may be in the interests of their constituents – generally to congratulate winners of *Pop Idol* or moan about *Big Brother.* Also, in DJ'ing, an abbreviation for Electronic Dance Music (see *D: Ream*).

Eggy bread

Laxative snack being prepared by Belinda Oaten for her young daughters when her husband chose to break news of his romps with a Polish rent boy.

see *Oaten, Mark*

WIGGINGS

"Mrs Gorman provided seriously misleading and inaccurate information to the committee… During our inquiry we have been gravely concerned by Mrs. Gorman's untruthfulness, her failures to provide the Commissioner with information, and false accusations she has made against others"

- the Commons Standards and Privileges Committee on Teresa Gorman, 2000

FROM THE BEAK

Emery, Sir Peter
b. Feb 27th 1926 / d. Dec 9th 2004 MP (Con), Reading, 1959-66 / Honiton, 1967-97 / Devon East, 1997-2001

Long-serving self-server Peter Frank Hannibal Emery once memorably described himself as 'a businessman rather than a politician.' Few were surprised when he opposed the 1995 Nolan Report recommendation that MPs declare extra-Parliamentary earnings: he'd raked in an eye-watering £500,000 in bonuses from property deals between 1989 and 1992 alone.

He was repeatedly censured by the Commons Public Accounts Committee for gross profiteering through his company, Shenley Trust Services Ltd. (formerly Emery & Emery). Slapped on the wrist in 1980 for raking in 70% gains on a government contract, he insisted the true figure was only 7% – but a weary committee reinstated the zero after pointlessly re-opening the investigation. Sir Peter earned especial notoriety through his close involvement with Bophuthatswana (*qv*), the unsavoury South African puppet territory which retained his services in 1981 to further its profile abroad. He promptly set up a lavish 'embassy' for it in London's Holland Park and began to lobby his Parliamentary colleagues on its behalf. Despite constant opposition from anti-apartheid protesters, he organised 'jollies' to Sun City for fellow MPs, as well as distributing brochures extolling its virtues, penning puff pieces for the *Times* without declaring his interest and – of course – trousering plump fees all the while.

The cosy arrangement began to unravel in the mid-80s, however. In September 1984 Sir Peter withdrew £75,902 from the embassy's Coutts account (of which he was the sole signatory) and deposited it in an account of his own in Geneva. In April 1986 the Bophuthatswanan authorities enquired as to the money's whereabouts, and Sir Peter replied that he'd deposited it secretly at the request of the territory's President, Leon Mangope. Mangope furiously denied this, and his writ was only withdrawn when the money was repaid with full interest. A lengthy UK police investigation into Sir Peter's conduct was also undertaken, but ultimately led nowhere, as a wary Mangope declined to testify in the UK.

English Manner Ltd., the

Bespoke etiquette and travel company set up by Jonathan Sayeed MP (*qv*) and his Commons assistant Alexandra Messervy, with the ultimate consequence of destroying his political career early in 2005.

Messervy was unequivocal about the clientele she deemed desirable: "These days, a lot of people have money but lack breeding, and those are the travellers I would like to educate," she sniffed. Part of their brilliant business plan was to show foreign visitors around aristocratic homes, but with 'a senior Member of the British Parliament' like Sayeed on side, this extended to government buildings too. He promised visitors a lesson in 'how the British Parliament works', and – having stumped up $1,500 – that's exactly what they got.

One Bob Morris (of American periodical *Travel & Leisure*) breathlessly wrote up how he'd visited the Commons, watched Prime Minister's Questions and wolfed dinner in its private dining room. The priceless piece was duly logged as part of a Standards and Privileges Committee investigation, which concluded that Sayeed – who maintains he never solicited or received money for showing tourists around Westminster – had been 'at the least negligent in failing to exercise sufficient care to safeguard the reputation of Parliament, and at worst to have acted carelessly, in a manner which has allowed that reputation to be injured'. He stood down at the May 2005 Election, but the business appears to be thriving still.

Enron

Once America's fastest-growing company, this energy giant was engulfed in a grotesque corporate fraud scandal late in 2001, which provoked worldwide investor misery. Though its collapse was the result of systematic accounting dishonesty across the Atlantic, it didn't obviate reports in the UK that our very own Labour Party was 'enveloped in sleaze' over the affair. Opposition parties demanded an inquiry to determine whether Enron's sponsorship of New Labour had influenced energy policy, and to establish why up-to-their-necks accountants Arthur Andersen had been taken off the government trade blacklist, where they had been festering since the DeLorean farrago of the early 80s. Enron's highly creative accountants had forged strong links with Labour, though the only ex-MP who actually held an Enron directorship – Lord Wakeham – was a Tory. To date, no coherent answers have been provided.

RED HOT

"I think you have to get someone to laugh in bed. You have to get a man to the point he laughs so loud that he can't even say, 'Oh, don't do that"

- Edwina Currie, quoted in the Sunday Mirror, September 2002

CURRIE

Euan Test, the

Benchmark applied to government initiatives by Tony Blair in 1997, whose simple requirement was that they passed muster with his 13-year-old son. Whether the test was foolproof is open to debate: when Blair declared the Euan-endorsed Millennium Dome "the greatest show on earth," it swiftly became a critical and PR disaster, which even the organisers admitted had 'fallen short'. It is not known on what other matters Euan's view was sought, but when he was found face down in Leicester Square on July 6th 2000, many interpreted it as a devastating critique of his father's controversial proposal for spot-fines for drunken louts.

A test Blair showed greater reluctance to run publicly past his children was the safety or otherwise of the MMR vaccine (*qv*).

Evans, Sir Christopher
b. Nov 29th 1957

Welsh BioTech pioneer who donated over £5k to the Labour party in 1998, upping the sum to £25k in June 1999. In January 2000 the Merlin Biosciences multi-millionaire was made a knight of the realm. Sir Christopher, who sits on several government task forces and was one of the bioscience bigwigs who signed a letter in support of

Labour to the *Financial Times* in May 2001, lent the party a further £1m between January and May 2005, on terms he always maintained had been commercial. His loyalty was sorely tested on September 20th 2006, however, when police arrested him as part of the ongoing Cash For Honours (*qv*) affair. He was not charged with any offence, but the turn of events left him 'disappointed'. "If I'd thought for one moment I would be placed in this embarrassing and mind-boggling position, I wouldn't have made the loan," he seethed in hindsight.

Evans, Craig

b. 1972

Strapping Welsh farmer who made headlines when John Prescott (*qv*) threw a punch at him during the 2001 Election campaign. The wild left hook – provoked by Evans's hurling of an egg – became a leading story on news bulletins worldwide, with foreign viewers marvelling at our country's hands-on canvassing style. Described as 'a mild-mannered giant who likes a pint' by fellow drinkers at the Golden Lion in Ffordd Las, the 29-year-old Evans remained tight-lipped (and possibly thick-lipped) after the contretemps, despite sizeable tabloid offers for his story. The shy chicken farmer would only say that he opposed the hunting ban and that Prescott had drawn blood. The DPM (*qv*) was perhaps

grateful that Evans was slower to talk of pressing charges than he himself had been at the Brit Awards three years earlier (see *Nobacon, Danbert*).

Evans, David

b. April 23rd 1935
MP (Con), Welwyn Hatfield, 1987-97

Reluctantly remembered for his rancid views on subjects such as crime, race relations and women, this rottweiler was described as 'the incarnation of Thatcherite brutalism' by the *Guardian* in 1999, in an article that also called his voice 'a sound to chill the blood of any liberal'.

"If it was your daughter, or this lovely girl here, raped by some black bastard outside the school one evening? Let him out on bail again so he can go and do her sister?"

His parliamentary career was characterised by robust statements such as: "If I thought that it was remotely possible, I would advocate the death penalty for those in possession of drugs. That works in Singapore and Malaysia, so why not here?" In a taped interview with children at Stanbrough School in his constituency, meanwhile, he called for the castration of rapists, haranguing parents: "Come on, if it was your daughter, or this lovely girl here, raped by some black bastard outside the school one evening? Let him out on bail again so he can go and do her sister?" He was not so protective of women's rights when it came to politics, however, denouncing female MPs as promoted above their talents, and saying that Virginia Bottomley (*qv*) was "dead from the neck up" and "in the Cabinet simply because she's a woman." Getting the boot in 1997 did little to chasten him: the following year he was forced to apologise and pay damages to 'the Birmingham Six' for asserting in another eventful school appearance that they were in fact guilty of terrorism.

Extra Time

1. What Jeffrey Archer allegedly requested from Monica Coghlan (*qv*) on September 8th 1987 – by her account he required another few minutes to see the job through, incurring an additional £20 tariff on top of the £50 basic.

2. What Jeffrey Archer received from Mr Justice Potts on July 19th 2001 – his sentence of 2 years for perjury being extended for two years by other convictions, including perverting the course of justice.

Falconer, Charles
b. Nov 19th 1951

Cherubic Chancellor and defining 'Tony's Crony', whose immoveable loyalty to Blair led the *Sunday Times* to state in January 2007: 'Defending the indefensible is something Charlie Falconer has refined into an art form. Whenever Blair is in trouble, the PM can be confident that his portly, unelected lord chancellor will step forward to argue that black is white.' The socialist firebrand's bid to become Labour MP for Dudley West at the 1997 election foundered at the selection stage when it emerged that his four children were being privately educated. Instead he became Baron Falconer of Thoroton (the first peer to be created on Blair's recommendation) and joined the government as solicitor-general, then Minister of State at the Home Office, assuming responsibility for the dismal Millennium Dome (*qv*) after Peter Mandelson's 1998 resignation. At the Home Office he infuriated fellow lawyers by criticising their fees (he was comfortably clearing £500,000 a year himself in the 1990s), and during a subsequent stint as Secretary of State for Constitutional Affairs he vigorously supported the abolition of the ancient post of Lord Chancellor – a move he has subsequently admitted he regrets. As soon as Gordon Brown took over from Tony Blair, Falconer was binned as Secretary of State for Justice (a post he'd held for barely two months) in favour of Jack Straw.

Farage, Nigel
b. April 3rd 1964
MEP (UKIP), 1999-

Pinstriped striptease fan who became leader of Europe's daftest party in 2006. In January of the same year he demonstrated at least some sympathy for European integration when he made sweet love to Liga Howells (a part-Swedish, part-German, Latvian-born 25-year-old) seven times in one night, according to tabloid sources. If the sexpot polyglot was to be believed, UKIP's married boss also requested a sound spanking, perhaps in a brave bid to confront his long-held terror of European domination. "It was so weird," Howells expounded to the *News of the World*. "He went, 'smack me, Miss'. I have never, ever heard anything like this in my whole life."

Farage conceded he was 'in the dog house' with his wife for spending the night with the scorcher, but denied exchanging anything with Liga beyond telephone numbers.

"It is beyond belief some of the things he asked me to do. And I wasn't prepared to do what he asked me"

He had form, however: in 2004 he went on a champagne-fuelled lap-dancing binge in London and Strasbourg. Although she confessed to participating in ice-cube play, Howells – who pointed out in her defence that she was on the rebound – added: "It is beyond belief some of the things he asked me to do. And I wasn't prepared to do what he asked me" (see *Corish, Barbara*).

SLEAZE

"Why are you asking me about this? I don't care – it's a Welsh situation, I'm a national politician. Where do they get these amateurs from? You're an amateur, mate! Go get on your bus, go home! Bugger off – get on your bus, you amateur!"

– *John Prescott woos the press on the campaign trail, April 2005*

SLOT

Farmiloe, Sally
b. 1948

Veteran Sloane who became Jeffrey Archer's mistress in 1996 but got the Chelsea boot in favour of Hull fisherwoman Nikki Kingdon three years later. A bit-part actress who'd taken a minor role in vintage TV series *Howard's Way*, Farmiloe met Archer through Tory fund-raising work in the mid-90s. His initial approach at a Valentine's ball was not traditionally romantic ("he came up behind me, threw his arms around me and grabbed hold of my boobs," she reminisced), but their steamy affair was still active during his astonishing bid for the London Mayoralty in the autumn of 1999. "When we made love it was so frantic my naked back was rubbed raw on the carpet for half-an-hour," she later revealed. "I had these dreadful friction burns." At one Conservative ball in Mayfair during his campaign, he ushered the silicone-boosted 'socialite' to the car park for some earthy sex, unbeknownst to his campaign team. They also had sex in his Mini ("We tried to make love in the front seat, but it was very cramped and awkward," she later explained) and in a back room of London's Café Royal hotel, where Archer was conducting an auction. But when rumours surfaced about his perjury at the end of the year, he dropped her like an old kebab – something her friends said left her 'shattered', especially when unfounded stories leaked from Archer's camp that she had 'chunky' ankles.

"He came up behind me, threw his arms around me and grabbed hold of my boobs"

She'd recovered sufficiently by 2004 to peddle her woes to the *News of the World* for over £100,000, revealing that she'd dubbed Archer 'Wonderboy' (*qv*) for his staying power.

Appropriately for an Archer mistress, they'd enjoyed an active fantasy life. One golden memory was of the time they discussed who they'd each like to join them for a threesome. She picked busty *'Allo, 'Allo* beauty Vicki Michelle, while, unbelievably, His Lordship apparently nominated Lord Coe.

Farmiloe's own politics have yet to find formal expression, though the author of *Sensual Pleasures* did confess to the *New Statesman* in 2005: "I worry about immigration. We're an island. We need to maintain our national identity. We've been swamped."

Faud, Prince Mohammed bin

Nifty contact made by Jonathan Aitken (*qv*) at a Paris lunch in 1973. The Saudi prince fed Aitken odd jobs throughout the 70s (via his aide Said Ayas, *qv*), and gave him a Jaguar car in 1976 – though Aitken insisted that his various efforts on Faud's behalf had gone unrewarded. Aitken became his chief London functionary in 1978, in charge of a firm called al-Bilad. Faud continued to help the sleaze icon over the next two decades, from his 1981 takeover of TV-am (*qv*) right through to arms procurement in the 90s. The fruitful relationship ended as it had begun twenty years before – in Paris, on a meal ticket. The second occasion was Aitken's fateful meeting with two Faud associates at the Paris Ritz (*qv*) on 19th September 1993, when the tab was picked up by the Saudis. By this last act of kindness, however, Prince Mohammed ultimately did his old pal no favours.

Fayed, Mohammed
b. Jan 27th 1929

Litigious Egyptian shopkeeper whose public image lies somewhere between Santa Claus and Don Corleone, and whose open-minded approach to the democratic process prompted one of the defining episodes in modern British sleaze – Cash For Questions (*qv*).

Fayed's roots have been obscured by his own myth-making, but the age given in his *Who's Who* entry is a good four years south of the mark, and his affectation of the prefix 'al-' to his name is known to be bogus: despite claiming to belong to an old family, he's the self-made son of an Alexandria primary school teacher. After an apprenticeship wheeling and dealing (including flogging Coca Cola and sewing machines), his first big-money deal was marrying Samira, the sister of up-and-coming arms dealer Adnan Khashoggi, in the mid-50s. He is known to have worked in Haiti in the mid-60s, where he achieved the notable feat of turning over 'Papa Doc' Duvalier and getting away with it. He went on to amass a fortune as a financial adviser to the Sultan of Brunei in the 70s and 80s (though for some reason the idea was put about that it was old money from family cotton and shipping businesses), and grew determined to find a foothold in the British establishment.

Opportunity presented itself in 1985, when the House of Fraser group (including Harrods) came up for sale. He beat ruthless *Observer* chief 'Tiny' Rowland to the punch with a cash bid running to hundreds of millions – but, cast as the sore loser, the pugnacious capitalist promptly embarked on a dirty campaign to get the DTI to look into the deal. Rowland undermined the Egyptian in his newspaper and in Parliament (through the efforts of Tory MP Sir Edward du Cann, chairman of Rowland's equally dubious bidders the Lonrho group). Fayed retaliated by employing Ian Greer (*qv*), who recruited a quartet of British MPs – Neil Hamilton, Peter Hordern, Michael Grylls and Tim Smith – to defend his interests. He was later to claim that in the late 80s he received monthly bills for £8,000–£10,000 from Greer for questions tabled by them in Parliament.

Rowland finally succeeded in his quest to involve the DTI, and on April 9th 1987 Trade Minister

Paul Channon (qv) set the dogs on Fayed. The investigation, which continued under Michael Howard, spanned eight countries and cost the taxpayer £1.5m. When their report was published in 1990 it denounced Fayed at every step as a liar and unfit witness, pouring scorn on his invented family background ("We are satisfied that the image they created between November 1984 and March 1985 of their wealthy Egyptian ancestors was completely bogus"), dismissing his claim that Harrods was bought with his own liquid assets, and also turning up unsavoury incidents – like the fleecing of the Haitian Harbour Authority for $100k, and an attempted $2m bribe to his brother-in-law Adnan Khashoggi (to keep mum about his claim that Fayed had defrauded him).

"There are limits on my generosity"

Stung, and furious at the Tories, the foul-mouthed millionaire began to wonder whether his sizeable investment in backbenchers had been worth it. As he explained in October 1994: "There are limits on my generosity." It had taken sleaze geniuses Neil and Christine Hamilton to find them – the irascible hotelier says he grew tired of their relentless requests to be put up for the night, even pretending that the hotel was 'full' to fob them off. After one especially minibar-happy 1987 stay at the Paris Ritz (qv), he decided to call the *Guardian* in 1994.

Fayed would spend much of the next two years in court defending major libel actions: one from Greer and Neil Hamilton, the other an ongoing concern with former employee Christoph Bettermann, who – like Egyptian despot Potiphar – he had used his connections to see thrown in jail in the Middle East. In February 1996 he was forced in court to accept the claimant's contention that he had published allegations of embezzlement against Bettermann "knowing them to be completely untrue and having fabricated them as part of a wicked scheme to exact a cruel revenge on him for his resignation from the Al Fayed Group." This successful action, costing Fayed almost £1m and revealing damaging details of how his employees covered for him, was intended to be a cornerstone of the 'Cash for Questions' case. But later that year Greer would beat an embarrassing retreat from his libel action, forcing Neil Hamilton, who had the same defence team, to follow suit.

Fayed's dealings with the hapless Hamiltons had given the entire country cause for a good chuckle, and though attempts to revive gag rag *Punch* briefly stopped the laughter in 1996, mirth was restored when Hamilton took the feud back to the libel courts in 1999. Fayed's daily rants turned the Royal Court of Justice into the hottest panto in town: one moment suggesting Michael Howard had accepted millions in 'bribes' to investigate him, the next accusing the Royal family of murder and conspiracy. His farcical but frequent declarations that the all-powerful 'Nazi' Prince Philip had personally ordered the assassination of his son Dodi may have had something to do with the gaffe-prone Greek withdrawing his Royal Warrant from Harrods on December 21st 2001. In fact none of its Royal patrons had spent a penny there since 1997, and Fayed knew he could forget about a knighthood. Seeimgly accepting that even the more modest ambition of getting a British passport was now beyond him, he moved to Switzerland in 2003.

Fearon, Donald 'Boogie'
b. c1960

Hulking Rastafarian ruffian who greatly assisted the downfall of Welsh Secretary Ron Davies (*qv*).

"I just thought that he was a normal bloke who drove a digger and fancied a bit of gay sex"

Though shy about his exact age (some estimates placed the grizzled hobo as old as fifty when he hit the headlines), Fearon was anything but when it came to discussing the former Welsh Secretary's fateful trip to Clapham Common one miserable autumn night in 1998. According to the jobless Fearon, Davies approached him in search of 'gay sex'. Fearon said he'd made it clear that his own sexual services weren't for hire, but that he could arrange a meeting between Davies and a male prostitute of his acquaintance, on which basis they proceeded to a local housing estate.

In Fearon's account Davies then availed himself of the man's services, only to reveal that he had no money on him. When things turned nasty, Fearon continued, Davies arranged to pay the man the following day, volunteering his car as security overnight. Then, Fearon claimed, Davies panicked and went to the police with a garbled story about looking for his car and innocently accepting a kind stranger's offer of a curry. "The story is complete rubbish, and I stand by the formal statement I made to police at the time," retorted the hapless MP. "I have no intention of commenting further on a fabricated story bought from a street robber." In Davies's original account, he was sprung in a lift at a nearby housing estate by two of Fearon's pals, then kidnapped and robbed ("I had a knife held at my throat for, I don't know, 10 or 15 minutes, or whatever"). Fearon stoutly denied the allegation and, due to inconsistencies in Davies's story, all charges against 'Boogie' and his associates were dropped following a £24,000 police investigation.

Unusually, Tony Blair found his colleague's version of events as hard to swallow as the police had, and within hours of leaving Brixton Police Station the Welsh Minister was out of the Cabinet. "I am sick of this, man," Fearon went on to whine in the *Sunday Mirror* that December. "I'm the only victim of this whole thing... I just thought that he was a normal bloke who drove a digger and fancied a bit of gay sex." In March 2005 Fearon was sentenced to life imprisonment for possessing a firearm with intent to endanger life. Davies responded to the news by commenting: "Mr Fearon is a violent man and it was my misfortune to be, as far as I know, one of his first victims."

Fettes College

Styled 'the Eton of the North', this Scottish independent school (fees: £20,000 a year) numbers amongst its alumni actress Tilda Swinton, oil tycoon Bill Gammell and socialist icon The Rt Hon Anthony Charles Lynton Blair (*qv*). The latter is not swift to discuss his snooty education, and decided to send his own children to a gritty inner-city alternative, the London Oratory School (*qv*).

Fiddle

Not a muddle.

see *McLeish, Henry*

Fields, Terry
b. March 8th 1937
MP (Lab), Liverpool Broadgreen, 1983-92

Fireman-turned-firebrand who was jailed over an unpaid £373 Poll Tax bill on July 11th 1991. Though many applauded his stand, Labour leader Neil Kinnock (*qv*) was less supportive, declaring: "Law makers must not be law breakers." In the jug the defiant Fields was cheered by a visit from sleaze supernova Ron Brown (*qv*), who illicitly taped their conversation and further vexed Kinnock by playing it to waiting reporters. After 60 days' porridge, Fields returned to his seat – but was expelled by the party following an internal disciplinary hearing that December. At the 1992 General Election he stood on an independent Labour ticket, but (with 14% of the vote) couldn't defeat the official candidate, Jane Kennedy.

Filkin, Elizabeth
b. Nov 24th 1940

So-called 'parliamentary watchdog' who earned her spurs as a lecturer and community worker before becoming chief executive of the

National Association of Citizens' Advice Bureaux. She spent the 90s working for the London Docklands Development Corporation and the Inland Revenue, before landing the role of Parliamentary Commissioner for Standards in February 1999.

Her controversial tenure saw her probing the activities of MPs including Keith Vaz, Teresa Gorman, John Reid, John Major, William Hague and Geoffrey Robinson (all qv), and her work sharply divided the Commons. Betty Boothroyd bellyached that her profile was too high and Gorman griped that she was insufficiently impartial, while Tony Benn said it was 'a great mistake for the Commons to force her out when the need for transparency lay at the heart of her first appointment' and Peter Bottomley suggested that Labour's resentment of her tenacity had prompted her ousting. Others criticised her methods – notably the Commons' longest serving member, Tam Dalyell, who was incensed by media leaks of her reports.

Filkin was expected to be automatically reappointed in 2002, but was told that she would have to reapply. She responded by accusing senior MPs – including Cabinet ministers – of undermining her, and declined to stand, announcing in October 2004 that she was to lead the new Advertising Standards Advisory Committee instead.

Firebrand

Media term typically applied to anyone with roots in the old left, or the North of England, who shows the slightest inclination to deviate from New Labour's party line.

Flagrance

Conspicuous, shameless wrong-doing (see *Archer, Jeffrey*). Not to be confused with fragrance (see *Archer, Mary*).

For Better, For Worse

Moving pledge made at the altar in 1983 by 33-year-old Christine Holman to stick by her husband Mostyn Neil Hamilton, no matter what hardships or indignities came their way – and later the fitting title of her racy 2005 autobiography.

Forde, Helga
b. 1973

Swansea-born air hostess whose breasts proved of great interest to John Prescott (*qv*) on a Virgin Atlantic flight to Washington. "He told me a red lipstick would look good on me, which I thought was very unprofessional for a man of his power," she told the *Sun*. "I then went back to him with a bowl of fruit. As I asked him if he wanted any, he took a pear and replied, 'Oh, what a lovely pair', as he looked at my chest with his beady eyes."

"I was used to the normal male attention on flights. But Prescott took it further and made my skin crawl"

Unamused by the Deputy PM's wit, she took offence and resigned, stating: "I worked as an air hostess for several years, so I was used to the normal male attention on flights. But Prescott took it further and made my skin crawl."

Forth, Eric
b. Sept 9th 1944 / d. May 17th 2006
MP (Con), Mid-Worcestershire / Bromley & Chislehurst, 1983-2006

Said to be 'so right-wing it's barely possible to see him over the horizon', this hard-boiled Glaswegian caused a ripple in January 1997, when he was had up for bullying by 78-year-old war hero and school governor Monty Hughes, who'd had to eject him from the grounds of Wirral Grammar School for Girls. The incident occurred when Forth (flanked by Alan Duncan (*qv*) and Tory candidate Les Byrom) ambushed a school visit by up-and-coming Labour Education spokesman David Blunkett (*qv*), challenging him to a one-on-one debate in front of the goggling pupils. Though he was accused by Duncan of being a 'thug', it wasn't in fact pensioner Hughes who got the worst

of their behaviour. The main victims were a woman from the education authority (who was, according to Hughes, 'clearly being intimidated' when she asked them to leave) and Blunkett himself (who had to suffer Byrom's juvenile chanting of 'Blunkett's sca-red, Blun-kett's sca-red').

"I've faced tougher opposition in my life," stonewalled no-nonsense D-Day veteran Hughes. "These men are supposed to be the Government. They were acting like playground louts. It was deplorable. One has to be very careful as to who enters school grounds these days." Labour spokesman Martin Liptrot added: "They invaded the school itching for a fight, and baited a blind man to come out. I have never seen such bully-boy, loutish, behaviour from a Government minister. It was like the naughty boys from Bash Street coming up from their bunker to pick on the children of Wirral South.

In his spare time, the fervent filibuster backed hanging, low wages, NHS fees and topless modelling (he once spoke out in favour of Page 3). He was strongly opposed to too much money being poured into treating AIDS (a condition he described as 'largely self-inflicted'), but was sympathetic to the apartheid regime in South Africa – and slated the BBC for screening a Nelson Mandela concert in 1988. When trying to block equal opportunities legislation and anti-racism measures in the police, Forth defended his stance by saying he represented the "white, Anglo-Saxon and bigoted" majority. Upon his death the *Independent* remembered him as 'gloriously politically incorrect', the *Evening Standard* called him 'one of Westminster's most colourful characters' and the *Daily Mail* said he was simply 'magnificent'.

Fortune

1. Tacky, sub-*Dragon's Den* 2007 ITV format, involving millionaires such as Jeffrey Archer (*qv*) giving large sums of money to worthy causes.

2. A large sum of money, such as the £500k the *Daily Star* gave to Jeffrey Archer (*qv*) in 1987.

Forty-five Minutes

Length of time long believed to represent three-quarters of an hour, but redefined since September 24th 2002 to encompass a potentially unlimited period (see *Dodgy Dossier, the*).

RED HOT

"It gets better as you get older - you know where your knees go"

- *Edwina Currie, quoted in the Sunday Mirror, September 2002*

CURRIE

Foster, Peter
b. Sept 26th 1962

Aussie crook jailed on three continents for his rotten business practices and quack health remedies, and the man Cherie Blair turned to when looking for financial advice in 2002. Foster – acclaimed by Cherie's confidante Carole Caplin as 'the greatest lover I've ever known' – has earned a series of fines, trading bans and prison sentences in the US, UK and Australia, despite having generated millions in postal-sale confidence tricks.

After early offences as a teenage boxing promoter (including a £40k insurance fraud and a heavily-promoted but non-existent comeback fight for Mohammed Ali), Foster devoted his life to plugging a variety of worthless teas, creams and patches as miracle slimming products, through bogus companies like Slimweight UK and TRIMit. He first attracted UK tabloid headlines in the 1980s by dating pigeon-chested page 3 beauty and Bai-Lin tea (*qv*) champion Samantha Fox. Mrs Blair claimed only to have met the odious Aussie once, and in December 2002 released a statement insisting that the man who brought the world Cho-Low and Bai-Lin tea was emphatically not involved in her purchase of two Bristol properties. Foster, however, was only too happy to produce emails demonstrating not only that was this a lie, but that Cherie had described him as 'a star', stating: "We are on the same wavelength, Peter." This was not deemed a suitable tuning for the wife of a Prime Minister, and Cherie soon issued a public apology.

Despite asserting "I have never hidden my past from anybody", Foster has subsequently sued newspapers in his native Australia for describing him as a 'conman' and 'fraudster'. The court in each case decided the descriptions were 'fair', and added: "He has accepted that people did not have to embellish upon his past to make him look bad." His most recent cameo on the world stage came in October 2006, when – following two weeks on the run after a Fijian property fiddle

– he stripped to his smalls and leapt from a bridge on the outskirts of the capital Suva in a desperate bid to swim for freedom. Unfortunately he stunned himself on a boat, and was fished from the drink moments later. By December he was facing prison again, with the island's Director of Public Prosecutions describing him as 'a huge flight risk'. Apparently unable to learn from his mistakes, Foster once mused in a prison deposition: "I keep wishing I could turn the clock back and turn the clock back. And I keep going back and back and back, and before you know it I'm in the womb again. Where do you go from there?"

Fox, Dr Liam
b. Sept 22nd 1961
MP (Con), Woodspring, 1992-

Not to be confused with superstar deejay Dr Neil Fox, this moderate-right anti-abortionist caused a stir in 1999 when he suggested that foreign doctors, at the time being welcomed by the government to plug a 'skills gap' in the UK, should be forced to sit language tests. Fox received the benefit of the doubt until December 2000, when he admitted telling an offensive joke (see *Winterton, Ann*) about national treasures the Spice Girls ("What do you call three dogs and a blackbird?"). The 'widely circulated' rib-tickler did at least show that he was more up to date on the group's latest reshuffle than they were on the Shadow Cabinet's (remaining members Posh, Sporty, Baby and Scary released a statement saying they'd never heard of him). Incendiary red Denis MacShane did not accept the Stringfellows regular's guarded apology, linking it to his earlier comments and terming it 'open racism'. "Sigmund Freud said that jokes were the hidden signals about someone's real beliefs," he raged. "Now he makes a racist joke about Mel B and insults every black and Asian creative artist in showbusiness."

Fox, Samantha
b. April 15th 1966

Pint-sized topless model and 80s rock goddess who once described Cherie Blair's sometime business advisor Peter Foster (*qv*) as 'the love of my life' – despite his involving her in a slimming scam. Their on-off affair ended in 1994, before he fell for the charms of Carole Caplin (*qv*). Samantha is thought not to be related to Shadow Defence Secretary Dr Liam Fox (*qv*).

Francis, Ted
b. 1933

Former bit-part actor who played the role of his life in 1999, when he duped former friend Jeffrey Archer into talking about the time he'd told a 'porkie' for him twelve years before – live in a taped phone conversation for the *News of the World*.

Archer had asked Francis to cover for him over dinner in January 1987, when the Tory realised he'd fixed his alibi for the wrong day (see *Coghlan, Monica / Caprice, Le*). Archer later cunningly introduced him to staff, so they would remember 'the face but not the date.' He also got Francis to write a letter backing up the story, though it was never produced in the original libel battle. At Archer's 1999 perjury trial the court heard that Francis requested a payment of £20k 'unrelated' to the alibi agreement, to which Archer readily consented – but when the time came to upend the piggy-bank, he only coughed up £12k. He may have regretted his parsimony when Francis went to the papers, but things soon got even more complicated. Archer tried to brazen it out by admitting he did concoct an alibi, but only to conceal from his wife the fact that he was meeting an old mistress. The 'old mistress' in question, Andrina Colquhoun (*qv*), was appalled when she heard the lusty Lord's boast, and happily exploded the lie for the benefit of the court. Fortunately for Francis, however, a jury accepted that he genuinely believed he was only helping an old mucker through a marital pickle, and he was acquitted of perverting the course of justice on July 19th 2001.

Galloway, George

b. Aug 16th 1954
MP (Lab), Glasgow Hillhead 1987-97 / Glasgow Kelvin 1997-2005 / ('Respect'), Bethnal Green & Bow, 2005-

Peppery popinjay once acclaimed by the *Spectator* as 'the most eloquent left-winger since Bevan'. However, his questionable taste in friends and backfiring PR stunts have made 'Respect' – the name of his breakaway party – an increasingly difficult commodity for him to command.

Although he has taken pride in calling himself the 'best fighter' in school, he made his first real enemies as a young Labour activist in Dundee: in 1977 Bunty Turley, a rival for the historically safe Labour council seat of Gillburn, campaigned successfully against him as an independent under the slogan 'Enough is Enough'. By then Galloway – nicknamed 'Gorgeous George' for his attention to grooming – was already passionately interested in the Middle East. In the 1980s he travelled widely on behalf of the charity War On Want, at whose expense the *Daily Mirror* suggested he'd been living high on the hog. He was subsequently cleared of misappropriating funds, though he was obliged to pay back £1,720 in expenses. On becoming an MP in 1987 he made it clear that he would only toe the party line when it pleased him. In February 1988 the Executive Committee of his Constituency Labour Party passed a vote of no confidence in him, partly inspired by his boast (printed in numerous tabloids) that, in the course of his work for War On Want: "I travelled to and spent lots of time with people in Greece, many of whom were women, some of whom were known carnally to me... I actually had sexual intercourse with some of the people in Greece." He was narrowly reselected.

By 1990 he was the subject of further rumblings, this time over his alleged truancy from Parliament – a plaintive small ad in *Tribune* read "Lost: MP who answers to the name of George... balding and has been nicknamed Gorgeous." The accompanying telephone number was that of London media watering hole the Groucho Club. When Labour leader John Smith's heart gave out in 1994 – the same year Galloway visited Saddam Hussein in Iraq – he was one of only three

MPs to decline to vote in the ensuing leadership election, telling SNP leader Alex Salmond with his customary wit: "I don't give a fuck what Tony Blair thinks." This he amply demonstrated in March 2003 by calling Blair and Bush 'wolves' and advising British troops to disobey orders in combat ("the best thing British troops can do is to refuse to obey illegal orders"), comments some called treasonous and Blair called 'disgraceful and wrong'. He was finally expelled from the party on October 23rd 2003, prompting him to found his own crew, 'Respect', and cause one of the major upsets of the 2005 General Election by unseating Labour's Oona King in Bethnal Green and Bow.

Predictably enough, the campaign was controversial: Galloway was accused of stirring up an inflammatory atmosphere against his half-Jewish rival in the very Muslim constituency, and some commentators were surprised he'd chosen to unseat one of only two black women in the Commons (he responded with reference to 'the deaths of many people in Iraq with blacker faces than hers'). King objected to some of the 'Respect' rhetoric and claimed to have been physically threatened by their supporters, remarking that 'extremism breeds extremism'. She added with reference to Saddam: "What makes me sick is that when I come across someone who is guilty of genocide, I do not get on a plane and go to Baghdad and grovel at his feet." Another upset closer to home came from his wife, Amina Abu Zayyad (*qv*), who divorced him on the eve of the Election, citing his serial infidelity in a soul-baring *Sunday Times* interview.

"You are confusing me with someone who gives a fuck"

On May 17th Galloway faced the US Senate Sub-Committee on suspicion of having received thousands of pounds in oil tokens from Saddam under the Oil for Food scheme (*qv*). Though he aimed a series of well-rehearsed broadsides at the Bush administration, he seemed to forget that it wasn't the legality of the Iraq War that was under scrutiny, but his own financial arrangements. The Senate's report in October was severe: 'Despite Galloway's denials, the evidence obtained by the Sub-Committee, including Hussein-era documents from the Ministry of Oil, shows that Iraq granted George Galloway allocations for millions of barrels of oil... Moreover some evidence indicates that Galloway appeared to use a charity for children's leukaemia to conceal payments.' This 'charity' was Mariam's Appeal (*qv*) – not in fact a charity at all, but a controversial pro-Iraqi fighting fund set up by Galloway in 1998. Senator Norm

Coleman concluded that Galloway 'knowingly made false or misleading statements under oath before the Sub-Committee' and 'solicited and was granted eight oil allocations from the Hussein government from 1999 through 2003'. Talk of US perjury charges has thus far come to naught, however.

That November, the silvery cavalier's commitment to domestic politics was again called into question. Having urged 'Respect' supporters across the land to pressure their own MPs into attending the report stage of the Prevention of Terrorism Bill, Galloway himself failed to turn up: he was fulfilling what the *Guardian* called 'a lucrative speaking engagement' in Cork instead. And any remaining credibility he'd gained from squaring up to Uncle Sam evaporated when he appeared on TV freakshow *Celebrity Big Brother* in January 2006. He explained to stunned constituents watching at home that his aim was to politicise disaffected voters, but his decision to don a feline fetish outfit, cavort in a cheap vampire costume and taunt recovering alcoholic Michael 'Awight' Barrymore with the words 'Poor me! Poor me! Pour me another drink!' did little to further the goal. His presence in the house made little difference to his Parliamentary attendance in any case: the *Economist* reported the same month that the handful of MPs sharing his attendance percentile included the Prime Minister, five abstentionist Sinn Fein members and two cadavers.

His stock was little improved by the emergence of footage showing a jocular Galloway acclaiming Uday Hussein – Saddam's eldest son, and a noted rapist and murderer – as 'Excellency' at his palace in 1999. Further outrage ensued in May 2006, when lads' mag *GQ* published an interview in which Galloway remarked that the assassination of Tony Blair would be 'morally justified'. His former Labour colleagues were appalled: backbencher Anne Moffat called it "absolutely sickening, even by his standards", while Stephen Pound gasped: "Every time you think he can't sink any lower he goes and stuns you again." The publication of a eulogistic biography of Fidel Castro (*qv*) later that year seemed to confirm their fears. When taken to task over the latter by three state school students at the Oxford Union, Galloway reportedly accused them of being 'hunting, shooting and fishing types', telling them: "You are confusing me with someone who gives a fuck."

On July 17th 2007 a long-awaited Standards and Privileges Committee report concluded he was 'complicit in the concealment of the true source of the funds' arising from Mariam's Appeal, was 'clearly irresponsible' in refusing to check the sources of the donations and had 'damaged the reputation of the House'. It recommended that he be suspended from the Commons for a bumper 18 days. It wasn't the first House he'd been evicted from, and his response was predictably robust. "They should be cutting a medal for me for my work on Iraq, not suspending me," he fumed, characterising the investigating committee as 'Sir Humphrey, Sir Bufton and Sir Tufton' and adding that he preferred to rely on "the verdict of the people".

But for millions his image was irrecoverably tainted. The blurb to his 2001 auto-hagiography *I'm Not The Only One* might have described him as a 'political firebrand, bête noir of the right-wing tabloids and thorn in the side of New Labour', but posterity seems more likely to remember him as the whiskery old fruit in a crimson leotard, licking imaginary milk off Rula Lenska's hands on *Celebrity Big Brother*.

Garbage-gate

Wildean tag Tony Blair applied to the fuss over his intervention on behalf of a foreign businessman – Lakshmi Mittal (*qv*) – in a multi-million pound Romanian steel contract in 2001. Blair's letter to his Romanian counterpart on 30th July very nearly coincided with a substantial transfer of funds from Mittal's account to the Labour party, a fact which a Downing Street spokesman dismissed as 'irrelevant'.

Gibb, Robin
b. Dec 22nd 1949

Buck-toothed Bee Gee who treated Tony Blair and family to a luxury yuletide break at his multi-million Miami mansion in December 2006. While the Blairs tanned themselves at Robin's nest, however, Norman Baker MP (Lib Dem, Lewes) and Philip Davies (Tory, Shipley) were busy firing off letters to Parliamentary Commissioner for Standards Sir Philip Mawer, urging an investigation into whether the break conformed to Parliamentary rules. Davies argued that "Tony Blair is systematically bringing the office of Prime Minister into disrepute," while Baker stormed: "Surely him and Cherie have got enough money without ringing up the Bee Gees to borrow their home? It's just one freebie after another." Party officials insisted that the holiday was 'a commercial arrangement', but confusion mounted when Gibb's druid wife Dwina (a close confidante of Cherie Blair) broke ranks to insist it was a 'friendly' arrangement, and that nothing had changed hands. Either way, Baker was unmoved, insisting: "The problem is, he should not be star-struck by clapped-out pop stars" (see *Richard, Sir Cliff*).

Gifts

Euphemism for bribes, typically in the form of cash bungs, holidays or other freebies. Unlike normal gifts, which require only gratitude in return, MPs' gifts carry with them the expectation of advancement or favour, and are almost never acknowledged – least of all in the Register of Members' Interests (*qv*).

Gilberthorpe, Anthony

Former Gloucester councillor who stitched up his old pal Piers Merchant MP (*qv*) like a kipper in October 1997. Gilberthorpe – who'd been Merchant's Parliamentary Researcher in the 1980s – offered the randy MP the use of his flat in York as a love-nest for himself and his teenage mistress Anna Cox (*qv*). Merchant, who had consistently denied any romantic attachment to the former nightclub hostess, gratefully accepted – but what Gilberthorpe hadn't disclosed was that he'd been paid £25k by the *Sunday Mirror* to bug the place. "Anthony Gilberthorpe had set the whole thing up, ensuring that I was up in York in his flat with Anna, that the room was covered in CCTV and wired for sound," Merchant carped to the *Observer* in 2003 – and he was doubtless even more incensed by the fact that X-rated footage of their Spice Girl-soundtracked romps had appeared on the staggeringly bad Live! TV channel. The only solace Merchant could take came from the collapse of his erstwhile employee's antiques business later that year.

Gilligan, Andrew
b. 1968

Having honed his skills sweating over Cambridge student rag *Varsity*, this bungling bloodhound styled himself as a thorn in the government's side and soon made enemies of Downing Street Cerberus Alastair Campbell and Defence Minister Geoff Hoon with *Today* programme reports on the EU and the armed forces. He was vindicated in his spat with Hoon, but after Campbell labelled him 'Gullible Gilligan' in 2000, he carried the grudge into his coverage of the Iraq war in 2003. When he spotted a chance to expose the scurrilous Scot for 'sexing up' the government dossier intended to justify the invasion, he pounced. On May 29th 2003 he appeared on the *Today* programme, alleging that "the government probably knew the 45-minute figure was wrong even before it decided to put it in" and that "Downing Street, our source says, a week before publication ordered it to be sexed up."

"Downing Street ordered it to be sexed up"

Frenzied media coverage followed, and in a subsequent chat with the *Mail On Sunday* Gilligan fingered Campbell as the culprit behind the 'sexing up'. Unfortunately, there was no hard evidence linking Tony Blair's Director of Strategy and Communications to changes allegedly made to the dossier to make it more 'eye-catching' (the words later chosen by Lord Butler). Gilligan was then forced to reveal his source for the claim, Dr David Kelly (*qv*), who was neither a member of the Joint Intelligence Committee that had drawn up the dossier, nor had any personal dealings with Downing Street. This thrilled Campbell, who crowed in his diary: "It was double-edged but GH [Geoff Hoon] and I agreed it would fuck Gilligan if that was his source." Some found the spin king's crowing a little distasteful, since Kelly later committed suicide over the matter, and the Butler Report duly concluded that the dossier was seriously flawed – but the January 2004 Hutton Report (*qv*) was principally devastating for the BBC. It stated that whatever suggestions Campbell might have made, any final decisions over the content of the Dodgy Dossier had come from the appropriate committee. Hutton also slammed Gilligan's original conclusions on the *Today* programme: namely, how the government knew beforehand that choice tit-bits of the dossier were either 'wrong' or 'questionable'. An almighty stink led to multiple resignations at the very top of the BBC, which had backed Gilligan's fudged story all the way.

The spate of BBC resignations (including its Chairman and Director-General) was not aped in government, even after the Butler inquiry showed the intelligence dossier to have been more seriously flawed than the *Today* report. And, some have said, for his professional errors and personal score-settling, Gilligan – who also resigned – should shoulder much of the blame for letting the government off the hook.

Githins

Fictional drug company devised by the *Sunday Times* 'Insight' team for the purpose of beguiling MPs into accepting £1,000 bungs to table Parliamentary questions in 1994. Both Githins and 'Thising's' (*qv*), a supposed throat condition, were in fact witty anagrams of 'Insight'. Eighteen of the twenty members approached smelt a rat, leaving only Graham Riddick and David Tredinnick (both *qv*) to grab the cheques and earn sleaze immortality.

Goldfish Bowl, the

Plodding compendium of accounts of life in No.10, recounted to Cherie Blair (*qv*) by a succession of Prime Ministerial consorts and published in 2005. The work was co-written by Cate Haste, whose previous efforts include the seminal *Nazi Women*, but Mrs Blair embarked on her lucrative international lecture tour alone.

Goody, Jade
b. June 5th 1981

Hefty reality TV idol whose deportment in 2007's *Celebrity Big Brother* provoked uproar in the corridors of power. Within days of Goody referring to fellow contestant Shilpa Shetty as 'Shilpa Poppadum', TV watchdog Ofcom had received a record 50,000 complaints. Though Shetty quickly stated "I don't feel there was any racial discrimination happening

from Jade's end", government Chief Whip Jacqui Smith (*qv*) denounced the 'shameful' events on *Question Time*, a stance echoed by seasoned trash TV star Edwina Currie, while Ann Widdecombe called for the programme to be axed. On January 16th Keith Vaz tabled an Early Day Motion condemning the show, and before long Jack Straw, David Cameron and even Tony Blair's office had been forced into making official comments. Gordon Brown, on a tour of India at the time, joined the chorus of disapproval by terming it 'unacceptable', and urged viewers to boot Goody out. On January 19th his wish was granted, prompting London Mayor Ken Livingstone (*qv*) to tell the *Today* programme the following morning: "I think everyone is delighted that we got the result we did last night."

SLEAZE

"Is he [*Archer*] in need of cold, unloving, rubber-insulated sex in a seedy hotel round about quarter to one on a Tuesday morning after an evening at the Caprice?"

– Mr. Justice Caulfield addresses the jury, 1987

SLOT

Gorman, Teresa
b. Sept 30th 1931
MP (Con), Billericay, 1987-2001

Eyebrowless harridan who allegedly inflamed John Major's ardour, and famously proposed the castration of rapists. The House of Commons Standards Committee adopted a similarly uncompromising stance towards her in 2000, when it ruled that she had failed properly to register several properties in Portugal and South London. She was no stranger to embarrassment, however: when first reaching office (at the twelfth attempt) in 1987, it emerged that she was some ten years older than she'd professed.

In February 2000 the Committee slammed her for submitting "seriously misleading and inaccurate information" about her connections with offshore companies, and she was also censured for craftily tabling a bill to repeal the Rent Acts while not disclosing that she was three times a landlady herself. Added to charges of attempting to smear a tenant who'd complained about her to Parliament and improperly contacting witnesses while under investigation, it amounted to an irresistible case against the veteran. As increasingly-impatient Commissioner for Standards Elizabeth Filkin put it: "Mrs Gorman neither fulfilled the registration requirements nor observed the principles of honesty and accountability which it requires." The whole affair had lost her the nomination to run as Tory Mayor, a course she determined on after hearing rival Steven Norris (*qv*) would 'go soft' on homosexuality issues in local schools. Gorman was suspended for a month without pay – the longest stretch since the inception of the Committee – and wisely stood down at the 2001 general election.

"Mr Major grabbed my hand, laid it on top of his, and then placed his left hand on top of mine in a sandwich. He was very gentle, and then he started rubbing the side of my hand with his thumb"

That October she published a shoddy volume entitled *No, Prime Minister!*, which detailed a 'hot August afternoon' in 1993, when she'd taken tea with John Major. Given that she was one of the 'Maastricht Rebels' threatening to destroy his leadership, the glamorous gran didn't know what to expect. She put on a 'snazzy new outfit' with a split skirt, and when she teetered into his office Major instructed a civil servant to leave on account of a 'private matter'. "The minute he left," claimed Gorman, "Mr Major grabbed my hand, laid it on top of his, and then placed his left hand on top of mine in a sandwich. He was very gentle, and then he started rubbing the side of my hand with his thumb." At this point news of Major's affair with Edwina Currie (*qv*) had not broken, but his interest came as no shock to a woman of Gorman's experience. "I knew all about his flirtatious ways, and all about the art of seduction", she smirked. At this point, Gorman – who published *The Bastards: Dirty Tricks and the Threat to Europe* later that year – claims she began to ponder 'just what he'd invited me there for'. As the pair sat 'knee to knee', the HRT proponent "wondered if he was going to offer me a job or his body." But Major's passion seemingly cooled as soon as the subject of Europe came up, and his raw charisma was not enough to make the avowed Eurosceptic vote with the government.

Graham, Sir Alistair
b. Aug 6th 1942

Rigorous sleaze watchdog, with a distinguished public service record, whose criticism of the government over the conduct of ministers such as John Prescott, David Blunkett and Tessa Jowell (all *qv*) saw him effectively sacked from his role as head of the Committee on Standards in Public Life by Tony Blair in March 2007. This led to suggestions that the Prime Minister was planning to scrap the entire mechanism, and widespread bemusement that Graham was being punished for doing his job properly.

see *Filkin, Elizabeth*

Graham, Tommy
b. Dec 5th 1943
MP (Lab), West Renfrewshire, 1987-98 / (independent), 1998-2001

Triple-chinned bully who was finally expelled from the Labour party a year after being cited in the July 28th 1997 suicide note of Paisley South MP Gordon McMaster (*qv*).

McMaster's scrawled last words – 'I hope Tommy Graham can live with himself' – were widely perceived to refer to a smear campaign which had suggested the troubled alcoholic (and ME sufferer) actually had AIDS. Graham angrily shifted blame for the unpleasantness onto a sometime political ally, Renfrewshire councillor Paul 'The Knife' Mack (*qv*). "Gordon was a good friend of mine," he told the *Sunday Mirror* later. "I would never smear him by spreading gay rumours. But the truth was that he was a very sick man. He drank too much and was subject to depression." The party delayed their embarrassing investigation until after the vote on Scottish devolution in September 1997, asking the unapologetic Glaswegian MP (who had now been suspended) to keep mum in the meantime. Chief Whip

Nick Brown and Scottish Secretary Donald Dewar allegedly asked the 'big man' to ride it out and not rock the boat. Come the inquiry, however, his co-operation counted for nothing: having interviewed him for 18 hours in September 1998, Labour's National Constitutional Committee took just three minutes to boot Graham out after 33 years in the party. Following months of death threats and broken windows, Graham could only moan: "My back is full of knives." Although formally cleared of involvement in McMaster's death, the inquiry had extended to alleged bullying of a further local MP, Irene Adams (qv), and various matters of internal irregularity.

During the year-long wait for a decision, his charge of 'bringing the party into disrepute' was hardly helped by repeated stories in the *Scotsman* about 'Ferguslie Park Community Business Holdings', a Paisley community scheme run by a Graham associate, through which local drug barons were suspected to have laundered up to £360k. The MP was cleared of any charges connecting him to the drugs, but the party inquiry did find a 'substantial body of evidence' to suggest that Graham's cronies had systematically sought political advantage through him. Graham was found culpable on five counts, including rigging meetings, blocking access to public funds and 'stacking' council membership with yes-men to help unseat Paisley North MP Adams. He was also attacked for smear tactics – not just 'bad-mouthing' opponents, but, according to former friends on the committee, on one occasion acquiring 'pink' porn photos of a top union official to use as political ballast. The XXXL bruiser had supposedly offered them to Scottish executive members in exchange for the personal file on Brian Oldrey, a Labour councillor who planned to stand against him in Renfrew on an 'anti-sleaze' ticket – though Graham insisted there were no photos and none of the men concerned were even gay. Overall, he was found guilty of "a sustained course of conduct prejudicial to, and acts grossly detrimental to, the party." He vowed to clear his name, but the next day (heeding advice from his tired lawyer) he capitulated on all but the porno detail, and dropped the appeal.

Before the hearing he'd proudly announced: "I am convinced I will be back sitting on the Labour benches, fighting for the cause of a good Labour government." Asked afterwards where he planned to sit as an independent, he quipped: 'On my bum'. As it turned out, his flabby buttocks had to squash up on Opposition benches, alongside the Tories he'd so long despised – while powerful former allies like Gordon Brown, Donald Dewar and Robin Cook refused to speak to him.

"The fact that I am 20 stone, swear a bit, and have a big mouth seems to be the main reason for my downfall"

A month after the expulsion he was accused once more by Irene Adams of trying to undermine her – this time after his wife and two kids mysteriously joined Adams' constituency party in October. Despite defiant noises about carrying on 'till he was kicked out', by the next election he'd had enough and stood down.

First, however, he issued a swingeing September 12th 1999 attack on New Labour in the *Sunday Mirror*, to mark the anniversary of the 'Stalinist kangaroo court' which did him over. "I am big and bluff and have a Glasgow shipyard voice," he boomed. "The fact that I am 20 stone, swear a bit, and have a big mouth seems to be the main reason for my downfall."

Gray, James
b. November 7th 1954
MP (Con), Chippenham, 1997-

Galloping cad whose passion for bloodsports led to a more damaging dalliance – with Countryside Alliance filly Philippa Mayo. The horsewhip-and-horn fling, which emerged in September 2006, saw Gray branded 'unfit for office' by Mayo's incandescent husband and 'a real-life B'Stard' by the *Mirror* (after Rik Mayall's character in slapstick satire *The New Statesman*). The level of vitriol he experienced owed largely to the fact that his wife, the mother of his three children, had been battling cancer for many of the 19 months that he'd maintained the secret mistress.

While admitting "I'm not proud of myself," Gray saw no reason to resign over the incident, though he hadn't been afraid to in the past: on May 19th 2005 his position as Shadow Secretary of State for Scotland became 'untenable' after off-message remarks about the abolition of MSPs were widely perceived as anti-Scottish. "James Gray must be the first Shadow Secretary of State for Scotland whose term of office did not include setting foot in Scotland, or even Scottish Questions in the House of Commons," raged his government counterpart, Alistair Darling.

Gray – whose most public ride until his affair had been on May 31st 2004, when he steered a horse into parliament as a cheap stunt – did at least wait three weeks after his wife's all-clear before carving up both families in September 2006, but it wasn't good enough for his local Conservative association, who moved to deselect him that November. "Women are not at all happy about the way he's conducted the break-up of his marriage," huffed its chair, Margaret Histed. "We all feel desperately sorry for Sarah… How could one ever trust a man like that again?" Despite her doubts, Gray survived a deselection vote in January 2007, pledging: "I will be mending as many bridges as possible."

Greer, Ian
b. 1930

The man who made lobbying a dirty word was brought up by Salvation Army parents and became the youngest-ever party area agent (in Dartford) in 1954. He developed contacts with Conservative MPs throughout the 1960s, in part using his capacity as director of the Mental Health Trust, and in 1970 set up his first political consultancy business, in partnership with one John Russell. It flourished for a decade but they split acrimoniously in 1980, to some degree over Russell's disapproval

of the activities of Michael Grylls (*qv*), with whom Greer would work closely in years to come. Greer promptly set up the notorious Ian Greer Associates (IGA), moved into lavish Westminster offices and rode the wave of flamboyant greed that characterised the 80s. Within a few years its clients included British Airways, Coca Cola, the National Nuclear Corporation and, notoriously, the Fayed brothers. By February 1984 Neil Hamilton (*qv*) was able to describe it as "an excellent firm offering an excellent service to the client companies lucky enough to retain it."

"It would be very unwise of MPs to accept those sort of payments… I think that's really prostituting their profession"

Greer always maintained that 'the company does not retain any peers, MEPs, MPs or other political advisers, and never has.' Instead, he paid them undisclosed one-off fees (thought to have been between £5000 and £10,000 a pop) for bringing new business to IGA, thereby helping to create a generation of cash-rich, integrity-poor parliamentarians. Not everyone accepted the fees, though – Michael Colvin, a Tory MP from 1979 to 2000, introduced clients to Greer, but commented: "It would be very unwise of MPs to accept those sort of payments… I think that's really prostituting their profession."

Neil Hamilton and others had a less robust attitude, and as a result the Cash For Questions affair (*qv*) erupted in 1994. The Fayeds had first contracted with IGA in 1985, as part of their ongoing bid to defeat the efforts of their nemesis Tiny Rowland, who was enraged that Mohammed Fayed had gained control of the House Of Fraser group. Greer agreed to find MPs sympathetic to their cause, and eventually settled on Sir Peter Hordern, Neil Hamilton, Michael Grylls and Tim Smith (all *qv*). When the *Guardian* got wind of the arrangement, it published a series of damning articles, prompting Smith to resign and Hamilton to join forces with Greer in a £2m libel action, a flawed initiative that saw both men safely ruined. Greer went on to publish his side of events in 1997's little-read *One Man's Word*, and was cleared of provable corruption in that July's Downey Report (*qv*). He has kept a low profile ever since.

See *Cash For Questions / Grylls, Michael / Hamilton, Neil / Fayed, Mohammed*

Griffiths, Jane
b. April 17th 1954
MP (Lab), Reading East, 1997-2005

Hamster-cheeked rat-fancier who in 2004 became the first sitting MP of the century to be deselected by her own constituency, over what were described as 'personality issues'. Amidst ugly political manoeuvring on all sides, these included accusing a neighbouring MP (Reading West's anti-porn crusader Martin Salter) of being a 'racially inflammatory' bully, and her 'wild conspiracy theories' about a sexist coup – though female constituency activists signed a letter affirming she was just as unpopular among women. Her own party deemed councillor Tony Page (who boasted two convictions for indecency) a preferable candidate, but he promptly lost the seat to the Tories.

Griffith's last memorable act as a politician was to be solicited (unsuccessfully) for sex in the Commons by a drunken Marsha Singh (*qv*). Her first as a civilian was to be declared bankrupt over an unpaid £29,000 tax bill, avoiding the ignominy of being thrown out of the Commons by a matter of days. It wasn't her first financial slip; a county court judgement had been made against her back in 1999, followed by a series of disputes with everyone from landlords to the Treasury Office, and in 2001 there was even a dressing-down from the House Serjeant-at-Arms for misusing the parliamentary stamp allowance. A warrant for Griffiths's arrest was issued in September 2005, when she failed to attend a Reading County

Court hearing, and the absentee redhead – apparently somewhere on the continent – was swiftly dubbed 'The Scarlet Pimpernel'. "Perhaps critics have now got some idea of what we have had to put up with over the last six years," crowed a party insider to local media. "Denial after denial... the person responsible for the downfall of Jane Griffiths is Jane Griffiths."

"Denial after denial... the person responsible for the downfall of Jane Griffiths is Jane Griffiths"

She was eventually winkled from her Latvian bolthole to explain, and convinced the court she had the assets to make good the debt – though it wasn't the end of the matter, as the discharge was soon suspended for further lack of co-operation. "I can only say that I have had a lot of difficulty coming to terms with the situation I have been in," she told the court. "And I think that is probably the best explanation I can offer you."

The collapse of her political career has allowed her more time to spend with her beloved rats, about whom she provides regular updates in her blog – including an affecting account of how one of the loveable rodents practically took off a vet's finger.

see *Clark, Helen / Singh, Marsha*

Griffiths, Nigel
b. May 20th 1955
MP (Lab), Edinburgh South, 1987-

An early admirer of Gordon Brown (they attended Edinburgh University together in the late 70s), this fresh-faced Scot was appointed an under-secretary at the DTI by Tony Blair in 1997, sacked in 1998 and awarded the same post in 2001. That October he became embroiled in a remarkably tedious row over the use of his office in Minto Street, Edinburgh, for campaigning, in contravention of Commons rules. The initial fuss soon died down when Griffiths – who'd been paying rent and then reclaiming it at a rate of £10,000 a year since 1997 – apologised to the Fees Office. A couple of months later, however, it emerged that he actually owned the premises, and hadn't reported the fact in the Register of Members' Interests.

In February 2002 Elizabeth Filkin (*qv*) found that Griffiths had misused Commons allowances, and failed to register property and rental income. Though his rent claims were found to be 'technically defective' (he later repaid £31,000), there was no recommendation for him to be punished – much to his relief. "I am grateful to both Elizabeth Filkin and the committee for the swiftness and thoroughness of their report," he gushed. "I am delighted that they recommended that no action be taken." The public was equally grateful that the story ended there.

Grylls, Michael

b. Feb 21st 1934 / d. Feb 7th 2001
MP (Con), Chertsey, 1970-74 /
North West Surrey 1974-97

Former wine and tobacco importer who served on the Greater London Council and contested Fulham twice before winning his seat in 1970. He sat on the select committee for overseas development in the 70s, and chaired the Tory trade and industry committee from 1981 to 1997. In that time he also assiduously collected consultancies and directorships, many with the assistance of Ian Greer (*qv*), whom he'd known since 1959. It surprised few when he was disgraced in the Cash For Questions scandal (*qv*), and in its obituary five years later the *Guardian* called him 'the most senior and voracious Tory MP run by the lobbyist Ian Greer'.

By the 1980s his contacts in industry were predictably extensive. It is thought that the modus operandi was as follows: whenever businesses (from within his own constituency or not) approached Grylls for help, he directed them to Greer. If the business decided to retain Greer's services, then Grylls would receive a percentage of the fee, which he would traditionally not declare in the Register of Members' Interests. The tidy little pension fund started to come unstuck when then Tory transport secretary Nicholas Ridley sought to rechannel £20m worth of international flights from BA to ailing carrier British Caledonian in 1987. BA approached Grylls for help, Grylls directed them to Greer, Greer swung into action and Ridley's initiative was promptly scuppered, in no small part owing to Grylls's vigorous efforts. Questions began to be asked, and Fleet Street started to investigate.

In 1990 the Committee on Members' Interests grilled Grylls about the number and size of of Greer's payments to him, but he stalled them. By 1997, however, he'd admitted trousering well over £100,000 from Greer. The Committee slammed him for having 'persistently failed' to declare his interests in dealing with the House of Fraser, as well as having 'deliberately misled' them by 'seriously understating' the number of payments he'd received. That February Grylls stated to the Select Committee on Standards and Privileges: "I regret that I should be part of an inquiry which will give publicity to those people seeking to damage the reputation of Parliament on the eve of a General Election." By the time the Downey Report was published in July, he'd resigned his seat.

Gummer, John
b. Nov 26th 1939
MP (Con), Lewisham West, 1970-74 / Eye, 1979-83 / Suffolk Coastal, 1983-

This devout Christian (and author of the 1966 tract *When The Coloured People Come*) will always be remembered for his orchestration of one of the most misguided PR stunts in British political history. Attending a boat show in Suffolk on May 6th 1990, at the height of the 'Mad Cow Disease' scare, he paraded his four-year-old daughter Cordelia before the assembled cameras, a beefburger clutched in her little hand, in a bid to convince the public that British beef was still best. Though she suffered no ill-effects, the stunt did little to impress a public outraged by the government's slow response to the crisis, and the resulting image seems set to remain its most enduring symbol.

H

Hague, William
b. March 26th 1961
MP (Con), Richmond (Yorks), 1988-

Ale-swilling judo gimp whose tenure as the first Conservative leader in 80 years not to become Prime Minister was summed up by Tony Blair in 2000 as "good jokes, lousy judgement." Few of Hague's cracks would have passed muster in a student bar, but he could at least rest assured that between 1997 and 2001 he was presiding over the biggest joke in Britain.

"Good jokes, lousy judgement"

The 16 year-old Hague's precocious cameo as an archetypal 'Tory boy' at the 1977 party conference led the *Guardian* to comment on his 'surprisingly elderly-sounding Yorkshire accent' – and image has remained a perennial problem. His appearance in a personalised baseball cap at the Notting Hill Carnival is still recalled with horror by stylists, and further attempts to ingratiate himself with the public haven't won much acclaim either. These include calling for Heathrow Airport to be renamed 'Diana Airport' in August 1997, and bragging to *GQ* magazine in August 2000 that he'd sunk up to 14 pints of beer in a day as a teenager. The latter sat especially uneasily with the recollections of Terry Glossop, assistant manager of the Angel in Rotherham, Hague's family local. "Some of the old boys have been coming in here for donkey's years," he told the *Guardian*, "and no one can remember Hague coming in for as much as a half of lager." More embarrassment was to come a couple of months later, when he endorsed Jeffrey Archer (*qv*) as a candidate of 'probity and integrity' for the 2000 London Mayoral race – a pronouncement he later called the biggest mistake of his career. Perhaps there was a small favour being returned: Hague had long enjoyed regular grapples with fellow Judo enthusiast Sebastian Coe in Archer's Peninsula House gym – free of charge, to the other paying residents' annoyance. The arrangement failed to escape the beady eye of Labour snitch Fraser Kemp MP, who reported the matter, prompting Parliamentary Watchdog Elizabeth Filkin (qv) to tick Hague off in December 1999 for not declaring the perk. It wasn't his first error of judgement – the previous year he'd nominated Michael Ashcroft (qv) for a peerage, for example.

Hague was widely criticised for a speech at the 2001 conference in which he commented "Talk about asylum and they call you racist; talk about your nation and they call you Little Englanders… Elect a Conservative government and we will give you back your country." The remarks were widely interpreted as having a racist and xenophobic ring. Having gained just one seat for the Tories, Hague lost the 2001 Election and stood down ("we have not been able to persuade a majority, or anything approaching a majority, that we are yet the alternative government that they need"). Despite further accusations of cheap xenophobia (the French were "cheese-eating surrender monkeys," he read from *Have I Got News For You*'s autocue, and "if anyone has a history of

making themselves at home in other people's countries, it's the Germans") he was soon earning more than £1m a year as an after-dinner speaker, guest presenter, biographer and rabble-rousing columnist (his repellent 'He Knows – He's Been There' column for the *News of the World* regularly advertised his bluff Yorkshire support for the death penalty). By 2005 he was comfortably earning more for his extra-parliamentary activities than any other MP. A return to the Tory front bench as Shadow Foreign Secretary in December 2005 ensured him a sizeable wage cut and a return to anonymity – though it was at least conditional on giving up his column.

Hamilton, Christine
b. Nov 10th 1949

As consort to the least dignified politician in modern British history, Neil Hamilton's wife has had numerous crosses to bear. As an inveterate publicity seeker in her own right, however, she has helped parlay her husband's many tribulations into a barely-sustainable media career for the inseparable pair. Or, as she puts it on her website: "I am thrilled to have left the artificial world of boring old politics for the madcap fun world of the media and entertainment."

The first Neil in her life was future Fleet Street stallion Andrew Neil, whom she bedded as a student (he later described it to the *Telegraph* as 'a night of madness'). For 26 years the young Christine acted as a Conservative research assistant – including stints under extravagantly-moustachioed racist Gerald Nabarro and Register of Members' Interests-shy Michael Grylls (*qv*) – before wedding weedy, needy, greedy Neil Hamilton (*qv*) in 1983. "I proposed to Neil," she later explained. "It was not a question. It was an order."

"I am thrilled to have left the artificial world of boring old politics for the madcap fun world of the media and entertainment"

One of her less successful wifely acts was to introduce her husband to Ian Greer (*qv*), thus unwittingly setting in train the events that were to result in both men's ruin. For the most part, however, she was the model of the constituency wife, but began to emerge from her husband's shadow during his disastrous re-election bid in 1997. She attracted especial attention for the so-called 'Battle of Knutsford Heath,' at which she berated anti-sleaze candidate Martin Bell for no very good reason ('I mean, what sort of man wears a white suit? I just flipped,' she later wrote).

In 1998 she made an Oxford University Conservative dinner only too memorable for undersexed undergraduate Will Goodhand by treating him to a drunken postprandial snog, and by the end of her husband's ruinous libel trial in 1999 (see *Cash for Questions*) she was rapidly eclipsing his media profile.

As penury hit, it became clear that further cutbacks in the Hamiltons' dignity were going to be required. A welter of low-grade TV programmes followed, as well as bad books such as Neil's *Politics' Strangest Characters* and Christine's *Book of British Battleaxes*. These ventures in self-parody came to little until they inadvertently struck bronze during the filming of a 2001 documentary with Louis Theroux. A suggestible simpleton named Nadine Milroy-Sloan (*qv*), having enlisted the support of Max Clifford (*qv*), erroneously identified Christine as the late middle-aged swinger who'd sat on her face at a suburban sex party. The police acted swiftly, despite a total lack of evidence, and the Hamiltons were subsequently exonerated, even receiving a compo payout from Clifford. In May 2003 Milroy-Sloan was found guilty on two counts of perverting the course of justice.

Since then Christine has dressed in drag for cheap laughs, worn basque and suspenders on stage, performed *The Vagina Monologues*, had cosmetic surgery live on TV and posed naked with Neil as Adam and Eve for lads' mag *GQ*. An appearance on *I'm A Celebrity, Get Me Out Of Here* in 2002 led to her own chat show (enjoyed by a handful of digital viewers on BBC Choice), which featured guests ranging from disgraced MP Jonathan Aitken (*qv*) to disgraced comic Bernard Manning and disgraced royal rat James Hewitt. In her own words, she is "game for anything as long as it is legal, honest and faintly decent". The last of these will hopefully mean no re-release for *England Are Jolly Dee*, the duo's belief-beggaring attempt at a football anthem, blamed by many for the country's poor performance at the 2006 World Cup.

Hamilton, Neil

b. March 9th 1949
MP (Con), Tatton, 1983-97

Spineless political lightweight Mostyn Neil Hamilton was a torch-bearer for Tory sleaze for well over a decade, since when he has carved out a bleak career on the fringes of the celebrity media. His political career was snuffed out by an ill-advised association with Mohammed Fayed (*qv*), and he is now synonymous with the Cash For Questions affair (*qv*) that derailed John Major's administration in 1997.

Descended from Welsh miners, he became a Tory party member at the age of 15 and came last in a school mock election soon afterwards. In 1972 he attended a controversial Italian Fascist conference on behalf of a Tory students' group, and in 1979 sought election in Bradford North (of all places) on an anti-immigration ticket. Upon his 1983 election for Tatton, in the Tory heartland of Cheshire, he aligned himself with the hard-right, opposing trade unions and anti-apartheid agitation. A staple of the Monday Club (*qv*) and supporter of Chile's hated Pinochet regime, he first associated the family name with the Royal Courts of Justice in October 1986, when suing the BBC for libel after a *Panorama* special called 'Maggie's Militant Tendency' linked him to far-right groups across Europe. Though he laughed all the way to the bank (the two-year, James Goldsmith-funded action resulted in a £20k payoff), joker Neil never properly rebutted the most noteworthy claim: that he'd given a Nazi salute while 'messing around' on an official Parliamentary visit to Berlin in August 1983. The Tory boy's frothy put-downs from the back-benches (few of them original, it has to be said) earned him the title 'Parliamentary Wit of the Year' from the *Spectator* in 1988. One less acclaimed sally came when he jested to a Labour MP that the IRA could perhaps shoot pensioners dying from cold. His mind had soon moved onto weightier matters, though. In 1989 he rebranded himself as a crusader for civil liberties in the Skoal Bandits (*qv*) affair, but his tireless lobbying for the carcinogenic *amuses-bouches* turned out to be futile, and it wasn't until 1994 that he was to join the fast track to immortality in the field of parliamentary corruption.

Cash For Questions (*qv*) first reared its head in October 1994, when the *Guardian* alleged that Ian Greer (*qv*) had arranged for Hamilton and Tim Smith (*qv*) to ask questions on Mohammed Fayed's behalf in the House, in exchange for payments totalling up to £30,000 in brown envelopes (*qv*). Smith admitted plain guilt and resigned, but Hamilton steadfastly maintained his innocence, and continues to do so to this day. Flying in the face of his party's wishes and blaming a 'left-wing bias' in the media, the insanely optimistic MP decided to defend Tatton at the 1997 General Election. In doing so he successfully called his bumbling leader's bluff – John Major had delayed the potentially damning Downey Report (*qv*) until after the Party could be safely re-elected, and as a result Hamilton was still protected from the inquiry's full wrath – but his fears about media bias proved justified. The former BBC correspondent Martin Bell (*qv*) romped home on an anti-sleaze ticket, his 11,000-vote majority greatly assisted by Labour and the Lib Dems making the unprecedented decision to withdraw their own candidates.

When the Downey Report (*qv*) finally appeared in July, it reserved especial contempt for Hamilton. "It is difficult to escape the conclusion that, as the inquiry has progressed and more and more has been discovered, Mr Hamilton's credibility has suffered increasingly serious damage," it said. Regarding Skoal Bandits, it declared that the hen-pecked idealist 'persistently and deliberately failed to declare his interests' in putting US Tobacco's case to ministers – 'interests' that included trousering $10k to introduce the company to political lobbyists. Taken alongside undeclared fees from the nuclear and strategic sectors, the Select Committee identified 'casualness bordering on indifference or contempt towards the rules of the House' and concluded: 'Mr Hamilton's conduct fell seriously and persistently below the standards which the House is entitled to expect of its Members.' Especially 'compelling evidence' against his good name came in the testimony of three Fayed associates, whose word – crushingly – Downey deemed more reliable than the Honourable Member for Tatton's.

With little left to lose, Hamilton chose to strike at what he judged to be the cause of his woes – the man whose bribes he was said to have taken. Having sustained the humiliation of being asked to stay away from the 1998 Tory party conference by William Hague, in 1999 he took Fayed to court. The idea was to portray the ranting shopkeeper as a disgruntled conspiracy theorist who'd say anything for revenge after failing to win a British passport, but the kamikaze case was thrown out when the jury heard that Hamilton had enjoyed a string of perks paid for by him – including a notorious six-day jolly at the Ritz hotel in Paris, where they ran up a £2,120 extras bill. When his subsequent appeal also failed, he was left with legal bills of £3m and had no choice but to file for bankruptcy. The committed Eurosceptic promptly vowed to take his case all the way to the European Court of Human Rights, but in the end he focused on options closer to home – reality TV, for instance.

Since then the bow-tied buffoon has dwelt in the shadow of his formidable wife Christine, summarising his meal ticket on a 'celebrity' edition of *Mastermind* as being an 'object of professional curiosity'. He has dressed up as David Beckham for GMTV and a transvestite for BBC Northern Ireland, squatted in a bathtub full of jam as part of a British Heart Foundation campaign and appeared in an uncommissionable cookery pilot entitled *Posh Nosh*. But nothing symbolises his fall as succinctly as a May 2005 turn on Channel 4 Johnny Vegas vehicle *18 Stone Of Idiot*, when he was pelted with mackerel while cage-dancing. "The man will do anything... where's his fucking pride?" gasped the obese comic – a conundrum that could be Hamilton's epitaph.

Hammond Report, The

2001 report on New Labour's business links with the Hinduja brothers (*qv*), named after its author, Sir Anthony Hammond. Among those to whom big-hearted Sir Anthony gave the benefit of the doubt was Peter Mandelson (*qv*). Not to be confused with the Hutton report (*qv*), another New Labour whitewash from 2004.

Harkess, Judge James
b. 1932

Comprehensively humiliated Justice (and failed Tory candidate) who threatened to have Alan Clark (*qv*) 'horsewhipped' in May 1994 when it was revealed that not only had his wife Valerie had what she called 'forceful and selfish sex' with the rutting rotter, but so had both his daughters: Clark referred to the family as his 'harem' and 'coven'. The MP also used Valerie's name to set up a South African bank account through which he conducted share deals in arms firm Astra. Harkess's threat to use the horsewhip went sadly unfulfilled, and his wife's opposite number, Jane Clark, cruelly suggested that the Judge would be better off employing the instrument on his wife, while the ringmaster of the whole affair, Max Clifford (*qv*), gleefully summarised it as 'pure, pure panto'.

SLEAZE ——— **SLOT**

> "Whatever structures and procedures we have in the House, we cannot legislate for integrity, and individual members should act in such a manner whereby their integrity is not called into question"
>
> *- Speaker Betty Boothroyd, May 22nd 1995*

Hawking

1. Rarefied bird-based pastime, beloved of medieval rulers and wealthy Saudis – who occasionally invited sleaze giant Jonathan Aitken (*qv*) to participate.

2. Advertising your services for sale – to wealthy Saudis, for example (see *Aitken, Jonathan*).

Hayes, Jerry
b. April 20th 1953
MP (Con), Harlow, 1983-97

Cherubic self-publicist who ran into choppy waters in January 1997 when it was alleged in the *News of the World* (via the ever public-spirited Max Clifford) that he'd had an affair with young Parliamentary Researcher (*qv*) Paul Stone. For a fee of around £30,000, Stone helpfully furnished the newspaper with compromising correspondence, but the married MP denied any gay angle, describing their interaction as a 'lovely relationship' and 'an intimate friendship' and going only as far as to say: "I didn't understand the feelings I was having... I knew these affections for this boy were becoming unhealthy." The publicity, which clashed with Hayes's image as a family man, came at just the wrong time for his party, as it steeled itself for a foregone General Election.

"I didn't understand the feelings I was having... I knew these affections for this boy were becoming unhealthy"

The allegations also led to debate on the gay age of consent, as Stone was below it when the affair was said to have taken place in 1991. What they didn't do was change the affection in which the MP was held in the Commons and his constituency. Nonetheless, Hayes (who'd also goofed in 1994 by leading tributes to Michael Heseltine after a spoof death announcement by Chris Morris, *qv*) lost his seat at the 1997 Election. After a spell scribbling for Mohammed Fayed's hilarious revival of *Punch* magazine, he returned to the bar, where he still practises as a criminal lawyer. In that capacity he acted for sleaze stud John Hemming (*qv*) in a 2005 bid to challenge postal votes at the General Election.

Hemming, John
b. March 16th 1960
MP (Lib Dem), Birmingham Yardley, 2005-

The Lib Dems' answer to Steven Norris (*qv*), this minted Member is credited by his doting wife Christine as having had 'no less than 26' extra-marital affairs – a statistic that emerged soon after his election in 2005, when it was revealed that he was having a child with his Parliamentary Researcher (*qv*) and fellow Birmingham councillor Emily Cox. Though Hemming has since disputed the figure, he cheerily picked up the blower to vote for himself in a *News of the World* poll to find 'Britain's Biggest Love Rat' that October. "People used to think of me as a bit of a geek," swanked the unsightly computer millionaire. "But I now seem to have turned into some kind of James Bond character."

When not philandering, Hemming is a fierce campaigner in favour of public lavatories, and against electoral malpractice – perhaps because of ugly memories of his own. When standing as the Liberal candidate in the 1979 Oxford Student Union elections, the concupiscent swot (and Magdalen College Women's Representative) was denied his party's traditional third place when he scampered home fourth – behind an Airedale Terrier.

Hindujas, the

Billionaire quartet from Bombay, two of whom – Srichand and Gopichand – are now UK citizens, in no small part thanks to the Herculean efforts of MPs Keith Vaz (who first wrote to the Home Office in 1997 commending Gopichand's application) and Peter Mandelson (who helped out £1m Dome donor Srichand in 1999).

The ministers fared very differently after their efforts on the Hindujas' behalf. Srichand wrote to Tony Blair in the spring of 1999 complaining that there were no Asian Cabinet ministers, and Vaz was promoted at the very next reshuffle (Blair's office denied any link). Mandelson, however, was swiftly out of a job. This was to some extent because a huge corruption case was brought against the British Hindujas (and one of their brothers) in India in 2001 over the Bofors affair (*qv*), meaning that unwelcome questions were suddenly being asked about how the duo got their passports. But the sacking was largely because Mandy misled the House about his conversation with a Home Office minister on Srichand's behalf (see *Mandelson, Peter*). It scarcely helped matters that the Millennium Dome (*qv*) – Peter's pet project and the greatest beneficiary of the brothers' generosity – was already being derided as a money pit.

The Hinduja three were cleared of all Bofors-related charges in May 2005, and remain tight-lipped as to the exact nature of their income, which involves oil, banking, pharmaceuticals, telecoms and goods transport. In mid-2006 it was reported that Srichand and Gopichand were working on home improvements for a £100m (62,000sq ft) palace in Pall Mall – with the specific intention of outdoing the £70m pad (at a paltry 50,000 sq ft) owned by Britain's richest Indian, Lakshmi Mittal (*qv*). The brothers even hope to pip the Mall estate's former owner, the Queen, in boasting the single most luxurious private residence in London. The property will house up to 38 members of their extended family, including the less celebrated brothers: Prakash is based in Switzerland, while Ashok – the Zeppo of the clan – is left to run the Bombay office.

Hirst, Sir Michael
b. Jan 2nd 1946
MP (Con), Strathkelvin and Bearsden, 1983–87

Scots Tory whose dignified response to stories about his private life won him surprisingly little public sympathy. This was perhaps because revelations that he'd cheated on his wife with at least one other man came straight after John Major had proposed him as a 'sleaze-free' candidate at the 1997 Election. At the time Sir Michael was on a mercy dash to replace adulterer and Allan 'Axeman' Stewart (*qv*) in the safest Conservative seat in Scotland.

Having lost Strathkelvin and Bearsden to Labour in 1987, Hirst had enjoyed a relaxing ten-year break from the political coalface, despite a failed bid to regain the seat in 1992.

"If this is sleaze, then I'm a banana"

He was consoled with a knighthood and the Chair of the Scottish Conservatives – a post he held until March 1997, when Major decided that Glasgow Eastwood was such a dead cert Sir Michael could have another go. A senior Tory source said at the time: "It's a foregone conclusion." Hirst was seen as a safe candidate despite Ian Greer (*qv*) having named him in October 1996 as one of 21 Tories who had received money from his company. Hirst summoned the press to his door, told them it was a piffling £500 party donation, and declared: "If this is sleaze, then I'm a banana."

Fruitier rumours emerged within days of his nomination, suggesting that the married Church of Scotland elder had enjoyed love matches with up to two male party workers, one of whom the Scottish press later linked to a huge party payola scandal. All 'Sir Mickey' would admit in his letter to John Major was 'a past indiscretion'. An old colleague, Paul Clarke, then came out of the woodwork, accusing Hirst of having run a 'dirty tricks' campaign over 'some kind of sexual perversion' to stop his selection by the Welsh Tories (Clarke had ten years earlier been forced to resign his East Lothian seat and was delisted in Scotland after a smear campaign linked him with three MPs, two women and a man – as well as a made-up petition to legalise sex with children). As usual at the 1997 Election, nothing went the way the Tories had planned. Sir Michael abruptly withdrew his candidacy, and the 'safest seat in Scotland' was put onto a platter for Labour's Jim Murphy (*qv*). In a final humiliation, Sir Michael was asked two weeks later if he'd like to stand as a UKIP candidate for the same seat. "The UKIP must be desperately short of candidates to make such a clumsy approach to me," he observed.

Hodge, Margaret
b. Sept 8th 1944
MP (Lab), Barking, 1994-

Terrifying 'original leftwing firebrand' who will be forever associated with a child abuse scandal dating from her notorious reign over Islington Council (1982-92), when she was known as 'Enver' Hodge, after the brutal Albanian dictator.

While endorsing Poll Tax rebellion at the expense of a £16m shortfall in council revenue, she also sent her children to private schools outside her borough (see *Blair, Tony*). Stung by her critics, she sought to ban all office contact with the local paper while showering public money on what the *Guardian* later typified as 'lesbian self-defence classes and non-sexist jigsaws'. But what blew her reputation apart was the inadequate and unsympathetic response to an ongoing child abuse scandal during her decade in charge, in which 32 council workers and staff at Islington children's homes were implicated – of whom only four were disciplined, and just two prevented from going back to work. One social worker even resigned in 1992 because she couldn't prevent a child being placed under the care of a suspect individual. On October 6th that year, tales of 'degradation and exploitation' involving grooming, drugs and prostitution under her council's care were published in the *Evening Standard* – only to be dismissed by Hodge as 'gutter journalism'.

But the subsequent investigation backed the story, and Hodge's administration was panned by an independent inquiry in 1995 for having 'failed to respond properly'. SDP Councillor David Hyams commented: "She had her own solution to childcare problems, of course. As services were being cut, she was advertising in *The Lady* magazine for a nanny." Hodge, the daughter of a millionaire steel trader, ducked out of the firing line and headed for a lucrative consultancy post at Price Waterhouse in October 1992, from where she moved to Parliament in a 1994 by-election after the sudden death of Jo Richardson MP. It wasn't until June 2003 – when she was appointed Children's Minister, of all things – that trouble flared up again. As people questioned whether she was really the most sensitive candidate for the post, Hodge conceded a 'terrible error of judgement' when she'd failed to act back in 1992. But she tried to block a 'sensationalist' BBC investigation into her childcare record in November 2003, and wrote to the Chairman telling him their chief witness was an 'extremely disturbed person'. In fact Demetrious Panton, an abuse victim of Islington children's homes, had transcended his background to become an advisor to the office of the Deputy Prime Minister. Again Hodge tried to resort to legal threats, this time to prevent her offending letter reaching the press; a week later she was apologising for the slur in the High Court, making a £10k charity donation and covering costs.

Since then Hodge has held less high-profile posts, but hasn't lost her talent for giving offence. Having been given the 2004 Big Brother Award for 'Worst Public Servant' by an individual freedoms group called Privacy International, she was moved to Work and Pensions, where she caused a row on July 17th 2005 by suggesting that laid-off MG Rovers workers could go and work at Tesco. In April 2006 there were further calls for her resignation when she gave the BNP a boost ahead of the May 4th local elections. Her claims in the *Sunday Telegraph* that 'eight out of ten' working class voters would be considering the BNP, partly because 'they feel no one else is listening to them' (including her own party) was felt to have legitimised the far-right vote. "They can't get a home for their children, they see black and ethnic minority communities moving in and they are angry," she said of her constituents. "Go through the middle of Barking and you could be in Camden or Brixton." It was not a case of racism, she said, but people were 'not ashamed' to vote BNP any more. Sure enough, the race-issue party made record gains, especially in her own hood, Barking, where almost every candidate they put forward was selected. Suddenly the low-profile BNP campaign became the UK's biggest fascist success story since the 1930s. One Labour activist called her comments "little more than an advert for the BNP,"

adding "if I were Nick Griffin and I had a baby girl, I would be calling it Margaret." Griffin and his send-em-back brigade had a bouquet of roses delivered to Hodge's door the next day. "If I had paid her a million pounds I couldn't have asked her to do more," beamed one Barking extremist.

Homes For Votes

Alternative name for late 80s electoral scandal in Westminster.

see *shirleyportering*

Honourable Fool

Modest term used by Jeffrey Archer to describe himself at his 1987 libel trial, while busily defrauding the *Daily Star* of half a million pounds. He was referring to one particular act of chivalry towards damsel in distress Monica Coghlan (*qv*), to whom – though he was sure he had never met her – he gave a big bag of cash to go abroad with. This gave rise to the slang term 'an Archer' (*qv*).

Honours (Prevention of Abuses) Act 1925, the

Prompted by David Lloyd-George's rotten administration, this Act of Parliament took the controversial step of making the sale of honours illegal. Long dormant, it was invoked in March 2006 following suspicions it had been breached by New Labour during the 2005 General Election campaign.

see *Cash For Honours*

Hoon, Geoff
b. Dec 6th 1953
MP (Lab), Ashfield 1992-

Celebrated in the Commons for his liking for rock and pop, 'Buff' Hoon has also earned a reputation for disingenuousness second only to Stephen Byers (*qv*).

An academic, lawyer and long-standing MEP before entering the Commons, Hoon swiftly moved through the ranks, becoming Secretary of State for Defence in 1999. As such, he was at the helm during the WMD farce, becoming one of the most surprising beneficiaries of the Hutton all-clear (see *the Hutton Report)*, since the Ministry of Defence was widely suspected of underhand tactics in naming whistleblower Dr David Kelly (*qv*) before his infamous July 2003 suicide. Matters were hardly helped when it emerged that the Elvis fan would be holidaying in America during Kelly's funeral, despite having been his boss in the ministry (John Prescott went instead). But alt-country enthusiast Hoon had a history of this sort of thing: two days after the discovery of Kelly's body he'd attended the British Grand Prix, and in February 2003, while troops gathered in the desert for war, the greying rocker was skiing in France.

The *NME*-reading Defence Secretary also had previous with Andrew Gilligan (*qv*), the bulbous BBC journalist who'd ineptly provoked the Kelly scandal: he'd already demanded one public apology from the *Today* programme, following a suggestion that British troops were under-equipped and ill-prepared for combat in Iraq. This was retracted after an investigation by the National Audit Office backed the report, but no action was taken, despite Stones fan Hoon – known as 'Hoon Dog' to the public – denying the matter in Parliament. Hoon, who admits to having spent an age at his desk in the War Office trying to book last-minute concert tickets to a Brian Wilson gig, later had to apologise to the family of Steve Roberts, a soldier killed in Iraq on 24th March 2003. Sgt Roberts had been forced to go without proper body armour due to a kit shortage.

When not engaged in rendering UK arms procurement more 'competitive', or reinforcing nuclear defence, Hoon liked to relax to the sounds of his favourite album, *The Freewheelin' Bob Dylan*, and told the *Guardian* on April 15th 2005 how he'd recovered from one particularly 'wretched' week at the office by watching Britpop has-beens The Bluetones in Wolverhampton. Although he weathered demands for his resignation throughout 2004 (following the military equipment scandal, the Butler Report and his April admission that more could have been done to help save Dr Kelly), Hoon hung on till the 2005 reshuffle, when he was quietly replaced by fellow pop-picker John Reid (*qv*).

Hughes, Beverley
b. March 30th 1950
MP (Lab), Stretford & Urmston, 1997-

Immigration Minister whose first public blunder came when she denounced a July 2001 episode of *Brass Eye* (about paedophilia) as 'unbelievably sick' – then had to admit almost immediately that she hadn't seen it. Three years later she bowed out after accepting she had – 'however unwittingly' – given a wholly misleading press briefing over a visa fraud scandal. James Cameron, a British consul in Romania, had gone to the Tories in March 2004 with concerns over fraudulent asylum claims, frustrated that earlier attempts to blow the whistle seemed to have fallen on deaf ears at the Home Office. Hughes's mistake was then to insist on *Newsnight* on March 29th that the recent questions from the Tories were the first she'd heard of the alleged scam. She also assured the House that if she'd known about it, something would have been done.

In fact senior whip Bob Ainsworth had written to her a year before, raising serious worries about the issue, and Hughes had taken the time to write in response twice – something he didn't hesitate to remind her when they bumped into each other in Parliament the next day. Even Tony Blair admitted: "It's pretty obvious to me that something was seriously wrong." After consulting her boss David Blunkett over dinner, and checking the damning correspondence the next day, they decided that the best thing for her to do 'in good conscience' was to resign on April 1st – thereby taking the heat off the Home Secretary. All agreed that it would be monstrous to expect Blunkett to take responsibility for the goings-on in his department, but he was good enough to describe the day his underling took the bullet as the 'worst personal day' of his political life. It wasn't a claim he'd be able to make for long.

Hughes, Kevin
b. Dec 15th 1952 / d. July 16th 2006
MP (Lab), Doncaster North, 1992-2005

Ex-communist who presided over the Donnygate (*qv*) scandal, but shook off allegations of direct involvement. Hughes had publicly defended some of his corrupt councillors, but managed to ride out smears about his private life and the challenge of an official 'anti-sleaze candidate' in 1997. However, he dropped threats of legal action against *Private Eye* magazine for saying he'd assaulted ex-councillor (and anti-sleaze campaigner) Ron Rose, after Rose produced witnesses to the event. Hughes died soon after standing down from Parliament, but will be remembered for his Commons attack on "the yoghurt and muesli-eating, *Guardian*-reading fraternity" in 2001 – and, according to one colleague, for making "Joe Stalin look like a nursery school teacher" during his five-year spell as a party whip.

Hughes, Robert
b. July 14th 1951
MP (Con), Harrow West, 1987-97

Minister for John Major's vacuous Citizens' Charter who resigned in March 1995 after it emerged that he'd been enjoying a six-month affair with Janet Oates, his Parliamentary Researcher (*qv*). Oates, who'd met Hughes when she approached him as a constituent seeking advice over the early release from prison of a violent ex-boyfriend, went public when Hughes deputised his second wife, Sandra, to sack her.

The *News of the World* quoted Sandra saying he "was ready for sex any time of day or night", but – though his constituency association was scandalised – Mrs Hughes (dubbed 'the biter bit' by one newspaper) stood by her man, who found additional solace in religion.

"Ready for sex any time of day or night"

The tabloids, meanwhile, had a riot making jokes about Hughes 'getting his Oates'.

Hughes, Simon
b. May 17th 1951
MP (Lib Dem), Bermondsey, 1983-

Lib Dem whose bisexuality was revealed as part of a January 2006 tabloid pincer movement that also scuppered the credibility of Mark Oaten (*qv*). Hughes would undoubtedly have emerged from his 'outing' with greater public sympathy if he hadn't specialised in the non-denial denial (otherwise known as 'the loophole lie') to keep his sexuality under wraps. Prominent gay rights activist Peter Tatchell (see *Mugabe, Robert*) might also have had more time for Hughes's predicament if he hadn't personally suffered at his hands in "the dirtiest and most notorious by-election in British political history", as *Gay News* described the 1983 fight for Bermondsey. Then-Labour candidate Tatchell saw his campaign wrecked by gay smears and innuendo, while Hughes's people presented him as 'the straight choice'. On the 29th January 2006, the *Scotsman* quoted an unnamed Hughes volunteer on the February 1983 campaign as saying: "We were all happy to see the kicking [Peter] Tatchell took over his sexuality, when every one of us knew very well that Simon was gay too." It was a campaign for which Hughes had to apologise 23 years later, on 26th January 2006, when he finally conceded he was 'bisexual'.

The carefully-chosen word meant bachelor Hughes could keep a clear conscience over the many times he'd denied he was actually gay. When asked the question that very month, he had told the *Telegraph*: "The answer is no, as it happens, but if it was the case, which it isn't, I hope that it would not be an issue." Given the same question by the *Independent*, he said: "No, I'm not. But it absolutely should not matter if I was." He then repeated the denial to the *Guardian* on January 24th, just 48 hours before he came clean – and only did so then because the *Sun* possessed credit card bills in his name proving he was using the gay chatline 'Man Talk'. "I gave a reply that wasn't untrue, but was clearly misleading and I apologise," he squirmed to the tabloid on January 26th. "I apologise if I misled people, I apologise if I unintentionally gave the wrong impression." He also took care to point to past relationships with women – with unsubstantiated claims of having had numerous marriage proposals rejected – as evidence that he wasn't actually 'gay', and therefore had stuck to the literal truth of the matter. Setting semantics aside, many concurred with the *Independent* think-piece four days later, which called him simply 'a shameless liar'.

Humphrey
b. 1988 / d. 2006

Named after the Machiavellian *Yes Minister* character, this long-serving Downing Street tom was linked to a bloody robin binge in No. 10's garden in June 1994. PM John Major – who'd just launched his 'Back To Basics' initiative – furiously

rebutted the charge, stating: "I am afraid Humphrey has been falsely accused." But Major was strangely silent that September, when the piebald puss savaged a duck in an unprovoked attack in St. James's Park.

Humphrey returned to the public eye in 1997, when incoming first lady Cherie Blair was accused of deeming him 'unhygienic' and ordering his execution by lethal injection. After a photo call, during which she clutched the writhing pet to her bosom, his sentence was commuted to South London exile for his autumn years; it was later suggested that his banishment had been prompted by Alastair Campbell's cat allergy. In March 2005 a spokesman stated that "Humphrey has a small thyroid problem, but is otherwise in excellent health" – but months later the geriatric feline succumbed to a massive stroke.

Hunter, Andrew

b. Jan 8th 1943
MP (Con), Basingstoke, 1983-2002 / (independent) 2002-04 / (DUP) 2004-05

Hard-right hard-hitter with a consistent voting record against equal gay rights. A vigorous opponent of sanctions and sporting bans against South Africa, in 1987 the former Harrow schoolmaster chaired a lobby group dedicated to achieving full political recognition for the apartheid-sponsored territory of Bophuthatswana (*qv*). In October 1989 he assured his African friends that he and his supporters were using 'every conceivable means' of presenting Bophuthatswana's case – meaning parliamentary debates, 'informal lobbying on a personal basis', correspondence with the Prime Minister, and (of course) business-class 'jollies' with the wife to scorching Sun City. Somehow this all took forever, and despite Hunter having promised way back in March 1988 (in a self-penned paper entitled *A Foreign Policy for Bophuthatswana – A View From Westminster*) to give the matter 'highest priority', the freebies and junkets managed to outlast the hated apartheid regime. Still, at least he remembered to declare his dinner and travel expenses (unlike a 1985 business trip to Romania, when he'd met and presented gifts to President Ceausescu).

In 2001 Hunter was pressured into leaving the Monday Club (*qv*) by Ian Duncan Smith, and faced further adverse publicity over his involvement with *Right Now!* magazine, a far-right rag with links to both the Monday Club and reviled French politician Jean-Marie LePen. Piqued, in 2002 he announced his decision to leave the Tories for Ian Paisley's Democratic Unionist Party – a move even

Tony Blair condemned as 'entirely muddle-headed and wrong'. Though much of his energy was devoted to Northern Ireland thereafter, he also found time to champion the cause of psychopathic multiple-murderer Jeremy Bamber in Parliament.

Hurd, Douglas

b. March 8th 1930
MP (Con), Mid-Oxon, 1974-83 / Witney, 1983-97

Lanky egghead and Foreign Secretary from 1989-95, whose equivocal stance on matters such as Iraq and the Balkans led many to question his convictions. His legacy is especially tainted by the Pergau Dam affair (*qv*), over which he was ultimately found to have acted unlawfully.

Renowned as a fervent flogger at Eton, after graduating from Cambridge Hurd entered the diplomatic service, which he left for politics. Having worked his way through the party ranks, he had an unremarkable spell as Home Secretary (1985-89), during which he supported the sale of weapons to Saddam Hussein, before devising the distasteful policy towards Slobodan Milosevic and the Serbs for which he is most remembered today. Essentially, Hurd refused to concede that Milosevic was any worse than his opponents in the Balkan wars, and therefore declined to assist the Bosnians against the Serbs, imposing an arms embargo instead. While Hurd's apparent appeasement of Milosevic flew in the face of NATO, US and public feeling, it did pave the way for potentially lucrative British privatisation of Serbian utilities (they eventually went to Italy). Shortly after his retirement from frontline politics in 1995, Hurd became a director of NatWest, in which capacity he visited Milosevic in Serbia to discuss business opportunities – though these were sadly derailed by Milosevic's war crimes trial, at which the Bosnian government muttered about charging Hurd as an accomplice to genocide.

Yet Hurd's finest hour came with the Pergau Dam (*qv*), a Malaysian Hydroelectric project part-funded by a generous slice of the UK foreign aid budget. The concurrent undertaking by the Malaysian government to buy a colossal amount of UK arms caused the affair, already stinking to high heaven, to become the subject of a UK government inquiry in March 1994. That November the High Court ruled that Hurd had acted *ultra vires* (and therefore, in layman's terms, illegally), on the grounds that the project was not of economic or humanitarian benefit to the Malaysian people, and he retired from frontline politics soon afterwards.

Hussein, Saddam
b. April 29th 1937 / d. Dec 30th 2006

Iraqi dictator and romantic novelist (*Zabibah and the King* was a million-seller in his homeland), with whom Britain had a long and turbulent relationship.

see *Iraq / Arms To Iraq / Galloway, George*

SLEAZE

"I am stunned by the jury's verdict and continue to deny that I acted corruptly in the pursuit of my parliamentary and ministerial duties"

– Neil Hamilton upon losing his libel claim, December 1999

SLOT

Lord Lambton

b. July 10th 1922 / d. Dec 30th 2006

MP (Con), Berwick-upon-Tweed, 1951-73

Unabashed dandy and RAF minister who resigned his seat in 1973 when he was caught taking drugs and cavorting with hard-bitten prostitute Norma Levy – and paying by cheque. Anthony Lambton's confessed love of 'variety' in his marriage had seen him frolic with many vice-girls, but his downfall came in the booze-soaked form of Levy's husband Colin, who tipped off the police when arrested for alleged drug smuggling. The Yard wasn't interested enough for his liking, so he secretly filmed Lambton and showed the footage to the *News of the World*. It was too grainy, so a hack was despatched to hide in the wardrobe of the Levys' Maida Vale love nest and snap Norma's next pot-fuelled romp with the Under-Secretary for Defence. When the newspaper decided not to run the story, the desperate Levy hawked it to the German magazine *Stern* before finally making a cut-price sale to the *Sunday People*, who went to the police.

Lambton was well and truly in the soup, and released a statement calling Colin Levy a 'sneak pimp', admitting with disarming candour: "I have no excuses whatsoever to make. I behaved with incredible stupidity." This, however, was undermined by his subsequent rumination: "Surely all men patronise whores?" Matters took a further turn for the worse when the police searched his flat and found cannabis and barbiturates, for which he was fined £300. Prior to this, there had been some support for him in the Commons – as the Home Secretary put it, no MP wanted to admit it was a 'crime to have a mistress'. But he now had to go, and later blamed his frisky ways on 'the futility of the job'. The furore claimed another establishment scalp too: when the word 'Jellicoe' was found in Mrs. Levy's appointments diary, a panicked Lord Jellicoe, Leader of the House of Lords, spontaneously owned up to a 'casual' brass habit of his own, and resigned, ascribing his indiscretions to his 'exceptionally heavy burden of work'. As Lambton put it: "The way things are going, it will soon be clear that Heath is the only member of the government who doesn't do it." It later transpired that the 'Jellicoe' in question had been a mansion block on Levy's beat. Soon afterwards Lambton moved to Italy, where he pursued a life of debauched tedium, continuing to use the title which (like every other aristocratic MP) he'd been obliged to renounce in 1970. As for Norma Levy, she bore no ill feeling, commenting: "I vote for the Tories. They are my best clients."

Indefatigability

1. The quality of never being tired, never giving up, and unfailingly sticking to your principles.

2. Quality attributed to Saddam Hussein by George Galloway MP (*qv*).

see also *Courage, Strength*

Ingham, Sir Bernard
b. June 21st 1932

Described by insufferably pompous buffoon Piers Morgan as 'an insufferably pompous buffoon', this ruddy former journalist served for 11 years as Margaret Thatcher's fanatically loyal press secretary, and is regarded as a pioneering spin doctor. No amount of spin, however, could prevent him being hauled before the beak for criminal damage in March 1999. The charge arose from a long-running dispute with his Surrey neighbour, builder Barry Cripps, largely over planning. Things boiled over on December 13th 1998, when Cripps – reversing his personalised Mercedes into the garage at 'Nutcracker Gables' – strayed briefly onto Ingham's driveway. In a scene straight out of a 70s sitcom, Thatcher's doughty lieutenant steamed out of his property, yelling and gesticulating before kicking the vehicle.

When Croydon's constabulary arrived, Ingham endeared himself to the arresting officer by enquiring: "Are you sure you want to do this?" Having called Cripps 'extremely troublesome', he was bound over to keep the peace, and later paid £792 for damage to the car. "It is ironic that I am here," he steamed afterwards, "because I have sought over 11 years of problems to uphold decent people's rights and the planning system." Cripps, meanwhile, had this message: "We are weary of the constant bombardment that we have suffered. We are no match for Sir Bernard Ingham. Let's hope that he will now allow us to get on with our lives peacefully."

Integrity

1. Unshakeable personal standards of conduct. Steadfast adherence to a strict moral or ethical code.

2. Quality attributed to Jeffrey Archer by William Hague (*qv*).

see *Probity*

International Federation of Physical Culture

Defunct body-building club whose correspondence courses enabled nine-stone weaklings to display marginally-improved physiques on windswept British beaches in the 50s and 60s. Jeffrey Archer's youthful CV contained the pathetic boast that he was a 'Fellow' of the organisation – a non-existent honour and a notable early fib.

Iraq

Formerly known as Mesopotamia, this moderate-sized, oil-rich nation in the Middle East can boast the world's first civilisation, and was until recently armed by friendly nations such as Great Britain.

WIGGINGS

"She knew that it was unlawful and wrong for the Council to exercise its powers to secure an electoral advantage for any party… she was at least recklessly indifferent as to whether it was right or wrong"

– *District Auditor John Magill on 'Dame' Shirley Porter, 1996*

FROM THE BEAK

Irimia, Gabriela
b. Oct 31st 1982

Stick-thin warbler widely considered the second most frightening thing ever to have come out of Transylvania (the first being her twin, Monica). She first came to public attention as half of butt-slapping novelty act the Cheeky Girls, and – as of late 2006 – became love interest of goofy Liberal Lembit Öpik (*qv*).

2003 was good to the twins, with a string of holiday camp appearances, but by 2006 they were washed up in tabloid terms. Until, that is, Size-4 scarecrow Gabriela replaced weathergirl Siân Lloyd in Öpik's affections. The ensuing press circus ensured a welcome publicity boost for the tired turn, for whom deportation had become a real possibility. Concerned *Wright Stuff* sage Öpik duly brought up the matter with immigration minister Liam Byrne (*qv*) in the Commons, but broke no rules in so doing ("at no stage did he lobby anybody on this matter," confirmed a Lib Dem spokesman). Gabriela had little doubt that her new boyfriend would shortly be throwing the corridors of power open to the debt-ridden duo. "Monica can't wait until I am introduced to Tony Blair because she thinks his son, Euan, is really cute," cooed the pop corncrake in January 2007. "Who knows what will happen there?"

Irvine, Derry
b. June 23rd 1940
Lord Chancellor (Lab), 1997-2003

Preening kingmaker whose 'pompous, conceited and vainglorious' approach to the role of Lord Chancellor (as Ann Widdecombe MP saw it) was widely perceived as the major reason for New Labour rebranding a post continually occupied since 1066.

Irvine will also go down in history as architect of the love-match of the century, for introducing legal hotshots Tony Blair and Cherie Booth. 'Cupid QC' was always unpopular within the Labour party, to which he acted as legal advisor throughout the 80s (and where his brief included helping expel members of the Militant Tendency, *qv*), but he had the last laugh in May 1997, when his protégé gave him the top legal post in the land. It also meant that he was joining the same Cabinet as Secretary of State for Scotland Donald Dewar – an unwelcome reunion, given that Dewar's wife had left him for Irvine in 1970, and the shattered cuckold had neither forgotten nor forgiven.

"I would compare myself to Thomas Wolsey"

In his new position, Lord Irvine of Lairg preferred to think of himself as a Cardinal – 'I would compare myself to Thomas Wolsey', he puffed in 1997 of his 'important role', with responsibilities 'encompassing politics, religion, the economy, the military'.

Like Wolsey before him, Irvine felt his brief justified a taste for the finer things: his official residence at the Palace of Westminster was redecorated at the mind-blowing cost to the taxpayer of £650k, including £59k on the notorious hand-printed wallpaper that reminded so many of a Balti house. Defending the measures to the House in March 1998 was not Irvine's finest hour (he called it a 'noble cause', deserving of better than the rubbish 'down at the DIY store'). This arrogance led to awkward questions about his role itself, especially when he accepted a whopping £22,691 payrise in 2003, keeping clear daylight between his salary and that of the Lord Chief Justice. After an outcry he agreed to a more modest hike, but in June 2003 he was – like Wolsey to the last – reluctantly removed from power.

Iscariot, Judas
b. c1 AD

Notorious wrongdoer whose cause was taken up by fellow miscreant Jeffrey Archer in *The Gospel According To Judas*. Inspired by the challenge of rehabilitating the reputation of a man condemned by society and history, Archer said in a statement in January 2007: "This is the most important book I have ever worked on. It means an awful lot to me." He is thought to have received well in excess of 30 pieces of silver for his efforts, which were hailed by the *Times* on March 24th as 'supremely pointless' and 'remarkably tedious'.

J

Jellied Bloody Mary

Bizarre aperitif served to guests of Neil and Christine Hamilton, and marginally preferable to the other wobbly savouries Christine has been accused of offering at parties (see *Milroy-Sloan, Nadine*). The unappetising cocktails were to form a crucial plank in the Hamiltons' alibi when a spurious sexual assault allegation was made against them in 2001.

Jenkins, Lee
b. 1970

Disgruntled teacher who seemed to understand the rules on undeclared ministerial income better than his landlord – then-Education Secretary David Blunkett (*qv*). Of the shabby Wimbledon home he rented from the Cabinet Minister for £700 a month (and a £1000 deposit), Jenkins remarked in July 2000: "I assumed it was the sort of thing that should be declared if you are a Minister, because it is outside earnings." But Blunkett had informed no-one, least of all the Register of Members' Interests. His record as a landlord didn't escape censure, either. "It was in a terrible state of repair," moaned Jenkins, who'd moved in with his fiancée at the beginning of the year. "There were damp patches, the windows leak and the radiators are still not working properly." Though 'friends' of Blunkett were quick to counter with criticism of Jenkins's tenancy record, the catalogue of grievances just kept on growing: worn carpet, dust, smell, no effort to clean up after previous tenants, documents left in the drawers and – most damning of all – "rotting vegetables in one of the cupboards."

John is John

Catch-all phrase devised by Prime Minister Tony Blair on May 17th 2001 to explain why his Deputy, John Prescott (*qv*), had thrown a punch at a member of the electorate the day before.

see *Evans, Craig*

Johnson, Boris
b. June 19th 1964
MP (Con), Henley, 2001-

Alexander Boris de Pfeffel Johnson has studiously cultivated the image of a lovable buffoon – a Woosterish smokescreen that conceals his sharp mind and dubious personal morality.

Johnson was educated at Eton, where he was a King's Scholar (with friends including convicted fraudster Darius Guppy and pompous pulpiteer Earl Spencer) and Balliol College, Oxford, where he joined the bingeing Bullingdon Club (*qv*) and contributed to his sister Rachel's nauseating *Oxford Myths* book (see *Young Meteors*). It is unclear how far his student antics went, though he has admitted to attempting to snort cocaine ("I think I was once given cocaine, but I sneezed, so it didn't go up my nose"), and stated on the 2005 election trail: "I've forgotten my view on drugs." In 1985 he joined the *Times* as a cub reporter, but was swiftly sacked for falsifying a comment made by his godfather, Colin Lucas (later Vice-Chancellor of Oxford University). He later found a berth at the *Telegraph*, becoming EC correspondent from 1989-94.

Shortly after Guppy was jailed for six years in 1993, Johnson was secretly recorded pledging to him that he'd help an effort to have a *News of the World* journalist beaten up – an incident he has insisted he has no regrets about. His first marriage, to Allegra Mostyn-Owen, was dissolved the same year when it was discovered that he'd got barrister Marina Wheeler (now mother of his two sons and two daughters) pregnant. He married Wheeler the same year, and became assistant editor of the *Telegraph* from 1994–99 and a political columnist on the *Spectator* (*qv*), of which he was made editor in 1999. Following a bid to become MP for Clwyd South in 1997, he succeeded Michael Heseltine in Henley in 2001, and was appointed a Shadow Minister for the Arts in 2004. The honeymoon was short: a belief-beggaringly tactless *Spectator* leader of October 16th accused Liverpool of 'mawkish sentimentality' barely a week after Ken Bigley had been butchered in Iraq. Johnson was despatched to the city to apologise by party leader Michael Howard, and was relieved of his post a month later when it emerged he'd fibbed about getting his long-term mistress Petronella Wyatt pregnant (she had a termination). Employing his trademark archaism, Johnson described the press reports as 'an inverted pyramid of piffle,' but Howard begged to differ, and told the corpulent Casanova to clear his desk. A party spokesman commented that the sacking was 'nothing to do with personal morality, but rather with his personal integrity and honesty.'

"I think I was once given cocaine, but I sneezed, so it didn't go up my nose"

In December 2005 he resigned the editorship of the *Spectator* to take up an appointment as Shadow Higher Education Minister, but his rehabilitation was undermined by claims in April 2006 that he was enjoying another affair, this time with buxom journalist Anna Fazackerley. A filthy tackle during a friendly football game between celebrities and ex-German pros in May 2006 perhaps showed more of his true colours, and he was back in trouble in September when he characterised Papua New Guinea as a place that indulged in 'orgies of cannibalism and chief-killing'. The quip failed to tickle Jean L Kekedo, the country's High Commissioner in London, who commented: "I consider the comments, coming from a senior British MP, very damaging to the image of Papua New Guinea, and an insult to the integrity and intelligence of all Papua New Guineans." That August Johnson came second in a *Reader's Digest* poll to find Britain's biggest 'figure of fun' (edged out of the top spot by Ozzy Osbourne, but comfortably ahead of fellow love-rat Chris Eubank), and in April 2007 he escaped censure from David Cameron for describing Portsmouth in his *GQ* column as 'arguably too full of drugs, obesity, underachievement and Labour MPs'. Mike Hancock, the Lib Dem member for Portsmouth South, also failed to see the joke, calling the remark 'simply outrageous and beyond belief... an insult to the whole city' and stating: "David Cameron should immediately sack Mr Johnson from his post as a spokesman." This wasn't about to happen, though. With huge swathes of the public still swallowing the 'Bumbling Boris' brand whole, the party's paltry response was: "Boris speaking his mind, in only the way Boris can, is preferable any day to Labour and Lib Dem politicians who try to cover up the truth."

In July 2007 Johnson made a final bid for political significance when he announced his candidature for Tory Mayor of London. "In my case there are huge obstacles," he understated, having wisely left the 'personal character' section of his official application form blank. "It is hard to see how those difficulties could be overcome – but I am ruling nothing out." He could at least boast one prominent supporter, in the mulleted form of fellow ladies' man Peter Stringfellow. *OK!* magazine reported that the randy club owner would be backing Johnson 'to the hilt', quoting his remark that "underneath the buffoon there is a clever man" – if nothing else, a novel take on Johnson's famous sexual appetite.

Jolly

Parliamentary slang for a lavish trip abroad, typically euphemised as a 'fact-finding mission' and funded by the public purse or interested parties.

Jonathan of Arabia

Title of *World In Action* TV special on Jonathan Aitken's Saudi business links, screened on April 10th 1995 after its subject's feverish last-minute attempts to halt it failed. The documentary, which juxtaposed hard-hitting claims about Aitken's lifestyle with shots of a comedy camel wandering over dunes near Liverpool, provoked his infamous 'Sword of Truth' press conference (see *World In Action / Guardian* trial).

SLEAZE

"I think people will fall about laughing when they see it. And not just laughing at us, but laughing with us"

– Neil Hamilton on his World Cup 'anthem' England Is Jolly Dee, May 2006

SLOT

Jones, Fiona
b. Feb 27th 1957 / d. Jan. 28th 2007
MP (Lab), Newark, 1997-2001

Doomed 'Blair Babe' whose unsafe conviction for electoral malpractice was an early fly in New Labour's ointment. Despite seeing the result overturned, Jones never recovered from the battering she received from the press and her party, and – six years after her seat proved as vulnerable as the Court's verdict – she died of chronic alcoholism.

Having claimed the former Tory stronghold of Newark in the 1997 landslide, Jones was prosecuted for election fraud – the first time an MP had been hauled up for such an offence in 75 years. The month after her victory, rumblings were heard from the unsuccessful Lib Dem candidate, Peter Harris ("Labour ran their whole campaign on a theme of integrity and anti-sleaze, so they should come clean and show the full picture"), but were dismissed as 'sour grapes' by a party spokesperson, who insisted all election expenses would stand up to public scrutiny. Jones was equally bullish: "I am entirely satisfied the accounts conform with election law and are reasonable", she said. But by December fraud officers were involved, and the following August Jones and her Parliamentary agent Des Whicher were committed to Crown Court for trial.

The hearing began early in 1999, and centred on her claim to have spent a total of £8,514.94 on her campaign – just under the legal limit of £8,910.70, but roughly half what her opponents believed the true figure to be. As well as employing a team of professional telephonists to canvass every voter, she was accused of making ancillary expenditures such as hiring a bright New Labour red Toyota ("the acquisition of a smart red vehicle was all to do with the image the party wanted to project to the public," said the prosecutor). On March 19th she was convicted, stripped of her Commons seat and ordered to complete 100 hours' community service. She riposted: "I don't believe I have done anything wrong." Her appeal was indeed upheld in April (as was Whicher's), on grounds that the judge had not directed the jury appropriately as to the definition of election expenses, nor the date on which the campaign can be said to have started.

Jones returned to the House in triumph, but a mere 34 MPs signed an Early Day Motion welcoming her back. Faced with such lukewarm support, she soon became immersed in the notorious Commons drinking culture. Her husband Chris later told the *News of the World* that she had even witnessed a 'famous MP' tipping a generous serving of cocaine into his own drink. Jones got the boot in the 2001 election, when Patrick Mercer (*qv*) clawed her seat back for the Tories, and shortly afterwards she was successfully sued for rent due on her former constituency office. A civil case against the police for malicious prosecution resulted in failure in December 2005, landing her with a £45,000 bill.

The following April she returned to the news when she claimed that a senior Labour Cabinet minister had offered her career advancement in exchange for sex. Though she never publicly identified the individual, she felt she had been frozen out for rejecting his advances – and when the depressing details of her death emerged early in 2007, her descent into alcoholism was widely attributed to the lack of support she'd received from Labour colleagues. "This is a tremendous tragedy," commented Des Whicher. "I have absolutely no doubt at all that what brought it on was the appalling strain and stress she was put under as a result of the court case and people in the Labour party – particularly locally. It made her time as a Member of Parliament very difficult."

Jordan

Hashemite Kingdom in the Middle East that served as a useful staging-post for UK weapons en route for Iraq in the 1980s.

see *Price, Katie*

Jostlegate

Name given to the notorious 'attack' Helen Clark MP (*qv*) accused her Tory rival Stewart Jackson of perpetrating against her outside Peterborough's Buttercross Café in October 2004 – though some onlookers considered the supposed assault to have been little more than a mild jostling.

After an exhaustive investigation into the storm in a teashop, it was concluded that there wasn't enough evidence to prosecute – indeed, Jackson claimed it was Clark who'd pushed him (his pregnant wife was sufficiently distressed to involve the police). Jackson instigated proceedings against Clark in January 2005, seeking compensation for defamation and malicious falsehood, and pledging to give any damages to local charities. "Mrs Clark's allegations are – and always were – a politically inspired and malicious fabrication, designed to damage me as her opponent," he told the *Peterborough Evening Telegraph*. "She sought to ruin my reputation and destroy my good name." Clark countered by branding him a 'sad little man' and accusing him of 'resorting to the politics of the gutter', but made no comment on reports that she was to be investigated for wasting police time. In the end the fuss fizzled out – and Jackson got his chance to rough up his rival at the ballot box, turfing her from her seat in the Election later that year.

Jowell, Tessa
b. September 17th 1947
MP (Lab), Dulwich, 1992-

'Culture Secretary' since 2001, in which role many perceive her major contributions to British life to have been encouraging gambling and binge-drinking. The estranged spouse of David Mills (*qv*), Jowell is also an old-fashioned housewife who doesn't consider it any business of hers what her fella gets up to – for example, how £344k got into his bank account and paid off their mortgage.

After working as a social worker, Camden councillor and mental health charity assistant director, Jowell became an MP in 1992, acting as Shadow Spokesman for Health and Women before becoming Public Health Minister in New Labour's first term. As her department came under fire for seeking to soften drinking laws in 1999, Mills was handsomely profiting from pub chain The Old Monk Company, later giving rise to accusations of a conflict of interests – but with her husband's finances structured offshore, Jowell was able to state with confidence that there had never been one. In March 2006 she promised she "had never heard of this company until this weekend," but was careful to add: "I understand the shares were never owned by my husband". Having ridden this out, in the next reshuffle Jowell entered the Cabinet as Employment Minister, where she weathered the controversial deregulation of gambling laws (see *Anschutz, Philip*) and a row over misuse of lottery cash. It also emerged she had been barred from government meetings on Iran from 2003 onwards, owing to a conflict with her then-husband's 'Middle East interests': specifically Mahan Air, an Iranian aerospace firm, and BAe, of al-Yamamah (*qv*) fame.

With the press taking ever greater interest in her affairs, her continuance in public office hinged on the credibility of one story: that, for four years of marriage between 2000 and 2004, during which time she and her husband took out a £408k mortgage against their home, she was completely in the dark about his finances. And, moreover, that she never knew he had received a mammoth sum of money from an unnamed source, alleged to be Silvio Berlusconi (*qv*), in September 2000, and never thought to ask how he'd managed to pay off their entire mortgage just weeks after tying all the capital they'd raised into a hedge fund. She told Sir Gus O'Donnell (heading up the inquiry in February 2006), that it was only in August 2004 that she'd become aware her husband had banked a six-figure sum four years earlier, one "which he thought he had reasonable grounds to believe was a gift". She denied that there had been anything "unusual, improper or illegal" about her behaviour or the mortgage deal, and the inquiry generously allowed that, had she known about the payment, Jowell would have rushed to her desk to show her husband a copy of the Ministerial Code of Conduct (*qv*).

All the same, whenever she eventually did learn of the sum, she didn't register it – something the government conceded was a mistake. As raging Tory MP Nigel Evans pointed out, parliamentary rules state that ministers must make it their active business to ask their spouses about shareholdings so they can decide whether it's a problem. On March 1st 2006 he summed it up thus: "The fact is that she knew what the Code said. She should have told her husband what the Code said. He should have told her about the substantial gift and she should have declared it. The Ministerial Code is in tatters tonight unless she goes." Faced with the choice of losing her job or her husband of 27 years, the ambitious Minister knew what she had to do, and Mills got his marital P45 forthwith.

Cynics suggested that the until-further-notice separation had the useful effect of distancing Jowell from her worse half, but leaving what they described as "the hope that over time their relationship can be restored". It certainly saved an expensive divorce, which might have required yet more trawling through their financial records. For his part, Mills had it carefully put on record that he "fully accepts responsibility for the situation into which he put his wife, who he knows is entirely blameless in all of this... He is as mortified as she has been angered by the embarrassment he has caused her." Jowell, needless to say, received Tony Blair's full backing and remained in the Cabinet, charged with the appalling task of persuading the public that the Olympics (*qv*) were still a good idea.

Jowellgate

Name given to a stink centring on the husband of Cabinet Minister Tessa Jowell – one David Mills (*qv*) – which should perhaps be called 'Millsgate'. The Labour minister's main role in the affair seems to have been as a deaf and blind partner to her spouse, and the unwitting beneficiary of a massive boost in paying off their mortgage.

The scandal involved a $600,000 (£345,000) deposit in his bank account, which Mills told accountants in 2004 was from 'the

B people'. One of his clients was the man he liked to call 'Mr B', which some have suggested was code for 'Silvio Berlusconi'. Why he should have been so shy about working for Italy's leading citizen is anyone's guess – the generous statesman had provided him with legitimate employment for years. In particular, Mills had helped the media mogul avoid monopoly regulations in Italy in the 90s by setting up a company called 'Horizon', to which 'Mr B' could transfer his pay-TV channel.

In a February 2nd 2004 letter to his accountant, much of which was devoted to whining about having to share the £2m windfall from the sale of the company in March 1996, Mills put himself under suspicion with a series of curious statements. Most intriguing of all was that he had "turned some very tricky corners, to put it mildly" in court during one of Berlusconi's many trials, which "had kept Mr B out of a great deal of trouble that I would have landed him in if I had said all I knew."

When it emerged that Italian prosecutors preparing a case against Berlusconi believed the mystery payment might have been a reward for false testimony and evidence of corruption, Tony Blair swiftly moved to distance himself from the sweating lawyer, following the sensible lead set by Mills's own wife and another rich Italian client, Diego Attanasio, a shipping magnate whom Mills had by now remembered was the source of the 'gift'. "By sheer chance, the most extraordinary chance, last night," he told *Legal Business* magazine in April 2006, "I discovered a piece of clinching evidence that the money came from Diego Attanasio." Unfortunately Attanasio's adamant denial was backed up by a more convincing alibi than any Mills could come up with: he was in jail at the time ("someone is using my name to clear up their problems with the Inland Revenue," he thundered in a speech back home). As Milanese prosecutors then refused to accept the Englishman's documentary evidence, the main problem in bringing the case seemed to be whether anyone involved could be trusted at all. In July 2006 both Mills (who has described himself as a 'complete idiot' and a 'complete fool', and his actions as 'completely insane') and his old paymaster were indicted on fraud charges.

The awkward couple were reunited in Italy, with Mills left to explain why he signed a police confession, apparently under duress, admitting the outgoing PM "put a sum of money my way" in recognition of having "protected Berlusconi in various trials and investigations" – an admission he has since totally retracted. But there was at least one silver lining for the lawyer: because Mills 'forgot' to tell his wife about his dealings, she clung onto her job as Culture Secretary – with the full support of Berlusconi's old houseguest Blair. As of the time of writing, it it is unclear as to when the trial will proceed – if ever.

see *Jowell, Tessa* / *Mills, David*

David Lloyd George

b. Jan 17th 1863 / d. March 26th 1945

MP (Lib), Caernarvon Boroughs, 1890-1945 / PM 1916-22

Characterised by the line 'Lloyd George knew my father', Britain's only ever Welsh PM operated a Cash for Honours (*qv*) system that has made any subsequent counterpart seem a model of subtlety. 'The Hairy Corncrake' also distinguished himself in the courts - to say nothing of the bedroom. Nicknamed 'The Goat' for his brief, vigorous approach to coition, he was cited in a close friend's 1897 divorce case, and sued the *People* in 1909 for suggesting his name was to surface again in similar proceedings. Long before the birth of Jeffrey Archer (*qv*), he brazenly perjured himself to win the action, having persuaded his wife to sit by him in court while he dismissed the article as 'an absolute invention'. Their son Richard was later to recall a pre-trial parental summit at which his father appealed for her complicity, if only to enable herself to become the wife of a Prime Minister.

In fairness to DLG, his career differed from Archer's in many important respects: as well as winning a war and giving the country the old age pension, he wrote no bad novels and actually did donate his compo to good causes. Still, it's his heroic abuse of the Honours system for which he's chiefly remembered. Largely orchestrated by bloated conman Arthur Maundy Gregory, a string of unsuitable candidates (including known criminals), bought into the concept at once. Even those who'd actually earned gongs were invited to cough up, at a rate of around £10k for a Knighthood, £30k for a hereditary Baronetcy or £50k to join the Lords – notwithstanding Lloyd George's contempt for the institution, which he slammed as 'the ranks of the unemployed'. In private he maintained that selling honours was much the cleanest way for parties to raise capital, but in the face of public outcry he moved to distance himself from any knowledge (see *Blair, Tony*). The scandal accelerated his departure from office in October 1922. As for Maundy Gregory, he retired to Paris on a £2000 pension, widely interpreted as hush money, and died in mysterious circumstances in September 1941.

K

Abbreviation employed in private correspondence by former Alvin Stardust mentor Lord Levy, which some interpreted as a reference to knighthoods.

see *P*

Karadžic, Radovan
b. June 19th 1945

Having presided over the unambiguously criminal Bosnian-Serb regime in the 1990s, this genocidal brute (and bad poet) now tops The International War Crimes Tribunal's most wanted list. He's also a sometime acquaintance of John Reid MP (*qv*). In 1996 the *Sunday Times* alleged that a goodly portion of Conservative funding could be traced to Karadžic's businesses, flames fanned by the fact that Karadžic had once been escorted around London by pro-Serb sympathiser and prospective Tory candidate for Halesowen, John Kennedy. However, thanks to

Reid's undeclared three-day, five-star Lake Geneva hotel junket as Karadžic's guest in 1993, Labour will always remain as closely tied to him as the Tories. "He used to talk to Karadžic, he admired Karadžic," said Cambridge don and Bosnian historian Brendan Simms. "He mistook the Bosnian Serb project as the inheritor of the united Communist ideal."

see *Reid, John*

Keen, Alan
b. Nov 25th 1937
MP (Labour), Feltham & Heston, 1992-

Obscure 'McMP' who attracted a modicum of attention in May 2007 when it emerged that he'd signed an Early Day Motion aimed at persuading the *Oxford English Dictionary* to remove its definition of 'McJob'. His anger at the epithet – meaning low-paid, menial employment without prospects – was in no way connected to the generous hospitality offered to him by burger dealership McDonalds at the 2006 World Cup. "McJob is meant to be an insulting term," he railed to the press. "There is a lot of snobbery in much of the criticism of McDonalds, and I feel strongly about it." Other MPs who felt strongly about the matter included Clive Betts (*qv*) and Lib Dem John Leech, both of whom had also accepted World Cup treats from the chain. "This is not about McDonalds," insisted Leech, a former employee, "but the way its employees are labelled."

Kelly, Dr David
b. May 17th 1944 / d. July 17th 2003

Troubled boffin found dead on Harrowdown Hill, Oxon on July 17th 2003, shortly after he'd been named as the unreliable source used by Andrew Gilligan (*qv*) in his rash exposé of the 'Dodgy Dossier' (*qv*), on the strength of which the country had gone to war.

According to sources in the same British government which had chosen to employ him, Kelly wasn't so much a world expert in weapons of mass destruction (WMDs) as a deluded fantasist who should never have been let anywhere near a sensitive military document (see *Kelly, Tom*). His mistake had been to wander beyond his brief during his 'unattributed' chat with Gilligan (on the record, but anonymous) – this included his personal theory that Alastair Campbell was running the show, quoted as fact by Gilligan. In fact, Kelly was so surprised to hear the casual remark repeated that he told MoD bosses that he couldn't possibly have been the primary source on the story. He was the source, however, so everyone involved was done for – except the

government, of course. With his reputation so recently smeared, his death was assumed to be suicide, though he'd spent the morning of his death cheerily responding to emails of support. Conspiracy theorists like to point up signs of a state-sponsored assassination – Kelly had apparently told a diplomat four months earlier that if Britain invaded Iraq 'I will probably be found dead in the woods', and was also said to have mentioned 'dark actors playing games'.

All was smoothed over by Blair, however, when he announced on July 19th that Kelly's death had been 'an absolutely terrible tragedy', adding: "I'm profoundly saddened for David Kelly and for his family. He was a fine public servant who did an immense amount of good for his country in the past, and I'm sure would have done so again in the future… all of us, the politicians and the media alike, should show some respect and restraint. That's all I intend to say."

Kelly, Ruth
b. May 9th 1968
MP (Lab), Bolton West, 1997-

A staunch member of controversial Catholic sect Opus Dei, this throaty former economist has faced criticism both over her fitness to serve as a 'Minister for Equality' and Education Minister. She was absent from every government vote on equal gay rights since Labour came to power in 1997, causing scientists to fear she'd oppose vital stem cell research, and her decision to educate one of her children privately seemed to contradict her own policies. When asked on BBC Radio in May 2006 if she deemed homosexuality a sin, Kelly refused to answer directly, prompting activist Peter Tatchell to observe: "Tony Blair would never appoint someone to a race equality post who had a lukewarm record of opposing racism."

In fact, Kelly's record was lukewarm in several areas: as Secretary of State for Education she'd presided that January over a scandal where her department cleared registered sex offenders to work in schools. "This surely is a case of putting an alcoholic in charge of the bar," one complainant wrote to the *Times*. "Belonging to a religious organisation that holds extreme reactionary views invalidates this woman's objectivity. She should resign." It was a call she faced again in January 2007, when it emerged that she'd opted to send her son to a special private school – something Labour MP Ian Gibson called "a slap in the face for the teachers and pupils in the school the child has been taken out of". Kelly – who has the unusual distinction of having had four children since becoming an MP – commented: "It is not uncommon for pupils with substantial learning difficulties to spend some time outside the state sector to help them progress."

Kelly, Tom
b. 1955

One of Downing Street's oiliest spin merchants, this Prime Ministerial mouthpiece briefed journalists in August 2003 that Dr David Kelly was a bit of a 'Walter Mitty'.

No. 10's capacity to disgust us would seem positively boundless"

Kelly likened his unhappy namesake to the fictional daydreamer after admitting to No.10 Chief of Staff Jonathan Powell that he planned to 'tighten the screw' on the government's critics. The late Dr Kelly's outraged friends pointed out that if, as the government insisted, the weapons expert had never been to Downing Street, then a No.10 official was hardly in a position to make confident psychological assessments. "If he knew David Kelly, then he should have come out from under his stone and said so," stormed one. "If he didn't know him, then what on earth was he doing smearing him?" Double Oscar-winning Labour MP Glenda Jackson was equally unimpressed. "No.10's capacity to disgust us would seem positively boundless," she told the *Today* programme. "That this kind of smear tactic should be coming out of No.10 at this time is beneath contempt."

But the snide spokesman wasn't new to such criticism. Boasting methods Ian Paisley said made "Machiavelli look like a rank amateur", Kelly had claimed back in 2001 that BBC Middle East reporter Kate Adie had committed a major security breach and endangered Tony Blair's life by discussing his movements in a live breakfast interview. Adie successfully sought damages from the *Sun* for reprinting the allegations, and accused Kelly of "exacerbating the situation" by ensuring the reports would be reproduced across all media. More recently, he erroneously briefed lobby journalists that reports of Tony Blair's heart scare were "100% bullshit". It seems entirely fitting that in the wake of the David Kelly affair he was promoted to become Downing Street's chief spokesman, at a reported salary of £100,000.

SLEAZE

"I have only met Lord Archer on one occasion… He was worried about shaking hands with me, a retired villain, when the reality is I should have been worried about shaking hands with a practising scapegrace"

– 'Mad' Frankie Fraser, August 2001

SLOT

Kennedy, Charles
b. Nov 25th 1959
MP (Lib Dem), Ross, 1983-

A cheerful champion of the middle ground, 'chat-show Charlie' would perhaps occupy a fonder place in the hearts of the British electorate if he hadn't fibbed so consistently over the alcoholism many suspected was affecting his professional capabilities. Revelations from Anne Werrin, his aide and secretary of 20 years, that he'd ducked out of a planned press conference for confessing his problem as early as July 2003, do make certain public comments since that date smack of insincerity. On March 22nd 2004, for example, he told ITV news: "I certainly do not have a drink problem." Two days earlier he'd briefed the press that "alcohol is next to zero". A

week before Christmas 2005, he indignantly informed Jonathan Dimbleby: "I'm actually an extremely moderate and infrequent consumer of alcohol, as a matter of fact." Such bluster sat uneasily with his frequent parliamentary no-shows (a skived Commons debate on the Euro in June 2003, pulling a sickie for the 2004 Budget debate) and lapses in professionalism (being caught unprepared at the launch of his 2005 manifesto). It wasn't until January 5th 2006 that he decided to fess up – and even then only because ITN were planning a scoop about his recent clinical treatment. He stood down as Lib Dem Leader two days after the announcement, when he realised his lack of candour – despite numerous promptings both internal and public – had cost him his footsoldiers' respect.

He returned to the headlines on July 6th 2007, when he flouted the newly-imposed public smoking ban (which he'd backed in Parliament). Having boarded the 11:05 service from Paddington to Plymouth, he couldn't resist a cheeky gasper out of the window – and refused to extinguish it, despite the entreaties of fellow travellers. The train manager therefore summoned the British Transport Police, who persuaded him otherwise. It is not suggested he had availed himself of the trolley catering facilities on board before sparking up.

SLEAZE

"Remember Mary Archer in the witness box. Your vision of her probably will never disappear. Has she elegance? Has she fragrance? Would she have, without the strain of this trial, radiance? What is she like in physical features, in presentation, in appearance?'

– Mr. Justice Caulfield (qv) addresses the jury, 1987

SLOT

Kilroy-Silk, Robert
b. May 19th 1942
MP (Lab), Ormskirk, 1974-83 / Knowsley North, 1983-86
MEP (UKIP/Veritas), 2004-

Perma-bronzed smoothie with a solid record of penning inflammatory columns and losing his cool.

"They are backward and evil, and if it is racist to say so, then racist I must be"

In the 80s the tan-shop hardman's louche image made him a long-term target for the Militant Tendency (*qv*), who fought for over a decade to unseat him. He finally cracked when he allegedly right-hooked left-winger Jeremy Corbyn MP, though it was subsequently denied ('If I'd hit him, he'd have stayed down,' he bragged). He subsequently stood as Shadow Spokesman for Home Affairs, but left politics altogether in 1986 to present a vacuous chat show that afforded him ample opportunity to patronise the public. In 1991 he resorted to physical retaliation against a guest called John Edwards, who'd tapped him over the head with some documents, while his *Daily Express* column offered a gasket-blowing outlet for attacks on other races (HIV in the UK was the fault of 'the foreigners', the Irish were 'priests, peasants and pixies' and the Muslims 'suicide bombers, limb-amputators, women repressors'). His attacks on Islamic people were nothing if not consistent – "they are backward and evil, and if it is racist to say so, then racist I must be – and happy and proud to be so," he boasted on February 25th 1991, while on January 15th 1995 he raged, again in the *Express*, that "Moslems everywhere behave with equal savagery". He put the 'orgy of thieving' in Iraq in 2003 down to 'the character of the people', not the circumstances, and when another rant (positing that the Arabs had contributed zero to world culture) was republished in January 2004, it finally resulted in his sacking. This enabled 'Mr Tangerine Man' to focus full-time on Europhobia, getting involved with time-wasters UKIP before inevitably falling out and forming the still-sillier Veritas party (*qv*), giving a Cheshire man called David McGrath a chance to pour a bucket of slurry over his head 'in the name of Islam' on December 4th.

On the election trail in 2005 he mocked a voter who held his hand for too long by suggesting he was gay (in the same campaign he threatened to throttle a pensioner with his stick), while a water-squirting incident saw a furious Kilroy seeking to press charges, stating that his assailant had "smashed a bottle against the side of my head", which "could have caused serious injury" in a "violent attack". On this occasion TV crews were on hand to prove it was just a refreshing splash of H_2O. Kilroy's supporters still recognise him as a man of principle, however. They point to a political dinner party in the early 90s, when one guest supposedly made a racist remark. "Kilroy-Silk didn't say anything," said *World In Action* producer and witness David Jones. "He just got up and hit him."

King Rat

How amorous rodent Paul Marsden (*qv*) styled himself in email correspondence with crusading psychiatrist Rita Pal (*qv*).

see *Princess Rat*

Kinnock, Neil
b. March 28 1942
MP (Lab), Bedwelty, 1970-83 / Islwyn, 1983-1995

Long-time critic of the House of Lords who leapt at the offer of a life peerage on January 31st 2005. The ermine-trimmed taff, who dropped his toothless sinecure as an EU 'sleazebuster' to don the coveted robes, celebrated his new status by picking up a six-month driving ban in April 2006 (for repeat speeding offences in his wife Glenys's Audi A4). The flame-haired ex-firebrand claims he abandoned his old principles for 'practical political reasons', and it is anticipated that his career in the Lords will prove every bit as effective as his four-year stint eradicating corruption from European politics.

Knickergate

Term given to Labour liability Ron Brown's sozzled rampage around ex-lover Nonna Longden's Hastings flat on April 25th 1989.

When their three-year affair ended, the debt-riddled Longden was said to have demanded a cash pay-off from the turbulent MP, in exchange for not releasing 'politically sensitive' tape recordings. On the evening in question the pair had allegedly met to discuss the matter, along with Longden's new lover, straggle-bearded Oriental carpet swindler Dermot Redmond. According to Brown, trouble flared up when Redmond spotted two pairs of Longden's smalls in the Leith MP's pocket, and proceeded to trash the property. Both she and Redmond rejected this version of events at Brown's January 1990 trial. Longden furiously denied having planted the underwear, and was joined by her new beau in stating that it was Brown who'd gone 'berserk' while they were fetching the police, smashing mirrors and windows amongst other things. "Havoc rained around me," Brown told the police later that evening, his voice slurring. "Things were thrown. I was ducking and weaving. Wherever I went, he came after me. I was stunned by all the chaos. My glasses had been knocked off." He escaped with a £1000 fine, but was expelled from the party and deselected soon afterwards.

Krug & Shepherd's

Series of Christmas and conference parties held by Jeffrey Archer (*qv*), either in his Thameside penthouse or hotel suite, at which Cabinet ministers, newspaper editors, pundits, party donors, celebrities and even a few friends were served branded champagne and home-made shepherd's pie. When Archer was caged in 2001, his second son, disgraced city trader and chip off the old block James, assumed hostly duties – but few guests were available, and the tradition withered. Despite being *the* Tory invite of the 80s, several attendees have since maintained they only quaffed the perjuring peer's bubbly out of party duty – and the pie hasn't escaped censure, either. As Archer began his prison term in July 2001, *Observer* scribe Andrew Rawnsley vouched "I never touched so much as a forkful of his pie," while his shamed colleague Simon Hoggart (see *Quinn, Kimberly*) wrote: "It was important to get a proper meal and arrive after the shepherd's had finished."

Kurtha, Aziz

Businessman, former TV presenter and prostitute Monica Coghlan's third client on the evening of September 8th 1986. By naming Jeffrey Archer (*qv*) as the furtive fourth, he set in motion the Tory deputy chairman's downfall. The next day Kurtha concluded the easiest deal of his life – with the *News of the World*. Having relocated to Dubai, in 1999 he told the *Telegraph* he'd be willing to testify that an associate of Archer's calling himself Ali Mahmood had encouraged him to leave England at the time, promising he'd be 'looked after' if he did so.

L

Lamont, Norman

b. May 8th 1942
MP (Con), Kingston-upon-Thames,
1972-97

Bean-counting blunderer whose striking good looks were once compared by the *Guardian* to those of an 'overfed badger' (see *Davies, Ron*). Lamont's brushes with trouble were generally through unfortunate misunderstandings – the cannabis cake he scoffed by mistake as a young man, the black eye he sported in 1986 (allegedly inflicted by angry love rival Richard Connolly), the disputed bill for 'champagne and large breakfasts' at the Tory conference, the 'Threshergate' (*qv*) mix-up and the basement flat he unwittingly let to a call-girl in 1991 (see *Dale, Sara*). A still more unfortunate acquaintance was Augusto Pinochet (*qv*).

History is most likely, however, to associate Lamont's name with 'Black Wednesday' (*qv*), or September 16th 1992 – the most scandalous instance of Tory fiscal incompetence on record, in which he was ably assisted by a young David Cameron (*qv*). The result of this disastrous cock-up was UK financial meltdown (to the tune of £3.3bn) and the ruin of innumerable British businesses and individuals. The Chancellor's efforts to brazen it out were hardly spirit-of-the-blitz stuff – a story soon circulated that he was overheard singing in the bath that same evening and, after a careless press-conference quip in May 1993, legend now has it that the song was *Je Ne Regrette Rien*. In December of that year he appeared to hisses at the British Comedy Awards, an appearance chiefy remembered for Julian Clary's unlikely boast to have been 'fisting' him backstage. The *Times* claimed in 2005 that Lamont and John Major had used the Freedom of Information Act to hold up the release of papers relating to Black Wednesday – something both denied.

Kingston party members took out their frustration by ditching him in 1997, so Lamont went to embarrassingly public lengths to solicit a cosy new billet, eventually settling on Harrogate in Yorkshire. Being a long-time Londoner, however, the burly brock was seen as a shameless interloper in the Northern town, and local schoolteacher Phil Willis (*qv*) pinched the once-safe Tory seat for the Lib Dems. Lamont had to settle for becoming Lord Lamont of Lerwick instead, in which capacity he was arguably an even more vocal supporter of Pinochet than Thatcher was – though clearly not so well-known to the great man. After receiving a bottle of scotch from the big-hearted peer at Christmas, Pinochet is said to have asked hopefully: 'Is he a Law Lord?'. When not eulogising the Chilean brute's 'great contribution to freedom' or praising him for 'saving his country', Lamont beavers away as chairman of top-secret boys' club Le Cercle (*qv*). He's not above venturing from his sett, though: in August 2006 he told ePolitix.com that his former aide David Cameron 'has got to develop more policy... we do need more policies more quickly.'

SLEAZE

> "We will say to ourselves with pride: this is our Dome, Britain's Dome. And believe me, it will be the envy of the world"
>
> – *Tony Blair, speech at Royal Festival Hall, February 1998*

SLOT

Latimer, Clare
b. 1952

10 Downing St. caterer doomed to be remembered as the woman who *didn't* have an affair with John Major. Nonetheless, the story almost bankrupted two magazines (*Scallywag* and the *New Statesman*) in 1993, when Major decided to come down on the tittle-tattle like a ton of bricks.

"For two years after the story broke, my life was hell. John Major wrecked my life. I hope he's aware of it"

The ensuing press exposure succeeded in scotching the 'insolent undercurrent' suggesting Major might have played away (see *Currie, Edwina*), but many (including his real-life mistress) felt he'd treated Latimer very shabbily indeed. As Currie commented on the BBC in 2002: "My sympathies are still with Clare Latimer herself. I don't know her personally, but her business was wrecked... She was treated in an atrocious fashion."

Latimer, for her part, called Currie a 'brash extrovert' who 'tries to earn money out of everything she does', telling *Good Housekeeping* in 2004: "For two years after the story broke, my life was hell. That man wrecked my life. I hope he's aware of it." When news of the Currie affair broke in 2002, the magazines Major had earlier pursued reacted with fury, suggesting that their fate might have been very different had the PM's extra-marital form been known.

Law, Peter

b. April 1st 1948 / d. April 25th 2006

MP (independent), Blaenau Gwent, 2005-06

Former Labour councillor who stood against Labour at the 2005 General Election, and whose untimely death from a brain tumour was swiftly followed by allegations that he'd been offered a peerage not to oppose the party.

His grieving widow, Trish, told BBC Wales's *Dragon's Eye* ('the programme that dares to breathe fire into Welsh politics and public life'): "There was pressure put on him. He had quite a number of phone calls from high-ranking politicians not to do it, he would be silly to do it, there was no way that he would win." However, she added, her ailing husband "could not be bought."

Labour, needless to say, strenuously denied the allegation, which coincided neatly with the Cash for Honours affair (*qv*).

Legg, Barry

b.1949

MP (Con), Milton Keynes South West, 1992-97

Controversial Eurosceptic whose CV is summarised, even by the kindest observers, as 'something of a mixed bag'. As a Westminster councillor in the late 1980s, he was implicated in the machinations of Shirley Porter (*qv*), and though cleared of wilful misconduct in the 'homes for votes' scandal, he was heavily criticised for failing to blow the whistle. District Auditor John Magill's massive report concluded: "I find as fact that Councillor Legg knew that it was wrong for the Council to exercise its powers to secure an increase in the number of likely Conservative voters." Legg, it continued, had shirked his "duty to speak up." Still worse – though his memory fails him on this point – Council minutes have him chairing a meeting in February 1989 when the fateful decision was made to move 200 homeless Westminster families into high-rise blocks known to be insulated with asbestos. The families lived there for seven years without reprieve, a move subsequently condemned in a coruscating public inquiry.

Legg's business record was little better: as company secretary of food giant Hillsdown Holdings, he was involved in the decision to cream off an £18.4m surplus in their pension fund, condemned by the High Court as 'unjust and unauthorised'. Legg claims he was overruled when he suggested that a 'proportion' of the windfall should reach the people entitled to it – but he wasn't prepared to resign over it. His out-of-the-blue 'legg-up' from pal Iain Duncan Smith to become party Chief Executive in February 2003 provoked widespread astonishment – which turned to outrage when the BBC's *Today* programme prepared a damning dossier on his chequered career.

Not long after his promotion, the former Maastricht rebel was distancing himself from reports that he'd been meeting UKIP members, causing 'horrified' fellow Tory MP Derek Conway (*qv*) to storm: "I think he [Duncan Smith] allowed friendship to cloud his judgement, frankly. And I think that's wrong… it's a wrong appointment." Conway vowed that party members would not rest "as long as Barry Legg is Chief Executive," but they were soon back to a full night's sleep: 'Gammy' Legg was a lame duck.

Having lasted just three months in the role, he tendered his resignation following a 'strategic review' in early May – just before the humiliation of an emergency meeting convened to review his disastrous appointment.

Lehaney, 'Sir' Barry
b. 1943

Wheezy Ilford pensioner whose rampant online fantasy life – as chauffeur to non-existent swingers Lord James and Lady Joan Hamilton – prompted Nadine Milroy-Sloan (*qv*) to bring a false accusation of sexual assault against sleaze megastars Neil and Christine Hamilton (both *qv*) in 2001.

After encountering Lehaney – who'd awarded himself a knighthood – in a chatroom, Milroy-Sloan decided she'd stumbled upon an upper crust sex ring that would earn her a fortune. Acting on the advice of Max Clifford (*qv*), that May she boarded a bus from London to Essex to meet Lehaney, in the hope that he'd help her tape explicit conversations with the Hamiltons. Instead, she claimed, an orgy took place during which Christine Hamilton had sat on her face while Lehaney assaulted her. At Milroy-Sloan's subsequent trial for perverting the course of justice Lehaney admitted to having 'an extensive criminal record', as well as prompting sniggers by confessing to taking Viagra because he 'couldn't raise a gallop'. It was quickly established beyond doubt that the Hamiltons were nowhere near Ilford at the time, and that Lehaney couldn't have attacked her in the manner described – he was too arthritic.

By 2006 Lehaney had rebranded himself as something of a political commentator, popping up on talksport.com to say he found George Galloway (*qv*) 'anti-English and anti-semetic [*sic*]… I find his politics a great danger.'

Levy, Lord Michael
b. July 11th 1944

Having made millions from Alvin Stardust, Bad Manners and Chris Rea (who called him 'one of the hardest bastards I have ever met'), this spry salesman became New Labour's so-called 'Mr Cashpoint' at the 1997 Election and beyond, charged with handling loans and donations, including £1m from Bernie Ecclestone (*qv*) and thousands from Sir Christopher Evans (*qv*). He and Tony Blair apparently became 'like brothers' after meeting over dinner in 1994, and as the Premier's long-time tennis partner he is said to have challenged businessmen to a knock-up on the basis that 'Tony might just turn up'. He was made a life peer in 1997, though he hasn't condescended to address the Upper House since delivering his maiden speech that December.

On July 12th 2006 Levy was arrested by police investigating the 'Cash for Honours' (*qv*) allegations, following suggestions that he'd been bartering baubles for cash, and was released on bail after six hours' questioning.

On September 20th he was rearrested and again released on bail, maintaining all the while that he had done nothing wrong. January 30th 2007 saw his collar felt yet again, this time on suspicion of conspiracy to pervert the course of justice. To his unbounded relief, however, it was announced in July that he was not to be charged with any offence – and he made it clear that his fundraising efforts on behalf of the party would end when Blair left office.

Lewis, Ivan
b. March 4th 1967
MP (Lab), Bury South, 1997-

Ambitious family man and Health Minister who flew in the face of

Parliamentary tradition in 2006 by leaving his wife for an older woman – married local councillor Margaret Gibb. The move was especially bold given that Lewis, as chief executive of the Manchester Jewish Foundation, figured prominently in the tightly-knit local religious community. Even Gibb's dignified husband admitted the affair had become 'common knowledge' in the area, though Lewis maintained: "It won't affect my commitment and my sense of responsibility to make Bury South a better place."

Liddell, Helen

b. Dec 6th 1950
MP (Lab), Monklands East, 1994-97 / Airdrie & Shotts, 1997-2005

Former Secretary of State for Scotland, known locally as 'Attila the Hen' or 'Stalin's Granny'. The title that embarrassed her most, however, was 'personal aide to Robert Maxwell' (*qv*) – so much so that she told an interviewer in June 1994: "The truth is I have never worked for Robert Maxwell. It is a smear to suggest I was ever employed by him." This unequivocal claim sat awkwardly with the time she spent between 1988 and 1992 working for Maxwell at the *Daily Record* and *Sunday Mail* – and not just at the office. Personally recruited by 'the Bouncing Czech', she became his official companion at local Scottish jollies and business trips abroad,

and at one such function a BBC TV crew even filmed her briefly accompanying the pension-pilferer into the gents' (nothing unseemly transpired). Liddell – who also found time to write a bad novel, *The Elite*, in 1990 – became an MP upon the death of Labour leader John Smith, and swiftly earned a name for herself as a campaigner for her tireless efforts to have monastery-brewed tramp-fuel Buckfast Tonic Wine banned from sale. When she became Secretary of State for Scotland in 2001, her personal diligence came under scrutiny. Dubbed '*Minister for Monarch of the Glen*' after countless visits to the set of the Sunday night drama, she was criticised in 2002 when it emerged that private French lessons were being slotted into her less-than-packed ministerial diary, and the office was shut down for good in 2003. Liddell promptly accepted another cosy billet, as High Commissioner to Australia.

Livingstone, Ken

b. June 17th 1945
MP (Lab), Brent East 1987-2001
Mayor of London 2001-

Newt-fancying socialist and inaugural London Mayor, with a consistent record of failing to connect brain and mouth in public.

'Red Ken' first marked his card whilst working for Camden Council at the fag-end of the 1970s, by authorising the settlement of a local government strike by offering higher pay – a move later ruled illegal by the District Auditor. He courted further controversy as leader of the Greater London Council in December 1982, when he invited Sinn Fein terrorists Gerry Adams and Danny Morrison over as official guests. The distasteful duo were denied entry to England under the Prevention Of Terrorism Act, so Livingstone had to go to Northern Ireland to visit them instead. When Adams was elected to Parliament in 1983, Livingstone promptly stated that the history of British policy in Ireland compared unfavourably to Hitler's policy regarding the Jews.

"If they're not happy here, they can go back to Iran and try their luck with the Ayatollahs"

Having reneged on an earlier pledge not to run as an independent if not given Labour's official nomination, he was expelled from the party on April 4th 2000 (and readmitted in late 2003). In March 2002 he was accused of constructing his own 'secret Cabinet' by appointing six cronies to highly-salaried jobs as 'special advisers', including PR and media communications posts. Two months later, in the early hours of May 19th, Livingstone was seen brawling in the street with Robin Hedges, a friend of his partner Emma Beal, at her sister's

birthday party. The *Evening Standard* suggested in June that the well-oiled Mayor had fled representatives of his own London constabulary after thrusting Hedges down some steps and manhandling Beal, who was pregnant with their first child. A Standards Board inquiry failed to establish exactly what had happened, due to considerable disagreement in the witnesses' recollection of events: Beal backed Ken up and denied that he'd manhandled her, and the board ruled in his favour 'on the balance of probabilities'.

The hated Congestion Charge, widely seen as a stealth tax on motorists, was instituted in February 2003 and aroused virulent feelings against him amongst London drivers. In April 2004 he was back in trouble for expressing his desire to see the Saudi Royal family 'swinging from lamposts', and in July he was criticised for hugging controversial cleric Yusuf al-Qaradawi, whom the BBC reported 'has been criticised for condoning suicide bombings and having anti-Semitic and homophobic views.' But the gaffe that would cause him greatest trouble occurred in February 2005, when he tipsily likened *Evening Standard* hack Oliver Finegold to a 'German war criminal' and a 'concentration camp guard' for taking orders from Associated Newspapers. Livingstone hated the newspaper group "because of its past record of pre-war support for anti-Semitism and Nazism", despite penning his own well-paid restaurant column for *ES Magazine*. Upon realising that Finegold was Jewish, he persisted with his remarks, in a manner that the Adjudication Panel for England deemed 'unnecessarily offensive'. Panel Chairman David Laverick pointed out that the investigation had been prompted by the Mayor's ongoing refusal to apologise for what the London Jewish Forum called 'the pain caused to so many Jewish Londoners who have been affected by the Holocaust' – but Livingstone was firm in his contention that "this decision strikes at the heart of democracy." He was found guilty of bringing his office into disrepute and handed down a four week suspension. He promptly appealed to the High Court, where in a less-than-ringing endorsement the judge decided that the Mayor had not been acting 'in his official capacity' when he made the admittedly 'offensive' and 'indefensible' remarks. His suspension was quashed and the Standards Board was ordered to pay his costs, on the grounds that the Adjudication Panel had misdirected itself – but no one disputed that his original comments had been unacceptable.

In March 2006 he faced fresh accusations of anti-Semitism following a press conference at which he was alleged to have insulted the Reuben brothers, a pair of Indian-born British businessmen (of Iraqi-Jewish descent) involved in a property development for the 2012 London Olympics. He is reported to have said: "If they're not happy here here they can go back to Iran and try their luck with the Ayatollahs if they don't like the planning regime or my approach."

True to form, once cleared of misconduct he resolutely declined to apologise, despite calls both from the press and his colleagues, and proceeded to compare Brian Coleman (a Tory delegate to the GLA) to club-footed Nazi PR boss Josef Goebbels. Yet his own department's prodigious city-wide propaganda – branding him 'Mayor of Lond-ON' and the like – would have done the Third Reich's publicity machine proud.

Lobbygate

Alternate name for the storm in a teacup that was 1998's 'Cash for Access' affair.

see *Draper, Derek*

London Olympics

Ruinously expensive exercise in guaranteeing sporting humiliation will occur on home soil in 2012. Cost estimates for the glorified PE tournament have ballooned since the Olympic Board was handed a figure of £2.3bn in July 2005. In November 2006 Culture Secretary Tessa Jowell (*qv*) announced that the figure had been hiked by a billion, and two months later an all-party Select Committee placed the likely tally as high as £8bn. By March 2007 Jowell had announced that the figure was £9.35 bn. "There will always be pessimists who claim every setback is a catastrophe," roared Tony Blair in the *Guardian* that January, going on to baffle readers with talk of 'reducing the carbon footprint' by using unspecified 'sustainable building methods'.

London Mayor Ken Livingstone (*qv*) was quick to reassure the public too, stating on the *Today* programme in November 2006: "Nothing is a mess, everything is going exactly according to plan." Not everyone was as bullish. "It is inexcusable that the Government failed to budget accurately for VAT and contingency, or make a proper estimate of security costs," huffed Shadow Sports Minister Hugh Robertson in January 2007. "I fear that other good causes will pay for their financial incompetence." His fears appeared to be confirmed when it emerged in April that lottery funds earmarked for the arts would be diverted to shore up the Olympics. Jowell was quick as ever to defend the decision, stating: "The Olympics will provide an opportunity like no other to showcase not just sports, but also arts and culture. The investment is not just in sport and the regeneration of east London, but also in the cultural Olympiad."

Whether the inevitable future funding shortfalls will be covered by Londoners' council rates, taxpayers nationwide or lottery cash originally earmarked for charities, all will doubtless be forgiven when a British mixed pair scoop the bronze in badminton.

see *Millennium Dome, the*

WIGGINGS

"I have come to the clearest possible conclusion that Mr Allason has told me untruth after untruth in pursuit of this claim"

– *Mr Justice Laddie on Rupert Allason, 2001*

FROM THE BEAK

London Oratory

Selective, voluntary-aided London comprehensive school which opted out of local education authority control (under a policy opposed by the Labour Party), but to which Tony Blair opted to send his three older children, instead of the local school near their family home in Islington. "Any parent wants the best for their children," he explained to the Commons in December 1994. "I am not going to make a choice for my child on the basis of what is the politically correct thing to do."

Lord's

Venerable institution presided over by the MCC and beloved of cricket buffs such as Jeffrey Archer (*qv*). Following his perjury conviction its respected committee, including John Major (*qv*), voted decisively in 2002 to ban the peer for seven years – thereby denying him his coveted seat in its famous Long Room.

Not to be confused with another ancient institution, which lacked the authority to prevent Archer from resuming his seat on release from jail.

Lucy

David Blunkett's guide dog between 1994 and 2003, and half-sister to her successor Sadie (*qv*). Though untainted by the former Cabinet Minister's darkest days of sleaze, the black labrador displayed a similar tenacity in the face of public disgrace: she clung to her position for four years after eloquently vomiting in the Commons during a speech by the opposition's David Willetts (*qv*).

Mack, Paul
b. 1957

Former Renfrew councillor with a conviction for assaulting a girlfriend (with a video camera, she said), who was also named by peers as the 'common denominator' in the 'web of intrigue' at Labour's Scottish stronghold of Paisley (*qv*) – a story embracing electoral malpractice, a long-running feud and an MP's suicide.

Mack 'The Knife' was a constant thorn in his party's side after his suspension in 1995, for breaking election rules by standing unofficially. He became so animated in the council chamber that he was ordered from it on ten separate occasions, even requiring a police escort. Mack maintains that the 'quasi-masonic' Labour council group, of which he had been deputy leader, undemocratically blocked any and all points of order raised by other parties. He was embroiled in the 1997 demise of Gordon McMaster (*qv*), and roasted along with Tommy 'Golden' Graham (*qv*) in the former's suicide note – seemingly for rumouring that McMaster was gay and dying of AIDS. Graham was quick to lay the blame for the smear at Mack's door, despite allegedly owing him numerous political favours dating from his selection in 1987. Mack, whilst conceding he'd called McMaster 'spineless and treacherous', in turn blamed Paisley North MP Irene Adams (*qv*) for going public with the whispers. The egregious councillor admitted he'd briefed journalists just before the 1997 General Election, but added cruelly: "It would strike me as slightly improbable, given the fact it would be the first case in medical history where the AIDS victim actually put on weight" (McMaster was 18 stone when he died, just a shade lighter than the 20-stone Graham).

Mack, who now refers to Paisley as 'A Town Called Malice', had a failed shot at becoming an MP in 1999. His campaign literature read: "I have one major flaw; justice is written across my heart." In an August 1997 interview with Scotland's *Daily Record*, his battered ex, Catherine Mackin, took a different view : "He was a total nutcase, a real Jekyll and Hyde character... He is power crazy. He's a nut job. He belongs in a zoo."

SLEAZE

> "The green belt is a Labour achievement, and we intend to build upon it"
>
> – *John Prescott, 1998*

SLOT

MacNeil, Angus
b. July 21st 1970
MP (SNP), Na h-Eileanan an Iar, 2005-

Hebridean Cash For Honours whistleblower who became the subject of unwelcome scrutiny himself when Glasgow's *Sunday Mail* revealed in April 2007 that he'd enjoyed what was described as a 'drunken romp' with a pair of teenagers from a Celtic girl band (one was 17, one 18) as his heavily pregnant wife rested at home. "It was a lapse of judgement two years ago, for which I am sorry," squirmed MacNeil, gleefully described by the *Times* as an 'anti-sleaze champion… the last MP anyone might have expected to be tainted by personal scandal'.

The native Gaelic speaker – whose formal complaint to police in March 2006 had triggered a police investigation into suspected abuse of the honours system – elaborated thus: "Some foolishness took place at a post-ceilidh party, which was wrong and stupid. There is no allegation that anything further

happened, and I wish to make that absolutely clear." One of the multi-instrumentalists involved, Judie Morrison (daughter of a Church of Scotland minister), confirmed: "He was excited, but we did not have full sex – we were all too drunk."

see *Teine*

Major, John
b. March 9th 1943
MP (Con), Huntingdon, 1983-2001

Master and Commander of the Mother of Sleaze Parliaments, John Major's defining moment came with the catastrophic sloganeering of 1993's 'Back To Basics' initiative (*qv*), a ludicrous call for a return to core family values that triggered an unprecedented public unravelling of his administration (see *Clifford, Max / Hayes, Jerry / Mellor, David / Merchant, Piers / Milligan, Stephen / Yeo, Tim* etc). Throughout, Major managed to project the image of a harmless drip unable to control his degenerate subordinates – but the 2002 revelation of his own affair with publicity-seeking missile Edwina Currie (*qv*) exploded his credibility once and for all.

The son of a travelling showman turned garden-gnome maker, the future PM was academically undistinguished and was rejected for a job as a bus conductor before working as an insurance clerk and banker. His political awakening is frequently credited to the influence of Jean Kierans, a divorcée 13 years his senior, with whom he enjoyed an affair for much of the 1960s ("we were so very passionate and he was wonderful in bed", she later reminisced). In 1968 he was elected to Lambeth council, and – having failed in his first crack at Parliament in 1974 – romped home for safe-as-houses Huntingdon in 1979, beginning his remarkable ascent. After stints as Foreign Secretary and Chancellor, Major assumed Margaret Thatcher's mantle in November 1990, having fatefully won her around to joining the ERM as Chancellor. He seemed a spotless candidate – an 'honest, decent man' in the words of Paddy Ashdown (*qv*) – and an antidote to the sneaks who'd knifed Thatcher. Major had in fact systematically cheated on his sainted wife Norma with Currie during his rise to prominence (1984-88), something only revealed in the one-time junior health minister's numbing journals (see *Dirty Diary, the*). Currie was openly nostalgic for Major's manly physique, but his recollections were less rosy. "It is the one event in my life of which I am most ashamed," he declared shortly after she published in September 2002. Even the loyal Sir Bernard Ingham (*qv*) conceded the affair would have smacked of 'utter hypocrisy' in the political climate of the time, and former chief whip Michael Brown (*qv*) – himself no stranger to sleaze – fumed: "Had we known about it, Major would never have been Prime Minister. History has been changed in Major's favour by Edwina keeping her trap shut for so long."

Hypocrisy was another value Major embodied: in 1993 he won a libel case against the *New Statesman* and *Scallywag* magazine over a rumoured affair with Downing Street's caterer, Clare Latimer (*qv*). The gossip was false; but he went to some lengths to imply talk of his adultery 'had no basis in truth'. "Such was the atmosphere at the time that I judged that if I took no notice of the story, it would echo around from magazines to the serious pages of newspapers," he pompously wrote in his gruelling memoirs, *John Major: The Autobiography*. "I was not prepared to put Norma, Clare

Latimer, my children or myself at risk in this way." Latimer's take was rather different – she told *Good Housekeeping* in 2004: "I believe I was used as a decoy. It was convenient for John Major that the press turned their attention towards me, instead of discovering the real identity of his mistress." Teresa Gorman (*qv*) also claims Major made a pass at her while Prime Minister, though possibly only in a desperate bid to get her to vote with him on Maastricht. "He would come up behind you, put his arm round your waist or on your shoulder," she tutted. "He was more like Cecil Parkinson than you think."

"Had we known about it, Major would never have been Prime Minister"

The future Premier was discreetly referred to as 'B' throughout Currie's smutty memoirs, prompting rife speculation as to what the letter might stand for. Until then, the only B-word associated with Major had been 'Bastards' (*qv*), the term he'd been overheard using in July 1993 to describe three Cabinet ministers (Michael Portillo, Peter Lilley and Michael Howard) who were holding him to ransom over the Maastricht Treaty. Amazingly, it was this outburst that seemed to tarnish Major's 'nice guy' image, rather than the near-treason of the

'Arms to Iraq' affair (*qv*): this had first emerged the previous year, and the 1996 Scott Report (*qv*) would show his government to be rotten to the core (see *Arms to Iraq / Matrix Churchill / Project Babylon / Supergun*, etc). Despite a self-imposed leadership challenge in 1995, which he survived due to a lack of any credible opponents (see *Redwood, John*), Major reeled on to steer his party to a record defeat in 1997 (Labour won 418 seats, the Tories 165). He then stepped down, muttering through gritted teeth: "When the curtain falls, it is time to get off the stage." There would be no encore for the tomato-spattered leading man; and, perhaps out of some belated sense of penance, he has yet to accept the traditional peerage offered to ex-PMs. It has been suggested that this is because he's holding out to be made a Knight Of The Garter – but his affair with Currie may well have scotched any such hope.

Mandelson, Peter

MP (Lab), Hartlepool, 1992-2004
b. Oct. 21st 1953

Slippery architect of New Labour who was once Minister Without Portfolio' and twice Minister without job. Despite a string of lapses in judgement, however, the scheming fixer kept making comebacks to Blair's government

– until public pressure finally put paid to his lucky streak. As moral crusader Max Clifford commented: "The public views him as slimy, and he has only himself to blame."

After flirting with Communism as a student in the early 70s, Mandelson worked for the TUC and the British Youth Council before moving to LWT in 1982. There he was able to refine the genius for style over substance that was to sustain him as Labour's 'Director of Campaigns and Communications' from 1985. In 1990 the high-living bachelor became a candidate for the safe seat of Hartlepool, where urban legend has him pointing to a tray of mushy peas in a fish and chip shop and asking for guacamole. He won the seat in 1992, but his machinating personality did little to endear him to his parliamentary colleagues, with the crucial exception of Tony Blair. Indeed, Mandelson's decision to back Blair's leadership bid following John Smith's 1994 heart attack is said to have angered Smith's other protégé, Gordon Brown, who – as usual – felt betrayed.

Having masterminded the sound and fury of the 1997 landslide – with responsibilities ranging from electoral strategy to Tony's wardrobe (see *Disappointing Diary, the*) – Mandelson spent a few months as Minister Without Portfolio before landing his first high-profile government job: overseeing the wretched Millennium Dome (*qv*), in the face of almost universal Cabinet opposition. His unpopularity was reflected in his struggle to get onto the national executive, and John Prescott struck a chord with many in August 1997 when he compared him to a crab. Few tears were shed among the voters when the *Guardian* revealed in December 1998 that he'd avoided a small fortune in interest payments by accepting a free loan of £373,000 in 1996 from fellow MP and businessman Geoffrey Robinson (*qv*) to put towards a pad in trendy Notting Hill – though both he and Alastair Campbell are said to have blubbed openly when push came to sack over the sleazy deal. Given that Robinson's dealings were supposedly the subject of an investigation by the DTI at the time – and that Mandelson was heading up the very same Department – the question of a conflict of interests arose too. Mandelson, needless to say, had not declared the loan in the

Register Of Members' Interests, or seen fit to mention it to the mortgage company. In the face of intense press criticism he resigned on December 23rd 1998, commenting in his letter of resignation to the Prime Minister: 'I do not believe that I have done anything wrong or improper. But I should not, with all candour, have entered into the arrangement'.

Most assumed that his ministerial career was over – but his old pal Tony hadn't forgotten him, and a mere ten months later he was reinstated as Secretary of State for Northern Ireland (or 'Ireland', as Mandelson clumsily put it in his inaugural address in October 1999). He managed to avoid scandal for just over a year, but in January 2001 it all fell apart again when the *Observer* suggested he'd put a call through to Home Office minister Mike O'Brien on behalf of billionaire Srichand Hinduja (*qv*). At the time Hinduja was seeking British citizenship, and was also under investigation back home, for his role in the Bofors scandal (*qv*). As the Hinduja cartel had been surprisingly keen to sponsor 'the Faith Zone' at the Millennium Dome (which they eventually did, to the tune of £1m), this didn't look good. And quite how they decided Mandelson's pet project was a credible overseas investment opportunity has never been revealed either.

Had Sir Anthony Hammond been able to deliver his whitewash report before January 2001, it might have saved the reluctant Northern Ireland Secretary's skin – but instead, Mandelson received his second government P45, protesting all the while that he had done nothing wrong. "I have been unable to come to any definite conclusion about the suggestion that Mr Mandelson wanted his contact with Mr O'Brien kept private," concluded the otherwise generous-to-a-fault Sir Anthony a couple of months later. He also suggested, however, that: "It is not difficult to see how the *Observer* article, combined with Mr Mandelson's omission to mention the conversation with Mr Straw, may have given the impression that he had not given an honest account of his role."

In his own mind at least, Mandelson was vindicated that summer when he was re-elected in Hartlepool, seeing off anti-sleaze candidates including mining minnie Arthur Scargill. Thrilled with his success, he seized the opportunity to big himself up in front of a live television audience, paying moving tribute to his own 'inner steel' and smugly asserting: "I am a fighter, not a quitter!" This was, of course, perfectly true: neither of his high-profile resignations had been voluntary. His ambitions to return to the Cabinet were met coolly by his colleagues and in 2004 he resigned his seat in order to sidle under his current rock: a European Trade Commission sinecure in Brussels, where he has been lurking almost tax-free ever since.

Mariam's Appeal

Fund set up by George Galloway (*qv*) in 1998, ostensibly for the purpose of flying 4-year-old Iraqi orphan Mariam Hamza (no relation of 'hook-handed preacher of hate' Abu) to Britain for an operation. Despite appearances, however, Mariam's Appeal was never officially registered as a charity: it raised funds using the leukaemia-stricken orphan as its tragic symbol, but did so as a political pressure group. "It is not a charity," admitted Galloway, who would attach a postcard of Mariam to all his requests for money. "It is a political campaign, and it always has been."

The idea was to lobby for Iraqi trade sanctions to be lifted by using Mariam as a symbol of human suffering in Iraq. "The appeal's target is £100,000," he wrote to donors on Commons notepaper, "with the balance being sent back to Iraq in medicines and medical supplies for the children she has had to leave behind." Galloway could, and did, argue that it was not unusual for campaign managers to use campaign funds to cover their own expenses; he was thus unruffled by claims he'd raided the coffers for his own cigars, luxury hotels and first-class travel on regular trips to the Middle East (14 of them registered in total between September 1999 and January 2002, encompassing Jordan, the United Arab Emirates, Lebanon and Iraq). No accusations of misuse were therefore upheld. However, the first year-long inquiry by the Charities Commission, published in June 2004, did find that, because it was raising funds on the back of charitable work, Mariam's Appeal should properly have been registered as a charity. The report also noted that the Commission had been 'unable to obtain all the books and records of the Appeal', and that 'Mr Galloway confirmed that the Appeal did not produce annual profit and loss accounts or balance sheets'. His lack of helpfulness would later be cited again in a Commons inquiry.

The Appeal was 'exhaustively investigated' – Galloway's words – amidst stories that funds were being diverted to pay his wife and driver. In the end, Galloway admitted receiving hundreds of thousands of pounds from one Jordanian businessman alone (see *Zuraiqat, Fawaz*), and to having spent £800k of the Appeal's money on political campaigns and expenses, rather than on Mariam and her fellow invalids. By April 2003, according to the *Daily Telegraph*, it had even stopped giving its £65 a week to the child. But the *Telegraph* lost a substantial libel claim over the body of their accusations, based as they were on unreliable documents (see *Oil for Food*).

The US Senate's 2005 investigation of the Oil-for-Food affair picked up the scent. "Galloway may have used the charitable organisation to conceal payments he had received from the Hussein regime," it proposed, using letters provided by the Iraqi state.

"Galloway may have used the charitable organisation to conceal payments from the Hussein regime"

Galloway insisted he had never personally profited, adding he'd never heard of the company linking the Appeal and the Oil-For-Food scheme in the documents. But one name there was the fund's major donor, Fawaz Zuraiqat – whom Galloway had made Appeal chairman in 2001, and had most certainly heard of. When the Standards and Privileges Committee finally published their findings in July 2007, damning his 'connivance' in accepting funds which had almost certainly stemmed from Oil-for-Food, he admitted he'd never enquired where the money was coming from. "Mr Galloway has consistently denied, prevaricated and fudged in relation to the now undeniable evidence that the Mariam Appeal, and he indirectly through it, received money derived, via the Oil For Food programme, from the Iraqi regime," slammed the report, whilst accepting he had not benefited personally.

Marlow, Tony
b. June 17th 1940
MP (Con), Northampton North, 1979-97

Hard-right former army captain and flogging fanatic who favoured family values and fornication in equal measure. His other interests ranged from farming to fascism – fellow MP Paul Flynn remembers a cosy chat with Marlow on the way to a 1988 meeting, when: "He told me that Nazism is a defensible philosophy... He spent most of his time at the meeting doodling swastikas on a notepad." In 1994 the hardliner called for Radio 4's *Women's Hour* presenter Jenni Murray to be sacked for her anti-traditionalist views on marriage, accusing the BBC's 'self-declared feminist' of having 'an unrepresentative lifestyle' for one in her position. Marlow had evidently forgotten that his own lifestyle was not strictly conventional: he was dividing his time between two families and nine children (five by his wife, four by his mistress).

The following year he consolidated his status as a national figure of fun by standing alongside John Redwood during his hopeless 'leadership challenge', confusing TV sets up and down the country with a deafeningly loud striped blazer. He then dedicated himself to protecting the rights of handgun owners in the light of the 1996 Dunblane shootings, and one of his last acts before losing his seat was to table a January 1997 amendment proposing the reintroduction of caning without parental consent – a concept described by opposition spokesman Peter Kilfoyle as 'State-sanctioned assault on children'. He has been no stranger to opprobrium since leaving the House, either: in 2001 a hundred local farmers marched on his garden in protest, after landowner Marlow embarked on a GM experiment which endangered the organic crop status of neighbouring fields.

Marsden, Paul
b. March 18th 1968
MP (Lab / Lib Dem), Shrewsbury & Atcham, 1997-2005

Floor-crossing former sewage engineer whose decision to publish some startlingly bad erotic verse (*'Then that smile so devastating in its might / Tongue rippling across teeth so white / Breasts rising as I feel the urge to bite…'*) on his website in 2003 led to a flurry of claims about his personal life, not all of which were welcomed by his seriously unwell wife, Shelly.

The pitiful MP admitted to two affairs, one with his Commons researcher Fiona Pinto, 24, and another with an unnamed BBC political reporter, and was accused of making advances to other Lib Dem employees ("Whips were aware of Marsden's advances to a number of researchers, and have dealt with it," growled a party source). That December things flared up again with psychiatrist Rita Pal's allegation in Birmingham's *Sunday Mercury* that Marsden (styling himself 'King Rat') had sent her ('Princess Rat') a flurry of seedy emails.

"I'm just a weak, flawed man with a very high sex drive"

Pal had contacted him shortly after his defection to the Lib Dems in December 2001, when he pledged to assist her crusade to improve NHS care for the elderly. By April 2002 he'd upped the ante, allegedly writing to her 'You do know what you have missed? Us making love all night on a bed strewn with rose petals,' adding: 'I'm just a weak, flawed man with a very high sex drive.' Pal went on to allege that Marsden had masturbated whilst on the telephone to her ('To my utter amazement he did what he needed to do, and then promptly fell asleep on the phone, leaving me flabbergasted'). When her claims broke in November 2003, Marsden responded with the words 'I can totally and utterly deny this', but undermined his position by bragging to the *Sunday Times*: "Westminster is fabulous if you want to wine and dine someone. It's easy to sweep someone off their feet." Such charms were lost on Sandra Gidley, the Lib Dems' spokesman for women's affairs. Branding him 'devious', she added that the mystery BBC mistress "must be someone with no taste… He certainly doesn't do it for me."

"He is a ratty little weasel, a serial womaniser, a serial liar and he is not fit for public office"

Soon afterwards Shelly's first husband, roofing manager Jim Bayley, gave both barrels to Marsden – whom he'd met in 1990 – in an interview with the *Sunday Mirror*. "He seemed like a normal lad, although he was a bit of a wimp," he railed. "I had no idea that they were having an affair. I should have realised what was going on after she took him in as a lodger… He is a ratty little weasel, a serial womaniser, a serial liar and he is not fit for public office." The article also reported Marsden's surprising claim that Westminster was 'full of coke-snorting, alcohol-soaked, totty-chasing MPs'. Shelly was quick to reassure the public about the home front, though. "Yes, we have made love in the past few weeks," she told the *Daily Mail*. "Paul has always promised me he hasn't had full sex with these women… He told me their relationship had been sexual, but not full penetrative sex."

Infuriated by Marsden's defection, his local Labour party sued him for failing to keep up payments on computer equipment he was renting from them, and in December 2003 he was ordered to pay them £900. By July 2004 he'd had enough, and announced to widespread indifference that he wouldn't be standing at the next Election. If the news was intended to deflect further sleaze allegations, he was being optimistic: in November it emerged that his children's nanny, Sophie Richards, had been paid out of public funds to act as his researcher for six months. Constituency sources had no recollection of seeing her in his office, and the claims echoed existing complaints about payouts totalling up to £30,000 made to Shelly for secretarial work. In April 2005 Marsden sparked further apathy when he announced his intention to rejoin Labour, a decision Mark Oaten (*qv*) called 'slightly bizarre', adding: "He has not been around in Parliament now for six months or so."

On December 18th that year

Marsden returned to public attention when the *Mail On Sunday* ran an article by him about party leader Charles Kennedy's drink problem – something the Lib Dem boss had yet to fess up to. Perhaps Kennedy was also the subject of another substandard poem, entitled 'Demon Drink': '*Get life's buzz through sport / Don't be fooled by alcohol's draw / Otherwise another binge ends up in court / Stop and think, every island has its shore*'. Either way, Kennedy wasn't the only senior MP to suffer at the point of Marsden's restless quill – another effusion, 'Thirty Minutes', was aimed at Tony Blair: '*Tony knows the game is up / A string of figures refutes the cost / And a roar of approval follows the witty riposte.*' Indeed, with his political career well and truly over, he could still find solace in his literary abilities. "I'm not ashamed of my poetry," he told the *Independent on Sunday* that May. "If I was a French politician, people would probably admire me for it." The claim would perhaps apply more convincingly to other aspects of his career.

Marsh, Jodie

b. Dec 22nd 1978

Bottle-blonde bombsite and *Celebrity Big Brother* outcast (see *Galloway, George*) whose 2006 appointment as a representative of charity BeatBullying prompted Lib Dem Education Spokesman Phil Willis to ask Schools Minister Jacqui Smith on March 24th "if she will take steps to deny Jodie Marsh access to schools for which her Department is responsible."

"A fit girl with her own money, a sense of humour to die for, the brain of a scientist, the kindness of a saint and who can shag like a porn star"

Smith was swift to reassure the nation that Marsh – who describes herself on her website as 'a fit girl with her own money, a sense of humour to die for, the brain of a scientist, the kindness of a saint and who can shag like a porn star' – "does not represent the Department for Education and Skills in any way." Essex-born Marsh, memorably accused by Jordan (*qv*) of having 'a nose like a builder's elbow', riposted on her blog that Willis 'knows that if he starts a public war with an already famous person he can suddenly be in all the papers and magazines, and hey presto – overnight fame.'

RED HOT

"If we weren't meant to enjoy sex, God wouldn't have given us the dangly bits that get us turned on"

- Edwina Currie, quoted in the Sunday Mirror, September 2002

CURRIE

Mates, Michael
b. June 9th 1934
MP (Con), Petersfield, 1974-83 /
East Hampshire, 1983-

Caterpillar-browed blue who led the Tory rebellion over the Poll Tax (*qv*) and played a key role in toppling Margaret Thatcher, but had to go when his links to Polly Peck poltroon Asil Nadir (*qv*) became explicit. The portly Lt. Colonel first attracted accusations of sleaze in 1989, when his colleagues Jonathan Aitken and Alan Clark (both *qv*) tipped off his Labour opponents about a conflict of interests. This arose from Mates's accepting commercial interests in the defence sector (chiefly for arms contractors Link-Miles) whilst sitting on the Defence Select Committee throughout the late 80s. The double-dealing duo were motivated by revenge, following Mates's support of Michael Heseltine against Thatcher, but he was unfussed by their efforts: he still declined to declare his defence interests, and indeed went on to accrue others.

It wasn't until the end of May 1993 that he was to earn sleaze immortality, however, by gifting a watch to Asil Nadir which bore the immortal inscription 'Don't let the buggers get you down'. Quite whom he was referring to was unclear (the press? the police? Nadir's creditors? the serious fraud office?), but he reluctantly stood down from government on June 24th 1993 after he'd been spotted dining with a Nadir aide at the Reform Club. He vigorously maintained that he had done nothing wrong ("it was a misjudgement, but it is not a hanging offence"), and later stated that he believed Nadir was the victim of a plot by the security services. The claim could not be heard in open court, however: three days after receiving the watch Nadir jumped bail and fled to Cyprus. It is not known whether the two have kept up their friendship.

Matrix Churchill

Coventry-based aerospace firm acquired on October 23rd 1987 by an Iraqi company with designs on its longstanding weapons expertise. Because two of Matrix Churchill's senior officials were providing information to MI6, the Ministry of Defence became privy to a great deal of Iraq's secret military procurement activities over the next three years, including the dreaded Supergun (*qv*) device: nevertheless the British government decided to rubber-stamp most of Matrix Churchill's sales (see *Arms to Iraq*). Advice was even trotted out on how to deal with customs regulations and gain export licences.

After the 1990 Gulf War questions were unsurprisingly asked about the company that had helped tool up Britain's enemy, and in 1991 the government duly organised what some cynics saw as a show trial for four Matrix Churchill directors. One of them, Paul Henderson, claimed he was following specific government policy, disclosed to him but not to Parliament. However, 'in the interests of national security' Kenneth Clarke (*qv*) signed an immunity certificate enabling MI6 to keep mum about anything they didn't want to reveal. Nevertheless, the trial collapsed when former defence minister Alan Clark (*qv*) admitted under oath that he had been "economical with the actualité" over policy on arms exports to Iraq. The comment prompted an outcry and, in time, the 1996 Scott Report (*qv*) that helped bring down Major's government.

That might have occurred five years earlier if the trial hadn't been put into motion the moment questions were asked, conveniently ensuring that much of the damning information was *sub judice* until after the 1992 Election. The feeble case against the four men the government had offered up as traitors was dropped, since their defence was able to show that they were only acting under orders.

Maxton, John
b. May 5th 1936
MP (Lab), Glasgow Cathcart, 1979-2001

Proud dad accused alongside John Reid (*qv*) during a 2000-01 investigation into misuse of parliamentary funds. Maxton had taken Reid's lead by employing his own son, Jamie, on party business – but, as it seemed, on public money. As the inquiry unfolded, rumours abounded that witnesses were coming under undue pressure from the MPs involved, and tough guy Maxton – though ultimately not convicted of wrongdoing – was required to apologise for his bellicose manner during the investigation. Sleaze hawk Elizabeth Filkin (*qv*) remained convinced that she'd been right to pursue the pair, and there were efforts to reopen the case to force Maxton to testify under oath; but it was ultimately decided not to act on her recommendations, especially once her prey had stood down in 2001 to enjoy the rest of his days as Baron Maxton of Blackwaterfoot.

Maxwell, Robert
b. June 10th, 1923 / d. Nov 5th 1991
MP (Lab), Buckingham, 1964-70

Obese, pension-pinching tycoon whose links to the political elite were desperately downplayed when it emerged after his death that he'd been practising fraud on a scale commensurate only with his girth.

Born Jan Ludwik Hoch in the Ukraine, he fled to England when the Nazis invaded, changed his name, built up a publishing business and became Labour MP for Buckingham in 1964. Ever sanctimonious, he gave evidence against Hubert Selby Jr's *Last Exit To Brooklyn* at its notorious obscenity trial in 1966, and made many enemies in his party for his hectoring manner. He was unseated by the Tories in 1970, amidst a welter of claims about his business practices, and the following year a DTI investigation concluded 'he is not in our opinion a person who can be relied on to exercise proper stewardship of a publicly quoted company.' Still, his empire bulked out almost as fast as he did. By 1984 he was able to acquire Mirror Group Newspapers for £93m – and it was then that his sausagey fingers really began to get into pies.

Under his ample wing was the *Daily Mirror*, the *Sunday Mirror*, the Scottish *Daily Record* and the *Sunday Mail*, as well as various other papers, publishing companies and media interests, including a half-stake in MTV Europe. At MGN he employed numerous names familiar to sleaze fans – Alastair Campbell (whose loyalty stretched to punching the *Guardian*'s political editor, Michael White, for disrespecting the slob's memory in November 1991), Helen Liddell (who oversaw his media interests in Scotland for years on end, only to deny categorically ever having been employed by him), Geoffrey Robinson (who was suspended from the Commons in October 2001 for failing to disclose to the standards committee a £200,000 payment from him), Lord Donoughue (the Labour peer who served on the board of Mirror Group Newspapers), Ken Livingstone (who wrote a column for his *London Daily News*) and numerous others. Margaret Thatcher was another declared admirer, and even Gordon Brown penned a weekly column in the *Sunday Record*.

Though Maxwell's empire seemed to be flourishing, it was in fact widely suspected to be floundering. But his appetite for litigation was such that he was able to strong-arm most people out of making allegations against him. As it happened, he was dipping into his employees' pension funds to shore up his ailing interests. He responded to increasing pressure to clarify the situation by desperately attempting to borrow money, then flopping overboard his yacht. His bloated corpse was fished from the sea off the Canary Islands on November 5th 1999. Despite vague suggestions that his death was an accident or a Mossad / CIA assassination, there is little rational doubt that it was suicide, and a £420m deficit in Mirror Group pension funds was exposed almost at once.

He was accorded a lavish funeral in Israel, and tributes poured in from loyal British politicians. Then-PM John Major called him 'a great character' and expressed gratitude for his advice on foreign policy, pointing out that "no-one should doubt his interest in peace and his loyalty to his friends." Douglas Hurd (then Foreign Secretary) praised his "real flair for business", adding that "the world will be poorer for his absence," while Neil Kinnock (then Labour leader) averred: "I valued his personal friendship."

Maxwell's gift for haemorrhaging other people's money continued well after his death: the inconclusive trial of his nauseating sons Ian and Kevin was one of the most expensive in history, and the official inquiry into his dealings set up in 1992 still hadn't announced its findings by the end of the decade, by which time it had cost the taxpayer well over £8m.

McCombes, Alan
b. 1955

Scottish Socialist Party mainstay who was jailed for 12 days for contempt of court in May 2006, after refusing to hand over crucial evidence in the Tommy Sheridan libel trial. An old Militant Tendency buddy of Sheridan, he co-authored their radical leftist vision *Imagine* in 2001 (drawing from the same tired well as old mucker George Galloway's Lennon-inspired *I'm Not The Only One*). The friendship soured during the build-up to the trial, however, after the SSP Executive openly requested that Sheridan withdraw from the action before any more members were required to give awkward evidence. Sheridan declined, and while McCombes languished in jail, his home and offices were raided.

The evidence in question included the disputed minutes of SSP meetings at which Sheridan had reportedly admitted visiting Manchester sex club Cupid's. McCombes duly had to testify in the 'sordid little squabble' against his former friend, stating that Sheridan had indeed confessed his patronage of Cupid's during the meeting. He made it clear that he was a reluctant and hostile witness, "here under the strongest possible protest," and suggested both parties should have settled "before innocent people were dragged into this bizarre pantomime," telling the defence: "Your client, the *News of the World*, symbolises everything I have stood against my whole adult life." Another act was added to the panto when the jury upheld the libel claim by a 7-5 majority, prompting a *News of the World* appeal (at which it may not wish to call upon McCombes to testify again).

McConnell, Jack
b. June 30th 1960
MSP (Lab), Motherwell and Wishaw, 1999-
First Minister of Scotland, 2001-

Renowned for his incoherent public speaking, this Arran islander surprised many colleagues when he put his name forward for Scotland's top job. He surprised the rest of Scotland by revealing that he'd had an affair with a party secretary seven years earlier. The disclosure, he admitted, was calculated to limit the damage it might cause later, and only fuelled his reputation as 'Jack the Lad' – a nickname that principally reflected his inexperience at the highest level of politics. Indeed, McConnell's Christian name has inspired many wits north of the border: he has also been called 'Jumping Jack Flash' and 'Jack the Ripper' (the latter for his vicious filleting of those loyal to his predecessor Henry McLeish,

qv), as well as 'Union Jack', for his sycophancy towards London – until he cynically announced he'd be supporting Trinidad and Tobago against England at the 2006 World Cup.

McCririck, John
b. April 17th 1940

Obese, bewhiskered tipster who hijacked an invitation to speak about racing at Robin Cook's funeral in August 2005 to unleash a crude and ill-judged tirade at stay-away holidaymaker Tony Blair. "I believe the Prime Minister's snub to Robin's family, and to millions of New Labour voters, demonstrates a petty vindictiveness and a moral failure – opting to continue snorkelling instead of doing his duty!" ranted the man-breasted misogynist, to widespread condemnation.

Having established his credentials as a childish brute on *Celebrity Big Brother* (see *Galloway, George*) that January, the Old Harrovian appeared on *Celebrity Wife Swap* in October 2006. This time it was sleaze pin-up Edwina Currie's turn to suffer: when he wasn't sprawled across his bed in jumbo Y-fronts, gulping champagne from a silver goblet, the angry, unhappy beast goaded the poor boiler to the point of tears over her 'grubby' affair with John Major.

McDaid, Tricia
b. 1961

One-time Labour aide who opened the floodgates for backdated sexual harassment claims against hands-on Deputy PM John Prescott (*qv*) after alleging in 2006 that he'd pestered her publicly and turned up uninvited at her door late at night, lusting for sex. He'd introduced himself in late 1992 by crashing a Christmas party at the Victoria & Albert Museum and leering down her top. "He used to get really drunk on whisky," she reminisced to the *Sunday Times*. "He was a boastful, arrogant pig. He just jumped on you when he felt like it at a party. He had no manners whatsoever." McDaid also claimed that, when fully-oiled, Prescott (who branded her revelations 'completely and utterly untrue') would claim to possess "a dossier about people in the Labour party sleeping with one another." She filed for harassment on 30th July 2006, suggesting that he will face a formal inquiry – during which sleaze scholars can only hope and pray that the dynamite document will come to light.

see *Temple, Tracey / Forde, Helga / Bissett-Scott, Sarah*

McLeish, Henry
b. June 15th 1948
MP (Lab), Fife Central, 1987-2001 / First Minister of Scotland, 2000-01

Donald Dewar's successor as Scottish First Minister, this canny landlord's steady rise to the top went belly-up when it emerged in 2001 that he'd been sub-letting his Fife constituency office. The case earned notoriety mainly because 'safe pair of hands' McLeish refused to accept he'd done anything wrong, calling it a "muddle rather than a fiddle" (meaning he'd spent the undeclared revenue on tarting up the office, not treating himself). He was only forced to resign, however, after weeks of fudging each and every opportunity he had to come clean over the bonus £36,000 his department had picked up in rates over the years.

The affair was dubbed 'Officegate' (*qv*) by sleaze-starved Scottish newspapers, and the ex-footballer's career unravelled live on television when he 'muddled' his own figures during a disastrous BBC *Question Time* appearance on November 1st 2001. On November 6th he made a 'full and frank disclosure' of some five separate sub-lets, but appeared to 'forget' yet another – charity tenants Third Age, who'd spent two years living under his nose from 1995-97, and to whom McLeish had personally written letters demanding prompt payment. One of the directors of the charity at that time was a Labour councillor, and the other was his election agent of 1997, Lynda Struthers – so it was 'plain as a pikestaff' he knew of the arrangement, said top Tory David McLetchie (*qv*). "If Henry McLeish deceived the Parliament and, more importantly, his constituents, he should be forced to resign his seat immediately," raged SSP rival Jim Balfour in a sanctimonious frenzy. "If he has a condition which results in severe memory loss, such as forgetting close colleagues, I would also question his suitability to continue as an MSP."

McLeish did step down from office, and – following further investigations into the affair, which implicated several more party members – Labour lost control of the seat in a by-election the next year, after a 49.6% swing to the independent candidate. In March 2002 the police were called in. An agonisingly slow investigation followed, finally concluding with a slap in the wrist in 2003 and a statement that McLeish had not intended deliberately to defraud the taxpayer. According to friends, McLeish felt the punishment far outweighed his crime, and remained sanguine in disgrace. That could have been because of the generous £34k First Minister's pension he was entitled to (after barely a year in office), on top of his sizeable pay-off and numerous other perks and salaries – though sob-stories still somehow made it to the press that he and his wife were 'struggling' to cope with the wage cutbacks.

McLetchie, David
b. Aug 6th 1952
MSP (Con), Lothians, 1999-2003 / Edinburgh Pentlands, 2003-

Expenses-happy top dog of the Scottish Conservative and Unionist Party, who had to hail one final taxi on October 31st 2005 after it emerged how he was spending taxpayers' money. As leader, McLetchie had 'in good faith' run up a sensational £11,500 travel bill (more than any other MSP since the Parliament was created), despite having what is by common consent one of the most irrelevant jobs in politics. The bus-shy Tory might have got away with it, but many of the journeys were for fundraising purposes – including a flight to Bournemouth – and had nothing to do with constituency business. Furthermore, he had pursued Henry "muddlin' nae fiddlin" McLeish (*qv*) with great zeal over his expenses shame (see *Officegate*), tabling a motion damning 'the lack of candour and transparency' in his affairs and doing an impression of him (to wild applause from his own bench) thus: "Please Sir, it wisnae me, a big boy did it and ran away."

The eagerness with which McLetchie stood down over such a dull matter led many to wonder how much he was really enjoying 'the job from hell' anyway. Some thought the decision was coloured by dark mutterings from earlier in the year, when he refused to reveal the clients at the law firm, Tods Murray, where he was declared as partner.

"Please Sir, it wisnae me, a big boy did it and ran away"

The worry was, the firm had apparently consulted on matters of national interest – like Edinburgh Airport and whether or not alcohol could be consumed at Murrayfield sports ground. Whether or not McLetchie was personally involved, MSP conduct rules forebade being paid by any outside party; only, despite earning £30k a year on the side, he couldn't reveal the exact nature of his work without breaching client confidentiality. Whatever the circumstances, it was clear his real interests lay beyond running the Scottish Conservatives.

Maddeningly for headline writers, 'the Letch' has never been implicated in a sex scandal.

McMaster, Gordon
b. Feb 13th 1960 / d. July 28th 1997
MP (Lab), Paisley South, 1990-97

Tragic figure who presided over scandal-hit Paisley (*qv*) during the 90s, amid allegations that a council project had been infiltrated by organised crime, and finally committed suicide by inhaling exhaust fumes in his garage. McMaster was distressed by rumours that his poor health – ME and depression allegedly triggered by exposure to garden chemicals – was being put down to AIDS, and had started to drink heavily. One MP compromised by the affair, Tommy Graham (*qv*), was blamed for McMaster's death in several quarters, following an unflattering reference to him in the suicide note.

It was subsequently suggested that the true reason for his unhappiness was Scott Anderson, a teenage Labour Party member working for bitter rival Graham. Anderson – who has never talked about his relationship with McMaster – was well under the age of consent at the time of the MP's death (turning seventeen the day afterwards), but it remains unclear whether this was just another smear.

Meale, Alan
b. July 31st 1949
MP (Lab), Mansfield, 1987-

Former PPS to John Prescott (and a fellow Merchant Navy alumnus) who served up four courses of sleaze over planning applications in the late 1990s. As an hors-d'oeuvre, Meale wrote a letter to the Department of the Environment, Transport and the Regions (where he himself worked) concerning third division football club Mansfield Town, of which he was the 15th largest shareholder. The shares were declared in the Commons register, but Meale failed to disclose his financial interest in the matter in the letter, which emphasised his 'total support' for the scheme. His efforts to lobby for an inquiry into its £30m redevelopment plans also raised awkward questions about his relationship with club chairman, Keith Haslam. By September 1997 Prescott, the new planning secretary, announced that he had approved the proposal. A week later, Meale attempted to intervene with the police on Haslam's behalf over a car fraud case, prompting Detective Constable Malcolm Moss-Ward to write to the Commons Speaker, Betty Boothroyd, saying: "I am concerned that Meale should use his position to make an inquiry on behalf of a close friend without disclosing his interest or that he himself was a potential witness in the case."

It was time for the entrée: in October 1998 Meale penned a flurry of letters in support of an application by another pal, Tony Kleanthous (Chairman of Barnet FC), to build a new stadium for the club, despite the proposed green belt site being located fully 140 miles from his constituency. This caused the relevant MP, Andrew Dismore, to remark: "I do not regard it as appropriate for an MP from another constituency to correspond over planning applications in a different constituency and not even have courtesy of copying the documentation." This had barely been digested when dessert was served: it emerged that Meale had meddled in a third planning inquiry, this time concerning an equestrian centre, also located in the Barnet green belt. The stables in question were owned by a millionaire chum of his, Andrew Reid, who subsequently confirmed that Meale had been part of a committee which organised Labour fundraising events involving his Mayfair legal firm Reid Minty.

After a short breather, coffee and mints arrived in the 61-year-old shape of Haris Sophoclides, a multi-millionaire who had the unusual distinction of being both the most prominent Greek-Cypriot lobbyist in Britain and Meale's researcher, thereby having privileged access to Parliament. Meale, it emerged, had enjoyed a series of jollies to Cyprus funded by Sophoclides, as well as receiving a contribution to his 1997 Election chest. Meale, who openly admitted to not having read the Ministerial Code of Conduct, was delighted to clarify matters for the British public. "All I need is his advice on matters related to Cyprus or I just wanted to ask his advice on one or two other things," he explained.

Mellor, David

b. March 12th 1949
MP (Con), Putney, 1979-97

Inaugural Heritage Secretary (or 'Minister for Fun') in John Major's notoriously fun-loving government, who will be forever associated with the strip of his beloved Chelsea FC following an affair described by former *Sun* editor Kelvin Mackenzie as 'the quintessential modern tabloid scandal'.

Though the snaggle-toothed soccer nut was considered one of Major's abler sidemen, Mellor is best-remembered for his affair with talented actress Antonia de Sancha (*qv*), revealed in the *People* in July 1992 after they'd bugged her flat. The rag's thin justification for running the story was that Mellor had described himself as 'knackered' by the affair in one of their recordings, and that as a result he might be unequal to his government duties. Days later, de Sancha accepted £30k to tell the *Sun* how the classical music buff had ravaged her in Chelsea kit (a fabrication devised by Max Clifford, *qv*), just so they could run a mocked-up picture. She also claimed that the father-of-two had been keen on toe-sucking, though both parties have since denied this. Despite his father-in-law's rage ("if he'll cheat on our Judith, he'll cheat on the country"), the family rallied for a particularly nauseating photo call days later. Major, perhaps aware that he was in a glass house (see *Currie, Edwina*), rejected Mellor's resignation – but the reprieve was brief. On September 24th he quit, following tabloid reports that he'd accepted a Spanish holiday from PLO official's daughter Mona Bauwens, just as Iraq invaded Kuwait. It's widely taken as read, however, that the true cause was his affair – as reflected in the *Sun*'s gleeful headline of September 25th: TOE JOB TO NO JOB.

"Rather than have this turn into a trial of strength between the Government and some sections of the press about my future, I have decided to resolve it myself by resigning," he groused in his pompous resignation letter. "It is too much to expect of my colleagues in Government and in Parliament to have to put up with a constant barrage of stories about me in certain tabloid newspapers." It was too much to expect of Mellor to keep his fly-buttons done up, either: two years on, cricket-loving toff Viscount Cobham was left shattered ("I didn't stop shaking for a year") by his effervescent wife Penelope's shock elopement with 'the Mellorphant man', for whom she'd acted as a special advisor. In subsequent years, Mellor has carved out a career as a journalist, his musings appearing in the very papers that formerly excoriated him.

Mercer, Patrick
b. June 26th 1956
MP (Con), Newark, 2001-

"They prospered inside my regiment," this Tory spokesman for Homeland Security boasted to the *Times* on March 8th 2007, referring to black people. "But if you'd said to them 'Have you ever been called a nigger?', they would have said 'Yes'." The former Lt. Colonel went on to cite "Come on you fat bastard, come on you ginger bastard, come on you black bastard!" as equivalent means of motivating soldiers. Though his remarks were clearly not racist in intent (he added that people with red hair would have "a far harder time than a black man, in fact"), comments such as "I came across a lot of ethnic minority soldiers who were idle and useless," and the suggestion that such recruits cried racism as a cover for their laziness and philandering, did little to further the agenda of David Cameron's Compassionate Conservatives. The party could offer no quarter to a man who'd used the phrase 'black bastard' in a national newspaper and, despite a groundswell of support, the Tory leader announced later that day: "The comments made by Patrick Mercer are completely unacceptable, and I regret that they were made. We should not tolerate racism in the Army or in any walk of life. Patrick Mercer is no longer a shadow minister."

"Come on you fat bastard, come on you ginger bastard, come on you black bastard"

The news may have nonplussed Labour: they had no minister for Homeland Security anyway.

see *Winterton, Ann*

Merchant, Piers
b. Jan 2nd 1951
MP (Con), Newcastle Central 1983-87 / Beckenham, 1992-97

A month before the Mayday Election, in what looked suspiciously like a tabloid sting, this wedded wimp was caught on a telephoto lens snogging 17-year-old Anna Cox in a public park, while his wife was out canvassing for him. The *Sun* described Ms Cox as a 'Soho nightclub hostess', but Merchant insisted she was in fact a dedicated Young Conservative and valued Parliamentary Researcher (*qv*), and refuted claims that she'd stayed at his flat. He maintained this position for roughly as long as it took for the paper to produce more compromising photographs. At this point he changed his plea to 'yes, but only on the sofa', and staged a kamikaze camera-call outside his home with his wife, Helen. The French kiss that followed had little effect other than to put voters off their dinner.

The tabloids scented blood, and when Merchant fell for another set-up involving Cox (see *Gilberthorpe, Anthony*) during party conference week that October (filmed, this time), Merchant feebly claimed she was helping him compile a book about tabloid intrusion, only to forfeit office by taking the title of Steward of the Manor of Northstead. His decision may have been hastened by a recording in the possession of the *Sunday Mirror* on which he referred to party leader William Hague as a 'useless wanker who looks as if he is 19 going on 90'. His appetite for office was not quite sated, though; in 2004 he stood for the hopeless UKIP at the European Elections, only to provoke revelations of a further affair by the *News of the World*. Vote-strapped UKIP could not afford the luxury of ditching the hapless former MP, stating instead: "Piers's private life is a matter for him, and does not affect his work for the party."

Meyer, Sir Anthony

*b. Oct 27th 1920 / d. Dec 24th 2004
MP (Con), Eton & Slough, 1964-66
/ West Flint, 1970-83 / Clwyd North
West, 1983-92*

Distinguished MP and diplomat who for upwards of 26 years enjoyed vigorous massages (incorporating corporal punishment) from a West Indian blues singer named Simone Washington.

"Darling, it's the Daily Sleaze asking about Simone"

Washington had the prescience to keep a journal detailing their sex games, which somehow found its way into the *Sunday Mirror* early in 1992, at the same time that Meyer was being deselected by his constituency association following a hopelessly optimistic November 1991 leadership challenge to Margaret Thatcher. Meyer and his wife were apparently untroubled by the revelations – when the tabloids called, she is said to have called to him: "Darling, it's the *Daily Sleaze* asking about Simone."

Militant Tendency

Considered the loony left's answer to the Monday Club (*qv*), this Trotskyite infiltration movement gave the world SSP firebrand Tommy Sheridan (*qv*), Poll Tax-dodging firebrand Terry Fields (*qv*) and menswear-modelling firebrand Derek Hatton. In the 80s and early 90s Derry Irvine and Neil Kinnock (both *qv*) expelled a series of entryist MPs from the Labour party, eventually causing the radical faction to splinter (it would in time give rise to 'Respect' – see *Galloway, George)*. Arguably the movement's greatest legacy was effecting the political suicide of then-Shadow Home Affairs Spokesman Robert Kilroy-Silk (*qv*) after a sustained campaign against him. In 1985 their perma-tanned nemesis finally cracked, assaulting bearded firebrand Jeremy Corbyn MP before embarking on a new career in daytime TV and xenophobic journalism.

Millennium Dome, the

No amount of wistful statistics about schools or hospitals will ever come close to articulating what a puerile waste of resources this vacuous vanity project was.

Originally conceived by John Major's Tory government, the idea was expanded by Tony Blair's incoming Labour administration from 1997.

"If we can't make this work, we're not much of a government"

Built without public referendum at a public cost pushing £800m, Blair declared that the Dome would be "a triumph of confidence over cynicism, boldness over blandness, excellence over mediocrity." In fact it turned out just as cynical, bland and mediocre as the rest of New Labour's vote-winning incentives, and stands as a permanent symbol of party hubris. Overseen by Peter Mandelson (*qv*), it proudly declared itself the largest single-roofed structure in the world; but the problem of filling its vast space (861,000 square feet) proved insuperable. In the end, it was decided to run with a combination of right-on installations divided into 'zones' ('Faith', 'Home Planet',

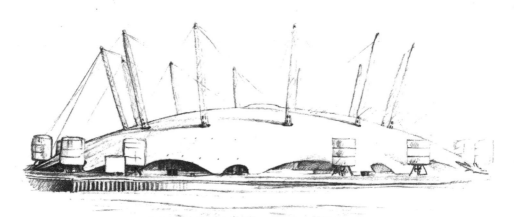

'Journey', 'Living Island', 'Self Portrait', 'Shared Ground,' etc) and branded attractions such as the 'McDonald's Our Town Story'. The impossibly-high projected visitor number of 12 million guaranteed that it could never break even, and it stood empty for the best part of a decade, as the government haemorrhaged up to £1m a month on its maintenance whilst attempting to beguile big business into taking it off their hands. As this went on, perhaps they had time to reflect on John Prescott's June 1997 statement: "If we can't make this work, we're not much of a government."

It seemed doomed to end up being a vast casino, but in June 2007 it finally reopened as a music venue called O2, with David Campbell, chief executive of developers AEG, announcing: "We don't want any reference point back to the Dome. We want to have a very clean break from the past."

see *London Olympics, the*

Milligan, Stephen
b. May 12th 1948 / d. Feb 7th 1994
MP (Con), Eastleigh, 1992-94

BBC journalist, Parliamentary Private Secretary to Jonathan Aitken (*qv*) and promising Tory MP whose sudden death in what the media called 'unusual sexual circumstances' – just two years after his election for Parliament – became a cruel symbol of Tory degeneracy. It's hard to deny that the extraneous details of the scene (which have passed into schoolboy legend) did little to help the Tories in the subsequent by-election, at which the vacant seat fell crushingly to the Lib Dems. Though most reports happily spoke of bondage, plastic bags and ladies' underwear, an internal BBC memo at the time instructed hacks: 'on no account mention fruit'. Many saw his passing as nothing more than a personal and political tragedy, but its manner can also take credit for heightening public awareness of the pitfalls of auto-erotic asphyxiation.

Mills, David
b. 1944

As celebrity lawyer, pal to Tony Blair and husband to Tessa 'Irritable' Jowell (*qv*), this former Camden Labour councillor has proved a thoroughgoing embarrassment to New Labour. In February 2006 his amnesia over the small matter of $600,000 – which Italian prosecutors suspect was given to him by former Italian premier Silvio Berlusconi (*qv*), possibly to bear false witness in his trials of 1997 and 1998 – very nearly cost his wife her career. Having been publicly dumped in March, 'Dark, Satanic' Mills's *annus horribilis* plunged to a new low in October, when he was committed for trial in Italy for corruption, having been indicted that summer on charges of tax evasion and embezzlement.

"I have the support and sympathy of very many people in public life, from the Prime Minister down"

Mills first aroused public censure in 1998-99, when his wife was Public Health Minister. As representative of diminutive motor-racing mogul Bernie Ecclestone (*qv*), his close ties to government embarrassed his wife's colleagues when they unveiled their astonishing tobacco advertising exemption for Formula One. Then Mills almost doubled his money on 90,000 shares in a firm called Old Monk, at a time when the government was meant to be addressing public fears about binge drinking. Owing to his structuring his finances offshore, however, in March 2006 Jowell was able to state that there had never been a conflict of interests.

In 2003 Mills was back in the soup when the *Observer* discovered he'd sought advice on pushing through a huge British Aerospace deal to Iran the year before, when a strict embargo was in force – prompting Tory anger when it was revealed that senior minister Dame Elizabeth Symons (whose portfolio extended to international security and the Middle East)

had given him an immediate personal response. He admitted to looking for loopholes, but denied considering anything illegal, nor receiving express treatment ("I sought no favours and had none," he was quoted in 2005).

In February 2006, investigation into his dealings brought to light his fondness for namedropping his well-positioned better half. One pitch, addressed to contacts in Dubai, even boasted: "I have the support and sympathy of very many people in public life, from the Prime Minister down." Unfortunately, however, Dubai banned him from practising there because of fraud investigations in Europe.

Worse was to come. For some years Mills had operated effectively on behalf of the man he called 'Mr B' (*qv*), in particular helping him avoid monopoly regulations in Italy in the 90s by setting up a company called 'Horizon', to which the media mogul could transfer his pay-TV channel. In a letter to his accountant dated February 2nd 2004, he damned himself with a series of admissions. The worst of them was the claim that he "had kept Mr B out of a great deal of trouble" by holding back much of what he knew.

It was too much for the Italian

authorities, and in July 2006 Mills (who subsequently described himself as a 'complete idiot' and his actions as 'completely insane') and his ex-paymaster were indicted on fraud charges. The lawyer's heroic battle to clear his name has subsequently been stalled by Mr B's mystery illness, however, and it is unclear when the trial will proceed – if ever.

see *Jowellgate*

Milroy-Sloan, Nadine
b. 1973

Unstable fantasist and web-sex fan slammed as 'a gold-digging little slut' by Neil Hamilton, the man she falsely accused of sexually assaulting her. Petite blonde Milroy-Sloan – who has a string of convictions for offences including pilfering from a Butlin's chalet and brawling in a chip shop – encountered 61-year-old pensioner 'Sir' Barry Lehaney (*qv*) online early in 2001. Mistakenly inferring from the upper-crust pen-names he used that she'd stumbled upon a sex-ring of the rich and powerful from her terraced home in Grimsby, she excitedly contacted Max Clifford (*qv*). Taking his advice to obtain proof from Lehaney, she travelled to Ilford on May 5th 2001.

Among her hazy recollections of the orgy she claimed ensued

was the suggestion that a 'Lady Hamilton' had sat on her face. Ever rigorous, Clifford swung into action with allegations about Neil and Christine Hamilton, but the devoted couple had a rock-solid alibi – they were serving Jellied Bloody Marys (*qv*) to dinner guests in Battersea – and the squalid affair ended with a substantial out-of-court settlement from Clifford (for calling the Hamiltons perverted), and three years' bird for Milroy-Sloan (for perverting the course of justice).

"If we were going to go to a sex party, we would go to one in Kensington or Chelsea – we wouldn't go to one in Essex"

Christine herself won little sympathy by selling her side of the story for a reported £35,000 and telling friends: "If we were going to go to a sex party, we would go to one in Kensington or Chelsea – we wouldn't go to one in Essex."

Ministerial Code of Conduct

Parliamentary diktat which states with crystal clarity: "No minister should accept gifts, hospitality or services from anyone which would, or might appear to, place him or her under an obligation." It really is that simple.

see entries *ad nauseam*

Mintogate

Stultifying stink involving the use of the use of Nigel Griffiths MP's office in Minto Street, Edinburgh for campaigning, in contravention of Commons rules.

see *Griffiths, Nigel / Officegate*

Mitchell, Austin
b. Sept 19th 1934
MP (Lab), Grimsby / Great Grimsby, 1977-

Ruddy backbencher who changed his name by deed poll to 'Haddock' in October 2002 to highlight the plight of the UK fishing industry. A still fishier claim to fame is that John Prescott (*qv*) once groped his wife, Linda. She was quoted in the *Sunday Times* on May 7th 2006 recalling an incident in 1978 when the randy lump 'pushed me quite forcefully against the wall and put his hand up my skirt'. It was her first introduction to the future Deputy PM. In these more enlightened times, a woman in her position might be entitled to pursue such an assailant through official channels (see *McDaid, Tricia*) or a lucrative tabloid spread (see *Temple, Tracey*).

Amateur photographer Mitchell has felt the strong arm of the law himself: at the 2005 Labour Conference, over-zealous stewards pounced as he snapped delegates peacefully queueing for their passes. Frightened onlookers gaped as armed policemen systematically deleted the incendiary images from his camera. "The party has given the security staff absolute carte blanche, and they have gone mad," he gasped. "It's completely over the top."

see *Wolfgang, Walter*

Mittal, Lakshmi
b. June 15th 1950

President and Chief Executive of the world's largest steel company, Arcelor Mittal, Labour donor, and proprietor of LNM Holdings – an Indian company tax-registered in the Dutch Antilles, yet championed by Tony Blair as a 'British' success. Of the estimated 100,000 people the firm employed worldwide in 2001-2, fewer than 100 were in the UK. Other than the small matter of being chased up on an unpaid £471,000 VAT bill from 2001 (since settled), Mittal's holdings have rarely troubled the UK taxman. As of 2006, his total donations to the Labour Party stood at over £2m – but he wasn't finished. In January 2007, the *Sunday Times* reported that Mittal was preparing to bail out Labour 'by pledging £2m to save the party from financial ruin': in short, providing the money it needed to pay back other controversial donors from the Cash for Peerages scandal (*qv*). It was still small beer compared to the £30m he reportedly splurged on his daughter Vanisha's 2004 wedding.

see *Garbagegate*

MMR

Acronym for the combined measles, mumps and rubella vaccine, administered to children at the age of around one since the early 1970s, and dogged by controversial claims that it can lead to side-effects including autism. Tony Blair refused to say whether or not his son Leo, born in May 2000, had received the jab ("I'm not going to enter into any public discussion on the health of my children", he said, ducking the question in December 2001). An alternative was available to the family, anyway – Cherie's 'healer' Jack Temple (*qv*) had this to offer: "If women follow my advice, their children will not need the MMR injection – end of story... For children who have been born by caesarean section, or those who have not been breastfed immediately after birth, I offer an energy-giving homeopathic remedy which eliminates the need for vaccines."

Mobil

Multi-national oil company on whose behalf Neil Hamilton (*qv*) tabled an amendment to a Finance Bill in 1989, aimed at saving them millions of pounds in tax. He then astounded them by requesting payment of £10,000 for his services, which they eventually euphemised as a consultancy fee (there was no arrangement in place). Peter Whitehurst QC, Mobil's tax expert who'd first put them in touch with Hamilton, later confessed even he was 'taken aback' by the request – and the payment was seen as a solid indication of corruption when dramatically submitted as evidence at Hamilton's disastrous 1999 libel action against Mohammed Fayed (*qv*).

Moderate

1. Term used to describe a tolerant individual in the political centre, such as Charles Kennedy (*qv*).

2. Term used by Charles Kennedy to describe his alcohol intake in December 2005, three weeks before confessing he had a serious problem.

Monday Club, The

Firmly right-of-centre Conservative pressure group, whose membership numbers about 3,000 Conservative Party members and supporters. In the words of playwright David Edgar, the Club "proselytises the ancient and venerable conservative traditions of paternalism, imperialism and racism." Founded in 1961 in reaction to the 'threat' of decolonisation, the club has remained nothing if not consistent: anti-immigration, pro-repatriation, soft on apartheid, and in favour of abolishing the Commission For Racial Equality. Though long a hothouse for Tory policy, it exerts an increasingly feeble influence on Westminster in the era of 'compassionate Conservatism'.

"If you say I am a racist, yes, I certainly am, and proud of it"

Tory chairman David Davis formally suspended party links in 2001 on account of its 'extreme' views, and hopes that it would find its way back into the political mainstream have not been helped by outbursts from its blue-blood officials in exile. Club President Lord Massereene (full name John David Clotworthy Whyte-Melville Foster Skeffington, 14th Viscount Massereene and 7th Viscount Ferrard) told the *New Statesman* on December 10th 2001: "If you say I am a racist, yes, I certainly am, and proud of it." Chairman Baron Sudeley, meanwhile, found his remarks in addressing the Club's AGM unsympathetically quoted by the *Times* in June 2006: Sudeley first of all supported the veracity of the idea that some races were superior to others, and went on to express admiration for Hitler (who "did so well to get everyone back to work").

Well-known veteran members have included Enoch Powell and Lord Tebbit; more recent alumni are Neil Hamilton, Geoffrey Rippon, Harvey Proctor, Michael Brown and Andrew Hunter (all *qv*). No current MPs are members.

Montrose, Petrina
b. 1969

Leggy former call girl entertained by the Blairs at Chequers, in her capacity as consort to dreadlocked pop troll Mick Hucknall ("Tony's a friend. I've said to him, 'You should have waited on Iraq'. He listens..."). The February 1998 soirée was also attended by Alastair Campbell, Gordon Brown and Salman Rushdie (whom the revealingly-clad Montrose claimed slipped her his phone number). "We had a light starter and a main meat dish," she revealed to the *Mail On Sunday* in June 2006. "I remember being disappointed that there was no fish."

Moore, Jo
b. 1963

Former assistant to Stephen Byers who came a creditable joint 59th (with her boss) in Channel 4's *100 Worst Britons* poll in 2003. The reason was simple: at 2.55pm on Tuesday, September 11th 2001, as the West tried to assimilate the news that America was under attack, Moore was coolly tapping a memo to her boss: "It's now a very good day to get out anything we want to bury. Councillors' expenses?"

"It's now a very good day to get out anything we want to bury. Councillors' expenses?"

Spin doctors are not employed to act on conscience, and it wasn't suggested for a moment that Moore wasn't doing her job – but her diplomacy hadn't improved much by the time the story broke on October 10th. Deciding it was a good day to make a televised apology, she took full responsibility for the email. Her words were undermined, however, when cameras caught her smirking moments after finishing. Despite the best efforts of veteran Byers apologist Tony Blair – who stepped in to say it would be 'too heavy a penalty' to end her career over one 'horrible, wrong and stupid' email – the media ran with the image of the cynical spin queen, and Moore was watched like a hawk thereafter. The axe finally fell on February 15th 2004, after word escaped that Byers' Director of Communications Martin Sixsmith (*qv*) had criticized her for planning to bury further bad news along with the late Princess Margaret. Dizzy from spin, Moore decided on a change of career, and is now a primary school teacher.

Morris, Chris
b. Sept 5th 1965

Highbrow Beadle whose japes have given gyp to numerous MPs, starting with Jerry Hayes (*qv*), who led tributes to former deputy PM Michael Heseltine when Morris announced his death in 1994, and subsequently had to apologise. Next up was David Amess (*qv*), who unwittingly turned the Commons into a vessel for surreal drug jokes on Morris's *Brass Eye*, with the assistance of Sir Bernard Ingham (*qv*). A 2001 episode concerning paedophilia, meanwhile, saw Portsmouth North MP Syd Rapson warning that perverts were using 'an area of internet the size of Ireland' to snare kiddies, and prompted a humiliating climbdown from Home Office ministers goaded by the media into condemning a show they hadn't even seen: among them were Beverley Hughes (*qv*) and David Blunkett (*qv*).

Morrison, Sir Peter
b. June 2nd 1944 / d. July 13th 1995
MP (Con), Chester, 1974-92

Margaret Thatcher's final Parliamentary Private Secretary, who was, according to woolly liberal

Simon Heffer, "a constant trial to the whips, who were afraid that his late-night cruises around and skirmishes in Sussex Gardens would come to the attention of the press" (*Daily Telegraph*, Aug 4th 2002). Had Sir Peter not stepped aside to allow Gyles Brandeth his shot at political obscurity in 1992, it is likely that the former Deputy Party Chairman would have become another high-profile 'Back To Basics' sleaze scalp. It was left to Tory closet-opener Alan Duncan MP to 'out' Sir Peter, who succumbed to a heart attack aged 51.

Mountford, Kali
b. Jan 12th 1954
MP (Lab), Colne Valley, 1997-

Sharing a name with the Hindu goddess of destruction, this mumsy former team-player on the Social Security Select Committee abused her position by leaking a sensitive draft report on childcare benefit to the Treasury, via Gordon Brown's Parliamentary Private Secretary, Don Touhig MP. When asked if she'd done it by the Standards and Privileges Committee on July 15th 1999, she replied: "My answer is no, I did not." Once the investigation was over, the confused Mountford accepted she'd been 'rather silly', resigned her post (pleading illness and inexperience) and enjoyed a five-day Commons suspension that October.

Muddle

Not a fiddle.

see *McLeish, Henry*

Mugabe, Robert
b. Feb 21st 1924

Zimbabwean tyrant who ousted the odious Reverend Canaan Banana as President in 1987, since when he has systematically brought the ex-colony to its knees. He'd instigated his vicious programme of ethnic cleansing in Matabeleland when still Prime Minister in the 1980s, but it was the turn of the millennium before the UK government decided his friendship wasn't worth having (though his money evidently was: the UK had cheerily flogged fighter plane parts to his regime as recently as 2000). Despite the savage treatment meted out to white farmers in his country, the only serious attempt to bring him to justice was made by gay rights campaigners Peter Tatchell and Chris Morris (not the TV prankster) during his 1999 visit to Britain: they tried to execute a citizen's arrest for breaching international human rights, only to be apprehended by British security forces themselves (for a 'breach of the peace' – see *Wolfgang, Walter*). Mugabe was quick to accuse the 'gay gangsters' of being the agents of a UK government conspiracy, though in light of Labour and Tory spinelessness towards him in the past twenty years, the theory never held water.

"The gay government of the gay United gay Kingdom"

The police's decision to cuff Tatchell and Morris won Blair's Britain little credibility with Mugabe: back home, he wittily denounced New Labour as "the gay government of the gay United gay Kingdom," and hasn't been back since. Despite this vicious slur, both Jack Straw and Prince Charles saw fit to shake his hand, in 2004 and 2005 respectively.

see *Shiri, Perence / Zimbabwe*

Murphy, Jim
b. Aug 23rd 1967
MP (Lab), Eastwood / East Renfrewshire, 1997-

'Lucky Jim' holds the possibly unique distinction of having been roasted in an Early Day Motion for 'intolerant and dictatorial behaviour' before becoming an MP. It was widely assumed that he'd been nominated as cannon fodder in what seemed an unassailable Tory stronghold at the 1997 Election, but he became a shock success for Labour after a succession of Tory sex scandals in the constituency left the Blues a laughing stock (see *Hirst, Sir Michael / Stewart, Allan*). The unprecedented EDM had arisen during Murphy's tenure as NUS President in 1996, when he sacked his Vice-President (the convenor of the Black Students Campaign) for speaking out in favour of free education.

In the ensuing storm, eight Labour MPs (including party heavyweights Tony Benn and Dennis Skinner) tabled a Commons motion slamming the tyro's actions, and one Campaign for Free Education member growled: "Murphy is nothing but a bullying, undemocratic mandate-breaker." Since settling in, young Jim has only been involved in one refreshingly petty stink: in December 2001, he was forced to admit that, while the House of Commons refunded the full rent for his constituency office, he still claimed half from his room-mate, none-the-wiser Eastwood MSP Ken MacIntosh. This undeclared back-hander amounted to a tidy profit on rent-free office space, and one of the most trivial political scandals of modern times.

Reginald Maudling

b. March 7th 1917 / d. Feb 14th 1979

MP (Con), Barnet / Chipping Barnet, 1950-79

Gaffe-prone soak whose memoirs contained the visionary statement that politicians 'cannot reasonably be expected to neglect their interests and those of their families'. As good as his word, he went on to prompt the inauguration of the Register of Members' Interests (qv) in the aftermath of the Poulson affair – arguably the greatest political scandal of the 1970s. Matters kicked off with Maudling's unexpected resignation as Home Secretary in 1972 when Scotland Yard began to investigate one of his former business associates, bent property developer John Poulson. His gesture lost its honourable sheen when it emerged that in pursuit of what he called his 'little pot of gold' he'd ducked income tax on his directorship of Peachey Property Corporation from 1965, by waiving his annual fee, selling them his house and renting it from them at £2 a week instead.

It soon emerged that further directorships had quadrupled his ministerial salary to £20,000, and that some of them were decidedly suspect. Poulson's canny offer of a directorship to Maudling's motor-mad son Martin and a donation to his wife's pet theatre project had made his quarry purr: soon the MP was currying foreign investment for one of the Yorkshire fraudster's dodgy businesses, the Real Estate Fund of America. When it crashed with £4m debts in 1970, Maudling seemed to have lost little except his 250,000 shares – but when Poulson's bankruptcy hearing came up a couple of years later, it was time for the Home Secretary to have a fireside chat with PM Edward Heath. In March 1974 Poulson was jailed for seven years for corruption. Though Maudling was not himself prosecuted, a 1977 Commons report under James Callaghan's Labour administration accused him of behaviour 'inconsistent with the standards which the House is entitled to expect of its members', further slamming him for only declaring the largesse Poulson had shown his wife and son. The likeable Maudling only outlived the humiliation by 18 months, though he was at least the subject of a Tory party 'Save Reggie' campaign – a feature decidedly absent from the travails of David Mellor, Jeffrey Archer, Jonathan Aitken and others.

Nadir, Asil
b. May 1st 1941

Aptly-named Tory donor (to the tune of £440,000) who came to prominence in the 1980s as CEO of the explosively successful Polly Peck conglomerate. As a result of his mismanagement, however, it spectacularly crashed in 1990. In 1993 Nadir was charged with various counts of theft and fraud, but jumped his £3.5m bail and absconded to his native Northern Cyprus, which has no extradition treaty with the UK. In his wake lay the seeds of the downfall of Northern Ireland Minister Michael Mates (*qv*), who was accused of advancing his cause in parliament and who had gifted him a watch engraved with the words 'don't let the buggers let you down' only days earlier.

In a 2003 interview with the BBC, Nadir vowed to return to the UK to clear his name (he's still wanted on charges relating to the theft of £34 million), but has yet to trouble passport control. As for the Tories, Party chairman Sir Norman Fowler pledged on June 16th 1993 that they'd repay any monies whose provenance proved dubious. Evidence proved hard to come by, however, and to date no cash has been returned.

Nannygate

Tag given to the 2004 brouhaha over David Blunkett's lover's nanny's UK residency application.

"No special favours... but a bit quicker"

Essentially, Blunkett was accused of abusing his position as Home Secretary to speed up Leoncia 'Luz' Casalme's application for permanent UK residency – a claim he strenuously denied, despite the discovery of a notorious memo including the phrase "no special favours... but a bit quicker." His prodigious memory seemed to have let him down again: there was no doubt that he'd handled paperwork relating to the application, and though he insisted to journalists at the Passport Office on December 1st that "I wouldn't be standing here if I thought there was any doubt whatsoever about what I've done," a fortnight later he resigned. On December 21st Sir Alan Budd (who'd conducted the official investigation into the affair) gave the press an early Christmas present when he announced: "I believe I have been able to establish a chain of events linking Blunkett to the change in the decision on Mrs Casalme's application."

National Lottery

14-million-to-1 bingo game decried as 'a tax on the poor' by the left and 'a tax on the stupid' by the right. Both agree it's a tax of sorts, and the government's distribution of its proceeds has been a constant source of controversy since its inception under John Major in 1994. Many feel that causes such as asylum and crime, covered by certain targeted Lottery charities, should be the responsibility of central government. Operator Camelot's sophisticated lobbying campaign at the 1999 Labour Conference, at a time when its contract was under review, led to suggestions that the sacred event was becoming a giant trade fair: in terms of MPs 'onside', the successful bidder outnumbered Richard Branson's 'People's Lottery' 10 to 1. Others argue that the government's endorsement of a lottery mentality – whereby instant enrichment is dangled as a viable substitute for hard graft – undermines Whitehall's integrity. And few could find any excuse for the lotto's TV ad campaign featuring Billy Connolly sporting a purple goatee. Lucky winners have included 'National Rotter' Lee Ryan (1995), 'Lotto Lout' Mikey Carroll (2002) and 'frenzied rapist' Iorworth Hoare (2004).

Nicholas Soames Day

Scheduled for May 14th each year, this fatuous festival was in fact only celebrated once – in 1996 – when right-on TV nuisance Mark Thomas orchestrated a public viewing of the four-chinned MP's three-tiered mahogany buffet, in accordance with the 1982 'Conditionally Exempt Works of Art' scheme. This allowed the gentry to duck death duties on art treasures so long as they let the public view them. Soames was onto the wheeze like a rat up a drainpipe, registering a variety of family coasters and salt-cellars, as well as antique furnishings such as the 'magnificent three-tier mahogany buffet with partially-reeded slender baluster upright supports' that was to undo him. When Shadow Treasury Spokesman Alistair Darling complained that "the system has been abused, people are getting exemption from works of art that are never going to be seen," Thomas saw his chance, and encouraged the viewing public to bombard Soames with viewing requests. This presented the member for Mid-Sussex with an agonising choice – cough up or have the hoi polloi inspect his treasures at will – and he decided he could afford the £8000 bill after all.

see *Soames, Nicholas*

Nicholls, Patrick
b. Nov 14th 1948
MP (Con), Teignbridge, 1983-2001

Choleric Eurosceptic who briefly became a junior environment minister in 1990. This allowed him to enjoy a jolly (*qv*) to Indonesia as leader of 'the UK-Indonesian All-Party Parliamentary Group', after which he controversially acclaimed the country's dictator 'General' Suharto for having 'raised the condition of its people' in a Commons debate.

A drink-drive conviction during that year's Tory conference killed his ministerial career, but he was soon appointed party Vice Chairman. That, too, proved short-lived: following an ill-advised newspaper article in which he branded the Germans 'warmongers' and the French 'collaborators', as well as postulating that Germany's sole contribution to European integration had been forcing other countries into two World Wars, he was obliged to step down in December 1994. It is thought that the colossal sums he was raking in from directorships cushioned the blow.

SLEAZE

"If I make a fool of myself, what does it matter? The most important thing is that it means a £2,500 donation to the Sheffield Hospice"

– David Blunkett on his 'forthcoming' appearance on Celebrity Mastermind, in The Blunkett Tapes (see page 330), December 2003

SLOT

Nixon, Richard
b. Jan 9th 1913 / d. April 22nd 1994

Transatlantic sleaze paradigm who served as especial inspiration to Jonathan Aitken (*qv*). His turgid 1993 biography of the disgraced US President analysed Watergate thus: 'What transformed an incident into a crisis was Nixon's endorsement of the cover-up, which began clumsily and continued stupidly.' It was a blueprint he would follow to the letter.

see *World In Action / Guardian trial*

Nobacon, Danbert
b. 1962

Transvestite vocalist with radicalised indie flash-in-the-pan Chumbawumba, who took advantage of his group's brush with fame to cool John Prescott's ardour at the 1998 Brit Awards.

The Deputy PM was contentedly swilling champagne at the bash as part of New Labour's move to capitalise on the vote-winning Cool Britannia (*qv*) initiative, while staunch vegetarian Nobacon (pronounced 'no bacon') had been invited on the back of numbing novelty hit *Tubthumping*. In upending a bucket of ice over Prescott, the former Chimp Eats Banana singer – real name Nigel Hunter – claimed to be acting out of concern for the plight of striking Liverpool dockers. Perhaps because he was seated at the time, hard-man Prescott did not retaliate, as he later would against egg-lobbing Craig Evans (*qv*). Subsequent talk of an assault charge came to nought, though New Labour's connections with Britpop cooled almost as swiftly as Prescott's crotch.

Nobacon's own convictions had come under the microscope a year earlier, when Chumbawumba signed to EMI – a move that confused fans of their 1989 release *Fuck EMI*.

SLEAZE

"Tough on sleaze, tough on the causes of sleaze"

- *Tony Blair, Labour Party conference, 2007*

SLOT

Nolan Report, the

Chaired by Lord Michael Nolan, this wide-ranging investigation into 'standards in public life' was commissioned in 1994 by John Major (*qv*) in desperate response to his cataclysmic Back To Basics (*qv*) initiative.

In May 1995 Nolan dropped the bombshell that 'people in public life are not always as clear as they should be about where the boundaries of acceptable conduct lie' – but by no means all his recommendations were implemented. The Report acknowledged 'a fall in public confidence in the financial probity of MPs', which 'coincided with an increase in the number of MPs holding paid consultancies which relate to their Parliamentary role', as well as 'some confusion among MPs as to what conduct is acceptable.' It also advised a straightforward ban on 'paid advocacy' or consultancies with lobbying firms, and the creation of the first Commissioner for Parliamentary Standards (Sir Gordon Downey, let loose on November 15th 1995). It boldly concluded: 'We cannot say conclusively that standards of behaviour in public life have declined', and clarified what was expected of MPs. Nonetheless, Nolan's 'Seven Principles of Public Life' – selflessness, integrity, objectivity, accountability, openness, honesty and leadership – are qualities that remain elusive to many British politicians.

Three further reports covering other aspects of public office followed, before the Nolan Committee became the Committee for Standards in Public Life in 1997. That year Tony Blair made a rod for his own back by extending the Committee's remit to encompass 'issues in relation to the funding of political parties' (see *Cash for Honours*).

Norris, Steven

b. May 24th 1945
MP (Con), Oxford East, 1983–87 / Epping Forest, 1988–97

Durable blue who was acclaimed as 'an extremely good kisser' by Edwina Currie (*qv*) and earned the nicknames 'Shagger' and 'Yes! Yes! Yes! Yes! Yes, Minister!' for his sexual exploits, which stood out as brazen even in the 90s Tory sleaze bonanza.

In 1996 he jumped the long queue of those undermining John Major's Back To Basics (*qv*) initiative when it emerged that he was juggling no fewer than five mistresses at the same time as a wife, with none of the individuals concerned cottoning on – until the tabloids intervened, that is. It was a feat not even Alan Clark (*qv*) could rival, though Norris insisted the affairs spanned some 25 years. The lucky women included doctor Clare Marx, saleswoman Lynn Taylor, *Times* correspondent Sheila Gunn, magazine executive Jennifer Sharp and parliamentary secretary Emma Courtney.

His multi-tasking clearly impressed Conservative high command, who advanced him as their candidate for the 2000 mayoral race when Jeffrey Archer dropped out. Norris's bounce-back reiterated the British public's open-mindedness where sexual morality is concerned – so long as the protagonist is at least moderately attractive (see *Mellor, David / Merchant, Piers*). That same year, Norris divorced his wife and married Courtney. Principles remained a weak point, however: by his own admission he only stood down from parliamentary politics in 1997 in order to earn 'serious money' as director general of the Road Haulage Association. He is currently thought to be gearing up for a third successive failure in the London Mayoral race (2008, this time).

Nutcracker Gables

Spacious bungalow in Purley, Surrey, proudly owned by prosperous builder Barry Cripps and his family. His decision to accessorise the property with an outdoor sauna, loft conversion and yellow, two-storey Wendy house ultimately led to the fateful events of Sunday, December 13th 1998.

see *Ingham, Sir Bernard*

Cecil Parkinson

b. Sept 1st 1931

MP (Con), Enfield West / South Hertfordshire / Hertsmere, 1970-9

Self-made millionaire and former Tory golden boy whose 1983 sex 'n' secretary scandal firmly established him as a sleaze heavyweight. Sara Keays first entered Parky's life as a 23 year-old Commons Secretary in June 1971, and their affair kicked off soon afterwards. By 1974 she was working directly under the married MP, from whom she claimed to have received her first proposal on moving jobs in 1979 – but as his career was flourishing, he concluded the timing was wrong. He duly became Party Chairman in 1981, and in October the next year was given a surprise casting vote as to whether his politically-ambitious mistress should contest Bermondsey at a by-Election. To her stupefaction, he rather thought not, and she lost the nomination to Robert Hughes (*qv*).

Nonetheless, their dalliance continued until 1983, when Keays announced (on May 21st) that she'd fallen pregnant. The news was especially unwelcome in light of the June General Election, which Parkinson had personally orchestrated for his mentor Margaret Thatcher. Instead of spraying bubbly over the PM, the eve of triumph found him confessing all to her. She promoted him regardless – but her faith in his tact was misplaced. Having assured Keays's father, an harrumphing Colonel, of his good intentions, big-hearted Cecil paid £5k into her account and jetted off to the Bahamas with his wife, Ann. By the time the Secretary Of State for Trade and Industry returned, bronzed and refreshed, he'd resolved to stand by his blameless spouse of 27 years. Keays was incensed, and even more so when the MP's decision initially endeared him to the public.

When she revealed the affair's less sympathetic details – the promises of marriage, the suggestion that the pregnancy be terminated ('I was not aware that political expediency was sufficient grounds for an abortion') – he resigned from DTI, though he remained a trusted Thatcher lieutenant and was unexpectedly re-appointed Tory chairman by William Hague (*qv*) in 1997. By 2002 his daughter by Keays, Flora, had come of age and a long-standing media gagging order had expired – giving Keays a long-denied chance to hit out in a TV documentary about the girl's troubled life, cataloguing a series of missed birthdays and Christmases. The week after saw Parkinson denounced as 'weak', 'pathetic', 'cruel', 'vicious', 'cowardly' and 'a 24-carat bastard' in a *Daily Mirror* column - but he rarely comments on the affair, except to say: "I'm not the bastard she has made me out."

Oaten, Mark
b. March 8th 1964
MP (Lib Dem), Winchester, 1997-

Mid-life meltdown MP whose credibility was minced by tabloid revelations about his unorthodox sexual predilections, including what the *News of the World* called 'a bizarre sex act too revolting to describe'.

> *"It's a gross act of humiliation which only a few punters ask for. It's quite revolting, really"*

Family man Oaten first came to national attention after the 1997 Election, when TV cameras caught him assaulting rival candidate Richard J. Huggett at 7am (round about the fourth recount). Electoral terrorist Huggett had stood as a 'Literal Democrat', thereby polling some 640 votes. Oaten's majority was just two at the latest count, and it wasn't looking likely that the result would stand. Huggett's goading finally made the balding balloteer flip, and provoked a self-

confessed 'attempt to throttle one of my opponents'. Oaten was asked to stand aside pending an inquiry into electoral malpractice, but won the subsequent by-election. Two unremarkable terms followed.

His downfall began with a doomed tilt at the party leadership. Despite insisting with hindsight that he'd long since lost all enjoyment and ambition in politics, the member for Winchester was among the first to toss his hat into the ring when good friend Charles Kennedy stepped unsteadily down from office in January 2006. The top job was always a faint hope, however, and he received scant party support beyond stargazing oddball Lembit Öpik (*qv*). Oaten was out of the race by January 19th, but had lingered above the parapet too long for the *News of the World*'s liking. The virulent rag had his card marked, and within 48 hours he would be forced to resign from the front bench altogether.

The problem lay with a 23-year-old ballet dancer and rent boy named Tomasz. Watching the news one evening, the Pole dancer recognised the hapless Oaten as a regular client and picked up the phone. Receiving a panicked brush-off, he took revenge in traditional style. "He was very specific about something special he wanted us to do to him," Tomasz told the tabloid on January

21st. "It's a gross act of humiliation which only a few punters ask for. It's quite revolting, really." When the ensuing frenzy had died down, Oaten's wife Belinda (who was famously preparing an eggy bread treat for the family when the MP broke the unhappy news), decided to stand by him. The same cannot be said of his electorate; the *Southern Daily Echo* reported that 58% of polled readers thought he should resign, and he duly announced that he would not seek re-election.

The central mystery of the affair remained obscure for a further four months: why had a successful MP with a solid family and promising future risked all by bedding down with rent boys? All was revealed in May 2006. "I was turning 40 and I really felt that I was losing my youth," he explained to the *Sunday Times*. "And the problem was undoubtedly compounded by my dramatic loss of hair in my late thirties."

SLEAZE

"Nowadays you are in danger of being in difficulty if you don't register a doughnut you've had at some entertainment or other"

– *Teresa Gorman on expenses, February 2002*

SLOT

Officegate

Rib-tickling title given to a spectacularly drab 2001 sub-letting 'scandal' involving a grace-and-favour office in Fife. The affair did at least offer welcome clarification of the age-old confusion between a 'muddle' (forgetfulness about important details) and a 'fiddle' (deliberate misleading of press and public over inappropriate use of parliamentary resources).

see *McLeish, Henry*

Oil for Food

$32bn scheme devised by the UN in 1995 to enable Iraq to buy humanitarian supplies from the proceeds of regulated oil sales, without flouting the sanctions imposed after its 1990 invasion of Kuwait. The unworkably corruptible system was picked apart by the 2004 Volcker inquiry, in which many European politicians and UN officials were implicated. British MP George Galloway (*qv*) was also linked, in a separate investigation by the US Senate, provocatively labelled '*Oil-for-Influence: How Saddam Used Oil to Influence Politicians Under the United Nations Oil For Food Program*'. Though no hard evidence of corruption could be found in the small amount of reliable paperwork (and certainly not around 20 million barrels' worth, as has been suggested) Galloway has been criticised for his lack of transparency.

In April 2003 the *Telegraph* claimed the 'Respect' boss had cleaned up to the tune of £375k per annum from the scheme, basing their allegations on seemingly falsified documents supposedly retrieved from bombed-out government buildings in Baghdad. At a libel hearing in December 2004, he was awarded £150k compensation and £1.2m costs, not least because the fusty rag interpreted the alleged transactions as personal gain by the MP. In July 2007, however, the Standards & Privileges Committee's four-year investigation into his Mariam's Appeal (*qv*) raised the intriguing possibility that the *Telegraph*'s documents might have been authentic after all ('I find no evidence that they are forgeries or altered,' wrote Sir Philip Mawer, 'and I find this possibility to be most unlikely'). On July 18th the paper crowed that 'Scotland Yard is to take the first steps toward a possible criminal investigation against George Galloway'.

As of 2006, it was reported that prosecutors in the US were considering a perjury charge against Galloway, though nothing has yet come of this. It was easier to link the MP to Iraqi money through Mariam's Appeal – the Charity Commission's damning June 2007 report suggested that some donations were sourced from 'improper transactions' connected to the Oil for Food programme, and the following month Galloway was recommended for suspension from the Commons. "There was strong circumstantial evidence that the Oil for Food programme was used by the Iraqi government, with Mr Galloway's connivance, to fund the campaigning activities of the Mariam Appeal," it stated in part.

Öpik, Lembit
b. March 2nd 1965
MP (Lib Dem), Montgomeryshire, 1997-

Lop-sided liability whose support in a leadership contest is regarded as the kiss of death (see *Kennedy, Charles / Oaten, Mark*), and who established his off-beam credentials in 1999 by expressing fears in Parliament that Earth was under threat from rogue asteroids. "What's worrying is that the last one impacted 65 million years ago and wiped out the dinosaurs," he explained to BBC News Online in March 1999. "I'm sorry to say that we're next in line for extinction." Until late 2006 the Estonian-descended amateur pilot was best-known for his appearances on TV programmes including *Have I Got News For You* and *The Wright Stuff*, as well as for dating weathergirl Siân

Lloyd. That all changed, however, when he took up with Gabriela Irimia (*qv*), one half of cash-strapped pop sensation the Cheeky Girls. News of their relationship stunned Parliament and public alike, and led to unkind speculation that leggy Gabriela's immigration status had inspired her attraction to the goofy parliamentarian. In the January 25th 2007 number of *Hello!* magazine, Öpik defied the critics by calling her 'insightful, bright, sharp, challenging, very funny and pretty strong-minded', while she pledged that 'if we do decide to get married one day, *Hello!* will be the first to be invited'. Elsewhere in the same issue, Lloyd stated: "I think the Parliamentary drinking culture traps a lot of people there... My hope is that Lembit will reflect on his choices and get himself back on track."

"If we do decide to get married one day, Hello! will be the first to be invited"

On July 31st, *Hello!*'s wedding invitation still hadn't been issued – Gabriela told *London Lite*: "We haven't been together for very long and we're not ready."

Osborne, George
b. May 23rd 1971
MP (Con), Tatton, 2001-

The current member for UK sleaze capital Tatton (see *Hamilton, Neil / Bell, Martin*) graduated from gag-writing for William Hague to become Shadow Chancellor under his old chum David Cameron. In late 2005 he weathered a tabloid snowstorm (to say nothing of Dennis Skinner's heckling) while masterminding Cameron's leadership challenge, when the *News of the World* ran a front-page picture appearing to show him at the same table as a young woman and a heap of cocaine. Osborne dismissed raddled vice girl Natalie Rowe's accompanying claims as 'pretty desperate stuff' – though, like Cameron, he has not denied taking the drug.

P

Abbreviation employed in private correspondence by former Bad Manners mentor Lord Levy, which some interpreted as a reference to peerages.

see *K*

Paisley

1. West Scottish design with a spotted motif, associated with fabrics and ties.

2. West Scottish council with a spotted reputation, associated with fabrications and lies. The 1997 suicide note of local MP Gordon McMaster brought years of distrust and chicanery between Labour and SSP figures to the surface. The powers that be were accused of '*prima facie* malficience' by councillor Paul 'The Knife' Mack (as spattered as anyone in the mudflinging), who admitted: "This once great town has become synonymous with sleaze."

see *Graham, Tommy / Mack, Paul / McMaster, Gordon*

Pal, Dr Rita
b. 1972

Outspoken NHS whistleblower and former crush of one-man sleaze epidemic Paul Marsden (*qv*), who dubbed her 'Princess Rat' in emails soon after getting behind her anti-euthanasia campaign in April 2000. She wisely resisted the married MP's charms (unlike her close friend, researcher Fiona Pinto, who went as far as 'drink-fuelled fumbles'), despite what she perceived as his offer to 'help out' and 'ring a few people' in exchange for an affair. The psychiatrist took revenge for his unwanted overtures by telling the *Birmingham Sunday Mercury* on December 7th 2003 about his feckless attempts at phone sex. However, Dr Pal insists that, were it not for their friendship, she could have embarrassed him a lot more, warning: "If I wished to fully expose Marsden I could easily create a website called 'Paul Marsden Exposed' and drive traffic through it." Instead, she has kept the story alive through her blog – the entry of June 30th 2007 re-lives the morning the story went semi-national in 2002, when it was picked up by the *Daily Express*. "I was sitting on my bed eating Rice Krispies," she wistfully recalls, "and I suddenly choked when BBC *Breakfast* read out the article... it all whizzed around me."

SLEAZE

"Tony's favourite food is fish and chips. He gets a takeaway whenever he is at home in his constituency"
– *feature on Tony Blair in Labour's in-house magazine, 1999*

"Fresh fettuccini garnished with an exotic sauce of olive oil, sun-dried tomatoes and capers"
– *what Tony Blair told The Islington Cook Book on the same topic, 1998*

SLOT

Parkinson, Michael
b. March 28th 1935

Fawning Yorkshireman who could barely contain his delight when Tony Blair agreed to grace his soporific chat-show in February 2006. On it the PM explained his decision to invade Iraq: "I think if you have faith about these things, you realise that judgement is made by other people … and if you believe in God, it's made by God as well." This from the man who told the *Daily Telegraph* on April 7th 1996: "I can't stand politicians who wear God on their sleeves." Blair later denied to the less accommodating Jeremy Paxman

that God had anything to do with his decisions. Parky has recently seen his crown slip to a slightly younger model, the relentlessly lowbrow Jonathan Ross (see *Cameron, David*).

Parliamentary Researcher

Dogsbody role in the Commons, offering youngsters the opportunity to perform demeaning tasks under MPs.

see entries *passim*

Pelling, Andrew
b. Aug 20th 1959
MP (Con), Croydon Central, 2005-

Former investment banker accused in May 2005 of leaving his wife and three children for a 24-year-old Tory activist named Lucy Slaytor. His spouse of 18 years, Sanae, raged to the *Evening Standard*: "He throws us money through the letter box. He has no respect for us. All he cares about is that new woman of his."

"It will be a pleasure to have you both not voting for me – why don't you go and vote for the BNP?"

Sanae spent ten months of 2004 in Japan caring for her father, and returned to face her husband's new arrangement. Before long Pelling – whose majority was a mere 75 – had moved in with Miss Slaytor's parents, prompting Sanae to add: "He treated me like a doormat. As far as he was concerned, I was there to clean up after him, raise his children and cook his food. I loved him and needed him to love me, but his only love is politics." Their daughter Elizabeth was also quoted in the newspaper, saying: "We all felt awful. We couldn't believe he was doing this to us. She asked us to convince our mother to give him a quick divorce so that they could get on with their lives. It was sick." The party declined to comment, but Pelling – who went on to marry Slaytor – stated: "My wife's allegations are mistruths. She left me and my children a long time ago. I'm now happily engaged."

He attracted further attention in February 2007, when he stunned elderly constituents Alfred and Angela Litten by recommending that they support a far-right party rather than the Tories. The Littens' brief correspondence with him (prompted by their asking if he would sign an Early Day Motion objecting to Israel's trade ties with the EU) was concluded when the MP wrote: "It will be a pleasure to have you both not voting for me – why don't you go and vote for the BNP?" He explained to the *Independent*: "Often MPs obfuscate when corresponding with the public. I prefer to be straightforward. If constituents want to dish it out, they ought to be able to take it when it is dished back." The BNP, however, were quick to express their gratitude, writing on their website: "Thank you very much Andrew Pelling for promoting the only genuine party committed to withdrawing from the EU in Croydon" (see *Hodge, Margaret*).

Peppiatt, Angela
b. 1945

Jeffrey Archer's PA from 1985-7, when the duties he required of her included filing, photocopying, answering the telephone and falsifying evidence. In January 1987, at Archer's request, she obtained an unused 1986 *Economist* diary (with the help of retired advertising agent Gavin Pearce, further to distance His Lordship from the endeavour), and made bogus entries in it to support his alibi. She left Archer's employ five months after his £500k libel victory in 1987, when he disputed her meriting a £10k bonus. Peppiatt, however, had had the foresight to make a copy of Archer's genuine 1986 diary, which finally found its way into police custody in 1999. "You don't say no to Jeffrey," she whimpered in mitigation. "You're either part of his team, or you're out." Fortunately it was found in court that the unwitting assistant was only obeying orders.

see *Dodgy Diary, the*

SLEAZE

> "It was the most disgusting thing I've ever had a man say to me in my life. I had to stop straight away. It just killed all passion dead"
> – *Barbara Corish on Stephen Byers' pillow talk, the News of the World, June 2002*

SLOT

Pergau Dam

Perhaps the ultimate example of foreign aid coming with strings attached, this hydro-electric dam was built from 1991 on the Pergau River in Malaysia, near the Thai border, with £234 million from the UK foreign aid budget – making it the largest aid project ever financed by the UK. At the time Malaysia was buying up to £1 billion of arms from the UK a year, under terms negotiated by Defence Secretary George Younger – and it is strongly suspected that the dam cash was conditional on the arms sales continuing. The scheme was not universally supported by UK officials, and the decision to proceed was largely the doing of Foreign Secretary Douglas Hurd (*qv*). A National Audit Office report in late 1993 condemned the project as a waste of money, and it became the subject of a government inquiry from March 1994. It soon emerged that Younger had indeed given the Malaysians to understand that aid for the dam would be given in proportion to the value of the arms deal.

A Commons Select Committee later ruled that Younger had made 'a grave error of judgement', and criticised Margaret Thatcher and former aid minister Chris Patten for not co-operating fully with their inquiry. That November the High Court ruled that Hurd had acted illegally in allocating the cash, as the project was not of economic or humanitarian benefit to the Malaysian people. He was not censured, but resigned soon afterwards, stating: "I have never knowingly broken the law." In 2002, administration of the UK aid budget ceased to be the Foreign Secretary's responsibility, largely in response to this affair.

The scandal highlighted the ticklish fact that British aid is not always awarded disinterestedly, and that the most deserving countries do not always receive commensurate financial assistance – Oman, for example, is the third largest buyer of British arms, and receives more aid per capita than Ethiopia.

Pie-Man, the

Acclaimed erotic drama featuring Antonia de Sancha (*qv*) as a one-legged prostitute infatuated with a pizza delivery boy. Prints of the 1992 piece are nigh-on impossible to acquire, and it is not known whether her performance in it first brought her charms to the attention of David Mellor (*qv*).

Pinochet, Augusto

b. Nov 25th 1915 / d. Dec. 10th 2006

Brutal dictator of Chile from Sept 11th 1973 to March 11th 1990, and chum of Margaret Thatcher, Norman Lamont and Alan Clark, among others in Tory high command. In debunking his reputation, his detractors point to the bloody coup against democratically-elected Salvador Allende that won him power in 1973, the sale of literally tons of cocaine and cluster bombs to Iran and Iraq in the late 80s, and countless acts of extreme violence carried out by his secret police, the DINA. Supporters, meanwhile, prefer to see him as the man who delivered Chile from the evils of Communism.

Not even Pinochet's fans in the UK dispute that huge numbers of Chilean nationals were tortured and murdered under his iron rule. Thatcher dismissed his British arrest under Labour in 1998 as 'gesture politics', which author Alan Bennett suggested was also true of Thatcher's stance – 'the gesture in question being two fingers to humanity'.

Despite the wizened despot's supposed ill health (Labour Home Secretary Jack Straw declined to release his medical papers in 2000), he managed to live well into the new millennium. On his 91st birthday in November 2006, Pinochet admitted 'political responsibility' for the atrocities that had occurred in his name, but stopped well short of apologising. On his death a fortnight later, Thatcher declared herself 'greatly saddened', and extended her 'deepest condolences' to his family.

Porter, Shirley
b. Nov 29th 1930

Terrifying Tory grandee (even Mrs Thatcher called her 'really scary') who oversaw the 1989 Westminster City Council gerrymandering (*qv*) scandal, branded by Labour 'the biggest financial scandal in the history of local government'. In total 48 senior staff quit under her famously intrusive and hectoring leadership – not that it stopped her lobbying frenziedly for further ennoblement and promotion.

"The most corrupt British public figure in living memory – with the possible exception of Robert Maxwell"

After the 1986 local elections saw the Conservative council majority tumble to just four, the millionairess had to orchestrate a comeback.

The strategy her administration devised required altering the social composition of the various marginal wards in their favour. This they did by selling attractively-priced council homes to probable Tory voters, shunting around 100 poor, Labour-friendly families into asbestos-ridden tower blocks in already-unwinnable wards.

Following a *Panorama* investigation into the illegal practice, a formal investigation was launched by District Auditor John Magill in 1989. He concluded that it was 'a disgraceful and improper purpose,' and in 1996 Porter and five colleagues were slapped with the £31.6m bill to compensate the taxpayer (this included £13.3m of discounts on council homes offered to attract Tory-profile homebuyers). Tesco heiress Shirl, however – whose fortune has been estimated as anywhere between £69m and £300m – pleaded insufficient funds, and embarked on a long and ultimately fruitless legal battle to salvage her reputation (among her diminishing assets was listed a gold-plated lavatory seat). During this appeal period, interest pushed the bill further up to £42m.

Perhaps some of the shortfall could have been avoided if she'd kept a tighter tab on the value of council property – some of her 'sale prices' included three cemeteries for just 15p and adjacent properties at 85p a pop. In 2001 the House of Lords declared her policies a 'blatant and dishonest misuse of public power', and in 2004 she finally agreed to cough up £12.3m in final settlement. She'd been living in Israel and Florida for 12 years, but on August 7th 2006, under the headline 'SHAMELESS SHIRLEY', the *Evening Standard* reported that she'd found £1.5m down the back of the sofa to spend on a flat near Park Lane. That same year her achievements were aptly summed up in *Nothing Like A Dame*, an unofficial biography by *Today* journalist Andrew Hosken. In its review, the *Guardian* hailed her as 'by a considerable margin, the most corrupt British public figure in living memory – with the possible exception of Robert Maxwell' (*qv*).

see *Legg, Barry / shirleyportering*

Prescott, John
b. May 31st 1938
MP (Lab), Hull East, 1970-

John Leslie Prescott (not to be confused with sex-slur TV idol John Leslie Stott) is the tongue-tied, fist-first loverman who spent ten years nominally as Britain's second most powerful man. Long celebrated for his tenuous grasp of English, he was once considered an important link between New Labour and its socialist roots – but grubby junkets on behalf of the Millennium Dome (*qv*), tawdry revelations about his private life and a predilection for expensive cars and croquet have steadily eroded his credibility.

Prescott's political ambitions date as far back as 1948, when he failed his 11+ exams and vowed revenge on those who'd tried to keep him down. After two long decades as a waiter and union activist in the Merchant Navy, he KO'd Norman Lamont (*qv*) in a heavyweight battle for Hull East in 1970, entering the Commons a die-hard socialist. Twenty-seven years on, the glories of government had smoothed away much of his chippiness about wealth: he earned the nickname 'Two Jags' because his role as Deputy PM allowed him a ministerial Jaguar as well as his personal pride and joy, in which he'd already notched up a string of driving offences. His most notorious motoring moment, however, came at the 1999 Labour Party Conference. An official car ferried the Prescotts 200 yards along the seafront from their hotel, so the Minister for Transport and the Environment could deliver a sermon encouraging the British people to use public transport. His excuse was an instant classic: "The wife doesn't like to have her hair blown about."

Despite mounting evidence that he was a liability – including a 2001 assault on a member of the public (see *Evans, Craig*) – Prescott clung to high office. In 2003 he was in trouble again, this time over a grace-and-favour flat in Clapham, rented from the RMT Union at a token rate. Though he paid less each month than the flat might have earned in a week, he hadn't registered the fact among his interests. Under pressure he renounced the perk, but hadn't learned his lesson: the public had been picking up his council tax all the while, and on January 12th 2006 he was forced to apologise and repay thousands of pounds for nine years' duty-free accommodation at Admiralty House. Three months later, his glamourless affair with Diary Secretary Tracey Temple (*qv*) triggered a torrent of doubts about his long-term fidelity to his wife Pauline, and caused his nickname to be amended to 'Two Shags'. The *Sun*'s political editor Trevor Kavanagh guffawed on Radio 5: "Learning John Prescott's had an affair is a bit like learning that Simon Hughes (*qv*) is gay. I mean, everyone knew he has affairs. He's had a string of affairs throughout his life and this has come as no surprise." As with Robin Cook (*qv*), voters had no choice but to accept that one of the least enticing men in the public eye was having a lot of sex.

More damaging were the accusations of sexual harrassment. On April 30th, former Labour aide Tricia McDaid (*qv*) told the *Sunday Times* that the Deputy PM was 'a serial groper' who 'just jumped on you when he felt like it'. She referred to a catalogue of victims inside and outside Parliament, which may have included the wife of colleague Austin Mitchell (*qv*) and buxom air stewardess Helga Forde (*qv*). A month later, McDaid aligned her money and her mouth by formally filing for sexual harrassment. Many female members of the party expressed great discomfort with the allegations, and MPs including Kate Hoey and Geraldine Smith refused to back Prescott as calls for his sacking mounted. Tony Blair, however, was too wary of alienating the party's old guard to strip Prescott of his title or £134,000 salary. Nevertheless, it was stressed that the jowly clown wouldn't actually be doing anything important henceforth: his ministerial duties would be spread across other departments. It wasn't good enough, though, and on May 7th – under the headline 'NOW PREZZA IS SCREWING US ALL' – the *Sun* ran a story totting up Prescott's cost to the taxpayer. The final tally, incorporating expenses and perks such as the government Jag, the Admiralty House pad and the use of plush Buckinghamshire estate Dorneywood (where he entertained Ms Temple) – topped £600k per annum. Some taxpayers dimly recalled that it had been precisely to please the same Labour old guard that another public figure with largely ceremonial duties – the Queen – had forfeited her own grace-and-favour perks under New Labour.

In 2006, on his 68th birthday and under sufferance, the former firebrand agreed to give up his Dorneywood love-nest after long-lens pictures emerged of him enjoying a genteel game of lawn croquet in its lush grounds. This finally gave the lie to the official line that Prescott 'ran the country' whenever Tony Blair popped abroad. And any hope that he'd serve out his final days in dignity were shattered when the Philip Anschutz (*qv*) affair broke in July. That August it emerged that Prescott's son, John Jr (*qv*), was engaged in property development deals that could stand or fall on being rubber-stamped by his father's office. By now the juvenile bully had long since stopped being a laughing stock, and no-one who saw him blow an ironic kiss to the waiting photographers outside Downing Street at the end of the summer can forget the violent sensations the vision provoked.

"NOW PREZZA IS SCREWING US ALL"

As Labour prepared for power in 1996, Prescott delivered a passionate anti-Tory speech at the Labour Conference. "They are up to their necks in sleaze," he thundered. "We are a party of principle. We will earn the trust of the British people... We've had enough lies. Enough sleaze." Sadly for him, no single Labour MP has done more to ensure that the phenomenon remains classless and cross-bench. On August 27th 2007 he finally announced that he'd be stepping down at the next Election – but it wasn't all bad news. His memoirs were apparently on the way, and one of the contenders for his seat is his younger son David.

Prescott, John Jr
b. 1963

John Prescott's eldest son, and the man burdened with carrying on the family name. This caused confusion in March 2005, when the press got wind that a certain 'J. Prescott' was attending a property conference at an exclusive seafront hotel in Cannes, the Carlton – and assumed it was the Deputy Prime Minister on a jolly. In August 2006 it emerged that 'Junior' co-owned regeneration company Estate Partnerships (devoted to identifying areas of social housing likely to be awarded planning permission), and that decisions concerning certain developments could possibly be made by his father's department.

One project under scrutiny from government and developers alike was a proposed 600-house complex near Middlesbrough, and 'Little' John was tasked with taking a wild guess as to its chances of success. He said he 'wouldn't know' whether his clients' planning applications landed on his father's desk or not. In fact the final submissions were delivered in June 2006, a month after Prescott had lost his powers to make any decisions whatsoever – but it whiffed enough of clashing interests to have Tories baying for an inquiry, even if nothing illegal had taken place. "We never speak about my business," said John Jr at the time. "I respect my father too much."

see *Dustbingate*

Price, Katie
b. May 22nd 1978

Better known as Jordan, this über-boobed glamour model stood on an independent ticket for Stretford and Urmston in 2001, against Labour's Beverley Hughes (*qv*). "I know it will take a big swing to win the seat, but there's no bigger swinger than me," she promised at the outset of her campaign, whose slogan 'For A Bigger And Betta Future' seemingly referenced her vast breasts. The glands informed several of her policies too, such as more UK nudist beaches and free cosmetic surgery, though she also proposed (with surprising gravitas) an end to parking tickets. How the Page 3 slattern intended to make good the inevitable shortfall in council income was barely covered in her manifesto – and neither was she in the accompanying photos.

In the end it didn't matter. Labour comfortably retained the seat - though with a creditable 713 votes she was in no danger of losing her deposit, unlike her army of lonely male admirers. By December 2006 a certain despair seemed to have crept into the comely sage's views. "Take away politics and religion for world peace," the *Observer* quoted her. "I don't know anything about any of it, but it just seems to cause problems."

Princess Rat

Unflattering pet name employed by Paul Marsden MP (*qv*) in a failed bid to woo go-getting young doctor Rita Pal (*qv*).

see *King Rat*

Probity

1. Moral rectitude.

2. Quality attributed to Jeffrey Archer by William Hague (*qv*).

see *Integrity*

Proctor, Harvey
b. Jan 16th 1947
MP (Con), Basildon, 1979-83
Billericay, 1983-87

Icy blue whose weakness for spanking youths cost him his Parliamentary career, following a vicious tabloid campaign.

A vigorous opponent of immigration, right-wing hardliner Proctor was assistant director of the Monday Club (*qv*) from 1969-71, and Chairman of its Immigration and Repatriation Committee.

In 1981 he penned the squib *Immigration – An Untenable Situation* for the Club, and served on its Executive Council from 1983 until he stood down as an MP in 1987, shortly before being tried for gross indecency. The charges arose from a vendetta the *People* had decided to pursue against him, after he'd won damages from them over claims that Mrs Thatcher refused to refer to him as 'My Hon Friend'. In the summer of 1986 they splashed with a lurid spread concerning an alleged network of rent boys which Proctor was employing. The MP's dignified refusal to confirm or deny the stories merely fanned their flames, and in due course the *Mirror* joined the fray, running tales of his exotic conduct in Morocco ('NAKED ARAB UNDER MP's BED'). In April 1987, some months after the sanctimonious *People* had handed their dossier to Scotland Yard, the police arrested Proctor in an absurd dawn raid. Though he had the support of his constituency association – having been committed for trial for gross indecency – he announced in May that he would not stand for re-election.

The age of consent was then 21, and some of Proctor's companions had been younger (unlike the law on heterosexual sex, a belief that they were not underaged was no defence). He pleaded guilty, was convicted and fined £1450. The press showed little sympathy for the aloof disciplinarian, and he remained the subject of their attentions in his next venture, a pair of gents' outfitters named Proctor's Shirts and Ties. This was established with the support of investors such as Tim Yeo, Neil Hamilton and Jeffrey Archer (all *qv*), and sold goods including cufflinks cheekily named 'Harvey's Nuts'. The *Spectator* especially distinguished itself with a cartoon captioned 'shirtlifters will be prosecuted', but the smirks froze in 1992 when 'queer bashers' attacked his premises in Richmond. Hamilton emerged with unaccustomed credit from that episode, receiving a broken nose for his pains, while his formidable wife Christine chased the attackers down the street.

The shops had closed by 2000, owing to the recession and a spot of bother over an unpaid VAT bill, and Proctor is currently working for the Duke of Rutland at Belvoir Castle, where he can occasionally be found manning the gift shop.

Project Babylon

Mind-boggling scheme to destroy the world from space, jointly devised by the Iraqi and British governments in the late 80s.

see *Supergun*

Project LISI

Dubious mid-80s arms deal to Singapore, designed to circumvent the embargo on shipping guns to Iran, and brokered by BMARC – a firm under the directorship of Jonathan Aitken (*qv*). A DTI investigation at the time (led by Michael Heseltine) proved usefully inconclusive, until a 1994 article in the *Independent* reopened the worm-packed can and prompted the TV documentary *Jonathan of Arabia* (*qv*).

Pure, Pure Panto

How Max Clifford (*qv*) joyfully described the media circus surrounding Alan Clark (*qv*) and the family of Judge James Harkess (*qv*) in May 1994.

Purer Than Pure

Impossible standard of rectitude, supposedly cited by Tony Blair in 1997 as that which he expected of his administration. Some quote him as having said 'whiter than white', but both versions are paraphrased – and it proved an impossible dream in any case.

SLEAZE

"This House stands in utter ill-repute on the question of the funding of political campaigns. None of the parties here, and all three of them are culpable, ever asked the millionaires and billionaires who gave them and lent them money where they got the money from"

- George Galloway upon being suspended, July 2007

SLOT

Quinn, Kimberly
b. 1961

Man-eating publisher of the *Spectator*, and former mistress to – amongst others – journalist Simon Hoggart and Labour minister David Blunkett (*qv*), by whom she had a bouncing baby son, William, in 2002. Legend has it that her opening gambit at a dinner hosted by sometime Boris Johnson mistress Petronella Wyatt was: "I've always wondered what it would be like to have sex with a blind man." Before long she'd found out – but in March 2005 DNA tests established that Blunkett was not the father of her second son, leading the *Telegraph* to speculate about 'a media figure who is prominent in India' and 'another media figure in Britain'. Following the end of their affair in mid-2004, the shattered Blunkett described her as 'sensual and intellectual' to the *Edinburgh Evening News*, adding: "She was the great love of my life – she meant everything to me." By December 15th he sadly admitted: "I misunderstood what we had, that someone could do this." Meanwhile Quinn – who had reportedly kept a diary of their three-year affair – returned to her second husband, Stephen. One man who had no sympathy with him was his predecessor, Michael Fortier. "Her affair with Stephen Quinn destroyed our marriage," he told the *Sunday Mirror* that August, "so naturally I am very bitter towards him."

Kimberly subsequently became embroiled in a taxpayers' revolt when it emerged that Blunkett had splurged £179 of public money to treat her to a first class railway ticket to Doncaster in August 2002 – a perk reserved only for spouses. The Parliamentary Standards Committee duly upheld a formal complaint against him, calling it "a clear breach of parliamentary rules," and he repaid the cash. It is not known whether he and his estranged lover went Dutch on the debt.

SLEAZE

"We spent too long in the Westminster palace of variety, so we're now in the REAL world of showbiz entertainment"

- *Christine Hamilton,*
August 2006

SLOT

John 'Jack' Profumo

b. Jan 30th 1915 / d. March 9th 2006

MP (Con), Kettering, 1940-45 / Stratford-on-Avon, 1950-63

Dapper sleaze tornado whose 1963 sex-and-spying affair riveted the nation and became the subject of a star-studded 1989 farce, *Scandal*, in which he was played by Coronation Street panto dame Sir Ian McKellen. The bother began with a July 8th 1961 party at Cliveden, home to Viscount Astor (*King Ralph* star Leslie 'ding-dong' Phillips). Among the call-girls present was Christine Keeler (*Willow* siren Joanne Whalley), who – prior to her brief, passionate affair with Secretary of State for War Profumo – was sharing a bed with senior Russian naval attaché Yevgeny Ivanov (*Living Daylights* hardman Jeroen Krabbé). Although rumours of the indiscretion were soon all over London, it took a shooting in December 1962 involving another of Keeler's lovers, Jamaican ponce Johnnie Edgecombe (Roland 'Fine Young Cannibals' Gift) before press and Parliament took real interest. In March 1963 mischievous Labour MPs took it upon themselves to raise the matter in the Commons, nominally on grounds of national security. Profumo thereupon made a self-exculpatory statement to the House on March 22nd 1963, including the fatal fib: "There was no impropriety whatsoever in my acquaintance with Miss Keeler."

Come June 5th he was forced to admit that the phrase 'no impropriety whatsoever' should not have been taken literally, and resigned. Matters took a tragic turn on August 3rd, when society osteopath and Cliveden 'fixer' Stephen Ward (*King Ralph* star John Hurt) committed suicide rather than be convicted of living off the immoral earnings of Keeler and another vice girl, Mandy Rice-Davies (*Doc Hollywood* beauty Bridget Fonda). Profumo, meanwhile, devoted himself to the field of community sanitation at London's Toynbee Hall, of which he eventually became chairman. As he embarked on the long road to redemption, his party was voted out: many felt the affair had been a decisive factor in the defeat, but its protagonist never spoke publicly of it again, and by 2006 obituarists were hailing him as a rare example of an MP who'd acted with complete integrity after his fall.

Redmond, Dermot
b. 1942

Persian rug dealer and convicted fraudster who was named as 'the other man' in Ron Brown's stormy affair with Commons researcher Nonna Longden. Irish-born Redmond had been best man at Longden's wedding to her estranged husband Peter, who told the *Sunday Mirror* on January 14th 1990: "I couldn't believe that Dermot could do that to me... he was very sneaky because he rang me to ask for Nonna's phone number. The next thing I knew, he had moved into her flat."

see *Knickergate*

Redwood, John
b. June 15th 1951
MP (Con), Wokingham, 1987-

Pointy-eared goon whose moment in the sun came when he resigned from John Major's Cabinet in 1995, in protest at the direction of the government. Until then his principal claim to fame had been fudging the words to Welsh anthem *Land of My Fathers* just after becoming Welsh Secretary in 1993 (the Tories' tight victory at the 1992 election had left them with no genuinely Welsh MPs of any standing). When Major pretended to resign in July 1995, the uniquely unappealing Redwood was the only MP who thought it worth having a crack at the top job. Crushingly, he proved even less popular than his rival, and was trounced 89 votes to 218. Redwood

claimed his beef with Major was over Europe, but it might just as easily have been 'Back To Basics': in 2003 the All Souls swot would leave his wife of 29 years for his Parliamentary Researcher (*qv*) of six years, former glamour girl and failed mayoral candidate Nikki Clarke, with whom he appeared in a *Hello!* spread in January 2004.

His devastated spouse (see also *Cook, Margaret*) later claimed he'd dumped her by phone and locked her out of the family home. "Wokingham voters beware!" she raged in an open letter to his constituents at the 2005 Election. "He can be very rude and arrogant. My experience also teaches me that he is heartless and capable of awful cruelty… The torment to which he subjected me shows the utterly inhuman nature of this man's personality. He is a Vulcan, not a human being." The volume of memoirs she said she was preparing – provisionally entitled *Living With A Vulcan* – had not found a publisher by 2007.

Regan, Gaynor
b. 1956

Successively diary secretary, mistress and second wife to Robin Cook (*qv*). Cook never publicly commented on Regan's clerical abilities, but her parking planning left much to be desired. If leaving her car on a meter was a ploy to cajole her lover into leaving his wife, however, it worked brilliantly: early one July morning in 1998 *News of the World* hounds snapped Cook furtively stuffing coins into the machine, prompting him to chuck long-term spouse Margaret almost immediately. Within weeks of his 'quickie' divorce the next January he'd married Gaynor in a Tunbridge Wells registry office.

Register of Members' Interests, the

Amnesty for bribes, gifts and bungs, regulated by the Committee on Standards in Public Life and The Advisory Committee on Business Interests. Despite its compulsory status, an astonishing number of MPs seem unaware of it.

see *Aitken, Jonathan / Blunkett, David / Hamilton, Neil / Prescott, John / Reid, John* etc

Reid, John
b. May 8th 1947
MP (Lab), Hamilton North / Motherwell North / Airdrie and Shotts, 1987-

Brutish bulldog who weathered a reputation for drunken thuggery to emerge as a key player in the crumbling New Labour regime.

The son of a Lanarkshire postman, Reid led a schoolboy strike only to lose his prefect's badge for smoking. After Stirling University (where he was a notable belter of Irish Republican songs and also obtained his mysterious PhD), he flirted with Communism for a couple of years in the 1970s before masterminding Neil Kinnock's years of failure from 1983. On gaining his seat in 1987, he quickly established a reputation as 'hardest man in the Commons'. The subjects of his booze-fuelled thumpings included fellow MP Gerry Bermingham and the doorkeeper of a party division lobby (when Reid was late for a vote in 1991). Having switched to Diet Coke in the mid-90s, the reformed tippler quipped "I didn't have a drink problem. I loved the stuff." But one parliamentary press officer remembers it less jovially: "He was a terrible drunk." Perhaps the demon drink explains his astonishing decision to enjoy an undeclared three-day junket as the guest of Radovan Karadžic (*qv*) at the five-star Le Richemond Hotel on the shores of Lake Geneva in 1993, which he forgot to declare in the Register of Members' Interests.

"It's mate-ocracy. It's about looking after yourself and your mates and not being accountable to anyone"

Though the booze was behind him by 1999, the old hackles were in evidence when he had a stand-up row with Donald Dewar (his rival for supreme jurisdiction over Scotland) at the Labour Party conference. Tensions were running high because Reid's lobbyist son Kevin had been caught boasting into a reporter's concealed microphone: "I know the Secretary of State very, very well – he's my father." It wouldn't be Reid's last embarrassment. In an investigation held from 2000-01, Parliamentary Standards Commissioner Elizabeth Filkin (*qv*)

initially upheld a claim that Reid and colleague John Maxton (*qv*) had misled the Commons Fees Office over the employment arrangements of two assistants, one of whom was his son. Effectively, Labour campaign salaries were being augmented by the taxpayer, through channeling of office expenses. But the heavily-Blairite Commons Committee found in Reid's favour – while admitting no fault with the fairness of the commissioner's original investigation. More serious were claims that the minister had 'discussed' the matter with potential witnesses. Even the pro-Reid Committee conceded: "it was at best unwise for Dr Reid to have discussed the investigation with any of the parties to it." The Scottish editor of the *Sunday Times*, Dean Nelson, who broke the story, angrily pointed out that Reid had not been exonerated, but that the burden of proof had been raised so high that the result he'd sought was impossible. "It's mate-ocracy," he fumed. "It's about looking after yourself and your mates and not being accountable to anyone." Filkin herself had her authority so badly undermined that she stood down soon after.

After assuming stewardship of the Home Office from Charles Clarke in May 2006, Reid distanced himself from his predecessor's incompetence by disclaiming responsibility for the department's shortcomings. Embarrassment ensued the same month when a derisory and probably ancient quantity of hashish was found in the spare bedroom of his Scottish holiday home (no one suggested it was his), and he came in for further stick in September 2006 (just after declaring he had 'no interest' in the leadership of the Labour party) for the inscrutable proposal that Muslim mums should shop their kids if they showed 'tell-tale signs' of militancy.

"I didnae have a drink problem. I loved the stuff"

His problems hadn't let up by the New Year: in January 2007 he was facing loud calls for his resignation over overcrowded prisons, lost sex offenders and a lightening of sentencing guidelines for judges. He was uncowed, though, telling the *Today* programme: "There's one thing that's certain. I'm not going to quit." In that, at least, he differed from David Blunkett.

Respect

1. A state of profound deference, regard or appreciation.

2. Political party founded by a leotard-wearing *Celebrity Big Brother* contestant (see *Galloway, George*).

Reverse Gear

Control mechanism permitting backwards movement and the covering of old ground. An attribute Tony Blair insisted he did not possess at the 2003 Labour Conference.

Richard, Sir Cliff
b. Oct 14th 1940

Spry bachelor boy, by his own account "the most radical rock star there has ever been", whose £3m colonial-style mansion in Barbados – purchased with the spoils of almost 50 years of insipid pop recordings – has repeatedly accommodated the family of Tony Blair.

"The most radical rock star there has ever been"

Cynics have drawn a link between Sir Cliff's generosity and his desire to have UK copyright protection on recorded music extended to 70 years from the existing 50, with the end of the line approaching for the gravy train on late-50s classics such as *Living Doll* and *Travelling Light*. A memo mentioning Cliff and fellow Caribbean tourists The Rolling Stones has Blair on record addressing these concerns a July 2005 Downing St. meeting, but aides insist it wasn't the PM who brought up the subject.

see *Gibb, Robin*

Richards, Rod
b. March 12th 1947
*MP (Con), Clwyd North West, 1992-97
/ Welsh Assembly, 1999-2002*

The very antithesis of John Major's 'Back To Basics' dream, this Welsh lout's wild ways earned him the nickname 'Rod the Rottweiler' well before he was muzzled by Tory bosses.

Richards, a burly former marine, worked as a Welsh-language newsreader, minicab driver and publican before achieving public office. His hectoring manner endeared him to few – he once described local Labour councillors as 'short, fat, slimy and fundamentally corrupt' and is said to have revelled in the title 'The Most Hated Man In Wales'. He lost his job in the Welsh Office when it emerged that he'd cheated on his wife with PR bimbo Julia Felthouse in 1996, upon which the tabloids assembled a cross-bench chorus of Welsh MPs to celebrate the self-confessed sex addict's downfall. Lib Dem Alex Carlile spoke for them all when he chirped: "No-one will regret his resignation – as a minister he was sanctimonious, arrogant and odious." He wasn't finished, though. In 1999 he won the Tory nomination for a 'top-up' place in the new Welsh Assembly (having been defeated in his own constituency during the democratic phase of the election), and managed to defeat William Hague's preferred candidate to become its Tory Leader.

He'd barely warmed his seat, however, before he faced serious allegations of assault (and not for the first time: he'd already been convicted of ABH in 1975). The charges stemmed from an evening he'd spent with sisters Tiffani and Cassandra Melvin in a Richmond pub in July 1999. After sharing pizza, they'd repaired to the girls' nearby home, but Richards was ejected when it became apparent that their intentions didn't square up, and was accused of having broken Cassandra's arm in the ensuing brawl. "There were two girls in their 20's, and I thought I'd shag them," he later explained to the *Mail On Sunday*. "To shag two women is a male fantasy." His QC was more circumspect: "The events of that night provide a classic cautionary tale for a middle-aged man at a loose end in London," she told the court. He was cleared in June 2000, but the trial left his credibility in pieces (he had been less than 'frank' with the police, he conceded in the witness box). At the end of the month the chairman of the Welsh Tories, Henri Lloyd-Davies, announced that "a number of requests have been made for Mr Richards to be referred to the Ethics and Integrity Committee," and confirmed that the complaints "relate to conduct over a period of time".

"I'm a serial shagger. I love women. I can't help it"

Having already lost the Conservative whip at the end of 1999, Richards served as an independent until 2002, when he stood down on 'health grounds'. The Tories' failure to put him on the list for the next intake caused him to rail bitterly at them, but their stance was perhaps vindicated when he was found celebrating Christmas face down in a Cardiff park a few months later. Things hit a new low the following year, when he was declared bankrupt with debts of around £300k, and was driven to flogging his tawdry reminiscences to the Sunday papers. "I'm a serial shagger," he raved. "I love women. I can't help it."

SLEAZE

"Being lectured by the current House of Commons on the question of the funding of political campaigns is like being accused of having bad taste by Donald Trump, like being accused of slouching by the Hunchback of Notre Dame"

- George Galloway upon being suspended, July 2007

SLOT

Riddick, Graham
b. Aug 26th 1955
MP (Con), Colne Valley, 1987-97

Greedy gull who had to resign as a Parliamentary Private Secretary after a *Sunday Times* sting in 1994 caught him out over Cash For Questions. Out of ten Labour and ten Tory MPs approached by the rag's investigative team on behalf on non-existent drugs firm 'Githins', only he and colleague David Tredinnick *(qv)* showed themselves willing participants, following a short meeting on the Commons terrace. Nonetheless, on 11th July, the day after publication, the defiant Riddick chose to attack "the so-called *Guardians* of the public interest" for entrapment. He had some support on the benches, having undertaken to return his £1,000 cheque just before the story went to press, but by July 13th he'd issued a grovelling apology to Parliament, pending an investigation by the Privileges Committee. Riddick would receive only half the fine of his less conscience-stricken colleague, after his plea to the Committee that he backed out before any intimation that he'd been 'had' – though perhaps with a little research he might have discovered there was no such firm as 'Githins', nor any such thing as 'Thising's Disease', the throat infection for which they claimed to have developed a lucrative cure, 'Sigthin' (all creations of the wordsmiths on the *Sunday Times* 'Insight' team).

In April 1995 the Committee's report found that the *Sunday Times'* journalistic methods 'fell substantially below the standards to be expected of legitimate investigative journalism'. Sadly, a similar verdict was delivered on the MPs' conduct, and Riddick – having already been suspended for ten days without pay – was forced to stand down from his minor government role. Though he won a Press Complaints ruling in his favour in 1996, citing a 'random attempt to lure MPs to accept payments by a direct invitation to behave improperly', the question remained as to why he'd been susceptible to the invitation in the first place, and he lost his seat at the next Election. His usurper, Labour's Kali Mountford (*qv*), carried on the constituency's proud history by getting herself suspended from the Commons in next to no time.

see *Cash For Questions*

Rippon, Geoffrey
b. May 28th 1924
MP (Con), Norwich South 1955-64 / Hexham 1964-1987

Tory stalwart who became an MP in 1955, penned an odious pamphlet for the Monday Club (*qv*) entitled 'Right Angle' and amassed a mind-boggling 48 directorships by the time he stood down in 1987, including the chairmanship of financial services group Blue Arrow, whose £60,000 emolument was considerably more than his parliamentary wage packet.

Ritz Hotel, Paris

Glitzy hostelry in which Lady Diana spent her final evening in 1997. Other melancholy events to have occurred within its sumptuous confines are Neil Hamilton's notorious blow-out at hotelier Mohammed Fayed's expense in 1987, and Jonathan Aitken's date with destiny (in the form of two Arab businessmen) six years later. Fayed was later to express disgust at the £2,120 extras bill run up by Hamilton and his wife Christine (*qv*), and remarked that the sight of government minister Aitken with two Saudi arms dealers "was like seeing the Attorney-General sitting with Al Capone." Both MPs would have saved themselves an awful lot of bother had they only reached for their own wallets when the bills arrived.

Riviera Gigolo, the

Nom de plume under which the young Alastair Campbell (*qv*) published his erotic fantasies in pocket-sized jazz-mag *Forum*. The highly competitive former Downing Street aide claims he filed the mucky missives from his student retreat in the South of France purely in order to win a bet, but no doubt they amply qualified him for the tabloid employment he found under Robert Maxwell (*qv*) upon graduation.

Robinson, Geoffrey
b. May 25th 1938
MP (Lab), Coventry North West, 1976-

Portly financier whose dealings have been a reliable source of embarrassment to New Labour.

After a chequered career at British Leyland and Jaguar, Robinson (who, according to Commons legend, never carries anything smaller than a £50 note) amassed a fortune with the support of an exotic Belgian recluse named Madame Joska Bourgeois. He was the principal beneficiary of her 1994 will, many of whose millions were held in Guernsey – in stark contrast to Labour's line on offshore trusts. With unlimited funds at his disposal, Robinson became fairy godfather to the nascent New Labour movement, and – having bought the *New Statesman* magazine, thereby ensuring its broad support for the regime – by 1996 was suddenly 'everywhere', according to party insiders. He threw lavish parties for politicos in his Park Lane penthouse, offered colleagues perks at football games (he's a long-term director of Coventry City) and even lent them his Nice flat – though only the very cream of the party was given the keys to his Tuscan villa (Tony Blair, for example).

But with prominence came public scrutiny. As Paymaster-General Robinson (who was once quoted as saying "everybody has conflicts of interest in the Treasury") was the subject of three different investigations by the Parliamentary Standards Commissioner in 1998 alone (non-declaration of the offshore trust in Guernsey, failure to register a four-year company directorship back in the 80s and a more recent shareholder irregularity). He denied using his position to further his commercial interests, but conceded to the House in November 1998 that he had not declared all his interests. What scuppered him was secretly loaning £373,000 to cash-strapped comrade Peter Mandelson back in 1997. The helping hand-out had come at a time when big-hearted Geoffrey was also under investigation for fraud by the DTI – Mandelson's own department. When the story broke in December 1998, a month after his embarrassing grovel to the House, the dodgy duo resigned from government within hours of each other.

His champagne soured yet further from 1999 to 2001, as the Tories got wind of his extensive dealings with

Robert Maxwell back in the 80s. A former company of his, TransTec (which he'd sold to Maxwell in 1991), went into receivership on Christmas Eve 1999, leading to accusations that Robinson had concealed a ruinous £11m claim against the company by Ford. In January 2000, while Tories fumed that it was 'all part of one murky big picture', Steven Byers (*qv*) revealed that TransTec firms had over the years received £1.3m in government grants. Attention was also paid to a £200,000 payment, related to another deal with Maxwell, that hadn't made it into the Register Of Members' Interests (Robinson said he never received it, but a diligent hack turned up an invoice for the sum stamped 'Paid'). He had survived three 'strikes' with the Standards Committee, but this time the breathless businessman was found out and suspended from the Commons for three weeks for 'inadvertently' misleading the House.

His next appearance in the headlines came in December 2002, when he was stopped by the police for erratic driving. He failed to provide a breathalyser sample or produce his driving documents and – when cocaine was found in the police van he was interviewed in – suffered the indignity of having his house searched. No clear link was established between the Class A drugs and the 64-year-old, and those charges (but not the three relating to driving offences) were dropped. In August 2003, he changed his 'not guilty' plea over failing to provide a sample to one of 'guilty', and accepted a driving ban – pleading in mitigation that the seriousness of the drugs allegations had addled his good judgement.

Since then, doubtless to the relief of Labour's High Command, he has kept his profile down – though he did weather a brief furore after giving his extensive collection of plants a good soaking during the 2006 hosepipe ban. It turned out the green-fingered millionaire had shelled out something in the region of £10k to bore his own water privately from beneath the earth's crust, thus evading any liability to Thames Water.

SLEAZE

"The public wants cleaner politics and better value for money. Tony Blair's government has tarnished politics and eroded public confidence... We need to restore trust and tackle the public's underlying cynicism"

– *David Cameron,*
September 29th 2006

SLOT

Ross, Ernie
b. July 27th 1942
MP (Lab), Dundee West, 1979-2005

Toady MP once known as the 'Member for Moscow West' who became so loyal to New Labour that he was renamed the 'Trot-finder General', and was slated by the standards committee in July 1999 over the Arms To Africa affair (*qv*). In 1998 he astonished parliament by invoking an obscure Commons rule to protect Foreign Secretary Robin Cook from answering questions over the supply of weapons to Sierra Leone. By February 1999 it had emerged why: Ross, a member of the committee investigating the affair, had sneaked Cook a draft copy of their highly critical report a month before it was due to be published. Ross resigned as soon as MPs demanded an inquiry, but there was little quarter from the standards committee. "He must have known at the time that what he did was wrong," it stated in July 1999, docking him £1800 in pay. "We recommend that he should apologise to the House by a personal statement and be suspended from the service of the House for 10 sitting days." Though Cook denied making any use of the findings, angry opposition MPs called for an apology. Lib-Dem spokesman Paul Tyler spat: "Once again this indicates an arrogant contempt for Parliament." Ross – who, according to his friends, 'liked to be on first-name terms with Cabinet Ministers' – soon slipped back into obscurity, resurfacing only briefly in May 2001 when SNP rival Gordon Archer accused him of misappropriating £3000 of taxpayers' money to fund his own electoral newsletter. Ross branded the claims 'pathetic and wrong', and any interest in them soon died down.

Ryman, John
b. Nov 7th 1930
MP (Lab), Blyth, 1974-1986 / (independent) 1986-7

Disliked by colleagues and constituents in equal measure, this five-times-married confidence trickster entered Parliament in a hail of sleaze after a famously dirty 1974 campaign: following two years' investigation, his agent was jailed for submitting fraudulent election expenses. Ryman angered fellow Labour MPs by spending more time hunting or pursuing his career at the Bar than attending Parliament, and Chief Whip Bob Mellish once famously resorted to making an announcement on local radio, imploring listeners to phone in if they'd spotted him. He eventually stood down from the party in 1986 to mark out his remaining days as an independent. Proof positive that Ryman should never have held office finally came on April 23rd 1992, when he was convicted of defrauding two old ladies of their life savings. Marauding as director of a Swiss bank, he'd promised the guileless grans a handsome 22·5% interest rate on their hard-earned nest-eggs: in the event the money found its way to one of his ex-wives in lieu of maintenance payments, and he was banged up for 2½ years.

John Stonehouse

b. July 28th 1925 / d. April 14th 1988

MP (Lab), Wednesbury / Walsall North, 1957-76

Britain's last Postmaster-General was determined to become wealthy, but his business incompetence led to debts of £1 million instead. When he realised in 1974 that, despite years of dilligent book-cooking, his several failing companies were being investigated by the DTI (one pet project, 'London Capital Group', was later described by the Board of Trade as 'a debt-ridden pack of cards, saturated with offences, irregularities and improprieties'), he decided that desperate measures were called for. Having filched the identities of two dead constituents and shifted £100,000 into a Swiss bank account, he flew to Miami and staged his own drowning on November 20th, leaving a pile of clothes on the beach and a distraught wife and family back home. San Francisco was his next port of call, where he celebrated the sub-Frederick Forsyth ruse's brief success in a topless bar before travelling on to Australia, where he planned to meet Sheila Buckley, his diary secretary (*qv*). What he hadn't reckoned on, however, was the sheer amateurishness of the Melbourne police, who - acting on a tip-off from an over-zealous bank clerk - nicked him on Christmas Eve believing they'd found Lord Lucan.

When he and his stash of fake passports were finally returned to the UK in June 1975, Stonehouse – once tipped as a future Labour leader – stunned the Commons with an hour-long speech in which he damned the 'evils of humbug, hypocrisy, moral decadence and materialism afflicting England', and penned a ludicrous memoir entitled *Death Of An Idealist*. He also argued, bafflingly, that he'd acted honourably in leaving behind life insurance policies for his grieving wife to cash in. She rewarded his generosity by instituting divorce proceedings as he languished on remand in Brixton Prison – from where he continued to exercise his right to serve as a Labour MP. The decision to defend himself in court was not a wise one – he got seven years and resigned as an MP on August 28th 1976, in order to dedicate himself fully to the prison workshop. Much of his sentence was spent campaigning against the right of fellow lags to enjoy pop music as they worked, and he secured early release on health grounds on August 14th 1979. Marriage to Buckley and a decade of sub-Forsyth novels ensued, before he succumbed to the last in a spectacular succession of heart attacks.

Sadie

David Blunkett's guide dog and best friend following the demise of Lucy (*qv*). Described as 'very spirited, a real character' by her former trainer Val Woolrich, Sadie has steered her master through two resignations, an expenses furore, a clash of interests row and a host of awkward women troubles since he took up her reins in January 2003. She is also the author of 'Sadie's Week', a hard-hitting featurette in her master's otherwise comic *Sun* column.

Sarwar, Mohammed
b. Aug 18th 1952
MP (Lab), Glasgow Govan / Glasgow Central 1997-

Britain's first Muslim MP, an anti-war stalwart, was suspended during his first two years of office amidst cries of electoral fraud, but ultimately exonerated. The accusations included bribery of a political opponent, which Sarwar maintained was a £5k loan, and voting irregularities during the bitter Glasgow Govan campaign – centering on four possibly false addresses at which Sarwar was accused of registering voters' names between January 1st and March 31st 1997. Two women who might not have been eligible to vote in his constituency positively identified the MP as the door-to-door canvasser who'd helped them fiddle their registry forms, but later withdrew their story, admitting it could have been any 'middle-aged balding Asian man'. Sarwar was cleared of all charges, saving Labour the embarrassment of another by-election after the Fiona Jones (*qv*) fiasco.

WIGGINGS

"You brought shame upon yourself and a sense of betrayal among the honest people who worked for you. Your political career is in shreds"

– Mr Justice Jowett to Fiona Jones, 1999

FROM THE BEAK

SLEAZE

"For too many Tories, morality means not getting caught... Let's be clear, Morality is measured in more than just money. It's about right and wrong. it's about values... We are a party of principle. We will earn the trust of the British people... We've had enough lies. Enough sleaze"
– John Prescott at the Labour Party Conference, October 1996

"He pushed me quite forcefully against the wall, and put his hand up my skirt"
– Linda McDougall, 2006

"He just leapt on me at one party, and his tongue was halfway down my throat"
– Tricia McDaid, 2006

"I was used to the normal male attention on flights. But Prescott took it further and made my skin crawl"
–Helga Forde, 2006

"I know in the last year I let myself down, I let you down. So, conference, I just want to say sorry"
– John Prescott at the Labour Party Conference, September 2006

SLOT

Sayeed, Jonathan
b. March 20th 1948
MP (Con), Bristol East, 1983-92 / Mid-Bedfordshire 1997-2005

At a time when Labour seemed to be hogging all the sleaze, it came as a refreshing change to see a Tory back in the stocks. Early in 2005 the *Sunday Times* claimed that fleshy ex-sailor Sayeed had been offering behind-the-scenes tours of the Palace of Westminster on behalf of a company called The English Manner (*qv*), which specialised in social-climbing holidays for rich Americans. When it emerged that the company had been set up by Sayeed and his Commons assistant Alexandra Messervy (*qv*), who was accused of receiving a salary from the public purse whilst devoting her energies to the business, the Standards and Privileges Committee got involved. Though it didn't find that he'd received fees directly, it concluded that the duo had been 'at the least negligent in failing to exercise sufficient care to safeguard the reputation of Parliament, and at worst to have acted carelessly, in a manner which has allowed that reputation to be injured'. Their report also made the familiar observation that Sayeed's conduct had 'fallen well below the standards' expected of the House, and he was duly suspended for a fortnight. Party leader Michael Howard had already suspended him from the Tory group of MPs for a month, commenting that "such behaviour in a Conservative Member of Parliament is completely unacceptable, and I condemn it without hesitation." Sayeed, who was also slammed for failing to declare US trips funded by the company, maintained: "I have never used my access to the house or its facilities for commercial gain, neither has The English Manner." It didn't stop his local party attempting to deselect him, though, and – having escaped that humiliation – he announced his intention to stand down from Parliament at the 2005 election.

Scottish Parliament

This vast edifice was conceived as a proud symbol of Scottish independence, but ended up a vainglorious folly second only to the Millennium Dome (qv). Embarked upon in 1998 at an estimated cost of £55m, by March 2004 (after some eighteen thousand changes to the plans) the bottom line had crossed the £430m mark. An inaugural debate was finally held in the building on September 7th 2004, but work was far from finished. Over the next two years the cash total tiptoed towards half a billion, as some 890 further snags were ironed out. After a roofbeam collapsed during a debate on March 2nd 2006, more than two months of itinerant Scottish democracy ensued before the Parliament could return to its ruinously expensive new home. The 2003 Fraser Report was especially damning of the lack of disclosure and blind optimism surrounding the project, which couldn't even justify itself with the promise of becoming a super-casino or a pop auditorium.

Scott, Sir Nicholas

b. Aug 5th 1933 / d. Jan 6th 2005
MP (Con), Paddington South, 1966-74
/ Chelsea, 1974-1996

Genial, accident-prone womaniser who had a low-key but effective career as a liberal Tory minister until several regrettable episodes combined to unseat him in the mid-90s. As Minister for Disabled People in 1994, he was forced to apologise over revelations that he'd misled the House by claiming that attempts to quash Labour's Civil Rights (Disabled Persons) Bill had not emanated from the government. Added embarrassment came in the shape of his daughter Victoria, a parliamentary officer for the Royal Association for Disability and Rehabilitation (RADAR), who led calls for his resignation. "Professionally, I am very, very angry. Personally, I feel rather let down," she commented, and her father duly returned to the backbenches.

His caring image took another beating in June 1995, when his car careered into three year-old Thibault Perreard's buggy and he was arrested for drink-driving and leaving the scene of an accident. While he was on bail awaiting trial, his constituency association returned a vote of no confidence in him and opened the seat to all comers. Scott eventually scraped through in November, but 1996 proved to be his annus horribilis: in March he was fined £450 and banned from driving for a year, and during October's Tory conference in Bournemouth he was found sprawled in the gutter after an Irish Embassy party. He stoutly maintained that a meagre amount of wine had combined with his painkillers to lend him the appearance of an inebriate, but it wasn't good enough for his constituency association. They moved against him for the second time, and that December he suffered the unthinkable indignity of being deselected in favour of Alan Clark (*qv*).

SLEAZE

> "He was a big man with a big heart, helping sick employees in need and backing charities"
>
> – *Alastair Campbell mourns Robert Maxwell, 1991*

SLOT

Scott Report, the (i)

Not to be confused with the 1996 Scott Report (another highly critical inquiry into government arms dealing also involving Jonathan Aitken), this 1969 document revealed the surprising extent of British arms sales to Nigeria during the bloody suppression of Biafran separatists. It also afforded the idealistic young Aitken (*qv*) an early brush with the law, after General Henry Alexander, a British military observer in Nigeria, handed him a copy over dinner 'in the strictest confidence'. Aitken repaid his trust by making two copies, one of which went to the *Sunday Telegraph*, and the other to his friend, MP and fellow pro-Biafran Hugh Fraser. Aitken blamed Fraser for the media storm that inevitably followed, then slept with his wife.

At Aitken's 1970 Old Bailey trial, on charges under the Official Secrets Act, it was disclosed (to what the youthful crusader described as his 'greatest discomfort' in his 1971 volume *Officially Secret*) that General Alexander had felt it necessary to tape a conversation with him: it therefore emerged that their 'careless' friend Fraser was being unjustly fingered for the leak. Aitken was cleared, but the sleazy odour that had settled about his person would prove tough to shift.

Scott Report, the (ii)

The 1996 Scott Inquiry dealt with the Arms-to-Iraq affair (see *Aitken, Jonathan*), and the ensuing 1806 page-long report revealed at numbing length how Thatcher's government had dealt with Saddam Hussein – in every sense of the word.

Commissioned after the scandal arose in 1992, it described how £1bn of Whitehall money had been deployed in 'soft' loan guarantees for British exporters to Iraq, and revealed that Cabinet ministers had refused to stop lending guaranteed funds to Saddam even after he murdered British journalist Farzad Bazoft (*qv*). Mouthy backbenchers like Rupert Allason argued, without evidence, that Bazoft was a spy, and Cabinet minutes suggest they were hoping to protect British industry. After rifling through what little evidence had escaped the shredder, Sir Richard Scott found that during the Iraqi invasion of Iran in the 1980s, officials had destroyed documents relating to the export of Chieftain tank parts to Jordan. Once there, it was presumed they would only end up in one place – Baghdad. It was felt too that ministers were relaxing official guidelines to help encourage enterprising private companies to sell machine tools, which could be used in munitions factories. British company Racal, for example, exported top-of-the-range Jaguar V radios to Saddam's army on credit.

The Iraqi dictator's credit bottomed out after the invasion of Kuwait in 1990, though – and by the time Britain was sending troops in, British 'industry' looked set to start losing all the millions it had cleverly made, and questions were being asked of the main players. That meant most of the Thatcher Cabinet, it seemed, plus inadvertent whistleblower Alan Clark (*qv*), who responded to a query about cover-ups by saying certain people had been 'economical with the actualité' – a flippant phrase that summed up the whole sorry saga.

Shakespeare, Stephan
b. 1957

Fresh-faced apologist for Jeffrey Archer during his kamikaze 1999 Mayoral bid. Having changed his surname from the less redolent Kukowski, 'the Bard' stood and fell for the Tories at Colchester in 1997. After that setback he commanded a mixture of sympathy and awe for agreeing to run the peer's far-fetched campaign for the chains of office in 1999. As the row over his 1987 libel win sent Archer's skeletons spilling from the closet, Shakespeare spent much of the year defending his boss's record on everything from tax bills ('Jeffrey is known as a scrupulous taxpayer') to Tory membership ('Jeffrey Archer is not resigning from the Conservative Party' – which was true: he was expelled in February 2000). When more details about perjury and prostitutes emerged from the 1987 libel trial, Shakespeare's rebuttals became increasingly lyrical. Claims that late Archer associate Terence Baker had admitted lying under oath were "allegations from beyond the grave"; the tortuous press unravelling of Archer's web of lies was like "an Agatha Christie novel"; the press were "a pack of hounds and they want their fox, and they want to rip him to pieces," and so on. Regarding the mix-up over false alibis, Shakespeare debuted a new one: "He said he was with a girlfriend and trying to hide it from his wife." Since that fiery baptism, Shakespeare has made a fortune by co-founding media polling giant You Gov.

WIGGINGS

"These charges represent as serious an offence of perjury as I have had experience of, and have been able to find in the books… it has been an extremely distasteful case"

– *Mr Justice Potts on Jeffrey Archer, 2001*

FROM THE BEAK

Shephard, Gillian
b. Jan 22nd 1940
MP (Con), Norfolk South West, 1987-2005

Tory mainstay whose unglamorous career ensured disappointing sales for her punishing 2000 memoir, *Shephard's Watch* (*sic*). Its publication frustratingly predated her rare brush with controversy in September 2002, when she entertained celebrity con Jeffrey Archer to lunch at her Norfolk home on his day-release from North Sea Camp open prison. Wine flowed at the table and – though His Lordship denied touching a drop – he was accused of 'severely breaching the trust put in him by the Governor' and was relegated to a Cat-B slammer. It wasn't only his Governor's trust that Archer compromised. "When they accepted, I naturally assumed that the terms of Jeffrey's leave from prison permitted him to attend the event," his hostess spluttered afterwards, while Home Secretary David Blunkett (*qv*), perhaps galled at not being invited himself, accused the wily lag of "cocking a snook at all of us". It is not known whether she treated the shepherd's pie connoisseur (see *Krug & Shepherd's*) to her own variant – though it's a fair bet that if she did, it would have been named as wittily as her autobiography.

Sheridan, Tommy
b. March 7th 1964

Thrice-jailed Scottish Socialist Party figurehead, principally known for his sharp dressing, fake tanning and protests against the Poll Tax (*qv*) until he became the central figure in Scotland's murkiest, most outlandish tale outside Loch Ness. His old militant antics (including stints in the nick for causes including withholding of fines) were soon forgotten under a blizzard of what he called 'gristle and sleaze'.

'Tommy', as he was once fondly known in the media, is an old socialist hero and confirmed teetotaller – as outraged at the claim in the Scottish *News of the World* that he'd swilled champagne during a five-in-a-bed romp than he was at the sex slurs themselves.

"Anybody rolling an ice cube round your body would have had a hair ball in their throat"

Further claims involved cocaine and ice cubes, swinging, spanking, strippers, an ex-prostitute and an unnamed footballer, all featuring in a wild party of June 8th 2002. Tommy's Trotsky-loving family in Glasgow would have been partially mollified to see at least some working-class standards upheld in the allegations: the stag-night 'orgy' with his brother-in-law was supposedly conducted in the city's low-rent Moat House hotel, and subsequently outside in the back of a car – though Sheridan insists both men were at home playing Scrabble that evening. Other colleagues felt a true socialist would defend his name by means other than demanding megabucks from the *News of the World* – especially since one 'kiss and tell' girl, Ann Colvin, waived her own fee from the newspaper (another, Fiona McGuire, took home twenty grand). As Sheridan prepared to take the tabloid to court in July 2006, more stories started stacking up: visits to Cupid's (a voyeuristic sex club in Manchester), as well as a dalliance with the paper's own self-styled 'sexpert', Anvar Khan, who made another serious allegation: that he had 'bad breath'.

Disproving the allegations made Sheridan wealthy, but as a man who valued political reputation over money (he used to tithe half his £52k salary back to his party) he must regret the many lurid details of the case, which have deeply embarrassed his old party and numerous individuals. He was narrowly prevented by the judge from taking off his shirt in the stand to search for a thick downy layer of grey fluff. "You're like a monkey," Gail Sheridan purred to her husband during his cross-examination of her (dissatisfied, he had sacked his QC to defend himself). "Anybody rolling an ice cube round your body would have had a hair ball in their throat." At the trial Sheridan accused the parade of 11 SSP witnesses queueing up to testify against him (see *McCombes, Alan*) of engineering 'the mother of all stitch-ups'. The party members insisted he'd admitted to two visits to such clubs, in 1996 and 2002, but knew of no evidence against him. 'Tommy' claimed he'd only quit to save the rest of the party's MSPs from having to carry on living in his shadow, and also raised the possibility that MI5 were behind it all. The *News of the World* had to pay him £200k, and consequently embarked on a major appeal, still being prepared, along with a police investigation which could result in exactly half the courtroom being charged with perjury.

The bloodied paper showed no inclination to tone down its attacks, issuing a front page 'GUILTY' verdict on their nemesis and proclaiming in a leader of October 1st 2006: "Though he hoodwinked a jury, he is in truth a liar, a perverter of justice and a perjurer." In defiance of legal wisdom they went on to brand Sheridan 'the most debauched, lying hypocrite in British political life'. While he waited for their appeal to be heard, Sheridan followed in the footsteps of Neil and Christine Hamilton by putting together a novelty show for the Edinburgh Festival fringe, *The Tommy Sheridan Chat Show*, though he admitted to the *Times* on July 30th 2007 that he can't tell jokes any more than he can tell lies. With guests including Les Dennis, he couldn't rely on others for laughs, either. But at least no-one accused him of lacking a sense of humour: the opening music on his radio show on Edinburgh's Talk 107 incorporates the *Jungle Book* line: "I'm the king of the swingers."

see *McCombes, Alan* / *Trolle, Katrine*

Shiri, Perence
b. Jan 11th 1955

Zimbabwean mass-murderer who learned a few new tricks at the British taxpayer's expense back in 1986. Having commanded the brutal, North Korean-trained Fifth Brigade during its killing spree in Matabeleland from 1983-84, Shiri (who styled himself 'the Black Jesus') honed his military skills as a guest of the UK government at the MOD's Royal College of Defence Studies. The junket was an ill-conceived attempt to bring the thug to heel, but might at least be excused on grounds of Whitehall's ambiguous intelligence. The same cannot be said of Tony Blair's mind-boggling decision to reinforce 'Air Marshal' Shiri's fleet of Hawks in 2000 – especially after the Movement for Democratic Change's 1997 report into the Matabeleland atrocities had found him personally responsible for 'gross crimes against humanity' (up to 20,000 people remain unaccounted for in the region). Shiri has since overseen Zimbabwe's vicious campaign of land seizure from white farmers.

see *Mugabe, Robert* / *Zimbabwe*

Shirleyportering

Not to be confused with Gerrymandering – the redrawing of a voting area into different districts – this involves manipulating the composition of the electorate to one's own specifications. The effect is the same: to give a party an unfair electoral advantage.

see *Porter, Shirley*

Shit, Conniving Little

see *Allason, Rupert*

Short, Clare
b. Feb 15th 1946
MP (Lab), Birmingham Ladywood, 1983-

Slow-off-the-mark war protester and self-appointed conscience to others. Most of Clare Short's brushes with sleaze and malpractice have been on the side of the whistleblowers, starting with Alan Clark (*qv*), whom she bawled out for being drunk at the despatch box in 1983. A campaign against filth in newspapers backfired

in 1986 when the *Sun* chose to compare the morals of Page 3 to those of Sinn Fein, an organisation for which Short (the daughter of Irish Catholics) did not hide her admiration. Towards the end of the decade she became known as a rebel in matters of security, stepping down from the Labour front bench in 1988 and 1990 over the Prevention of Terrorism Bill and the first Gulf War respectively. She missed the boat when it really mattered in 2003, though, electing on March 18th to stay on with her 'reckless' government despite having pledged to resign if Tony Blair went ahead with plans for war without a second UN Resolution. Realising her credibility was fatally scuppered after two more months on the Cabinet payroll, she finally stood down on May 12th. She wasn't done as a sleazebuster, though, and was back in the news the next February, alleging on the *Today* programme that Britain was bugging UN Secretary-General Kofi Annan. Whilst Blair fell short of flatly contradicting her, he said she was being 'totally irresponsible' although 'entirely consistent'. There was talk of prosecution under the Official Secrets Act, and of Short becoming the first Privy Counsellor to lose that status since 1921 – but, like so much government talk over the Iraq war, this turned out to be flam – and she later backpedalled, anyway.

In September 2006 she announced to an indifferent party and public that she'd be standing down at the next Election, and was 'ashamed' of the Blair administration. The following month she resigned the party whip, vowing to sit as an independent Labour MP – but in July 2007 she indicated she'd changed her mind again, commenting that Gordon Brown's accession represented 'a new beginning'. A nation awaits her decision with bated breath.

Siam Sauna

see *Ashton, Joe*

Simple Truth, the

1. 1991 charity campaign for Kurdish refugees, organised by Jeffrey Archer (*qv*) and taking its name from a song by Chris de Burgh (*qv*). On June 19th of that year the master storyteller triumphantly proclaimed the appeal had raised over £57m.

2. Phrase meaning 'the plain facts' – such as that the campaign of the same name raised only £1m for Kurdish refugees. A commodity with which Jeffrey Archer was economical (see *Actualité*), eventually resulting in a 2001 jail term.

Singh, Marsha
b. October 11th 1954
MP (Lab), Bradford West, 1997-

Affable MP who blottoed his copybook in March 2005 with a booze-fuelled outburst during an all-night debate over terrorism laws, when he appeared to solicit sex from a colleague while waving £20 notes.

"I don't want a fucking fight, I want a shag"

Many Members, reported the *Mail On Sunday*, were feeling the effects of the long session of March 10th-11th in the Commons Smoking Room; one Labour MP lay sprawled on the floor, having fallen off his stool; two more (Bridget Prentice and Tony McNulty) had repaired to the tea-room to snooze in armchairs. But no-one was suffering like Marsha Singh. After he allegedly insulted veteran blue Sir Sydney Chapman, another Tory calmly reasoned: "For God's sake, it's been a long night, he's had too much to drink. There's no need to make a fuss." In stepped Jane Griffiths (*qv*), who suggested he should come with her for a cup of tea. According to her, Singh replied with lightning wit: "I'll come with you for a shag. How much do you charge?" Then he turned to onlookers crying: "How much does Jane Griffiths charge for a shag? What is she worth?"

As Singh pulled out his money, Griffith's old drinking buddy Helen Clark dashed off to find a whip. "I don't want a fucking fight, I want a shag," insisted the Member for Bradford West – before pointing at a less appealing 'Blair Babe' and shouting: "...but I don't want to shag you." The Iraq rebel grew bolder, barging over to a table where Bob Marshall-Andrews and John Cryer were arm-wrestling (Singh lost comprehensively). A ruse was swiftly devised whereby the tipsy troublemaker found himself locked in the Chess Room, but he didn't find it much to his liking, and was soon heard banging and shouting to be let out. Having escaped, he rejected the offer of being taken to the tearoom ("I don't want fucking tea, I want fucking wine. I want to talk about shagging. Why can't people talk about shagging?"), but met an obstacle in the form of hard-boiled whip Jim Murphy. The bruiser had been roused from his slumbers in the whips' office, and strode across the floor in nothing but a white vest and crotch-hugging jogging shorts. But even the old hand backed off when the punchy Punjabi offered to 'take him on' – before triumphantly offering 'drinks for everybody'. Neither would comment the next morning, as Singh blearily attended a surgery in his constituency. But Clark and Griffiths were firmly on message. "It is unlike Marsha," sighed the latter, poignantly adding: "When people are drunk they do things they regret." Clark confirmed: "I'm sure Marsha will regret it. It is utterly out of character. But it did happen." Singh – denying the 'major allegations' of soliciting – eventually stated: "There was a minor altercation in the early hours of Friday morning which has been blown out of proportion. I do apologise to colleagues if I caused offence." No one pressed any complaints, though the women stood by their story. Two months later the deselected Griffiths was out of a job; but Singh was returned at the May Election. Asked how he'd be celebrating, he replied: "With a cup of tea".

RED HOT

"John Betjeman's famous statement that he wished he'd made love more often does not apply to us. My husband believes significant parts of the body fall into disuse, then the brain begins to think that useful life is over and starts to decline."

- *Edwina Currie, the Daily Mail, Oct 23rd, 2006*

CURRIE

SLEAZE

"The Hon. Lady should remember that she was an egg once, and very many members on all sides of the House may regret that it was ever fertilised"

– Nicholas Fairbairn to Edwina Currie, 1988

SLOT

Sixsmith, Martin

b. 1956

Best-remembered as 'the man who never resigned', ex-hack Sixsmith was Steven Byers' Director of Communications at a particularly ruinous time for the then-Cabinet Minister's reputation. Sixsmith is most closely-associated with the embarrassing Jo Moore (*qv*) affair, so much so that when Moore was asked to step down on February 15th 2002, she insisted to permanent secretary Sir Richard Mottram that her immediate boss should fall with her. He agreed – but the problem was, Sixsmith hadn't. He was startled on returning from a hospital appointment to find that an announcement had already been made. His position was untenable, but a doughty denial of all reports of his own professional demise confirmed his tenacity. On May 7th the Department was forced to admit that their Director of Communications had not, in fact, resigned. Ultimately, Sixsmith clung on marginally longer than Stephen Byers – the man who'd supposedly signed his death warrant – and he now writes turgid experimental novels instead.

Skinner, Dennis

b. Feb 11th 1932
MP (Lab), Bolsover, 1970-

Monarchy-hating caricature who has repeatedly been barred from the Commons for his intemperate outbursts. Favoured targets of 'the Beast of Bolsover' include the House of Lords, Black Rod and George Osborne (*qv*), on whose account he was chucked out on 8th December 2005. Commenting on Tory economic growth in the 1980s, he barked that "the only thing that was growing then were the lines of coke in front of boy George and the rest of the Tories." He justified his remarks to the Speaker with the immortal riposte: "That was in the *News of the World*, and you know it!" But Skinner had been fair game himself in February 1994, when the crusading rag reported an extra-marital affair with his well-heeled Parliamentary Researcher (*qv*) Lois Blasenheim, under the headline 'Beast of Legover'. And, as he clearly knows, the paper's sources are infallible.

Skoal Bandits

'Suck'em and sue' tobacco pouches earmarked by US Tobacco for aggressive marketing in the UK in 1989 – but banned before licence for sale. The concept was unappealing (tea-bag-like devices that fitted over the gums to unleash a devastating nicotine hit) and the product was directly linked to a range of oral cancers, but the Scottish Office still gave an astonishing £200,000 grant for them to build a European distribution centre at East Kilbride.

In February 1988, Edwina Currie (qv) announced the government's intention to ban them outright, but two die-hard libertarian MPs sniffed an infringement of consumer rights, and furiously took up the cudgels on UST's behalf: Neil Hamilton (qv) and Michael Brown (qv). Health Secretary Kenneth Clarke was later to record that they were 'very ferocious in their private representations' on the matter, but their flimsy arguments were undermined when it emerged that arch-lobbyist Ian Greer (qv) had negotiated them $10k each to push for the pungent pochettes' sale in Britain. Even discredited junior health minister Currie could smell a genuine threat to Britain's well-being, and their efforts were for naught. Still, Hamilton couldn't consider the affair a total dead loss: he enjoyed a three-night stay as US Tobacco's guest in a top New York hotel that October. And, one imagines, as many Skoal Bandits as he could stuff into his face.

Smith, Des
b. 1944

Former headmaster and former member of the council of the Specialist Schools and Academies Trust. He resigned the post in January 2006 following revelations in the *Sunday Times* about the funding of 'City Academies', which helped open the can of worms that was 'Cash for Honours' (qv). "Basically… the Prime Minister's office would recommend someone like Malcolm [a fictional potential donor] for an OBE, a CBE or a knighthood," he happily chirruped to an undercover reporter over champagne. When the report appeared he resigned, and Downing Street countered that it was 'nonsense to suggest that honours are awarded for giving money to an Academy'. In April

Smith was arrested under the 1925 Honours (Prevention of Abuses) Act, questioned, and released on bail pending further enquiries. In December he furiously told the *Mail On Sunday*: "I demand that Blair is arrested at 10 Downing Street at 7:20 am, that he is taken to a police station – hopefully Stoke Newington, which is a very unpleasant, Bastille-type place – and treated the same way that I have been treated." He also distanced himself from his earlier comments, admitting: "What I did on that occasion was 'big myself up'. I pretended I knew something I did not. Little did I know that at the time I was naively blundering into such a politically sensitive area." In February 2007 Smith was cleared of any wrongdoing by the CPS, and he promptly slammed Blair in the *News of the World* as 'a shallow, fairweather friend' who 'never uttered one word of support or encouragement'. He added: "I wanted to die... I now know the depths of despair Dr Kelly reached."

SLEAZE

"One day open prison, next day legislating; it is just not a very sensible basis for British public life to be conducted"

- David Mellor on Lord Archer's attempts to rejoin the Upper House, November 2005

SLOT

Smith, Sir Dudley
b. Nov 14th 1926
MP (Con), Brentford & Chiswick, 1959-66 / Warwick & Leamington, 1968-97

Veteran Tory who achieved a modicum of notoriety in 1992 when a young Matthew Taylor, later to become Tony Blair's head of policy in September 2003, devised the 'Apathy-Greed Index' and placed him at its summit. The result was achieved by multiplying the number of an MP's outside interests by the sum of their Commons votes missed. By sheer coincidence, Labour candidate Taylor was Sir Dudley's constituency rival when he stumbled across his magic formula.

Smith, Jacqui
b. Nov 3rd 1962
MP (Lab), Redditch, 1997-

Ultra-safe pair of hands whose statesmanlike response to the January 2007 *Celebrity Big Brother* crisis ("I think the editing is wrong and I think it's shameful to make money and publicity out of that sort of thing") earned her major Brownie points with the PM-in-waiting. He appointed her Home Secretary when he took over in July, but a few days later she stunned a nation by admitting she'd attended cannabis-fuelled student parties in hedonistic 1980s Oxford, and even had the odd puff herself. "I am not proud about it. I did the wrong thing," revealed the former Hertford College JCR president in a GMTV interview – thereby firing the starting pistol for a relay race of Cabinet Ministers eager to talk about their youthful soft drug use. Only devout Catholic Ruth Kelly (*qv*) provoked greater surprise than Smith, who was largely remembered by contemporaries as 'the quiet and boring one', 'dull' and 'something of the schoolma'am'. "Posh people had proper drugs," roared one boorish oaf to the *Times*. Whilst at least a few Cabinet members proudly claimed not to have dabbled, top brass saw no problem with those who'd strayed. "On the whole I think people think human beings should do jobs like this," Smith argued, hastening to add that she had 'not particularly enjoyed it' at the time and hadn't partaken since.

Smith, Tim
b. Oct 5th 1947
MP (Con), Ashfield 1977-79 / Beaconsfield 1982-97

Tory golden boy whose career was shredded when he admitted accepting bribes from Mohammed Fayed during the Cash For Questions (*qv*) affair. Having served as PPS to Home Secretary Leon Brittan from 1983-85, in the late 80s Smith settled into a tidy backbench career, collecting outside interests and forging close links with arch lobbyist Ian Greer (*qv*). In particular, Smith acted as a paid consultant for accountancy juggernaut Price Waterhouse, on whose behalf he bombarded the government with detailed questions. Smith did not declare his interest when putting them, and was unapologetic when challenged in 1988. "I am entitled to ask whatever questions I want of the government," he insisted. "I do not think there is any principle involved." And indeed there wasn't – not on his part, at any rate.

Greer encouraged him to table questions, sign motions and lobby on Fayed's behalf until 1989, when the Harrods owner's nemesis Tiny Rowland accused him of being rewarded for his activities. Smith then entered a reference to working as 'a consultant to the House of Fraser' in the Register of Members' Interests, and was duly made a party Vice-Chairman and then a joint Treasurer. His climb continued with a January 1994 appointment as a junior minister in the Northern Ireland Office, but he abruptly left the Government when the first 'Cash For Questions' allegations were aired in October: it emerged he'd admitted pocketing up to £25,000 from Fayed's brown envelopes (*qv*). "The way in which these payments were received and concealed fell well below the standards expected of Members of

Parliament," rebuked Sir Gordon Downey, investigating. Smith could only reply: "I am very sorry. I can only say in my defence that it seemed less obvious at the time than it does with the benefit of hindsight what was the right course of action to take." His swift departure was perhaps the only honourable act to emerge from the entire farrago, and he stood down from Parliament altogether in 1997.

see *Cash For Questions / Downey Report, the*

Soames, Nicholas
b. Feb 12th 1948
MP (Con), Crawley, 1983-97 / Mid-Sussex, 1997-

Grandson of Winston Churchill and best mate of Prince Charles, this bloated toff held his dream job between 1992 and 1994, when John Major appointed him to the Ministry of Agriculture, Fisheries and Food. 'Nickers' – as he was known at Eton, where he described himself as having been 'bone idle' – entered the army before becoming an MP and went on to become a Defence Minister, with a hearty appetite for military exports. He oversaw the official inquiry into 'Gulf War Syndrome' in 1996, and was forced to apologise for 'misleading' Parliament about the extent of British troops' exposure to chemicals during the conflict. He also forgot to reveal that when the war broke out, he was a non-executive director of UK chemical firm Hoffman La Roche, which supplied the ingredients for 'Naps' (Nerve Agent Pre-Treatment) tablets for British and US troops. "The tablets were being blamed for playing a part in these illnesses from very early on," pointed out the solicitor acting on behalf of hundreds of sick veterans. "Mr Soames should have known that they were developed by Roche, and he should have made clear to the Commons select committee that he had an interest in one of the manufacturers of one of the prime suspects for Gulf War illness." The great man could only wheeze in reply: "I had no idea it was even made by Roche. Plainly if I had I would have declared an interest."

It was a theme he would warm to: despite campaigning against the building of new housing in his leafy constituency (he has warned that such development will "bulldoze green spaces and put areas like Sussex at risk of being covered in concrete"), he is chairman of the Farmlington Second Dual Trust plc, which has significant shares in housebuilders Persimmon, Crest Nicolson and Berkeley, all of which have extensive interests on his patch. Soon after stepping down as Shadow Defence Secretary in May 2005 ("I want to take an important role on the backbenches"), it emerged that he'd accepted a non-executive directorship at the controversial Aegis Defence Services Ltd. More direct embarrassment had occurred in July 2004, when Soames was named 'Fat Boy Dim' by the *Sunday Times* after clashing with Jewish retail ogre Philip Green at London's Dorchester Hotel, over what was perceived by some as an anti-Semitic slight as Green supped with BBC business editor Jeff Randall and a *Sunday Times* journalist. Although Soames's sally was widely reported as "their kind keep it all together, as ever – it's the same as it ever was," he afterwards puffed: 'I have never said anything anti-Semitic,' admitting only an 'exchange of views', a 'minor remark' and an 'altercation'. Green's only rejoinder has been philosophical: "Life moves on. They are what they are, these people."

Soapbox

A crate which can be used to increase the physical standing of an unimpressive individual, so his voice might better be heard – on the election trail, for example. "People say that you cannot do it these days," John Major (*qv*) puzzlingly asserted in March 1992. "It is fashionable to say, for security and other reasons, that you cannot get up on a soapbox. I think you have to, and I am going to do it." He'd first experimented with the concept in Brixton market in the 1960s, but by 1997 its returns had diminished considerably – he was rewarded with one of the most crushing Election defeats in British political history. For the record, he was not actually standing on a soapbox, but a Central Office document box, which had been tested by Special Branch to ensure it wouldn't collapse under the sheer weight of sleaze when the PM stepped onto it.

Solidarity

1. Polish dissident party founded by Lech Walesa in 1980, following years of repression, in a bold bid to shatter Communist rule.

2. Scottish dissident party founded by Tommy Sheridan (*qv*) in September 2006, following his sex-slur libel action against the *News of the World*, in a bold bid to shatter the Scottish Socialist Party (SSP).

SLEAZE

"I feel a deep sense of responsibility and humility. You put your trust in me and I intend to repay that trust. I will not let you down"

– Tony Blair addresses the electorate, Election night, May 2nd 1997

SLOT

SLEAZE

"The allegation that I or anyone else lied to this House or deliberately misled the country by falsifying intelligence on WMD is itself the real lie"

– *Tony Blair, Commons debate on the Hutton report, January 28th 2004*

SLOT

Spence, Laura
b. 1982

Straight-A Whitley schoolgirl whose failure to get into Oxford to read medicine sparked a major political row, fuelled by Chancellor Gordon Brown's choleric May 2000 assertion that Magdalen College's decision was an 'absolute scandal', and that she was a victim of 'an interview system more reminiscent of an old boy network and the old school tie than genuine justice for society'. The University begged to differ, with the don who'd interviewed her – Professor John Stein – writing to the *Telegraph* in June: 'It is ironic that I get pilloried for alleged discrimination when my life's work has been devoted to widening access to education at all ages.' Later that month Lib Dem peer Lord Jenkins blasted Brown in a Lords higher education debate, stating "nearly every fact he used was false." Tory Baroness Young, meanwhile, felt it was "an ultimate disgrace to use a young girl, a sixth former. in this way." Even Harvard student Spence disagreed with Brown's stance, informing middle England's paper of record, the *Daily Mail*, in July 2001: "I don't think I was a perfect example of what he was trying to point out, because I don't feel that being from the North or a comprehensive mattered in my case."

Spring, Richard
b. Sept 24th 1946
MP (Con), West Suffolk, 1992–

Former Vice President of financial services behemoth Merrill Lynch, who resigned as PPS to the Ulster Secretary on April 9th 1995, when Sunday school teacher Odette Nightingale sang like a canary to the *News of the World* about a threesome she'd enjoyed with him and her boyfriend Chris Holmes – to the extent of covertly recording it. On the tape Spring could clearly be heard gossiping about John Major's sex life ("I think he and Norma only do it about 1.1 times a year"), thus well and truly scotching his chances of promotion anytime soon. Nightingale was unmoved by the unusual speed and dignity with which Spring fell on his sword, branding him 'no better than a dirty old man'.

SpyCruise

Tour company offering colossally expensive espionage-themed jaunts for overgrown schoolboys, boasting cabaret from so-called 'professor' Rupert Allason (*qv*), under his nom de plume 'Nigel West'. Their website promises that 'in the ship's lounges each night after dinner, you'll be able to meet our SpyCruise professors to ask them more about their lectures, or about their spy careers and experiences.' Allason has proved less willing to meet court officials to discuss his assets, following Mr Justice Neuberger's 2005 High Court ruling.

Stacpoole, Michael
b. 1938

Archer stooge who told the BBC's *Panorama* programme in 2001: "He paid me £40,000 to keep my mouth shut." The hapless PR man had been a friend to the squat fibber for two decades ("We would often go to clubs looking for girls. He liked black women – it seemed to give him a big thrill") when he foolishly agreed to meet pocket-sized prostitute Monica Coghlan (*qv*) in October 1986, in order to hand over a cash-stuffed envelope.

"We would often go to clubs looking for girls. He liked black women – it seemed to give him a big thrill"

Unlike her, Stacpoole did actually leave the country at the novelist's behest, and continued to receive hush money for years afterwards.

He concluded to *Panorama*: "Archer does what the hell he wants to do… how long has he lied for? How many times have people helped this man out with lies? I mean, he has lied and lied and lied."

Star

How Cherie Blair (*qv*) described international con-man Peter Foster (*qv*) in an email of October 31st 2002. The Aussie scapegrace became involved in 'Cheriegate' (*qv*) for what Mrs Blair called 'a couple of weeks' – namely, between October 20th and November 29th. Foster had recommended an accountant, Andrew Axelsen ("He will not charge you for his services as I will pay him for his time and efforts through my company") and a solicitor, Martin Williams (who would finish the year jointly charged with conspiracy relating to suspected money laundering). For this Cherie gushed gratefully: "You're a star". The admiration was mutual, with Foster telling her: "Your pleasure is my purpose".

SLEAZE

"The fact that there is serious disagreement between Zimbabwe and the UK does not mean we should be discourteous or rude"

– Jack Straw on shaking Robert Mugabe's hand, September 2004

SLOT

Stewart, Allan

b. June 1st 1942
MP (Con), East Renfrewshire, 1979-83
/ Glasgow Eastwood, 1983-97

Dedicated right-winger and former MP for 'the safest Tory seat in Scotland' who resigned as a junior Scottish Office Minister in February 1995 after an unfortunate incident at an anti-motorway protest in Glasgow's Pollok Park.

"Useful weapon, a pickaxe! There's a lot you can do with a pickaxe!"

During an altercation with the 'Pollok Free State', a group of activists who'd set up camp in defiance of the Criminal Justice Act and a proposed motorway that would have cut through the park, Stewart wrenched down a banner, seized a pickaxe, brandished it at the protestors and barked: "Useful weapon, a pickaxe! There's a lot you can do with a pickaxe!" He was promptly charged with a breach of the peace and fined £200 for 'threatening and abusive behaviour'. In response he wrote to then-Home Secretary Michael Howard, requesting information about the immigration status of protesters with 'funny foreign accents', an angle that got him nowhere. Further negative press about his relationship with married mother-of-four Catherine 'Bunny' Knight, whom he'd met at an alcohol treatment clinic, prompted his retirement as an MP just before the 1997 Election, a step that his constituency chairman Ian Muir improbably described as 'a human tragedy of immense proportions which will touch the hearts of all but the most hardened'.

Straw, Jack

b. Aug 3rd 1946
MP (Lab), Blackburn, 1979-

New Labour mainstay whose liberal ideals have been sorely tested by the demands of high office. Certainly his 'zero tolerance' Home Office policy against 'beggars, winos and squeegee merchants' seemed a little out of whack with the claim that his name derives from a medieval peasant revolutionary.

As a stroppy Jack-the-Lad in 1966 Straw was branded a 'troublemaker with malice aforethought' by his future department, the Foreign Office, for disrupting a student visit to Chile with his 'childish politicking'. It is not thought that he met future dictator Augusto Pinochet (*qv*) during his brief troublemaking spree in the region, but some 34 years later he would grant the murderer safe passage back to his homeland. Straw's most famous brush with dictatorship came as Foreign Secretary in September 2004, when he clasped the hand of Zimbabwean brute Robert Mugabe and muttered 'nice to see you' at a conference in New York. The cosy exchange came minutes after Mugabe had delivered a thunderous speech condemning the British government, and Straw's subsequent fudge tried to combine a desire to show 'courtesy' to a fellow statesman and the dubious claim it was so dark that he couldn't recognise who he was greeting. Tory Michael Ancram wasn't convinced: he branded the handshake 'shameful' and the excuse 'unbelievable'.

As the Foreign Secretary who oversaw the Iraq War, then lost his job after describing any scheme to bomb Iran as 'madness', Straw has enjoyed a mixed relationship with his Muslim constituents. As Shadow Education Secretary in the late 80s he played a leading role within Labour in defending the Islamic record on women's issues, and the right of Muslim schools to opt out of the state system on public funding. But he attracted controversy in October 2006 by calling for a ban on the hajib to promote better integration. One female constituent telephoned Radio Ramadan to complain how Straw had barracked her for covering her face in his office, despite the MP's earlier protestations that he had never put pressure on any individual to remove the veil. "The Muslim community does not need lessons in dress from Jack Straw, any more than it needs lessons in parenting from John Reid," stormed one spokesman from the controversial anti-Zionist group Hizb ut Tahrir.

Strength

1. The state, property, or quality of being strong; the ability to maintain a moral or intellectual position firmly; the power to resist strain or stress; durability.

2. Quality attributed to Saddam Hussein by George Galloway MP (*qv*).

see also *Courage, Indefatigability.*

Stringfellows

Long-standing Soho strip joint which made a cameo appearance in the Register of Members' Interests (*qv*) in 2000. Surprisingly, the culprit wasn't Liam Fox (*qv*), whose enjoyment of its facilities has been well-documented, but Tory frontbencher Nigel Evans, who proudly declared free membership – only to have it rescinded a year later. "If I had been invited again I would have renewed my membership," he sighed to the *Lancashire Evening Telegraph* in December 2001, "as it's quite impressive to tell people you are a member there." The club's viagra-fuelled owner Peter Stringfellow – who once boasted he'd slept with over 3000 women – is himself a confirmed blue, whose Conservative fundraisers have attracted guests including Margaret Thatcher. "She has always been a heroine of mine," he gushed after her April 2005 visit. "I was genuinely humbled to welcome her to the club."

Strudwick, Paula
b. 1947

Call girl and dominatrix with whom Jonathan Aitken enjoyed an affair from 1980-83. Miss Strudwick, who kept a cellar that would have made Sara Dale (*qv*) blanch, eventually sold her unedifying recollections to the *Sunday Mirror* in July 1995 "In the beginning, his lovemaking was very gentle," she reminisced. "But that soon changed. Within a few weeks, all he was interested in was whips." One cherished memory was of the time Aitken instructed her to collect armfuls of birch twigs. "As soon as I was home," she sighed, "he was on the phone saying: 'Soak them in a bath and get them really pliable. I'll be over on Monday at 7pm.'"

"Soak them in a bath and get them really pliable. I'll be over on Monday at 7pm."

Aitken, meanwhile, heroically maintained that he'd never known she was a pro.

Suard, André

Upmarket hairdresser who stunned the nation by invoicing almost £8000 for keeping Cherie Blair's tresses in order during the 2005 Election campaign. Suard – a senior stylist at Mayfair's Michaeljohn salon who is also said to have acted as babysitter for the younger Blairs – charged a special daily rate of £275 between April 6th and May 6th, in stark contrast to the estimated £65 splashed out over the same period by dashed Tory hopeful Michael Howard's wife Sandra. "Mrs. Blair worked fantastically hard during the election," whined an on-message Labour flunkey when the press got hold of the story, but not everyone in the party was so understanding. "We are almost accepting by stealth a First Lady," carped MP Peter Kilfoyle. "That £7,000 (*sic*) could have been spent on political campaigning." His words might have been harder still had he heard the claim made in ex-US ambassador Christopher 'Red Socks' Meyer's 2006 memoirs DC Confidential that 'the cry went up: Cherie's hairdresser is missing! Her French stylist had been left behind at Camp David. A US marines helicopter brought him post-haste as the rest of us kicked our heels.'

Such claims seem to have done little to dampen Cherie's friendship with the Parisian: in June 2007 it was reported that he'd asked her to give him away at his civil partnership ceremony.

Super Casino

The largest category of casino currently permitted under UK law. In 2005 Labour relaxed the laws on mass gaming, leading to fears that sleepy seaside towns such as Blackpool would become like Las Vegas or Sun City (see *Bophuthatswana*). The government's major hope, though, was that its own reckless gamble, the Millennium Dome (*qv*), would finally be put to good use (see *Anschutz, Philip*). But everyone put their chips on the wrong colour: to the disbelief of Prescott, Jowell et al, in February 2007 the licence was awarded to Manchester – only to be voted down in the Lords a month later. And then, in July, the very idea seemed doomed when PM Gordon Brown told the Commons it would be "subject to reflection over the next few months" – meaning the whole embarrassing to-do could have been avoided.

Supergun

Pipe dream of Canadian nutcase Gerald V Bull, whose dearest wish was to create a device capable of raining fire from space on any given inch of the earth's surface. Sadly, he was assassinated on 22nd March 1990, before his scheme could come to fruition. Up till then, 'Project Babylon' (*qv*) had been progressing nicely with the help of Iraqi dictator Saddam Hussein and government-backed UK firms. Just days later, eight sections of pipe bound for Basra on the Iraqi-chartered Gur Mariner were confiscated by customs in Middlesbrough, after an anonymous tip-off. At 40 metres in length, with a range of 1000km, this would have constituted by far the biggest gun in the world – and was due to arrive in Iraq just in time for Saddam's invasion of Kuwait. The doomsday device was constructed under commission by Matrix Churchill (*qv*) – a Midlands-based aerospace firm with strong government connections, then under Iraqi ownership – and the parts were designed by a Sheffield firm, Forgemasters. The official cover was that the steel hoops were intended for a petrochemical plant, but in 1992 John Major's government was forced to admit (as the case against Matrix Churchill mysteriously collapsed) that it knew a lot more than it had ever let on.

Superwoman

A female possessed of sufficient judgement to resist accepting financial advice from a notorious swindler; something Cherie Blair (*qv*) has modestly admitted she is not.

Swayne, Des
b. Aug 20th 1956
MP (Con), New Forest, 1997-

Technophobe Army Major and advisor to David Cameron, whose inability to get to grips with the internet made him the Tories' answer to Jo Moore (*qv*) in July 2006. Rather than sending memos by email, Swayne had a preference for computer 'print outs', a pile of which fell into enemy hands – to Cameron's great embarrassment. As well as describing Shadow Leader of the Commons Theresa May as 'neither liked nor trusted across the party' and claiming Tory Chairman Francis Maude was 'not yet trusted by the parliamentary party', the hapless aide also suggested joining the African debt relief bandwagon as a 'diversion' to take attention from his perceived failure to attack the EU. After warning that the old right were getting restless, Swayne pondered: "One way we might offer some comfort (or merely diversion) would be to up the ante on the Make Poverty History agenda." Cameron was soon under fire for cynicism, as weeks after the date of the memo he weighed in with a speech on the West's 'sacred promises' to the lives of millions of starving children.

T

Tebbit, Norman

b. March 29th 1931
MP (Con), Epping, 1970-74
Chingford, 1974-92

Rent-a-quote hardliner, Monday Club stalwart and pioneer of the 'on yer bike' approach to unemployment, who was memorably likened by Michael Foot in a 1978 Commons debate to a 'semi-house-trained polecat' – which o n l y prompted him to incorporate the m a l o d o r o u s rodent into his c o a t - o f - a r m s when he entered the House of Lords. Among the targets for his wrath over the years have been the BBC, the *Guardian*, immigrants, homosexuals, aid to Africa, the BBC again, Europe, civil partnerships, sub-continental cricket fans, Michael Portillo, 'libertarian' Conservative

student associations, 'modernisers', the 1960s, the 21st Century, Islam, the BBC yet again, and David Cameron. In 1986 he had an active role in the Westland Affair (*qv*) and fell out with Thatcher over the bombing of Libya. In February 1990 he termed his nemesis, the BBC, "insufferable, smug, sanctimonious, naive, guilt-ridden, wet," and so concerned were his colleagues about his inflammatory outbursts that in June 1991 party whips prevented him from delivering a paper on 'The Future of the Conservative Party' at the Monday Club.

Tebbit did not mellow with age. In 1996 Oxfam was furious over what they called his 'simplistic and unhelpful' criticism of charities. Sparks also flew when he made a point of praising lame duck Iain Duncan Smith as a "normal family man with children" during the 2001 Tory leadership race, in what was perceived as a less-than-subtle message to party traditionalists about Portillo's same-sex experiences as a student. In 2004 he fought furiously against bills for transgender recognition and homosexual rights – and then, on August 19th 2005, in the wake of the 7/7 bombings, he dragged his risible 1990 'Cricket Test' (*qv*) back into the political agenda.

"I've been opposing the concept of a multicultural society for 10 years or more"

The infantile maxim, which would require everyone from newscaster Sir Trevor MacDonald to tennis brat Andy Murray to leave the country, will not recognise as 'British' anyone who does not support the England cricket team. "I do think, had my comments been acted on, those attacks would have been less likely," Tebbit posited in an online interview, adding "I've been opposing the concept of a multicultural society for 10 years or more" before reaching his Kilroy moment: "The Muslim religion is so unreformed that nowhere in the Muslim world has there been any real advance in science, or art or literature, or technology in the last 500 years" (see *Kilroy-Silk, Robert*).

Indeed, time is of the essence for Tebbit, whose thoughts often tend backwards. "Would it not be a better idea to drag us back perhaps into the 19th century," he mused in a November 15th 2005 debate on Lords reform, "which in many ways was a very much better one for this country?"

Teine

Stomping all-girl four-piece from Stornoway, half of whom fitted snugly into bed with married SNP anti-sleaze champion Angus MacNeil (*qv*). At a party in July 2005, weeks after Catriona Watt (vocals, whistle and fiddle) and Judie Morrison (clarsach, vocals and fiddle) had left school, the Cash For Honours whistleblower challenged them to a game of darts, and a bout of drunken 'foolishness' ensued. Judie confirmed MacNeil was 'excited', though the incident went no further than 'heavy petting'. The unlikely threesome share a love of music – fittingly enough, since Catriona is also a whistle-blower (her solos are much admired) and both girls are talented fiddlers. The romp did little to damage their reputation: according to Hebridean reviewers the folk quartet – pronounced 'teen' – have already 'gained a reputation for themselves as a fresh, vital and ambitious band'.

Temple, Jack
b. July 1st 1917 / d. Feb 13th 2004

Muddle-headed medicine man to Cherie Blair (*qv*), responsible for giving the world 'Bio-Electric Shields' – essentially bits of stone he'd foraged from a Pembrokeshire landfill in the 1970s (Cherie has been said to wear a £40 chunk of the neolithic rock about her neck). Temple, who claimed to have "helped the lame to walk, the barren to conceive and the sad to smile", could also trace his origins back 97,000 years through 120 former lives. Although he failed to live up to his confident predictions of immortality, his mastery of dowsing is credited with reducing Mrs Blair's swollen ankles.

see *Caplin, Carole*

Temple, Tracey
b. Oct 10th 1962

Charmless Diary Secretary (*qv*) to John Prescott, whom she later claimed "exploited power for his own sexual gratification". From her own less-than-enthusiastic notices of the affair, however (see *Dirty Diary (ii), the*), it's hard to know what Temple saw in her married boss if not for his position in the government. The unsightly pair had long flirted openly around the office, and alongside more traditional photocopier games at their Christmas party in 2002 the Deputy PM was photographed hoisting ditzy drunk Temple over his shoulders. From this night on they became an item for two years, and Temple claims the groping continued apace, ranging from podgy fingers up her skirt to oral sex at his desk with the door open. The salacious details were flogged to the *Mail On Sunday* for a fortune in mid-2006, with some estimates running

as high as £250k – almost enough to run Prescott for six months. However, the DPM's bitter attack on Temple afterwards – 'much of her recollections' he dismissed as 'simply untrue, and clearly motivated by a desire to maximise financial gain' – only led to the most embarrassing story, the 'cocktail sausage' remark that even the *Mail* considered beneath its dignity (and left to a right-wing blogger to leak). Prescott's troubles didn't end there: Temple did not keep an exclusive relationship with Britain's second most powerful man, and lorry driver Barry Humphries – uncowed by Prescott's form as a pugilist – made public threats against his rival. The secretary – who admitted of her boss, "I loved him... I still do really... I also loved Pauline though, I do feel bad about that" – has returned from gardening leave to a low-profile civil service backwater, since a sacking might have provoked embarrassing sexual harassment charges.

see *McDaid, Tricia / Forde, Helga*

SLEAZE

"I am happy to confirm that Lord Archer is my friend, has been my friend and will remain my friend in the future"

– John Major, the House of Commons, 23rd March 1995

SLOT

SLEAZE

> "We did have a sexual relationship before her marriage, but it became very infrequent indeed afterward"
>
> - *Simon Hoggart on Kimberly Quinn, December 2004*

SLOT

Thatched Tavern, The

Torbay pub-restaurant praised on www.holidaytorbay.co.uk for its 'deceptively roomy bars' and 'ideal surroundings for the ideal Devon pub lunch'. Also a pilgrimage site for sleaze tourists: Tory MP Rupert Allason enjoyed a slap-up dinner there in mid-April 1997, but failed to leave a tip, little realising that the move would cost him his political career. For the pub's staff and their families, sickened by his cheeseparing ways, decided to switch their allegiance from Tory to Liberal Democrat, causing him to lose the previously impregnable seat by 12 votes.

Thatcher, Margaret

b. Oct 13th 1925
MP (Con), Finchley, 1959-92
Prime Minister, 1979 – 1990

Corvine harridan whose overlong stint as Premiere ushered in the modern sleaze era. The grocer's daughter and devout Methodist originally worked as a food chemist, but retrained as a barrister in 1953 and made the Commons six years later. There she became a scourge of liberal opinion by supporting the death penalty and birching in schools, as well as voting against a move to make divorce simpler. When the Tories romped home in 1970 she became Secretary of State for Education and Science, overseeing the controversial abolition of free school milk (admittedly not her own policy). In 1975 she became Leader of the Opposition, and spent the rest of the decade espousing the robust policies that would characterise her tenure at No. 10. When she wasn't building unemployment to

record levels, forcing pit closures or rampantly privatising industry ("No one would remember the Good Samaritan if he'd only had good intentions. He had money as well," she remarked in January 1986), Thatcher provoked criticism by inviting South Africa's President, apartheid guru P.W. Botha, to Chequers – to say nothing of her friendship with Chilean psychopath Augusto Pinochet (*qv*). Her hawkish inclination was reaffirmed in 1986 when she backed US bombing raids on Libya, flying in the face of the UK's NATO allies: the strong whiff of currying yankee favour also lingered over the murky Westland affair (*qv*) that same year. Domestic policy was no less volatile – Section 28 and the Poll Tax, for example, both outraged social justice campaigners, and even her daughter Carol ducked the latter. Thatcher was ousted in a coup in November 1990, but wasn't afraid to communicate her dim view of her successor, philandering clot John Major.

On leaving the Commons in 1992 she was elevated to the Lords (as Baroness Thatcher of Kesteven), and instantly cashed in by becoming a 'geopolitical consultant' to tobacco dealers Philip Morris (aka the Altria Group) for a salary of half a million dollars ($250,000 to her and a similar annual contribution to her charitable foundation). The passing of years in no way blunted her aptitude for controversy: the 1996 Scott Inquiry into Arms-to-Iraq (*qv*) left half her inner circle reaking of sleaze, and she demonstrated her ongoing solidarity (*qv*) with Pinochet by paying him a home visit during his house arrest in Surrey in 1998.

Thatcher, Mark
b. Aug 15th 1953

Bratty twit who has enjoyed the full support of an indulgent mother throughout his unsavoury career.

The hapless Old Harrovian first advertised his comic gifts in 1982, when his maiden attempt at the Paris-Dakar rally resulted in a six-day sojourn in the desert, at the end of which he singularly failed to thank his rescuers. In subsequent years, those who acclaimed Mrs. Thatcher's meritocratic principles were at a loss to explain how such a nincompoop managed to amass a £60m fortune. It certainly wasn't on account of the three-times-failed accountant's many failed ventures in the Far East, and he strenuously denies it stemmed from a commission on the £20bn al-Yamamah (*qv*) arms deal his mother signed in 1985, for which it has been reported he received a £12m payout as 'broker'. One clue comes from his 1987 marriage to Texan heiress Diane Burgdorf, whom he met while serving as a luxury car envoy in Dallas. They were forced to start a new life in South Africa when a £4m racketeering suit had to be settled out of court in 1994, alongside tax evasion charges that were eventually dropped – but he couldn't stay out of trouble in the colonialists' playground either. In 1998 he lent huge sums of money at exorbitant interest rates to more than 900 Cape Town police officers and civil servants, causing local uproar.

When his bluff dad Denis died in 2003, Mark became Sir Mark, fulfilling the fear of those who'd opposed the 1991 hereditary title in the first place. It wasn't until 2004 that he was to achieve his defining sleaze moment, however. On August 25th he was nicked at his luxury family home in Constantia for his part in funding a coup in Equatorial Guinea, in direct contravention of South Africa's 'Foreign Military Assistance Act'. Plea-bargaining enabled him to escape with a three-figure fine and a four-year suspended sentence in 2005, on the grounds of ignorance (convincingly enough), but the episode led to renewed pleas for his hereditary baronetcy to be discontinued. Further humiliation came in December, when the principality of Monaco deemed the nefarious Thatcher 'undesirable'. "The Prince made things very clear during his investiture in July, when he said that ethics will be at the centre of life in Monaco," said a spokesman, confirming that the nomadic ninny was no longer welcome there.

Things Can Only Get Better

Early 90s pop pap (sample lyric: 'I'm too weak to fight you / I got my personal health to deal with / Things can only get / Can only get / Things can only get better / Can only get better') adopted by the Labour Party in 1997 to herald the end of a decade of Tory sleaze and the dawn of a new age of political rectitude - and belted out to a cringing nation at the victory party by the likes of Robin Cook and Peter Mandelson. Given the fog of scandal and incompetence that had engulfed the previous administration, it shouldn't have been difficult to live up to – but Blair & Co. pulled together and managed not to.

see *D:Ream*

Thising's Disease

Non-existent throat condition devised by the *Sunday Times* 'Insight' team for the purposes of entrapping MPs into accepting £1,000 bungs to table Parliamentary questions. In fact Thising's, the drug that treated it (Sigthin) and the name of the firm supposedly lobbying for it (Githins) were anagrams of 'Insight'. Eighteen of the twenty members approached smelt a rat, leaving only Graham Riddick and David Tredinnick (both *qv*) to trouser cheques (though Riddick later returned his).

Threshergate

Storm in a teacup that brewed when Chancellor of the Exchequer Norman Lamont (*qv*) was unjustly accused of trying to use a maxed-out credit card to buy booze and fags from an off-licence.

In November 1992, the *Sun* alleged that Lamont was behind with his Access repayments, a suggestion he admitted was true. They gleefully went on to announce that his card had been used most recently in a branch of Thresher. John Onanuga, an assistant at the Praed Street store, in London's Paddington district, had obligingly identified the Minister as the bloke with the funny eyebrows who'd wandered in on Monday, November 16th, questing 20 Raffles and a bottle of cheap fizz. Onanuga

sought to lend credibility to the tale – concocted with the assistance of store manager David Newton – by adding that he'd espied a Commons pass in Lamont's wallet, but the Chancellor had a cast-iron alibi: he'd been at an official reception at 11 Downing Street. Despite weak media speculation that it had all been a conspiracy to discredit the Treasury, Thresher released the following statement soon afterwards: "Thresher has completed its disciplinary process, and John Onanuga and David Newton have again admitted that they fabricated the story of Mr Lamont visiting our Praed Street branch on Monday, November 16th, 1992. As a result, the shop manager David Newton has left our employment."

"It's so simple that even a Chancellor of the Exchequer can understand it"

Onanuga was deported to Nigeria as an illegal immigrant shortly afterwards (the government insisted that Threshergate had not expedited his departure), and the episode was sent up by former Labour Chancellor Denis Healey in an unfunny 1994 Visa ad. In it he strolled past a branch of Thresher, credit card in hand, accompanied by the slogan: "It's so simple that even a Chancellor of the Exchequer can understand it". The clip was withdrawn after well-known joker Lamont ("I have never been accused of lacking a sense of humour") complained it was based on a 'pack of lies'. Indeed, with his equally bushy eyebrows and well-fed physique, Healey can count himself lucky he didn't fall foul of the false attribution himself.

Touhig, Don
b. Dec 5th 1947
MP (Lab), Islwyn, 1995-

Born James Donnelly Touhig, this Welsh whip was unmemorably described by Labour rival Paul Flynn as the 'seamstress-in-chief of stitch-ups'. In October 1999, having already resigned as Gordon Brown's private secretary and apologised unreservedly to colleagues, he was suspended from the Commons for three days after requesting that a report on childcare be leaked to his department.

see *Mountford, Kali*

SLEAZE

"A day like today, I mean, it's not a day for sort of sound bites, really, erm, we can leave those at home, but I feel the hand of history upon our shoulder"

- Tony Blair on the Good Friday Agreement, April 1998

SLOT

Tredinnick, David
b. Jan 19th 1950
MP (Con), Bosworth, 1987-

Like Graham Riddick (*qv*), this MP was caught red-handed by The *Sunday Times* accepting a grand to ask questions in Parliament on behalf of a made-up pharmaceutical company. Unlike Riddick, he didn't return the money after a change of heart. Also unlike Riddick, he refused to apologise during the emergency debate called on 13th July 1994, three days after the story broke. Instead, he denied the allegations until the paper released a recording of him requesting the cheque be sent to his home address. As a result, his Commons suspension was twice as long as Riddick's, amounting to twenty days without pay; but once more unlike Riddick, he found a reprieve at the hands of the voters. Indeed Tredinnick, despite his record in this affair, was one of the few sullied Tories to ride out the 1997 Labour landslide.

Trend, Michael
b. April 19th 1952
MP (Con), Windsor, 1992-2005

Aristocratic former Tory Vice-Chairman whose political career hit a wall when he was required to pay back a total of over £90k in unlawful living expenses, following a *Mail On Sunday* exposé in December 2002. The maximum £20k a year, tax-free Parliamentary sub was intended only to support MPs needing London accommodation whilst travelling to Parliament from far-flung constituencies. As Trend's commute from Paddington took a mere 27 minutes – with one change and time for a quick croissant – it could hardly have cost much more than a London Travelcard. He would usually drive the 25 miles to spend 'most nights' at his home in Berkshire, however, and pocket the difference. Though Trend would not give details of his address in the capital, some MPs openly boasted in the tearooms how the whopping 'additional costs allowance' for overnight stays helped them rip through a mortgage on a desirable London property with public money. It should be noted that the sudden, heroic hike of nearly 50% in MPs' allowances was only pushed through in 2001 after a Labour-led backbench revolt. But Trend had blown his chance to fill his boots, and stood down at the next Election.

Trolle, Katrine
b. 1974

Pasty Danish who admitted she'd rather have lied than see Tommy Sheridan (*qv*) walk away from court with £200k in August 2006 – despite her embarrassing testimony against him. Sheridan insisted his relationship with the failed 2003 SSP candidate was purely political, yet she maintained she'd engaged in bawdy house visits, group sex and two-in-a-bed romps with the MSP (the latter in his marital bed while his wife was out at work). Trolle stood by her statements after Sheridan won the trial, and her two flatmates testified to seeing the pair nip upstairs, apparently for a quickie. The swarthy Sheridan, meanwhile, stated that his many mobile calls to Trolle were to discuss the Danish minimum wage (*qv*). "When I heard the verdict, my first thought was I should have lied," she later sobbed. "Then I'd still have my boyfriend, sordid details about me wouldn't have been all over the papers and, ironically, I wouldn't now be branded a liar." Described as a 'thoroughly nice woman' by those who know her from the SSP, Trolle – who had lived ten years in Scotland – told the *Observer* in August 2006: "My English doesn't stretch to say what I think of Tommy Sheridan."

Trousergate

Scrap that occurred between Alastair Campbell and Peter Mandelson at the 1995 Labour Conference, and was exposed in the latter's diaries in 2007 (see *Disappointing Diary, the*). Storm clouds gathered when the two loyal lieutenants got together to plan Tony Blair's outfit for a chilled get-together with young party activists. Mandelson favoured an open-necked look, accessorised with casual corduroy slacks, while Campbell wanted to see him in a suit, possibly offset with a tie. The entry, from February 1995, records the ensuing pandemonium: "[Mandelson] started to leave, then came back over, pushed at me, then threw a punch, then another. I grabbed his lapels to disable his arms and TB was by now moving in to separate us and PM just lunged at him, then looked back at me and shouted: 'I hate this. I'm going back to London'."

TV-am

Pioneering breakfast telly firm, subject to a tremendously unpopular 1981 takeover (without the knowledge of the other board members) by Aitken Hume PLC – the company set up by Jonathan Aitken (*qv*) with his cousin Tim. Discarded staff were so unhappy with the new management that presenter Anna Ford threw a glass of wine at Aitken the next time she saw him, telling the *Daily Mirror*: "He has treated me monstrously and ruined my life." What she didn't know was that Aitken Hume was a front: £2.1m of Saudi royal cash had been needed to raise the £3.3m controlling stake, but the source of the funding was concealed from the Independent Broadcasting Commission, since it would probably have scotched the bid. It wasn't until 1988 that the truth emerged (with characteristic reluctance) from Aitken's lips. He failed to apologise for the deliberate non-disclosure, expressing only his 'regret' at having valued 'the confidentiality of his clients above the candour that should have been offered', and stepping down as a director.

This should not to be confused with the Anglia TV (*qv*) takeover scandal, which involved Aitken's sibling-in-sleaze Jeffrey Archer, but no acknowledgment – however mealy-mouthed – of wrongdoing.

Ugly Rumours

1. Short-lived rock act based at Oxford University in the early 1970s (see *Blair, Tony*).

2. Malicious smears or gossip, such as putting it about that government scientists are delusional (see *Kelly, Dr David*).

UKIP (The UK Independence Party)

When Dr Johnson called patriotism 'the last refuge of the scoundrel', he could have been referring to this refuge for discredited right-wing MPs. The right-wing Eurosceptic party was founded in 1993 with the aim of withdrawing the UK from the EU, but most of its time has been spent on internal squabbling. Though it has enjoyed the support of sleaze idols such as Jonathan Aitken, John Browne, Robert Kilroy-Silk, Piers Merchant and Charles Wardle (all *qv*), it has not been endorsed by David Cameron, who branded them 'a bunch of fruitcakes and loonies and closet racists' in a 2006 radio interview. In full agreement with Cameron is UKIP's embittered founder Dr Alan Sked, who has penned articles before every General or European Election since 1997 to accuse them of incompetence, irrelevance and extremism. His most pungent piece came in the *Telegraph* in May 2004, in which he stated: 'UKIP is even less liberal than the BNP'. Its current leader is Nigel Farage (*qv*).

UK Passport

Document required to travel abroad as a British citizen. Much-coveted across all walks of life, from the rich and powerful (see *Hindujas, the*) to the lowly (see *Casalme, 'Luz'*), it is most strongly associated with Mohammed Fayed (*qv*), whose crazed attempts to obtain one have long served as cabaret for the nation.

RED HOT

"[*My husband*] was thrilled when we arrived in Warsaw at the end of the bike ride to find, shall we say, that despite some saddle soreness, everything was working normally. In fact, the chap next door banged on the wall and asked for a bit of quiet'

- Edwina Currie, the Daily Mail, October 23rd, 2006

CURRIE

Jeremy Thorpe

b. April 29th 1929

MP (Liberal), Devon North (1959-79)

No criminal wrongdoing was ever proven against this suave Liberal leader, but few political falls from grace have been as spectacular or salacious. The well-groomed MP first met sometime male model and psychiatric outpatient Norman Scott (né Josiffe) at a friend's estate in the autumn of 1961. He was instantly taken with the raven-haired stable lad, offering 'support' should it be needed. Within weeks Josiffe had popped up at the Commons with his Jack Russell, 'Mrs. Tish'. Thorpe listened to his tale of woe, involving a dead father (untrue), a vanished mother (untrue), penury (true) and losing his job at the stables (he'd been accused of rustling a horse), and promptly whisked him off to his mother's house, Stonewalls. There, alleged Josiffe, Thorpe christened him 'poor bunny' because he looked like 'a frightened rabbit' beneath his bedclothes, and had his way (Thorpe later denied their relationship was sexual, but as he never took the witness stand, his full version of events remains untold).

Thorpe went on to help his friend gain various jobs, but grew increasingly reluctant to provide references or foot his tailoring bills. Slighted, Josiffe began a campaign of troublemaking against him – in 1965 he write to Thorpe's mother to complain that her son was using him like a rent-boy, and proceeded to share his woes with police, press and even drinkers at the MP's local. By 1968, according to fellow Liberal Member Peter Bessel, the newlywed Thorpe had hatched a plan to have Josiffe – now styling himself 'Norman Scott', as it felt more aristocratic – 'dispatched'. "We have got to get rid of him," Bessel claimed his newly-crowned party leader had said. "It's no worse than shooting a sick dog." The words proved strangely prophetic in 1975, when a bungling 'hitman' named Andrew Newton – who may or may not have been hired by Thorpe – succeeded only in slaying Josiffe's arthritic Great Dane, Rinka (Mrs Tish had been put down years earlier for mauling ducks – see *Humphrey*). When Newton and Josiffe united in making claims against Thorpe, he resigned as leader – though not as an MP, to his colleagues' vexation. Josiffe proceeded to sell letters to the press, one of which (dated February 1962) included the celebrated assertion: "Bunnies can (and *will*) go to France." Thorpe finally lost his seat at the 1979 Election, a week before the start of his trial for conspiracy to murder. The proceedings proved triumphant for a youngish George Carman QC, who systematically undermined the prosecution witnesses and secured Thorpe's acquittal - but his career never recovered.

V

Vaz, Keith
b. Nov 26th 1956
MP (Lab), Leicester East, 1987-

Born Nigel Keith Anthony Standish Vaz and described by former Lord Chancellor Derry Irvine as 'the most incredible networker I have ever met,' this oily lawyer retired hurt from front-line politics, dogged by suggestions of impropriety.

As a spokesman for the British Asian community ('probably the most influential Asian in Britain', as he once modestly described himself), Vaz was active in protests over Salman Rushdie's *The Satanic Verses* in 1989, leading 3,000 demonstrators that March and hailing a rally against free speech in Leicester as "one of the great days in the history of Islam and Great Britain". Given that Vaz is Catholic and his constituency has a massive Muslim population, the absurd comment struck some as a crude ploy for votes. When he was done endorsing death threats against writers, he began to make a name for himself in the same 'godless party' (as he'd called it) where, eight years before they reached government, he'd been a rebel of conscience. Tipped in some quarters as a future leader, Vaz was known as a pro-European in favour of speeding up the immigration process – but became embroiled in the controversial affairs of Lakshmi Mittal (*qv*), failing to declare substantial cash sums from the steel baron's wife and being accused of accelerating the application process for the Hinduja brothers (see *Mandelson, Peter*). This was admittedly only in line with the promise on his website: "I am always happy to help, and if I can do anything for you or your family please do not hesitate to get in touch."

But he was less keen to assist when government bloodhound Elizabeth Filkin (*qv*) came knocking, brandishing a dossier with 18 separate charges of wrongdoing – ranging from ballot-rigging to pressuring local businessmen for donations, from interfering with council affairs to irregular use of party funds. Filkin later complained of being unable to complete her enquiries satisfactorily because Vaz failed to answer all her questions 'fully and promptly'. Although he was only found in clear breach on one count – failing to declare gifts from lawyer Sarosh Zaiwalla, whom he'd recommended for an honour – his evasive responses about his professional conduct did little to endear him to his colleagues or the public. At the 2001 Election he bowed to backbenchers baying for his resignation, and stood down from the Government (but not his seat) on 'health grounds'. In 2002 Vaz – known to some as 'Vazeline' for his slippery conduct – was suspended from the Commons for a month. Cited were his 'obfuscation, prevarication and delay', and he was accused of 'serious breaches' of the code of conduct and contempt of the House (in particular, he was fingered for attempting to obstruct the Standards Commissioner's inquiry into his affairs, and of not declaring financial interests stretching back as far as 1987). Since then he has stuck to the backbenches, from where he has vigorously campaigned to have violent video games banned.

Verdict

1. Roasting-themed reality TV show screened on BBC2 in February 2007, and slammed by campaign groups for 'trivialising rape'. In it 11 good men and true, and Lord Archer (sic, *qv*), lined up to deliver a 'not guilty' verdict on a fictional footballer.

2. Decision handed down in court, such as the 'guilty' reached at Lord Archer's 2001 trial for perjury. For this and other reasons, the peer would not have been eligible to join his fellow TV jurors (including dogging enthusiast Stan Collymore and So Solid Crew's MegaMan) in a real-life court.

Veritas

Political party founded and deserted by Robert Kilroy-Silk (*qv*), whose love of grooming, coupled with the suspicion that it was purely a vehicle for his views, led critics to rename it 'Vanitas'. Its website describes its target voter as someone who is 'fed up of being made to feel ashamed of being British' – but nothing like enough of them have been found to win them a voice in Parliament. In the 2006 local elections, Veritas advanced four candidates (two in Kingston-upon-Hull and two in Bolton); they raked in an average of 98 votes each, representing a heartbreaking 3.5% share of the total polled.

Viceroy Of Brunei

Non-existent position never held by Jeffrey Archer's father.

see *British Consul in Singapore*

Waller, Gary

b. June 24th 1945
MP (Con), Brighouse & Spenborough,
1979-83 / Keighley, 1983-97

Beefy backbencher who for a time vigorously denied siring a child by his lover, Commons Secretary Fay Stockwell, while in a long-term relationship with girlfriend Jane Thompson in 1986. His commitment to monogamy was further undermined at the height of 'Back to Basics' in January 1994, when the *News of the World* printed a personal description he'd given to a dating agency ('intelligent, humorous, career-oriented and youthful in approach') without mentioning his partner or child.

Gary is not thought to be related to unlucky-in-love reality TV icon Rik Waller, though he does share a heavy build with the singing cetacean – indeed, until his brush with scandal, his heroic efforts to complete the London Marathon were the only reason he was ever a talking-point in the Tearooms.

Wardle, Charles

b. Aug 23rd 1939
MP (Con), Bexhill and Battle, 1992-2001

Pie-faced snake-in-the-grass whose credibility was permanently shaken by involvement with Mohammed Fayed (*qv*). As an under-secretary at the Home Office in 1993, Wardle participated in the rejection of Fayed's passport application, but as the decade progressed he began to soften to the old boy. At an adjournment debate in July 1999 he raised a series of points in support of a full inquiry into the death of Fayed's 'daughter-to-be', Diana, Princess of Wales, 'with great force and clarity' (according to the House Of Fraser supremo, anyway). "He did so of his own volition," Fayed subsequently insisted – but Wardle nonetheless took delivery of a huge Harrods Hamper that Christmas. The treat was dutifully declared in January 2000, but come April it emerged that he'd accepted a £120,000 salary to act as consultant to the Harrods honcho, though he took care to reassure nay-sayers the post would not involve 'the provision of any services in my capacity as a Member of Parliament'. Given the Tories' recent history with the shifty shopkeeper (see *Hamilton,*

Neil), they promptly nominated Gregory Barker (*qv*) as a candidate in Wardle's place at the 2001 Election. Wardle was soon accusing Barker of having exaggerated his business credentials, and announced his backing for UKIP candidate Nigel Farage (*qv*). The party whip was therefore withdrawn, a move he branded 'vindictive and unjustified', and his sour grape binge continued at the next Election, when he sided with Labour in denouncing his former Home Office boss Michael Howard on immigration. Perhaps he was hoping Fayed would get one last shot at British citizenship under a UKIP administration – but it wasn't to be.

WIGGINGS

"Galloway's conduct aimed at concealing the true source of Iraqi funding of the Mariam Appeal, his conduct towards David Blair [*the Daily Telegraph*'s *correspondent*] and others involved in this inquiry, his unwillingness to cooperate fully with the commissioner, and his calling into question of the commissioner's and our own integrity have, in our view, damaged the reputation of the House"

– *Sir Philip Mawer on George Galloway, 2007*

FROM THE BEAK

Wareing, Bob
b. Aug 20th 1930
MP (Lab), Liverpool West Derby, 1983-

Puffy socialist rebel who shook hands with Radovan Karadžic (*qv*) in 1995 and managed to stir up New Labour's first business ethics row in July 1997, when he was found 'wrong' to have failed to register any interest in a company he wholly owned called Metta Trading – following a consultancy arrangement of September 1st 1993 that saw him bank a cool initial six grand. Much worse, argued Chief Whip Nick Brown (*qv*) in bringing the complaint, as he understood it 'the company was covered by a UN sanctions order' and was 'believed to be a front organisation for the Bosnian Serb regime'.

The company, however, had deftly ditched its former connections with the offending government weeks earlier (with Serbian Finance Minister Jovan Zebic stepping down as an official director) and thus side-stepped the UN sanctions. Wareing pointed out in his own defence that the DTI had confirmed the company's kosher status in July 29th 1993, before he signed up: and, by his own admission, he had never actually been prevailed upon to perform any consultancy work for them during his time under their obligation, and consequently had repaid the sum (with interest) by January 27th 1995. Despite some debate as to whether this constituted a genuine interest, he was still suspended from the Commons for a week and forced to make a statement, on the basis that his directorship should have been registered. It was a clear indication that the new government wouldn't tolerate the merest hint of sleaze in its ranks – so long as it came from a reactionary backbench crustacean who voted against them on everything from privatisation to gay rights.

Watson, Mike ('Lord Watson of Invergowrie')

b. May 1st 1949
MP (Lab), Glasgow Central, 1989-1997 / SMP, Glasgow Cathcart, 1999-2005

Staunch trade unionist whose career went up in smoke following two instances of attempted arson on the fateful night of 12th November 2004.

Watson, who received his peerage in 1999 after losing the nomination for his seat to Mohammed Sarwar (*qv*) in 1997, revived his parliamentary career in the Scottish elections and masterminded the Scottish fox-hunting ban in 2002. A couple of years later, however, his image as a friend to all creatures great and small took a severe beating. The venue was Edinburgh's prestigious Prestonfield

House Hotel, the occasion was the Scottish Politician of the Year Awards, and the problem was booze. The thirsty MSP (who hadn't been nominated for the the title) was visibly struggling at the VIP after-party, staring out of dark windows and demanding to know the way to the cloakroom despite having no coat. Trouble really kicked off when it was broken to M'Lord that the free bar had shut. Staff attest that the pissed-up peer "continued to forcefully request more alcohol" until he was packed off to bed with a bottle of wine for company. When the fire alarm sounded ten minutes later, nobody guessed that the blotto Baron had sidled back downstairs with a box of matches in his sporran and a pyromaniacal glint in his eyes. CCTV footage clearly showed him inspecting the lobby curtains with a torch, fishing out the matches and setting one ablaze. Having been apprehended for 'wilful fire-raising', he was suspended from both Holyrood and Westminster. Initially he stated "I categorically deny any wrongdoing. I have been shown still pictures from CCTV footage at Prestonfield House, and these do not show me doing anything wrong" – but on presentation of the evidence in court, he changed his plea from 'not guilty' to 'guilty', while continuing to deny responsibility for a further incident in the hotel's historic Yellow Room.

Presiding judge Kathrine Mackie wasn't impressed. The £4,500 bill could have been far more serious, she noted, and – citing a "significant risk of re-offending" – handed down a 16-month jail sentence on 22nd September 2005. "The potential for serious injury to guests and staff within the hotel, and for very significant damage to the property, was considerable," she continued, adding that his excessive consumption of alcohol "neither excuses nor fully explains your behaviour." That behaviour included returning to the scene of the crime to check on the progress of the blaze – all part of the 'booze blackout' Watson pleaded. The Labour party preferred his lawyer's explanation, and blamed the pressures of public life in expelling him. It was 'curtains' for his political career, but – following his early release in May 2006 – Sheriff Mackie's grim warning of re-offending hangs heavy in the Upper House, where he retains the right to sit (see *Archer, Jeffrey*). The diaries he is said to have penned in the slammer have not yet been published, which is some comfort to those who limped through Archer's.

West, Nigel

Rotten novelist and disputed espionage expert.

see *Allason, Rupert / Thatched Tavern, the*

Westland

The UK helicopter industry does not traditionally play a central role in national politics, but in 1986 it briefly threatened to dethrone Mrs. Thatcher.

Westland was an ailing helicopter manufacturer whose future bitterly divided the government, as it was feared that if it were bought by a US firm Britain would lose its footing in the lucrative industry. Thatcher and Trade & Industry secretary Leon Brittan wanted to see it merged with US company Sikorsky, while Defence Secretary Michael Heseltine urged that it should remain in Europe, by integrating it with British Aerospace and French and Italian companies. Heseltine's belief was that Britain, France, Germany and Italy should all undertake only to buy European-manufactured choppers, while Thatcher and Brittan thought the choice should be free and that Westland should sell to whoever it wished. It was agreed that Heseltine and Brittan should explore possibilities for a European rescue package, but ultimately the firm decided it preferred the US option. Thatcher pledged she'd still do business with the firm, something Heseltine took great exception to. Disagreements rumbled on and eventually became public knowledge, leading to a 'leaked letters' war. In January

1986 Heseltine stormed out of Downing Street and announced his resignation from the Cabinet. Awkward questions were asked in Parliament, and it emerged that Brittan had in fact authorised the leakage of vital information, prompting vociferous calls for his resignation, which he obliged them with on January 24th. On the 27th Thatcher finally made a statement in the House, narrowly managing to cling to her credibility thanks to a particularly feeble response from Leader of the Opposition Neil Kinnock (*qv*).

Whiplash, Miss

see *Dale, Sara*

Whistleblower

1. Someone who lifts the lid on what they consider unscrupulous activity, such as the SNP's Angus MacNeil (*qv*).

2. Someone who plays the whistle, such as teenager Catriona Watt of acclaimed Stornoway girl-band Teine (*qv*).

Whiter Than White

Impossible standard of cleanliness, supposedly cited by Tony Blair in 1997 as that which he expected of his new administration. The widely-repeated pledge is in fact a paraphrase (and more usually 'purer than pure') – but it proved an impossible dream in any case.

Wiggin, Jerry
b. Feb 24th 1937
MP (Con), Weston-super-Mare, 1969-97

Fondly known as 'Junket Jerry', Sir Alfred William Wiggin is a fearsome right-winger who straight-facedly told the *Times* in 1992 that he felt the public should underwrite the costs of an MP's extra secretarial assistance, "to keep his diary, deal with phone calls and help him in his outside business interests." Evidently lacking sufficient subs for his extramural interests, in 1996 he resorted to using an unwitting colleague to assist him instead. Wiggin was already well-known to sleaze fans for his lobbying activities – in November 1989, for example, he intervened in a Commons debate to seek government investment in a proposed British Sugar plant, without declaring himself a paid consultant to the British Sugar Corporation. "It's very difficult to get knowledgeable people if you get too fussy about what I would call general interests," he muttered when confronted by the *Sunday Correspondent*.

The fussiness of others was to trouble him again when he tabled several fateful amendments to a 1996 Gas

Bill in the name of one Sebastian Coe. For Wiggin was a paid adviser to the British Holiday and Home Parks Association, which stood to benefit from the proposed amendments, and – unlike the former Olympic gold medallist – he was not on the committee considering the Bill. When the story broke Wiggin was in sunny South Africa, as part of a parliamentary delegation studying 'fruit production'. In May 1995 he offered a grovelling apology ("I wish unreservedly to apologise to my Hon Friend and to the House for having tabled amendments to a Bill in Standing Committee in his name but without his knowledge or consent... an action which I acknowledge was at odds with the proper expectations of the House"), which prompted the speaker, Betty Boothroyd, to comment with touching idealism: "Individual Members should act in such a manner whereby their integrity is not called into question." Unfortunately just such questions were soon being asked in Weston-Super-Mare, and Junket Jerry resigned his seat at the 1997 election.

SLEAZE

"Unreconstructed wankers"

- *Tony Blair describes the Scottish press, December 1996*

SLOT

Willetts, David
b. March 9th 1956
MP (Con), Havant, 1992-

The fellow some call 'Two Brains' was described by Lord Hattersley as a young man 'whose genius is more discussed than observed'. He was a Treasury gopher for Margaret Thatcher, became a whip and then Paymaster-General under John Major in 1996 – before Cash For Questions (*qv*) came back to bite him on his 'two cheeks'. Specifically, he was accused of having tried to influence select committee chairman Sir Geoffrey Johnson Smith's investigation of Neil Hamilton (*qv*) – putting his possible tactics for damage limitation into a memo and adding that the chairman 'wants our advice'. When Sir Geoffrey denied the suggestion, Willetts claimed he'd been using the word 'wants' in its archaic sense ('lacks'), but his semantic quibbling held little interest for the committee, which accused him of 'dissembling.' When this emerged in November 1996, the harshest words came from someone then on his bench – de-flocked shepherd Quentin Davies (*qv*). "Either you were deceiving your colleagues in your initial memorandum," he seethed in the Commons, "or you are trying to deceive this committee now." 'Two Brains' resigned as soon as the report was published on December 11th 1996, though

William Hague eventually brought him back into the fold as a junior employment spokesman, and David Cameron briefly made him Shadow Education Secretary.

Willis, Phil

b. Nov 30th 1941
MP (Lib Dem), Harrogate & Knaresborough, 1997-

Unremarkable Lib Dem who fell foul of celebrity harridan Jodie Marsh in 2006.

see *Marsh, Jodie*

Winterton, Ann

b. March 6th 1941
MP (Con), Congleton 1983-

Extremist raconteuse with a list of racially-charged outbursts longer than Abu Hamza's right hook. Lady Winterton is a 'family values' Tory, which means she opposes pornography and abortion, Sunday Trading and embryo research, but applauds the death penalty and off-colour jokes. One of her favourite gags begins with an Englishman, a Cuban, a Japanese and a Pakistani sharing a railway carriage, and ends with the Englishman hurling the Pakistani out of the window in protest at UK immigration policy. The controversial 'Asians are ten a penny in my country' crack even succeeded in silencing 160 lairy drunks at a May 2002 rugby club dinner: the BNP had made record gains the previous day in Burnley, just 30 miles from her constituency. Bernard Manning's verdict on the jibe was not reported, but immigrants' friend Iain Duncan Smith considered it 'offensive and unacceptable' and banished the Shadow Rural Affairs Minister from the Tory front bench.

It wasn't long before Winterton was back in the swing, adding the Chinese to her hit-list with a famously offensive routine about dead cockle-pickers in February 2004, shortly after 20 Chinese wage-slaves had drowned in Morecambe Bay. When she refused to say sorry, new party leader Michael Howard – boldly claiming 'such sentiments have no place in the Conservative Party' – had to do so on her behalf, at the cost of her whip. A month later she came grovelling back. The restoration of her whip outraged black Tory peer Lord Taylor for one, but the Commission For Racial Equality was on her case again soon enough. In September 2005 she wrote an incendiary article for the *Congleton Guardian* in which she remarked that 'the United Kingdom is still, thankfully, a predominantly white, Christian country' and huffed about the 'so-called 'benefits' of the multi-cultural society we keep hearing about'. Chantelle Janes, director of Cheshire's Racial Equality Council begged to differ, calling the MP's comments 'inaccurate and nothing more than scaremongering', and saying she "failed to recognise the contribution black and minority ethnic people have made to this country and its development."

Winterton, who maintains on her website that she 'has always sought to represent the views of the people of the Congleton Constituency', still has a place in David Cameron's party – though she must wonder where she'll stand when the new leader's touted ethnic quotas kick in.

Wolfgang, Walter
b. 1923

Frail pensioner whose croaky heckling of Jack Straw's address to the 2005 Labour Party Conference led to his forcible removal from the auditorium, amidst fears that he'd somehow breached new anti-terrorism laws. The party quickly realised that, whilst acting in the best interests of national security, they'd made a critical PR blunder, and embarrassedly restored his conference pass the following day. Wolfgang returned to an ovation, obliging Tony Blair to apologise on the *Today* programme and John Reid (*qv*) to bluster: "We didn't want it, it shouldn't have happened, it's not the way we do things. Everybody is really sorry and we apologise for that."

Women's Institute

Locally-centred UK organisation offering over 200,000 women nationwide a chance to develop interests in subjects such as cookery, drama and history, as well as to perform charitable and social work and pose naked for calendars. Radical politics aren't typically on their agenda, but Tony Blair forced it to the top when he addressed their annual conference at Wembley on June 7th 2000. His glib words about traditional values ("let's hear no more rubbish about class war... We are unashamed supporters of excellence") rang hollow in the light of spiralling crime and NHS chaos, and provoked walk-outs, heckling and even a slow hand-clap. His humiliation was only allayed by the intervention of WI Chair Helen Carey, and the incident stands as one of the most embarrassing of his long premiership.

Wonderboy

Pet name given to Jeffrey Archer (*qv*) by his lover Sally Farmiloe (*qv*), on account of his alleged sexual prowess. "Jeffrey is the man who pressed all the right buttons," an anonymous friend of the former topless hang-glider told the *Evening Standard* when news of their affair broke in December 1999. "She gave him 11 out of 10 for sex because it was so magical."

Woodward, Shaun
b. Oct 26th 1958
MP (Con), Witney, 1997-99
(Lab), St. Helens South, 2001-

One-time Tory chairman whose 1999 floor-crossing (after he'd been sacked by William Hague over Section 28), led to a flurry of vitriolic stories in the press, many of which centred on his alleged claim to be the only Labour MP with a butler. He has also attracted criticism for never having asked a question in the Commons, and for not living in the working-class constituency into which he was parachuted on deciding not to seek re-election as a Labour candidate in Witney in 2001. It was thought that he preferred the palatial comforts of the Oxfordshire estate and London mansion funded by his wife, a scion of the Labour-friendly Sainsbury dynasty.

see *Davies, Quentin*

World In Action / Guardian trial

Ruinously expensive action brought in 1995 by Jonathan Aitken (*qv*) against Granada TV and the *Guardian* newspaper over a *World In Action* documentary, *Jonathan of Arabia* (*qv*), which lobbed a number of allegations in his direction. This led in turn to Aitken's own appearance before the beak – on perjury charges.

The slur which most animated Aitken was the suggestion that he'd enjoyed top-whack hospitality at the Paris Ritz on 19th December 1993, but left a Saudi royal to pick up the bill without thinking to declare it on the Register of Members' Interests. Or perhaps he simply thought that, with the unwitting aid of his wife and daughter, the claim would be the easiest to refute: other, more serious, accusations included pimping for Arabs and supplying arms to Iran against the embargo. In time, however, it emerged that the Ritz meeting was as shady as any of the above (see *Paris Ritz Hotel*). The *Guardian* eventually concluded in 1999 that the pow-wow had aimed to co-ordinate a plan for UK arms sales to Saudi Arabia, and was bankrolled by Prince Mohammed, who wanted to make sure that everyone involved got their dues. There seems no reason to dispute this, since the best alternative Aitken could float among his 'close friends' was hogwash about secret missions for MI6.

Lily-livered Cabinet Secretary Robin Butler was tasked by John Major with investigating the meeting internally in 1994, but he was no match for the detective skills of Mohammed Fayed (*qv*) and the *Guardian*, who smelt blood – particularly with Aitken's defensive bluster drawing attention to such an apparently trifling matter. Judicious snooping eventually pieced together a trail of credit card bills and hotel records that proved conclusively that Lolicia Aitken had not been in France on the crucial date, but in Switzerland – and therefore could not have been the mysterious woman who settled the bill. This incontrovertible fact turned the trial around, and left Aitken ruing his rejection of a modest offer by the *Guardian* to settle before the May 1997 Election – and the decision to make his wife and teenage daughter give evidence. The collapse of the trial in June 1997 sadly prevented allegations of Aitken 'entertaining' his guests in health spas and high-class brothels being investigated properly, to say nothing of BMARC and Project Lisi (*qv*). Not long afterwards Aitken was back in court, to be sentenced to 18 months' imprisonment.

X, Mr

Name used by Soraya Khashoggi, former mistress of Jonathan Aitken (*qv*), to describe another mystery lover during the 1979 Old Bailey trial of three detectives accused of blackmailing her. He turned out to be love rat Winston Churchill MP (*qv*).

Yeo, Tim

b. March 20th 1945
MP (Con), South Suffolk, 1983-

Conservative Member for Suffolk South and inaugural victim of the Back To Basics (*qv*) backlash.

The junior environment minister was on record as condemning the incidence of single-parent families in the UK ("It is in everyone's interests to reduce broken families and the number of single parents"), so the *News of the World*'s Boxing Day 1993 revelation that he was himself boosting the statistic left him wide-open to accusations of hypocrisy. Initially Tory HQ stood by him over his love-child with party activist Julia Stent (thought to have been conceived at the 1992 Tory Conference), and before long he was sunning himself in the Seychelles, perhaps hoping to earn an affectionate nickname like 'Pantsdown' or 'Shagger' back home. But neither the newspapers nor Max Clifford (*qv*) were letting go, and rent-a-quote MP David Evans (*qv*) was soon on the case too, saying the Conservatives could not tolerate 'people bonking their way around London'. Evidently the Prime Minister agreed, despite his own record on the subject (see *Currie, Edwina*) – and Yeo was left with little choice but to resign on 4th January 1994.

Young Meteors

Self-aggrandising work penned by Jonathan Aitken (*qv*) in 1967, rubbing his hands at how young, bright and ready to light up the sky he and his contemporaries (including David Steel, Norman Lamont and Roy Hattersley) were. The book (sub-titled 'An Inside Report on the Rising Stars of London, in Fashion, Entertainment, Modelling, Art, Politics, Journalism, Vice and Business') was, tellingly, dedicated to the various women in his life – 'Grania, Gill, Anne, Mary, Eithne' and also 'Caroline, who kept me going on her delicious paté'. Little can they have guessed how ingloriously the free-loving freeloader would burn out. "In terms of style, it was certainly the worst book I've ever written," he reflected to the *Guardian* in September 2003. "Apart from those young meteors who committed suicide or dropped themselves off buildings, it would be hard to find a greater crash than my own."

see *World In Action / Guardian trial*

Zayyad, Dr Amina Abu
b. 1966

"When he told me his new party was going to be called Respect, I went upstairs and cried. How can he call it this when he doesn't even treat his own wife with respect?"

That was the stark question posed by this glamorous Palestinian scientist of 'Respect' party founder – and erstwhile hubby – George Galloway MP in 2003. They'd met at a political gathering in Glasgow in 1991, at a time when she confessed "he was my hero", and wed in 2000. They say you should never meet your heroes, still less marry them; and in 2005, in the face of constant phone calls from younger women claiming to be either Galloway's mistress or a 'concerned friend', she became too disillusioned to carry on. "George said it was the intelligence services, his enemies, that were trying to get at me," sobbed Dr Zayyad to the *Sunday Times* in May 2005. She added that Galloway also helpfully suggested she hide in Beirut, at least

until the high-profile Election was over – but she demanded a divorce instead. Gorgeous George was not completely out of her life, however – later that year she appeared as a witness on his behalf before the US Senate sub-committee.

Zimbabwe

Former British colony of Rhodesia, named by Sir Cecil Rhodes after himself and granted unilateral independence in 1980. The then-Tory government's appeasement of the corrupt new regime, led by the obnoxious duo of Canaan Banana and Robert Mugabe (*qv*), has been a cause of embarrassment to every British administration since.

Mugabe's brutal repression of political opponents in Matabeleland – involving thousands of Ndebele people slaughtered, and thousands more beaten and tortured – swiftly established his credentials as a despot. But, despite this ethnic massacre within the Commonwealth, Mrs Thatcher's government still considered a stable Zimbabwe more important than a 'side-issue' like genocide (see also *Pinochet, Augusto / Hussein, Saddam*). A BBC *Panorama* programme in 2002 quoted Britain's High Commissioner at the time, Sir Martin Ewans, describing London's policy: "I think this Matabeleland is a side issue... We were extremely interested that Zimbabwe should be a success story, and we were doing our best to help Mugabe and his people."

Two years after the campaign (at its bloodiest from 1983-84), its orchestrator, 'Air Marshal' Perence Shiri (*qv*) – was invited to London to study at the Royal College of Defence Studies. The likes of Geoffrey Howe have since confirmed that the British government was aware of reported atrocities, but preferred to keep the madmen onside. On his return, Mugabe's chief bully turned his newly-acquired military expertise (and a troop of embittered war veterans) on the white farmers, a move which finally hardened the British government against the regime. But not before Shiri's Air Force had been given a hearty shot in the arm by Tony Blair: remarkably, the PM rubber-stamped the export of crucial spare parts for their Hawk jets in 2000, against the advice of his Foreign Secretary Robin Cook.

Cook's successor, Jack Straw (*qv*), was somewhat friendlier towards Mugabe – albeit by accident (in 2004 he mistook him for someone like, you know, that nice Nelson Mandela in a darkened Conference Hall) – but it really took something as important as the Cricket World Cup to politicise the issue back home. With England scheduled to meet Zimbabwe in Harare, the Government bravely left the moral decision of whether or not to endorse the regime to their cricket team. Later that year Mugabe quit the Commonwealth after it voted to maintain Zimbabwe's ongoing suspension 'indefinitely' – a measure initially taken after a typically unsound election victory in 2002.

see *Mugabe, Robert / Shiri, Perence / Straw, Jack*

Zircon

The British 'Star Wars', this hugely expensive Cold War defence project was systematically hidden from Parliament until it crashed to earth in 1987.

Named – appropriately – after an ersatz diamond, the spy satellite was to be a poor imitation of those operated by the superpowers, with which Margaret Thatcher dearly wanted to compete. Since America's National Security Agency already had space pretty much covered, it was questionable how a British vanity project would help shackle the Russian Bear. "I never thought they should even have tried Zircon – it didn't make sense," chuckled NSA boss Lieutenant-General William Odom. But it sure made sense when the NSA pocketed £500m as Britain's goodwill contribution. It was, said one senior British intelligence official, "part of the way we kept up our subscription to the US country club."

The public price of riding on NASA's coat-tails – almost literally, given that Britain had no other means of launch – was placed by one critic at £100m a year. He was investigative journalist Duncan Campbell, whose home was raided by the Secret Service (as were the offices the BBC) when the government got wind of a 1986 documentary on Zircon. Though there was a successful injunction, in January 1987 Campbell smuggled out his story in the *New Statesman*, and Robin Cook (*qv*) got hold of a video which he arranged to show in Parliament. Since it was thought that parliamentary privilege would override government sensitivity, there was a storm when the Speaker banned the offending VHS from Westminster.

Under increasing pressure from civil liberties groups, Chancellor Nigel Lawson cancelled Zircon on grounds of its ridiculous cost in February 1987 (though he maintains in his memoirs that he pulled the plug 'well before all this blew up'). Given that the project would probably not have been operational before the end of the Cold War, this was one of Lawson's more sensible moves; but given also that Zircon never got to intercept a single Commie whisper, it can scarcely be called money well spent.

Small wonder, then, that the mammoth cost of this Cold War madness was thought too important by Thatcher to put before the scrutiny of the Public Accounts Committee at any stage. And, in a neat prefiguring of the David Kelly affair, the scandal led to the resignation of BBC Director-General Alasdair Milne in January 1987.

Zucchini's

Mid-priced Lincoln eaterie (house speciality Pollo Prosciuto, buffet available at lunchtimes) where Jeffrey Archer (or FF8282, as he was then known) took a break from his strenuous community placement at a local theatre to dine with a senior prison warder, Paul Hocking, and an off-duty female police officer, Karen Brookes, in 2002. "The reason for the lunch was that Archer was providing information on the movement and the trafficking of drugs [in prison] in return for the pair providing him with material for his book," said an anonymous source at the time.

Whatever its motivation, the decision cost the gourmandising guard his job after 30 years' service, while Brookes was internally disciplined. Archer was promptly transferred to the considerably harsher Lincoln Prison, for 'not abiding by the terms of his licence' (taking into account a further offence at a lunch hosted by Gillian Shephard, *qv*). Archer thought the punishment outweighed the crime, whinging: "I was put in segregation, stripped, made to wear a red tracksuit and locked into a small isolation cell with a mattress on the floor." After completing his work in the theatre, Archer was known to persuade staff to let him pop into the Castle Inn, a gastropub on the way back to the jug (indoor or outside dining available, wide screen TV and a Friday quiz night).

Zureikat, Fawaz

b. 1954

Plump Jordanian businessman, trader with Saddam Hussein and associate of George Galloway (*qv*) who contributed over £900k to the non-charity Mariam's Appeal (*qv*). In 2001 Zuraiqat took over the Appeal's chair from Galloway and relocated its affairs to Baghdad, meaning that when the fund came under renewed investigation during the second Gulf War, the paperwork requested by the Charities Commission was 'no longer under the control of the original trustees' and 'cannot be located by them'. When the US Senate did find what they claimed was a letter from the Iraqi state oil commission in May 2005, it listed 'Fawaz Zuraiqat – Mariam's Appeal' next to a substantial shipment of millions of barrels of oil. When asked if he knew his Appeal's freshly-appointed chairman dealt oil with Saddam, Galloway said: "Not only did I know that, but I told everyone about it. I emblazoned it in our literature, on our website" (though this was not universally accepted). Generally, the 'Respect' MP's chief defence over the source of his funding is ignorance: he does do his best to keep his hands clean of the black stuff, telling BBC Radio 4 in April 2003 he had "never seen a barrel" of it (see *Oil-for-Food*).

On Boxing Day 2003, David Blunkett humiliated himself, his family and his party by giving a volley of incorrect answers on *Celebrity Mastermind*. Can you do better?

1. Which meteorological phenomenon is known as a 'twister' in the mid-west states of America? *David said: 'hurricane'.*

2. What was the nickname of the 12th Century Holy Roman Emperor Frederick I, because of his red beard? *David said: 'Red Beard'.*

3. Members of a North Yorkshire branch of which organisation posed nude for a charity calendar in 1999? *David said: 'Wonderful ladies who did the film Bottoms Up'.**

4. Later better-known for his work with young people, who became a national hero in 1900 for his 217-day defence of Mafeking during the Boer war? *David said: 'Pass'.*

5. Which gas first recognised by Antoine Lavoisier did he name 'azote' because of its inability to support life? *David said: 'Pass'.*

6. *Bos Grunniens* is the Latin name for the Tibetan Ox. What is the more common name? *David said: 'Pass'.*

7. In 1980 and 1984, which athlete became the only man to have won an Olympic gold medal for the 1500 metres at consecutive games? *David said: 'Pass'.*

8. In Greek mythology, who gave Theseus the thread that enabled him to escape from the Labyrinth after he slew the minotaur? *David said: 'Pass'.*

9. The *won* is the unit of currency in which two adjacent Asian countries? *David said: 'Thailand'.*

10. Which headstrong southern belle is the heroine of the novel and film *Gone With The Wind*? *David said: 'Pass'.*

* It is thought that David meant Calendar Girls.

CORRECT ANSWERS: 1. Tornado 2. Barbarossa 3. Women's Institute 4. Robert Baden Powell 5. Nitrogen 6. Yak 7. Sebastian Coe 8. Ariadne. 9. North and South Korea 10. Scarlett O'Hara